PRAISE FOR GARRETT PECK'S
A DECADE OF DISRUPTION

"The first decade of the new millennium was an epochal 'decade of disruption' as Garrett Peck convincingly describes it, setting the stage for the rise of Donald Trump in our current age of polarization and discord. A must read for anyone who wants to understand the opportunities, challenges and fault-lines facing America and the world today, and how we got here."

—Richard Florida, author of
The Rise of the Creative Class

"A lucid history of the first decade of the twenty-first century, which set trends in motion that are with us today. What to call that time? Washington, D.C.– based historian Peck suggests that the 'decade of disruption' is just about right to describe an era in which technology ravaged entire industries. In his nimble yet fact-dense account, the author enumerates many errors, from gerrymandering and the expansion of the imperial presidency to the ideological sclerosis of the Republican Party and the destruction of the middle class. A valuable road map that shows us how we got where we are today."

—*Kirkus Reviews*

A Decade of Disruption

ALSO BY GARRETT PECK

The Prohibition Hangover: Alcohol in America from Demon Rum to Cult Cabernet

Prohibition in Washington, D.C.: How Dry We Weren't

The Potomac River: A History and Guide

The Smithsonian Castle and the Seneca Quarry

Capital Beer: A Heady History of Brewing in Washington, D.C.

Walt Whitman in Washington, D.C.: The Civil War and America's Great Poet

The Great War in America: World War I and Its Aftermath

A Decade of Disruption

America in the New Millennium:
2000–2010

Garrett Peck

PEGASUS BOOKS
NEW YORK LONDON

A DECADE OF DISRUPTION

Pegasus Books, Ltd.
148 W 37th Street, 13th Floor
New York, NY 10018

First Pegasus Books cloth edition June 2020

Interior design by Maria Fernandez

ISBN: 978-1-64313-444-4

10 9 8 7 6 5 4 3 2 1

Printed in the United States of America
Distributed by Simon & Schuster
www.pegasusbooks.us

To Bishop Gene Robinson

Who makes a difference every day.

Contents

Introduction

The Cold War, an ideological battle between the democratic West and communist Soviet Union that erupted in the wake of World War II, ended in 1989 with the fall of the Berlin Wall. Two years later the Soviet Union itself collapsed, having been established during the darkest days of World War I as the first outpost of the proletarian revolution that was meant to sweep over the world. Instead, the communist empire fell apart and the West emerged victorious. Some thought that history was over. It wasn't. The end of the Cold War only closed one chapter in human history and opened a new one.

The 20th century was known as the American Century. As France was the great power in the 18th, and Great Britain the global power in the 19th, the 20th century was marked by American cultural, economic, and political dominance, particularly after the United States' victory in World War II. But by the end of the century, the U.S. had plenty of competition as other nations caught up.

America found itself in an increasingly crowded field, some of which would undoubtedly surpass the country one day. China was growing by such leaps that it overtook Japan as the second-largest economy, though still far behind the U.S. The European Union—closely allied to the Americans as democratic societies—drew ever closer economically and politically, and even launched its own currency, the euro. Russia was greatly diminished after the Cold War but still harbored aspirations to regain some of the lost glory of the Russian Empire. That said, by the end of the 20th century, the U.S. was still the only superpower on the block. But the Pax Americana was about to end.

The United States experienced a turbulent first decade of the 21st century, tumultuous years of economic crises, social and technological change, and war. The decade was bookended by two financial crises: the bursting of the Internet bubble in 2000, followed by the Great Recession in 2008. Americans earned tremendous sympathy after the terrorist attacks on September 11, 2001, but then squandered that global goodwill with an ill-fated invasion of Iraq eighteen months later. Banks deemed "too big to fail" were rescued when the federal government bailed them out, but meanwhile millions of people had lost their homes to foreclosure and witnessed the wipeout of their retirement savings.

Americans may have felt they were treading water economically, and they were right. The two economic crises represented years of lost opportunities: two wars paid for on the nation's credit card, and a major federal budget surplus changed to a deficit through tax cuts that largely benefited the wealthy. The fallout from the Great Recession helps explain the sharply polarized society in the years that followed, when populists ran amok on both the left and the right, and the country seemed to divide into two separate and hostile tribes.

Like many readers, I experienced the turbulent years of the first decade. I live about three miles from the Pentagon. On the morning of 9/11, I was working from home and had the windows of my apartment open, as it was just the most gorgeous day. I had the TV on, watching the horror unfold as the second plane struck the South Tower of the World Trade Center. I called my parents in Sacramento—they were just getting up—and told them to turn the TV on. *We're under attack*, I told them.

And then about forty minutes later came a loud *BOOM*. It didn't initially register—it sounded like a truck tire exploding. But within a few minutes CNN announced that a plane had hit the Pentagon. Looking out the window I saw a huge plume of black smoke rising. That really struck home. The fire department sirens wailed throughout the morning as trucks came from all over the D.C. area. I'm enormously proud of the Arlington County Fire Department, which was first at the scene and provided much of the manpower to fight the blaze at the Pentagon.

My office was in Pentagon City, and my window provided a direct view of the crash site. Over the next year I watched as construction workers toiled around the clock to rebuild the damaged wing of the Pentagon. They took a great deal of pride in this, and they completed the reconstruction before the first anniversary of 9/11.

While workers were rebuilding the Pentagon, my company, WorldCom, went into bankruptcy in 2002. The constant layoffs that followed were the most demoralizing thing I have ever experienced. It felt like we were undergoing a round of layoffs every three weeks, which pretty much halts worker productivity as you wonder who is next and mourn for the friends who've lost their jobs. I was never let go. But every time I hear the term "shareholder value," I shudder to think of how the company's leaders committed fraud to increase the stock price. It gives pause to think how many companies are beholden to Wall Street, rather than to their customers.

Later that summer, I distinctly remember Vice President Dick Cheney's saber-rattling speech before the Veterans of Foreign Wars, laying out the case for military action against Saddam Hussein and regime change. It immediately struck me that we were going to war, but as it turns out, Cheney had gotten ahead of where President George W. Bush actually was. In researching this book, I have left open the window of doubt as to when Bush actually made the decision to go to war. It's a question for future historians.

I count myself fortunate that I dodged the housing bubble. In early 2005, several friends and I were looking at condominiums at a superb location in D.C.'s Logan Circle. The real estate market was already quite overheated and the Federal Reserve was raising interest rates. Nevertheless, the saleswoman quoted a price that was twenty percent above where I figured the market was. When I asked what justified such a high price, she responded, "We think that's where the market will be in a year." I walked away. As the real estate market came tumbling down, the developer foreclosed.

One of my most vivid memories of the decade was on Monday, September 29, 2008, exactly two weeks after the investment bank Lehman Brothers collapsed and the economy was in freefall. I was in Provincetown, Massachusetts, for the fiftieth birthday celebration of a couple friends. That afternoon I went to the town hall, where mobile phone coverage was good, to interview Boston Beer Company founder Jim Koch over the phone for my first book, *The Prohibition Hangover*. During the interview, he suddenly announced, "Oh my God—the House has just rejected the rescue package," meaning the Troubled Asset Relief Program. "The stock market is *tanking!*" It was the moment that the American economy nearly went over the cliff in the Great Recession. Congress revisited TARP four days later and approved the bill. We can look back and realize just how close we came to another Great Depression.

Most of my ideas for this book came from a good read of the daily newspaper. Readers may forget that the newspaper was still delivered to the front door in the early 21st century; they gradually disappeared as content moved to the Internet. Newspapers are the first draft of history, followed by the second draft in autobiographies, biographies, and histories. This book fits squarely in the second draft, as a decade has passed and we can assess what mattered most in a decade of crowded events.

There was a remarkable amount of good literature that emerged in the 2000s that helped explain our times. It included Thomas Friedman's *The World is Flat* and its sequel, *Hot, Flat and Crowded*; Richard Florida's *The Rise of the Creative Class*; Chris Anderson's *The Long Tail*; and Andrew Ross Sorkin's *Too Big to Fail*. Michael Lewis published his terrific *The Big Short*, while Alan Blinder assessed the Great Recession in *After the Music Stopped*. The three men most responsible for the financial rescue in 2008—Ben Bernanke, Tim Geithner, and Henry Paulson—each published their memoirs of the bailout, a rescue that was deeply unpopular and yet necessary.

Many of the major players in the Bush administration published their memoirs within a few years of leaving the White House. Not just George W. Bush and Dick Cheney, but also Colin Powell, Condoleezza Rice, Karen Hughes, Karl Rove, Donald Rumsfeld, George Tenet, Tom Ridge, and others. In President Bush's memoir, *Decision Points*, he was suitably circumspect and offered candid accounts of what went right, where he made mistakes, and how he felt about his time in the Oval Office. Dick Cheney's memoir, *In My Time*, may as well have been called *I Ain't Sorry for Nothing*. There was little self-reflection or admission of mistakes; rather it was a justification of the administration's actions.

Numerous biographies of Barack Obama's rise to the presidency have been written as well. Journalist Bob Woodward published many books covering aspects of both the Bush and Obama administrations.

On the fiction side, Junot Díaz won the Pulitzer Prize for Fiction for his novel, *The Brief Wondrous Life of Oscar Wao*. And J. K. Rowling published the seventh and final book of her Harry Potter series, *Harry Potter and the Deathly Hallows*, in 2007 just as the very first Apple iPhone was being released. Rowling's books were turned into a staggeringly successful movie series.

This book is a narrative history of key events and trends that Americans shared together as part of our national experience, one that will be both fresh to readers, who largely lived through this time, but also objective, given that a decade has passed and we can reasonably weigh its historical importance. The first decade began with Bill Clinton in the White House and ended with Barack Obama, but the vast middle years belonged to George W. Bush, or "Dubya," as many called him because of his folksy Texas twang.

A Decade of Disruption paints a broad outline of significant events in American history in this first decade, including the Supreme Court decision in *Bush v. Gore*, the 9/11 terrorist attacks, the Iraq War, the Enron and WorldCom scandals, Hurricane Katrina, the disruptive nature of the Internet, the winning of civil rights for the gay community, an aging population, the lack of progress on fighting climate change, the housing bubble and the Great Recession, and the historic election of Barack Obama as the first African American president. It covers the period from the start of the new millennium in 2000 to the midterm election in 2010, when Tea Party Republicans captured the House of Representatives and hobbled the Obama presidency.

So what do we call this first decade? We don't have a name for it, like the eighties or the nineties. Some suggested the Aughts or the Naughty Aughties, but that seemed too Victorian and never took hold. Others called it the Double-Ohs for the two extra zeroes on the year 2000, or possibly the Zeros. Turning away from strict numerology, we might name it based on what happened—like how F. Scott Fitzgerald called the 1920s the Jazz Age. One might call this the Digital Decade for the dizzying pace of technological transformation, or the Decade of Disruption for how the Internet killed off so many business models and how automation eviscerated so many working-class jobs.

The Decade of Change or the Decade of Crisis were bandied about—but then again, when has there ever been a decade without change or a crisis? It could be called the Bush Decade, as George W. Bush was the American president during eight of these momentous years. Or the Borrowed Years for the massive consumer and federal borrowing—both to finance a lifestyle they couldn't afford, and to salvage the economy in part resulting from the bust after the housing bubble burst and the consumer spending spree ended.

Perhaps the Bubble Decade is more appropriate, or possibly the Double Bubble for the two investment bubbles that burst and brought the American economy into recession: the Internet bust in 2000, and the housing market crash that led to the Great Recession in 2008. *Time* magazine called it perhaps most appropriately the "Decade from Hell."[1]

Whatever you choose to call it, the first decade of the 21st century was a lost decade for the United States. It was an epoch of squandered opportunities, shattered economics, and increased polarization. Yet out of the crises there was always hope, and the American dream remained alive. "You can always count on Americans to do the right thing—after they've tried everything else," quipped Sir Winston Churchill, who himself had an American mother. Our republic is messy and often dysfunctional, but in the end we usually get things right. Usually.

1

From Dot-com to Dot-bomb

The first decade of the 21st century began with worldwide celebrations at midnight on January 1, 2000. As the world spun on its axis, citizens were treated to spectacular displays of fireworks from notable landmarks: the Harbour Bridge in Sydney, Australia, which was hosting the Summer Olympics in coming months; the Eiffel Tower in Paris; and the Washington Monument in the nation's capital, covered in scaffolding designed by architect Michael Graves. The celebrations were broadcast worldwide, meaning you could celebrate the New Year in every time zone from the comfort of your living room.

Or did we have it all wrong? Did the new millennium actually start a year later? Technically, yes, the third millennium started in 2001, but we still celebrated in 2000, as the counter clicked over from 19 to 20.

That counter was actually a core computer issue known as Y2K (that is, the Year 2000). Many early computers programmed the year as two rather than four digits, and thus many feared that the power grid, airplane tracking systems, water pumping stations, and more would fail when the year restarted from 99 to 00. They called it the Y2K bug, and companies and governments spent billions upgrading their equipment and software to prepare for New Year's Eve. But when the clock ticked over from 1999 to 2000, nothing happened. It was a huge relief. The world's computing systems in fact didn't fail; however, there was another crisis just around the corner.

Computers were the key reason why the American economy grew so strongly in the 1990s. The technology boom had pushed productivity ever higher, and the economy in turn boomed at a 4 percent annual growth rate. "It made America's freewheeling, entrepreneurial, so-what-if-you-fail business culture the envy of the world," explained Federal Reserve chair Alan Greenspan. "U.S. information technology swept the global market, as did innovations ranging from Starbucks lattes to credit derivatives."[1]

The nation was prosperous. Rising productivity produced a bonus of tax revenue for the federal government, which suddenly found a budget surplus in 1998 for the first time in thirty years. The surplus measured $70 billion in 1998, $124 billion in 1999, $237 billion in 2000, and was projected to grow to $270 billion in 2001. A debate ensued over how to spend it—or to return it to the taxpayers. Greenspan preferred a fiscally conservative policy to pay down the national debt, which then stood at $3.7 trillion. This was an opportunity to prepare for the retirement of the massive Baby Boom generation starting in a decade.[2]

The technology boom was in part driven by the adoption of the Internet. The Department of Defense created the platform in the 1970s as a communications platform that could survive a nuclear war. By the 1990s it broadened to the private sector with the widespread adoption of email and the World Wide Web, which created a graphical interface for people to find information. Websites were born, soon followed by electronic commerce. Consumers became comfortable with online transactions, such as buying books on Amazon. Internet-based companies—known as "dot-coms" for the .com on their website—claimed that they were the face of the New Economy, and that the business cycle was now a thing of the past. And presumably, so were recessions. It was a cocky time for people who worked in technology. They thought they could conquer the world.

A bull market erupted—a stock-buying binge that was nothing more than a bubble. And like all bubbles, it would burst. Investors scooped up shares in initial public offerings (IPO). Internet browser Netscape's IPO in 1995 touched off the Internet stock surge on the technology-heavy NASDAQ exchange. The discussion at cocktail and dinner parties was all about the latest stock tip. Amazon, AOL, eBay, and Yahoo were all darlings of the era. Valuations soared, far beyond profitable brick-and-mortar businesses, hyped by the hubristic belief that stocks could only go up.

In January 2000, a New Economy company America Online (AOL) merged with an Old Economy cable television company, Time Warner, in what was thought to be a harbinger of things to come. The deal was valued at a shocking $350 billion. It was poor timing (the dot-com bubble burst two months later), and an even poorer decision, as this merger turned out to have few synergies, and AOL's dial-up Internet business was fading. Ego-driven acquisitions made little business sense, but who cared when even secretaries were becoming millionaires with their stock options?

The Super Bowl, America's most watched television event, had possibly its most interesting commercials in 2000. Many of these were for dot-com companies that used humor and entertainment, such as the beloved sock puppet from Pets.com, cowboys herding cats for EDS, and a risqué "money out the wazoo" ad from E*Trade. Many of these companies soon would be out of business.

The dot-com boom was really two bubbles: Internet and telecom. Telecommunications companies required massive nationwide infrastructure: building a network was expensive, and thus investment in telecom was actually far greater than in dot-coms, which tended to be small startups. The hype was that you couldn't have enough bandwidth. Fiber optical cables had dramatically increased capacity as the Internet grew, but far more bandwidth was built than anyone needed. There were also too many competitors—everyone was overly leveraged as they had borrowed a staggering amount of money to build their networks.

Part of what fueled the dot-com boom were financial analysts like Henry Blodget of Merrill Lynch and Jack Grubman of Salomon Smith Barney, who were hyping stocks in public while panning them behind closed doors. There was supposed to be a firewall—what many referred to as a Chinese wall—in financial firms between analysts and traders, a wall that turned out to be nonexistent. Securities analysts became cheerleaders for stocks, knowing their firms would rope in juicy underwriting contracts and they'd get a fat bonus. They were hardly neutral players in an industry that needed dispassionate analysis. The conflicts of interest were legion.

"Shareholder value" was the mantra of CEOs of every publicly traded company. Driving the stock price up became the primary goal, not a secondary reflection of the company's merits. The stock option became a tool to promise rewards to managers and executives if they pushed the stock price up. This was especially popular in Silicon Valley technology companies, but soon others joined. Executives smelled money like sharks smell blood and they demanded options. Stock options were handed out to everyone from CEOs to secretaries. The rising stock market made everyone feel rich. Day-trading stocks became possible from home, and some adopted this get-rich-quick ethos that seems so destructive in human behavior. "The degree of hype was surreal," observed Alan Greenspan.[3]

CEOs and corporate boards engaged in peer benchmarking, comparing their pay to the median pay of other CEOs. As every executive believed they were above average, boards raised executive pay through the roof, often without the company's actual performance in mind. At the same time, worker compensation over the decade declined in real terms. This greatly widened the inequality gap and further concentrated national wealth at the top of the pyramid.[4] "Of course, the CEO was nominally supervised by the directors," noted Wall Street historian Roger Lowenstein. "But the typical board was larded with the CEO's cronies, even with his golfing buddies. They were generally as independent as a good cocker spaniel."[5]

Internet business centers developed around the country: the traditional technology incubator in Silicon Valley north of San Jose, California; Tysons Corner, Virginia; Boston; Raleigh-Durham; Seattle; and Silicon Alley in Lower Manhattan. These were technology hubs that attracted talent. As technology worker pay was so much higher, and often inflated through stock options, this pushed up the cost of living in technology-focused cities. California's Bay Area became especially unaffordable. Author Chrystia Freeland called the emergence of the technologists the "triumph of the nerds."[6]

The age of the Internet brought about a permanent shift in the office dress code. Through the 1990s, people generally dressed up for work. Men wore suits and ties, while women wore dresses, skirts, and jewelry. But with the advent of the dot-com era, business casual clothing was introduced into the workplace, and khakis, polos, sneakers and hoodies, and even jeans became normal. Every day became a casual day, not just casual Friday. While some expected this to be temporary, it was in fact permanent as the suit and necktie were relegated to the back of the closet, rarely to emerge again. Companies realized that relaxing work-related dress codes was good for employee morale, cost them absolutely nothing, and in turn, created a casual, hipster-friendly environment that attracted new talent. Millennials graduating college barely had to change outfits from college sweatshirts and jeans to fit right into the new workforce. And they were appropriately attired for the Ping Pong table in the breakroom.

In the dot-com boom, companies that had no earnings and no prospect of profitability saw their shares soar through the roof. Investors were simply infatuated with anything Internet-related, like the Dutch tulip mania of the

1630s. It was hubris to believe that the Internet party would never end. But end it did. And it was hubris to believe that somehow we had conquered the business cycle. The New Economy, as it turned out, was pretty indistinguishable from the Old.

On March 10, 2000, the tech-heavy NASDAQ reached an all-time high after doubling in one year. This was just five weeks after all those fabulous Super Bowl commercials ran. Stocks were far too expensive and companies too heavily leveraged with no profits. It was like someone taking the punch bowl away. Overnight the dot-com revolution turned into a dot-bomb. The bursting of the Internet bubble was as swift as it was sudden as investors raced for the lifeboats. Between the March high and year-end 2000, the NASDAQ fell 50 percent. The rest of the market was down as well, but not nearly as much: the Dow had fallen 3 percent, while the S&P 500 fell 14 percent.[7]

Things didn't improve in 2001, as the market selloff continued into its second year and extended into the broader market as the economy went into recession. By October 2002, the NASDAQ had fallen 78 percent from its March 2000 high. The S&P 500 fell 50 percent, and it took six years to return to its former high. The Dow Jones Industrial Average fell 40 percent to just above 7,000. An estimated $6.5 trillion in investment had been wiped out when the dot-com bubble burst.[8]

A huge shakeout took place as many Internet-based startups collapsed. Venture capital dried up. Hundreds of thousands of layoffs rippled through the economy in 2000 and 2001 as dot-coms folded. Sharks circled to sweep up the salvageable remnants. It turned out that the Old Economy way of business was the only way to do business: you still needed a business plan, paying customers, and to be profitable to survive.

Fortunately, the dot-com collapse didn't take down the broader economy—only a mild recession ensued, though many investors were hit hard. This was especially painful to future retirees, given that a growing number of Americans owned stocks in their retirement savings thanks to the 401(k). However, after the bubble burst there was no return to the heady economic growth of the 1990s. Economic growth slowed throughout the 2000s as productivity growth braked.

The Internet survived the meltdown, of course, and many dot-coms like Amazon, eBay, and Netflix continued and thrived. The survivors had good business models. The Internet launched many new successful businesses, and it had become a new channel for many existing businesses. It had permanently changed how companies operate with consumers, how consumers interact with one another, and how we research and share information. And most of all, pornography. Yes, pornography. The off Broadway musical *Avenue Q* had a famously ribald song called "The Internet is For Porn." Dr. Cox from the television comedy *Scrubs* said in sardonic seriousness: "I am fairly sure that if they took porn off the Internet, there would only be one web site left and it would be called 'Bring Back the Porn.'"

Indeed, the Internet had changed things. Customer service, information, music, publishing, research, shopping—so many things shifted online. By the end of the decade, for example, the album or compact disc would go extinct as consumers shifted to downloading music. People shifted from newspapers to the Web for their news. But these changes took time to evolve, rather than happened overnight.

In 1996, Federal Reserve chairman Alan Greenspan had warned about "irrational exuberance" in the stock market, but it took another four years before his warning came true. The phrase would be a hallmark for the first decade, not just in the bursting the dot-com bubble in 2000, but in the housing market collapse in 2007 and the stock market panic in 2008.

The New Economy meant a pink slip, a box to carry your stuff out of the office, and a humble phone call to ask if you could move back in with your parents till you got back on your feet. The thousands of stock options that would allow you to retire at thirty turned out to be worthless. The business cycle had conquered after all.

2

Dubya

The year 2000 marked many things: the supposed start of the new millennium, the Olympics, a leap year, and importantly for Americans, a presidential election. Bill Clinton, a charismatic but controversial Democrat, had been in the Oval Office for eight years, which coincided with the dot-com boom. It was said that his vice president, Al Gore, claimed to have invented the Internet when in fact it was really a Pentagon agency. This brought Gore widespread derision, even though he had said no such thing.

Every president elected since Bill Clinton has been known as a polarizing figure, but that is in part because of the increasing partisanship that poisoned the well of comity and good feelings that had existed since World War II. Americans became extremely polarized during the Vietnam War era, when the country sharply split over the war and nearly tore itself apart. The Watergate scandal created an enormous crisis of confidence and trust in the government, since President Richard Nixon had sabotaged a political opponent and subverted the constitution to get reelected in 1972. Still, politicians continued to act in a fairly bipartisan manner until the 1990s. The end of the era of good feelings in Congress coincided with the end of the Cold War.

Clinton badly stumbled in his first two years in the White House before hitting his stride. The result was a Republican Party takeover of Congress in 1994 led by Newt Gingrich, who turned the GOP into a hyper-partisan organization. Gingrich was only House Speaker for four years (1995–1998) before an ethics scandal sank him, but he forever changed the GOP into a party that shed its past as a mainstream, pro-trade, chamber of commerce party into a tribal organization geared more toward power. Four decades of Democratic dominance in Congress came to an end. With it came the rise of right-wing media like Fox News that was effectively a propaganda machine.

Clinton himself was certainly not innocent of partisanship or political shenanigans. He had an affair with a White House intern, which he lied about to the special counsel investigating him. The Gingrich-led House of Representatives impeached Clinton in 1998, a step that proved deeply unpopular to the nation. Clinton bounced back after the Senate failed to find him guilty, but the act of impeachment cemented Democrats and Republicans into their ideological corners. Impeachment is foremost a political act, and this backfired against Republicans who were scolded for prosecuting iniquity rather than illegality. "Partisan warfare had been the permanent condition of the 1990s," observed author Steve Kornacki.[1]

It was against this highly charged partisan environment that the presidential campaign of 2000 began to take shape. George "Dubya" Bush, the governor of Texas and son of former president George H. W. Bush, emerged as the Republican frontrunner. Bush had an upset victory over Ann Richards in 1994, despite never having been elected to public office before, and served two terms as governor of the Lone Star State. He championed education reform, something that Texas was failing at badly at the time. He roped in Karl Rove to serve as his political architect, a man who would follow him to the White House. Bush was folksy and likeable, and his record as governor was bipartisan and practical. He ran for the presidency as a "compassionate conservative," edging out Senator John McCain of Arizona, a Vietnam-era war hero and self-proclaimed maverick.

Dubya's father was a New England Yankee with a patrician background who had volunteered at age seventeen to fly navy torpedo bombers against the Japanese in World War II. Later as president, he caught the flu and embarrassingly threw up in the Japanese prime minister's lap. The elder Bush was a storied public servant. After making his fortune in oil, he served in Congress and was ambassador to the United Nations, headed the CIA, and was President Ronald Reagan's vice president before becoming a one-term president himself in 1989. His presidency witnessed the fall of the Berlin Wall and the end of the Cold War.

George W. Bush was born in New Haven, Connecticut, in 1946. He grew up in Texas, where his voice took on its distinctive twang, but he was sent to his father's elite schools, Andover and Yale, and later Harvard Business School. He was a mediocre student who had little interest in academics but much interest in people. Dubya became known for his smirk, a face he perfected as a youth. As an adult, he worked in the Texas oil industry and later bought the Texas Rangers baseball team. He married Laura Welch in 1977 and had twin daughters, named after their grandmothers.

Bush's Democratic opponent was Vice President Al Gore. "It looked like he had been running for president his entire life," Bush observed.[2] Gore was known for his wooden façade. He had a penchant for telling fables and stories, falsehoods that were easily fact-checked—especially now that we had the Internet at our fingertips. Gore's honesty became an issue on the campaign trail, and he ran an inept campaign, choosing not to harness President Clinton's popularity. Gore picked Connecticut senator Joe Lieberman as his running mate.

George Bush asked Dick Cheney, former Wyoming congressman, secretary of defense, and power player in several Republican administrations, to head the vice presidential search committee. Bush ended up picking Cheney to be his running mate. Cheney had plenty of political expertise, and both men had worked in the oil industry. (Cheney was the CEO of Halliburton, which counts oil and gas as its foundation.) He had heart issues, so there were concerns over his health.

American presidential campaigns are endless and exhausting, often lasting eighteen months and sometimes longer. The 2000 election was no different. Gore often vaulted ahead of Bush in the polls, but then Gore would state something that undermined his credibility. The election was ultimately Gore's to lose: the Clinton years had been good to the country. And then five days before the November election, the story broke of Bush's 1976 DWI in Maine. It nearly derailed his candidacy.

Election Day arrived, November 7. Most people were just glad it was finally over. As the state polls closed and reported their results, network television began coloring Republican-voting states red, and Democrat-voting states blue on election maps. This was used for the first time in the 2000 election, and these states became known as Red States and Blue States (and sometimes Purple States if they were narrowly divided).[3] However, pollster John Zogby believed the Red State/Blue State divide was artificial. He found instead a more reliable gauge for the divide: conservatives were much more likely to shop at Walmart than liberals.[4]

Florida became the decisive battleground. The Sunshine State was too close to call, and it was marked by controversy: some precincts still used old-fashioned paper ballots that required the voter to punch a small hole in their ballot choice. The small bit of paper did not always separate from the ballot (a phenomenon known as a "hanging chad"), and some voters were confused by the ballot layouts.

When it seemed that Florida finally settled on Bush, the vice president called the governor to concede the election. But as news came in about the hanging chads, Gore took an unusual step: he withdrew his concession and demanded a Florida recount. Thus began a thirty-six-day process that wound its way from the Sunshine State up to the U.S. Supreme Court with bitterness and rancor on both sides. Karl Rove, Bush's political strategist, called it the "thirty-six days of political hell." The Supreme Court decided the case *Bush v. Gore* on December 12 on a 5–4 decision to allow the Florida election results to stand. Bush had narrowly won the state, and thus won the presidential election.[5]

Al Gore won the national popular vote by about a half-million votes; however, George Bush won the electoral college by a single vote. The left-wing Green Party's Ralph Nader had served as the election spoiler. The nearly 100,000 people who voted for him in Florida, who presumably would have voted for Gore had Nader not been on the ballot, probably would have put Gore over the top in Florida—and thus cost Gore the presidential election.

Although partisanship was nothing new, the presidential election results rankled Democrats. The Supreme Court had intervened, Democrats angrily claimed, to make George Bush president. Bush admitted that the Democrats "never got over the 2000 election and were determined not to cooperate with me," but also acknowledged, "no doubt I bear some of the responsibility as well."[6]

Donald Trump Runs for Office

A long-overlooked episode from the 2000 election was that brash New York real estate developer and media celebrity Donald Trump briefly ran for the presidency on the Reform Party ticket. His party rival was Pat Buchanan, a deeply conservative populist with isolationist views. Trump denounced Buchanan on television: "He's a Hitler lover. I guess he's an anti-Semite. He doesn't like the blacks, he doesn't like the gays." He added: "It's just incredible that anybody could embrace this guy. And maybe he'll get four or five percent of the vote, and it'll be a really staunch right wacko vote. I'm not even sure if it's right. It's just a wacko vote. And I just can't imagine that anybody can take him seriously."[7]

Trump published the iconic book *The Art of the Deal* (1987), followed by *The Art of the Comeback* in 1997 after facing four bankruptcies, *The America We Deserve* for his 2000 presidential run as a Reform Party candidate, and finally 2004's *How to Get Rich*. Trump positioned himself as a self-made man, though he had inherited hundreds of millions from his real estate developer father, Fred Trump. He and his siblings had siphoned off most of their father's estate, thus evading a half-billion dollars in estate taxes when Fred died in 1999.[8] Trump had talked his way onto the Forbes 400 list of richest Americans in 1984 by leveraging his father's assets and boosted his public profile by praising himself in interviews with media outlets as the fictional representative "John Barron." As his casinos went bankrupt, Trump used intimidation to silence reporters who were investigating his business.[9]

Trump walked away from his Reform Party campaign with an op-ed in the *New York Times*: "I felt confident that my argument that America was being ripped off by our major trade partners and that it was time for tougher trade negotiations would have resonance in a race against the two Ivy League contenders," George W. Bush and Al Gore. "I leave the Reform Party to David Duke, Pat Buchanan and Lenora Fulani. That is not company I wish to keep." (Earlier in the week he had publicly stated, "So the Reform Party now includes a Klansman, Mr. Duke, a neo-Nazi, Mr. Buchanan, and a communist, Ms. Fulani. This is not company I wish to keep.")

Trump concluded, "I had enormous fun thinking about a presidential candidacy and count it as one of my great life experiences. Although I must admit that it still doesn't compare with completing one of the great skyscrapers of Manhattan, I cannot rule out another bid for the presidency in 2004." Or as it turned out in 2012 and 2016.[10]

Bush as President

George W. Bush was sworn in as the nation's forty-third president on January 20, 2001. He entered the presidency during the bursting of one financial bubble, and left office eight years later at the collapse of a far greater one. This was an unfortunate coincidence of history, and neither were his fault.

Both were speculative bubbles in the free market that collapsed and turned this into a lost decade.

After the drawn-out election saga, Bush promised to be a "uniter, not a divider." His track record would prove iffy on that, as he repeatedly took steps to appease his conservative political base, rather than consider what the broader country wanted. His base wanted tax cuts, a hawkish foreign policy, and a stance in the nation's culture wars to oppose abortion and gay marriage. He called himself "the decider" for his skill at making prompt, decisive decisions. Bush was not given to self-reflection or ruminating. He slept well every night. [11]

Bush was never a gifted public speaker—few will remember his speeches like those of Lincoln, FDR, Kennedy, or Reagan. But he was a decent man with a strong moral compass, warm, good-humored, and self-deprecating, and at times corny. With his folksy charm and Texas twang—he was fond of saying "nucular" instead of nuclear—liberals thought him dim-witted. That certainly was not the case. He was a devoted reader who could devour a book before bedtime, and after his presidency took up painting. Donald Rumsfeld captured this sentiment best:

> Presidents are often caricatured in ways that belie their true qualities. In the case of George W. Bush, he was a far more formidable president than his popular image, which was of a somewhat awkward and less than articulate man. That image was shaped by critics and by satirists, but also by his aw-shucks public personality and his periodic self-deprecation, which he engaged in even in private. His willingness to laugh at himself—and especially to poke at his occasional unsuccessful wrestling bouts with the English language—was a sign of inner comfort and confidence. Bush used humor to ease underlying tensions and was effective at it. [12]

James Comey, who served as deputy attorney general, witnessed the other side of Bush's sense of humor and teasing. "President Bush had a good sense of humor, but often at other people's expense," he wrote. "He teased people in a slightly edgy way, which seemed to betray some insecurity in his personality. His teasing was used as a way to ensure that the hierarchy in his relationship with others was understood." [13]

Bush was also gaffe-prone and at times a little too informal. He gave a very awkward back-rub in public to German chancellor Angela Merkel in 2006. For the four hundredth anniversary of the Jamestown settlement in 2007, Britain's Queen Elizabeth II visited the United States and Bush hosted a state dinner at the White House. He accidentally added two hundred years to her age (she was eighty-one), and she quipped, "I wonder whether I should start this toast by saying, 'When I was here in 1776 . . .'" The room erupted in laughter. [14]

The president may have seemed unsophisticated, but he wasn't. "With Bush, appearances were frequently deceiving," noted biographer James Mann. "He styled himself as a common man and tough-talking Texan, yet he came from a world of wealth, private schooling, and privilege. He was among the most unpopular of U.S. presidents, reviled by millions of Americans, yet those who met him in person usually found him to be likable and charming. He was caricatured as stupid, an impression furthered by his many mala-propisms, yet those who worked with or for him often reported him to be surprisingly canny." [15]

The modern executive branch is enormous, and the president makes thousands of political appointments to government positions, starting at the top with his or her cabinet. Bush had made an unusual selection for running mate: Dick Cheney, who had represented Wyoming in Congress, not exactly a populous state. Cheney was, however, the ultimate insider—he knew how the federal government worked. Bush had no experience at the federal level. "The problem was that Cheney was light-years to the right of Bush," noted Bush biographer Jean Edward Smith. Bush delegated many special projects to him with little oversight, and the administration was pulled to the right. He also became more partisan than his time as governor of Texas. [16]

Cheney was bald and unsmiling, a stone-faced mandarin who didn't like explaining himself to the public, and he was a powerful insider who could outmaneuver most people inside the administration. He was soft-spoken and a listener, but also had the president's ear. When former vice president Dan Quayle tried to coach Cheney on the VP's role, Cheney made it clear he had broken the mold: "I have a different understanding with the president." The Secret Service code-named him Angler for his love of fly-fishing. [17]

There was another unusual factor about Cheney: he was a vice president who did not want his boss's job. He wrote in his memoir, "I made clear early

on that I would not be running for president myself in four or eight years."[18]
He added:

> From day one George Bush made clear he wanted me to help
> govern. He had given a tremendous amount of thought, time, and
> attention to the issue of what his vice president would do. To the
> extent that this created a unique arrangement in our history, with
> a vice president playing a significant role in the key policy issues
> of the day, it was George Bush's arrangement.[19]

Cheney was perhaps the most powerful vice president in American history. He admittedly limited the press's access to him, which made him seem
secretive. Cheney wrote, "It became something of a journalistic sport during
my time in office to portray me as the all-powerful vice president." History
may judge the man harshly for his secrecy, bureaucratic maneuvering, and
promotion of legally dubious policies during the War on Terror.[20]

"Dick didn't care much about his image—which I liked—but that allowed
the caricatures to stick," noted Bush in his memoir. "One myth was that
Dick was actually running the White House. Everyone inside the building,
including the vice president, knew that was not true. But the impression was
out there." Bush was not Cheney's puppet—not by a longshot.[21]

Cheney's biographer, Barton Gellman, noted that, "He styled himself no
more than an adviser to Bush, but unlike every other adviser, he did not serve
at the pleasure of the president," as Cheney was an elected official, just as the
president was.[22] For example, he steered his own policy on global warming,
contrary to the president's—and eventually pulled the president to his side.
In the first months of the Bush administration, Cheney had chaired a secret
energy task force. He refused to discuss the decisions the task force made,
which in turn drew controversy, since Cheney came from the energy industry
and many worried what he might have given away to Big Oil.

Cheney knew he wasn't politically popular, but he didn't care. He was
there to serve the president and expand executive powers. Secretary of Defense
Donald Rumsfeld wrote about his friend: "The combination of keeping his
opinions to himself, and yet being influential, gave Cheney an air of mys-
tery. And for people who concluded that they did not like the substance of
his views—or concluded they did not like the views attributed to him by
others—this could make him seem to be a negative influence."[23]

The vice president was always loyal to Bush. He was more of a hawk than the president, and would have acted more aggressively, yet always backed the president despite his private beliefs. Gellman concluded about Dick Cheney, "He did not defy the commander in chief, but he certainly did not always wait for orders."[24]

Cheney's closest ally within the administration was Donald Rumsfeld. They were longtime friends who had served in Republican administrations since the 1970s. Rumsfeld was secretary of defense under President Gerald Ford. As Bush's secretary of defense, Rumsfeld came in to transform the Pentagon, which was still oriented toward a Cold War footing with heavy armor and heavy divisions. He often wore a disbelieving scowl on his face, and carried an acerbic, combative streak when he faced off with reporters. He was a man who asked deep, probing questions, but who seemed irritated when the same was done to him. Rumsfeld biographer Bradley Graham called him the "master of the tart zinger."[25] Richard Haass of the State Department described Rumsfeld as the "confident college wrestler, one who specializes at probes designed to keep others off balance. He did it by asking questions and more often than not by introducing issues that pushed the conversation in unintended directions." Rumsfeld earned a reputation for ruthless territoriality, an alpha dog in the cabinet who micromanaged his staff—which he constantly kept off balance with his endless memos and questions known as "snowflakes." He wasn't a *Let's work together to solve this problem* kind of leader. It was not long before his relationship with Secretary of State Colin Powell became dysfunctional, and he never got along with National Security Advisor Condoleezza Rice.[26]

One of Rumsfeld's more famous remarks was about the mind-bending *knowns and unknowns*. He spelled this this out in his memoir: "Reports that say something hasn't happened are always interesting to me because as we know, there are known knowns: there are things we know we know. We also know there are known unknowns: that is to say we know there are some things [we know] we do not know. But there are also unknown unknowns—the ones we don't know we don't know." This was the Rumsfeld intellect that drove many a Pentagon staffer to their wit's end.[27]

Bush recruited Colin Powell to be his first secretary of state. Powell was by far the most popular person in Bush's cabinet and the most esteemed African American in the country at the time. He had served as chairman of the Joint Chiefs of Staff during the 1991 Persian Gulf War that liberated Kuwait from

Iraq, and before that as National Security Advisor. The former soldier was popular for his long service to the country, his humility and decency, and his leadership skills. He had a compelling story, being the son of Jamaican immigrants who rose through the ranks to become a four-star general. In many ways Powell was an outlier in the Bush administration, having served in wartime and cautioned against war as a solution. The Bush administration had many hawks who viewed military intervention as a viable option for many of the world's problems.

For his attorney general, Bush named John Ashcroft, who was popular among evangelicals for his deep faith, but controversial in much of the country. Ashcroft was a former Missouri senator who had lost his reelection bid and was thus available. He was teased on *The David Letterman Show* about being photographed in front of a statue of Justice—a statue whose breast was uncovered. Up went a curtain before the statue the next day. The curtain hid Justice for the rest of Ashcroft's term, which was perhaps an apt metaphor for how far the Bush administration stretched the boundaries of law during the War on Terror.

❖

From the moment he was sworn in, Bush governed as if he had a landslide mandate, when in fact he had lost the popular vote in the election. But he boldly moved forward with a domestic agenda around education reform and tax cuts. He quickly saw success in both areas.

As governor, Bush had reformed Texas's failing schools, and he intended to do the same nationally. Bush bucked the GOP, which wanted to steer clear of education. He allied with liberal senator Ted Kennedy of Massachusetts, a younger brother of JFK. Within months Congress had passed the education reform bill known as the No Child Left Behind Act with strong bipartisan support. There was one immediate political consequence to the new law: when Bush refused to add additional funding for special education, Senator Jim Jeffords of Vermont abandoned the Republican Party in May 2001, shifting control of the Senate to the Democrats. This proved temporary, as Republicans recaptured the chamber in 2002.

The United States began the decade with a budgetary surplus—$237 billion—for the first time in three decades, thanks to the peace dividend at the end of the Cold War and rising employee productivity. It looked like the national debt would be paid off within a few years, a good thing given that the vast Baby Boom generation was getting older, everyday getting closer to the Medicare and Social Security entitlements that were promised them.

Bush inherited this rare federal surplus, but rather than pay down the national debt, he decided to return it to the taxpayers. This was standard Republican ideology: there was no problem that couldn't be solved by cutting taxes. Bush pushed for a supply-side tax cut, a mantra from the Ronald Reagan era, though it made little economic sense. The reality was simpler: some wealthy people didn't want to pay taxes for services that didn't benefit them, though taxes are the cost of what makes a society function. The Republican Party had increasingly viewed taxes as anathema, and were driven ideologically to oppose any tax increases, even if that made for bad fiscal policy. It had become a litmus test for Republican candidates: taxes could only go in one direction—down. Some ideologues even championed the idea of "starving the beast," that is, if federal revenue could be slashed, the government would be forced to downsize to its small, pre–New Deal size.

Bush's proposed $1.6 trillion tax cut went before Congress. He convinced numerous conservative Democrats to support the measure, though they whittled the cost down to an estimated $1.35 trillion over a decade. Federal Reserve chair Alan Greenspan endorsed the measure. Congress approved the 2001 tax cut and Bush signed it into law. And just like that, the budget surplus evaporated. Federal revenues fell into deficit as the stock market continued to fall in the wake of the dot-com collapse (the S&P 500 fell 20 percent in the first nine months of 2001), but federal spending continued apace. The economy was in recession, which would have wiped out the surplus anyway, but the tax cuts magnified the deficit. The Federal Reserve responded to the recession by lowering interest rates all the way down to 1 percent.[28]

The tax cut also reduced the estate tax, implemented after the Gilded Age to prevent the national wealth from accumulating in just a handful of families. Republicans framed the estate tax as the "death tax," a remarkable public relations coup in that they made the tax into a populist cause, though only the very rich were impacted by it. The estate tax was cut through 2010, then it was to revert to its full tax. The administration hoped to make the tax cut permanent, but first had to demonstrate that the budget would eventually be balanced. (It never was.)

Bush's second tax cut passed Congress in May 2003 as the Iraq War was unfolding. It is unusual to cut taxes during war when expenditures rise so much, but that is what Bush did. His 2003 tax cut was smaller, but it espe-cially favored the wealthy with a cut to capital gains and dividends taxes to 15 percent. The wealthy made most of their money from their investments, rather than from salaries, and Bush had just significantly reduced their taxes. The rich could now have a lower de facto tax rate than many working Ameri-cans. This tax cut in particular widened inequality and worsened the federal budget deficit. The billionaire investor Warren Buffett famously remarked in 2006, "There's class warfare, all right, but it's my class, the rich class, that's making war, and we're winning."[29]

If tax cuts fuel growth, then why did the American economy do so poorly after the Bush tax cuts? One would think all that extra income would have led to increased investment and many more jobs, but it did not. Instead, CEOs automated assembly lines, created jobs in China and India, offshored American talent, then rewarded themselves with big stock option grants for improving their company's profitability. The supply-side, trickle-down effect didn't work.[30]

The Bush tax cuts may have been ideologically beneficial to the political right, but they failed as economic policy. They did not stimulate the economy or foster new jobs. The country stagnated economically, with worker pay barely keeping even over the course of the decade. The biggest impact was on mounting deficits. The federal government cut its ability to raise revenue, even while it entered into three expensive wars (Afghanistan, Iraq, and the War on Terror) and contended with an aging population that demanded services. These things had to be paid for somehow.

In late 2003, Bush seized on a traditional Democratic program and made political hay: he convinced Congress to pass a prescription drug benefit for Medicare recipients, a crucial demographic of senior citizens, who are more likely to vote. Congress had no way of paying for it, as raising taxes was anathema to the GOP. They simply added it to the federal deficit. And it gave proof that George W. Bush was a big-government conservative.

Always a deficit hawk, Alan Greenspan pointed out that President Bush did not exercise a veto once in his first six years in office. This signaled profligacy. "To my mind, Bush's collaborate-don't-confront approach was a major mistake—it cost the nation a check-and-balance mechanism essential to fiscal discipline," Greenspan wrote. But deficit-fighting wasn't on the Bush White House's agenda. Dick Cheney said, "Reagan proved that deficits don't matter."[31]

No presidential administration within living memory was as politicized as the Bush administration. Ideology and party loyalty were more important than competency. While this may be fair under winner-take-all politics, it doesn't make for good government. The result, as we shall see, was disastrous with the federal response to Hurricane Katrina in 2005.

This politicization became all too apparent in the Justice Department. Conservatives feared they were losing the culture wars to liberal judges, so the White House set about recasting the judiciary with more conservative jurists. The Bush administration worked diligently to reshape the federal courts, appointing conservatives to appeals court positions until the system was heavily weighted. As many judiciary positions are lifetime appointments, it was a way to imprint a permanent conservative face on government.

Bush replaced two conservative Supreme Court justices in 2005, one of them a swing voter, Sandra Day O'Connor, the first woman to serve on the court. O'Connor announced her retirement and Bush appointed John Roberts to replace her. And then unexpectedly, Chief Justice William Rehnquist died. Bush shifted Roberts over to the chief justice position, and now had to find a second replacement for O'Connor. On an impulse, he nominated his personal counsel, Harriet Miers, who had no experience as a judge. Even the right cringed over this. It was one of Bush's few misfires. After Miers came under fierce criticism, she politely stepped aside, allowing Bush to appoint Samuel Alito to the bench.

In December 2006, Bush's second attorney general, Alberto Gonzales, fired seven United States attorneys and two others after they were determined not to be conservative enough. He came under a firestorm of protest and was hauled before Congress. Gonzales seriously waffled in his testimony. The damage was done, and he had to go. Gonzales and a dozen aides resigned under a cloud in 2007.[32]

In 2008, the Justice Department's inspector general's office revealed the extent that political appointees had illegally screened career applicants for positions under Gonzales. These jobs weren't political appointments, but rather career positions that the law required be selected on a nonpartisan basis. DOJ political appointee Monica Goodling screened out applicants, no matter how good their credentials, if they showed any liberal bias, such as by asking their opinion about abortion or same-sex marriage. Again, ideology trumped competency. The report also revealed that Gonzales's chief of staff, Kyle Sampson, had likewise politicized the process of hiring up to forty immigration judges.[33]

Protecting the environment had become a grassroots issue to Americans across the political spectrum, but the Bush administration sought to undermine environmental policies not by writing new laws, but rather in changing how they were enforced. This was especially apparent within the Environmental Protection Agency (EPA). Bush's allies in the energy industry wanted less stringent enforcement of the Clean Air Act, such as curtailing the states' ability to set more stringent pollution requirements, as it would cost them more money to produce clean energy. However, a series of court challenges by environmentalists rejected the administration's reinterpretation of the laws. The Supreme Court ruled in 2007 (*Massachusetts v. EPA*) that greenhouse gases were a pollutant under the Clean Air Act, and therefore the government had to regulate it.

Bush had acknowledged during the 2000 campaign that greenhouse gas emissions were warming the planet and that the U.S. needed to chart a fossil fuel–free future. However, once he entered the Oval Office he backtracked. Bush rejected the Kyoto Protocol, a 1997 international agreement to reduce green gas emissions. The fossil fuels industry were key Republican donors who stalled for time, even in the face of overwhelming scientific evidence, knowing that any action to fight climate change might be expensive or hurt the interests of their industry. Bush didn't become a climate-change denier, but he fell silent on the issue until near the end of his presidency, and he never put forth a plan for a carbon-neutral economy.

❖

As a born-again Christian, President Bush was close to the evangelical community, and they were an important part of his political base. He established what he called faith-based initiatives, social programs run through churches that were funded by federal dollars, which awkwardly blurred the line separating church and state. The values voters of the religious right focused on social issues, such as abortion, gay marriage, and the divorce rate, rather than bread-and-butter economic issues.

One of the key demands from religious conservatives was to ban or limit abortion. They wanted to restack the Supreme Court with conservatives to overturn the controversial 1973 decision *Roe v. Wade* that legalized national abortion. This was their holy grail. Women getting abortions tended to be lower income and minority women who could not afford a child. According to the Centers for Disease Control, the number of abortions performed declined from 857,475 in 2000 to 765,651 in 2010, and the trend continued downward. This was for a number of reasons, including education and access to contraception, such as the morning-after pill and RU-486, the so-called abortion pill. [34]

The religious right also believed that sex should be limited to marriage. It often opposed sex education in public schools, believing it promoted promiscuity, rather than arming students with the knowledge to make effective life choices. Abstinence was their only message. They believed that sex education should be taught at home by the parents, rather than by schools. The problem was, parents had proved terrible at providing sex education at home. No parent in this world has ever relished having a conversation with their child about sex—and children are mortified at having to discuss sex and their changing bodies with their parents. Most of society agreed: leave sex education to the education experts.

In order to appease its conservative Christian base, however, the Bush administration pushed abstinence-only sex education. Over time, the abstinence education movement was discredited as states moved away from federally funded abstinence programs. Independent studies of federal data showed that teenagers were not abstaining from sex, even if they had pledged to abstain until marriage. Instead, teenagers who had pledged to abstain had sex just as much as teenagers who had not pledged—and worse, they were far more likely to have unprotected sex, get pregnant, or contract a sexually transmitted infection (STI). The U.S. had the highest rate of teenaged pregnancies in the industrialized world. [35]

Even though the majority of Americans were Christian, the country continued its increasingly pluralistic streak. Americans modified their language, for example, by wishing others "Happy Holidays" instead of "Merry Christmas." The generic term *holidays* took over, such as "I went to Charleston for the holidays," as Americans gained a greater appreciation that the person they were speaking with might not share the same faith. Some called that being politically correct, while others said it was being culturally sensitive. Others angrily called it a "War on Christmas."

Another cultural debate emerged in the 1990s with the intelligent design, or ID, movement. It was the latest battle in a culture war that had gone on at least since the Scopes Trial of 1925 between fundamentalists who believed the

Biblical creation story was literally true, and Darwinian evolutionists who had the weight of science behind them. ID believed that life forms were so complex that some higher being must have designed it. It attempted to repackage creationism into a more secular package in the hopes that it could be taught in public schools, at least alongside the prevailing theory of evolution. President Bush believed both ID and evolution should be taught in schools.

Conservative columnist Charles Krauthammer denounced this kind of thinking. "Let's be clear. Intelligent design may be interesting as theology, but as science it is a fraud."[36] ID was simply Creationism Lite. Journalist Ray Suarez noted poignantly in *The Holy Vote*, "The same Americans who throng school board meetings demanding religious instruction cannot, by a vast majority, even recite the Ten Commandments."[37]

A court battle fairly silenced the nationwide debate over intelligent design. In 2004, the school board of Dover, Pennsylvania—a heavily Republican suburb of Harrisburg—became the first school district to require ninth grade biology teachers to teach ID. School board members acknowledged that they supported the concept of Young Earth creationism, an idea that the earth was only around six thousand years old. Eleven parents filed a lawsuit against the school board, and voters evicted eight of the nine school board members, replacing them with a board that supported evolution. Meanwhile, the lawsuit continued, and U.S. District Judge John E. Jones III struck down intelligent design teaching in no uncertain terms in December 2005. "The overwhelming evidence is that Intelligent Design is a religious view, a mere re-labeling of creationism and not a scientific theory," he wrote.[38]

The religious right had swung solidly behind George W. Bush, only to find it did not fully get what it desired in the way of public policy. *Roe v. Wade* was not overturned. ID was trashed in court. Although Bush governed as a "compassionate conservative," many religious conservatives saw him as a moderate. They grew disgruntled and channeled their disappointment into a new movement at the end of the decade, the Tea Party. Much of the country distrusted or simply tired of the evangelicals' uncompromising worldview, and other evangelicals rose from across the political spectrum to assert that the religious right did not speak for all of God's children.

Such were the major accomplishments and debates around the first years of the Bush administration. Dubya had expected to focus on domestic issues, and he had little foreign policy experience, but all that changed on a beautiful September morning in 2001.

3

9/11

September 11, 2001, was the most unbelievably beautiful day. The sun came up to warm the day into the low 70s across the mid-Atlantic states. There wasn't a touch of humidity in the air. It was the kind of day you opened up the windows to let the fresh morning air in. But within hours, the air was filled with smoke, terror filled the sky, and the nation stood aghast, for nineteen Arabic men had evil designs for this day.

Two jihadists from the al-Qaeda terrorist organization, Abdulaziz al-Omari and ringleader Mohamed Atta, set out that morning from the airport in Portland, Maine, where security was less stringent. They flew to Boston's Logan International Airport, where they joined three other terrorists and boarded American Airlines Flight 11. Another five terrorists boarded United Airlines Flight 175 in Boston.

At Dulles International Airport outside Washington, D.C., five terrorists boarded American Airlines Flight 77. In Newark, New Jersey, four terrorists boarded United Airlines Flight 93. All four airplanes were intercontinental Boeing 757 or 767s, and all were bound for Los Angeles or San Francisco. They were loaded with fuel to make the long-distance flight. The terrorists knew these planes were large enough to bring down a building, and with their fuel reserves they would burn all that much more intensely. The terrorists intended to turn the airplanes into fuel-filled missiles.

The al-Qaeda operatives sat in business class where they could be close to the cockpit. Once aloft, the terrorists stabbed airplane crew members with box cutters and stormed the cockpits, killing the pilot and copilot and taking over the controls. Trained at U.S. flight schools, they shut off the transponders and redirected the planes to their prearranged targets. The two Boston-based planes veered for New York City, aiming for the World Trade Center near the foot of Manhattan.

The World Trade Center was famous for its Twin Towers, two 110-story buildings that towered 1,350 feet above the city. About 50,000 people worked in the two buildings. The al-Qaeda terrorists intended to kill as many of these people as possible in a massive strike against the United States.

At 8:46 A.M., American Airlines 11, piloted by Mohamed Atta, crashed into the North Tower of the World Trade Center. At first there was great confusion in the media, as many people thought a commuter plane had accidentally crashed into the building. But there was no mistaking what happened seventeen minutes later, when United 175 struck the South Tower. This was caught on live television. When the plane hit, the top third of the building erupted in an enormous fireball. Hundreds of people were killed instantly, just like at the North Tower. It suddenly became clear that the nation was under attack.[1]

Aboard American 77, Solicitor General Ted Olson's wife Barbara called him from the flight to tell him that they had been hijacked. That flight had reached airspace over Ohio when the terrorists took control, turned the plane around and roared back toward the nation's capital. The terrorist pilot circled once over Washington to reduce his altitude, then followed Interstate 95 to the Pentagon, slamming the plane into the building's southwest face at 9:38 A.M., killing 184 people.

The fourth aircraft, United Airlines Flight 93 out of Newark, was delayed by heavy airport traffic. Aboard were seven crew members, thirty-three passengers, along with four hijackers. The terrorists had planned for all four planes to take off within a twenty-five-minute window. The delay had a major impact on the passengers: once they were hijacked, they started making phone calls from the plane and learned that three other planes had crashed into targets. They bravely took action, deciding to attack the hijackers.

As the passengers prepared to fight back, one of them, Todd Beamer, said—recorded over a telephone conversation—"Let's roll." Their assault on the cockpit finally resulted in the terrorist at the helm pitching the plane on its back and down, plowing into a field in Shanksville, Pennsylvania. The plane was probably targeted at the U.S. Capitol or White House. The bravery of the passengers and crew had saved possibly hundreds or even thousands of lives.[2]

The Air Force scrambled fighter planes to protect the cities. F-15s took off from Otis Air Force Base on Cape Cod, as well as fighters from Langley Air Force Base in Virginia. Vice President Dick Cheney, who had been moved to a secure location near the White House, gave the order for the fighters to shoot down any hijacked plane; however, the fighters were too far away to reach any of the planes.[3]

Hundreds of workers were trapped in the Twin Towers above where the planes had struck. They couldn't evacuate: the heat below them was too intense, and most, if not all, of the fire escapes were destroyed. Television cameras recorded a number of people poking out of windows, trying to breathe through the stifling heat. Eventually the heat and smoke grew so intense that some did the only thing they could do: they jumped. It was reminiscent of the Triangle Shirtwaist Factory fire in 1911 when burning workers leaped to their deaths as onlookers looked on helplessly—in this case, an entire nation on television. The sight of watching people jump to their deaths as the lesser of two evils was heartbreaking.

What probably saved more people than anything was the fact that the first plane hit the North Tower fairly high in the building, and that the attacks struck during the rush hour, before the World Trade Center was fully staffed. Many employees were still commuting to work. Of the 50,000 people who worked at the center, the 9/11 Commission estimated that 16,400 to 18,800 were actually in the WTC when the first plane struck at 8:46 A.M. For those already in the complex, New York's Fire Department (FDNY), Police Department (NYPD), and Port Authority Police Department (PAPD) worked feverishly to evacuate people from the burning buildings. The first responders had quickly arrived to help in the chaos. As workers scrambled out of the buildings, police and firemen climbed upward into the Twin Towers to evacuate people.[4]

Then the unthinkable happened. The South Tower collapsed, fifty-six minutes after being hit. It was the second building struck, but lower in the building than the North Tower, and the intense heat from the burning jet fuel had so weakened the structure that the floors above began to pancake downward, one after the next, until the entire building collapsed in a huge cloud of smoke, steel, and concrete. Television cameras caught it live as the collapse created a tornado of dust that enveloped lower Manhattan.

Twenty-nine minutes later, the North Tower collapsed at 10:28 A.M. The huge antenna atop the building seemed to keel over as the building fell under its own burning weight. It soon disappeared in a huge cloud of dust and smoke like its sister. The finance company Cantor Fitzgerald was nearly wiped out. It lost 658 employees in the North Tower, more than any other company that day.

The day became known as 9/11. It was a day of unspeakable tragedy but also remarkable human courage. "On September 11, the nation suffered the largest loss of life—2,973—on its soil as a result of hostile attack in its history," concluded the 9/11 Commission, a bipartisan group that investigated the attack. More people died on 9/11 than died at Pearl Harbor. A significant proportion of the casualties were first responders—firefighters and police—who had rushed into the Twin Towers to help evacuate people once the World Trade Center was hit. "The FDNY suffered 343 fatalities—the largest loss of life of any emergency response agency in history," the commission noted. "The PAPD suffered 37 fatalities—the largest loss of life of any police force in history. The NYPD suffered 23 fatalities—the second largest loss of life of any police force in history, exceeded only by the number of PAPD officers lost the same day." Americans gained a new appreciation for first responders. [5]

The Federal Aviation Administration ordered all flights over the country to land immediately. Some 4,500 planes landed at the closest airport they could find. The nation's skies were shut down. Travelers were stranded for days.

Since the start of the communications revolution that enabled nearly instant sharing of information through radio, television, and the Internet, people have been able to learn about important events in real time. An earlier generation could tell you exactly where they were when they learned that Pearl Harbor had been bombed on December 7, 1941. The same thing for President John F. Kennedy's assassination in 1963, or when the space shuttle *Challenger* blew up after takeoff in 1986. A similar moment impacted American society on September 11, 2001, which was the defining moment of the decade.

Telephone lines that day were swamped with people calling home or calling friends in the affected cities. Offices emptied out as employees scrambled home, lest their buildings be attacked like the World Trade Center. The subways were closed in New York and Washington, D.C. Workers were left stranded, and many of them had to walk all the way home. In any case, most Americans stopped working that day—and the next day and the day after that, as they were glued to their televisions, watching the crisis unfold as they tried to fathom what had happened. And everyone asked, *Who did this, and why do they hate us?*

The Pentagon reopened the day after 9/11, even though it still burned for days. The damage to the infrastructure of lower Manhattan was so severe that the New York Stock Exchange shut down for the rest of the week. The collapse of the Twin Towers had heavily damaged the surrounding buildings. Most of the area would have to be rebuilt. A new phrase entered the nation's lexicon: Ground Zero. It began as a phrase to indicate where the Twin Towers fell—the hallowed ground where so many died.

President Bush had started the day in Sarasota, Florida, where he was visiting an elementary school. The Secret Service quickly pushed him onto Air Force One headed for Louisiana, then on to Nebraska, before Bush insisted on returning to Washington, D.C. Two hours after touching down at Andrews Air Force Base, Bush addressed the nation from the Oval Office at 8:30 P.M. "Our way of life, our very freedom came under attack in a series of deliberate terrorist acts," he stated. "Terrorist attacks can shake the foundations of our biggest buildings, but they cannot touch the foundation of America." Bush ordered the intelligence and law enforcement communities "to find those responsible and to bring them to justice. We will make no distinction between the terrorists who committed these acts and those who harbor them." Though the perpetrators, al-Qaeda, were not mentioned, the message was clearly targeted at the Taliban, the Islamic fundamentalist movement that hosted al-Qaeda in Afghanistan. [6]

So began the War on Terror, an undeclared war that would have an indeterminate—and possibly no—end.

Who Was Al-Qaeda?

We can trace the beginnings of Arabic resentment toward the West to the end of World War I in 1918. The Arabs had been promised self-determination from the collapsing Ottoman Empire, but instead France and Great Britain drew the borders of the modern Middle East and won League of Nations mandates to govern them, in part because oil had been discovered in Mesopotamia. It was colonialism by another name. The creation of the State of Israel in 1948 in Palestine, a British-controlled mandate, drove further resentment. Radical Islamists built a hateful ideology that stoked Arabic anger. While a large number of groups could be considered Islamists, such as the Muslim Brotherhood in Egypt, none quite captured the world's attention as al-Qaeda.

Osama bin Laden, the son of a wealthy Yemeni-born Saudi developer, founded al-Qaeda in 1988 to fight against the Soviet occupation of Afghanistan. Once the Soviets withdrew from that country, he turned his sights toward the United States. The U.S. had increased its presence in the Persian Gulf region toward the end of the Cold War to counter the Soviet Union and revolutionary Iran. After the Gulf War liberated Kuwait from Iraq in 1991, some American armed forces remained in Saudi Arabia to patrol the no-fly zone over Iraq. Bin Laden resented this, believing that Saudi soil was sacred and that American forces were infidels.

After being expelled from Saudi Arabia, bin Laden took refuge in Sudan in 1992, where he directed and financed terrorism operations around the world with his group, *al-Qaeda* (meaning *the base* or *foundation* in Arabic). His goal was a radical form of Islam that would reestablish a caliphate and force the world to convert. The 9/11 Commission reported, "The extreme Islamist version of history blames the decline from Islam's golden age on the rulers and people who turned away from the true path of their religion, thereby leaving Islam vulnerable to encroaching foreign powers to steal their land, wealth, and even their souls." Al-Qaeda had a litany of grievances against the United States.[7]

In 1993, al-Qaeda bombed the World Trade Center parking garage. This was a tempting target, and they would hit it again. Three years later, bin Laden moved his operations to Afghanistan at the invitation of the Taliban, an extreme Islamist militia that had seized control of the country. There he began strengthening al-Qaeda and trained 10,000–20,000 terrorists in his camps for jihad, or holy war. Two years later, bin Laden and his Egyptian lieutenant Aymin al-Zawahiri issued a fatwa, an Islamic religious pronouncement, effectively declaring war against the United States and saying that jihad was every Muslim's duty. Neither bin Laden nor al-Zawahiri were clerics, nor did either have the religious authority to issue such pronouncements.[8]

It is difficult to believe that any just god would reward mass murder, but such is what the jihadists believed. The 9/11 Commission noted that al-Qaeda's "purpose is to rid the world of religious and political pluralism, the plebiscite, and equal rights for women. It makes no distinction between military and civilian targets. *Collateral damage* is not in its lexicon."[9]

On August 7, 1998, not long after issuing the fatwa, al-Qaeda exploded two massive truck bombs at the U.S. embassies in Kenya and Tanzania, killing hundreds of innocents. Just before the turn of the century, a terrorist cell was uncovered, thanks to alert U.S. Customs agents near Vancouver, Canada, that planned to detonate bombs at Los Angeles International Airport. Al-Qaeda bombed the destroyer USS *Cole* in Aden, Yemen on October 12, 2000, killing seventeen crew members and nearly sinking the ship. This was less than a month before the presidential election.

President Bill Clinton stepped up the nation's counterterrorism efforts, naming Richard Clarke as national coordinator for counterterrorism. Clarke served in the White House for a decade. In his 2004 book chronicling the rise of al-Qaeda and America's efforts to defend itself, *Against All Enemies*, Clarke painted a picture of the Bush administration, in its first eight months, as recalcitrant and disbelieving that al-Qaeda was a threat. He had worked for years to defeat al-Qaeda, yet claimed that the Bush administration was hard of hearing on the issue until after 9/11.[10]

Not so, countered National Security Advisor Condoleezza Rice. "When threat levels began to spike in the summer of 2001, we moved the U.S. government at all levels to a high state of alert," she wrote in her memoir. However, "the intelligence assessment was that an attack would most likely come in Jordan, Saudi Arabia, Israel, or in Europe."[11] Much of the chatter pointed to an impending al-Qaeda attack against American interests outside the United States. George Tenet, the director of Central Intelligence, told the 9/11 Commission, "the system was blinking red."[12]

Tenet led the CIA under Bill Clinton and stayed on under Bush. He was criticized for not anticipating and stopping the 9/11 attacks, and letting the Bush administration roll over him in the runup to the Iraq War. His agency provided faulty intelligence in both cases. Tenet's memoir, *At the Center of the Storm*, was widely criticized. It was an apology of sorts, written to defend his record in the face of the 9/11 Commission report.

Like Richard Clarke, Tenet noted that there were very clear signals that al-Qaeda was preparing a major terrorist attack. The problem was deciphering where that attack would come. Tenet wrote, "We—CIA, the intelligence community, investigative bodies, the government at large—missed the exact 'when and where' of 9/11. We didn't have enough dots to connect, and we'll always have to live with that."[13]

Several explicit dots were missed. Zacarias Moussaoui was arrested on August 16, 2001, after a Minnesota flying school alerted the FBI. Moussaoui demonstrated strange behavior: he only wanted to learn how to fly jumbo jets, but not how to land them. He may have been a backup or replacement pilot for one of the 9/11 hijackers. And two of the hijackers were on a government watchlist, yet they slipped into the country.

Richard Clarke had requested a meeting of principals within the Bush administration on January 25, 2001, to discuss the al-Qaeda threat, but this did not take place until September 4—just a week before 9/11. National Security Advisor Condoleezza Rice countered that she had given Clarke "a green light to develop a strategy," noting that Dick Cheney, Colin Powell, and Donald Rumsfeld had already been briefed separately on the terrorist organization. Briefed, yes, but they had made no coordinated decision on how to respond until it was too late. Rice concluded, "There was no silver bullet that could have prevented the 9/11 attacks."[14]

Why did the terrorists target the World Trade Center and the Pentagon? The Twin Towers were the largest, most potently visible symbol of American financial power, while the Pentagon reflected the nation's military might. Striking at those power centers was both symbolic and also very real. And al-Qaeda wanted to strike inside the United States, showing the country how vulnerable it was. The 9/11 attacks declared war on the U.S., and the country would be at war with the terrorist organization for at least the next decade.

The War on Terror

George Bush had championed a domestic agenda, but less than eight months into his presidency found himself as a wartime leader, facing an unconventional enemy. He would lead the United States and much of the world in the War on Terror. He penned in his memoir:

> The war would be different from any America had fought in the past. We had to uncover the terrorists' plots. We had to track their movements and disrupt their operations. We had to cut off their money and deprive them of their safe havens. And we had to do it all under the threat of another attack. The terrorists had made our home front a battleground. Putting America on a war footing was one of the most important decisions of my presidency.[15]

After 9/11, Bush quickly gathered a group of allies for the effort ahead. He traveled to the Ground Zero site to speak with the rescue workers who were digging through the rubble for any survivors and for the victims. A retired firefighter, Bob Beckwith, helped the president climb atop a truck, bullhorn in hand, so Bush could speak to the crowd among the wreckage. When a person shouted back that they couldn't hear the president, Bush responded, "I can hear you. The rest of the world hears you. And the people who knocked these buildings down will hear all of us soon." It was an electric, defining moment for his presidency.[16]

Besides the first responders, New York mayor Rudy Giuliani became known as "America's Mayor" in the wake of 9/11. In his first term as mayor (1994–1998), the hard-charging Republican and former prosecutor had cleaned up New York's finances, Times Square, and its streets. Tourists flocked back to what had been an ungovernable, unfathomable city. His second term (1998–2002) was marked by nannyism as Hizzoner tackled jaywalking, ticketed taxis, and settled petty scores. Giuliani was combative with a take-no-prisoners approach to governing. He had a temper, liked to grandstand, and was a bully, and he was not the kind of mayor who shared the limelight. Then 9/11 hit at the very end of his second term, which redeemed Giuliani in the public's eye and set in motion his continued political career on the national stage.

The 9/11 attacks showed that Giuliani was an impressive leader in a crisis. He was calm and resolute. He was one of the first politicians to enter the Ground Zero site. His daily press conference every morning in the aftermath of 9/11 reassured people that things were going to be okay, that the authorities were making strides in clearing the wreckage, as well as finding and identifying the bodies.

The United States is a complicated, heterogenous country, and national unity is difficult to achieve. The 9/11 attacks brought the country together, at least for a time, before partisanship reared its head again. The nifty World War II slogan, United We Stand, was trotted out. Confessional patriotism was everywhere, with people wearing the red, white, and blue on their lapels, raising a flag in front of their house, or posting a flag sticker on their car. This would be the last moment of national unity for the decade—and the decade after.

That said, the nation's culture wars still flared up on the wake of 9/11. Conservative evangelist Jerry Falwell, appearing on Pat Robertson's television program, *The 700 Club*, blamed American liberals for the terrorist attacks. "I really believe that the pagans, and the abortionists, and the feminists, and the gays and the lesbians who are actively trying to make that an alternative lifestyle, the ACLU, People for the American Way—all of them who have tried to secularize America—I point the finger in their face and say, 'You helped this happen.'" Falwell claimed that God withdrew his protective cloak from America because of American liberalism.

Robertson responded: "Well, I totally concur, and the problem is we have adopted that agenda at the highest levels of our government." Falwell was widely denounced for this remark. Even President Bush weighed in, calling Falwell's comment inappropriate for blaming fellow citizens rather than the terrorists for 9/11.[17]

National Public Radio broadcaster Scott Simon eloquently rebuked Falwell and Robertson. Noting that a gay rugby player, Mark Bingham, was on American Airlines Flight 77 and was likely part of the group that attempted to storm the cockpit, he asked: "Let me put it in the bald terms in which many Americans may be thinking right now: If your plane was hijacked, who would you rather sit next to? Righteous reverends who will sit back and say, 'This is God's punishment for gay Teletubbies,' or the gay rugby player who lays down his life to save others? And by the way, which person seems closer to God?" Simon might have also mentioned Father Michael Judge, a gay Catholic priest, who was delivering the last rites to victims when he was killed by falling debris from the Twin Towers.[18]

Much of the nation's national security efforts were now directed toward Afghanistan, where the Taliban militia harbored Osama bin Laden and his al-Qaeda terrorist network. Theirs was a symbiotic relationship. Just two days before 9/11, al-Qaeda suicide assassins, posing as journalists, blew up Ahmad Shah Massoud, the leader of the Northern Alliance. Bin Laden did this to help the Taliban, which was preparing an offense against the alliance.

Afghanistan was known as the Graveyard of Empires. It was a deeply conservative, multiethnic, and tribal society. The British Empire had disastrously attempted to conquer the lawless region in the 19th century, while the Soviets suffered their own version of the Vietnam quagmire after they occupied the country in 1979. They pulled out a decade later after losing tens of thousands of soldiers at the hands of the *mujahideen*, Islamic freedom fighters such as bin Laden.

On September 18, 2001, Congress passed a near-unanimous joint resolution, authorizing the president to use force against al-Qaeda and its allies. Bush addressed the nation before a joint session of Congress two days later, the most important speech of his presidency, a speech that painted the struggle in black and white terms: "Every nation, in every region, now has a decision to make: Either you are with us, or you are with the terrorists." Bush was now a wartime president. [19]

In rallying the country to fight terrorism, Bush made a vital appeal for Americans not to blame or discriminate against Muslims. The U.S. had a small Muslim population which felt embattled after the 9/11 attacks, and many Americans had a distrust of Islam. (Some went so far as to fear that Muslims were trying to establish sharia law in the country, an unfounded and irrelevant claim.) The U.S. had engaged in a vicious wave of anti-German hysteria during World War I and interned 120,000 Japanese American citizens during World War II. Bush was intent not to repeat that mistake.

On the other hand, Bush made a verbal misfire, calling the American effort against terrorism a crusade. That was a loaded term in the Middle East. While World War II was a crusade against fascism, this wasn't a proper term for the Islamic world. In the Crusades of the 11th through 13th centuries, European Christians sent armies to conquer Palestine from the Muslims and built a Crusader Kingdom. They were ultimately evicted. The Islamic world had largely forgotten about the Crusades—it had won those wars, after all. The memory of the Crusades was resurrected in early 20th century colonialism. Al-Qaeda referred to American forces as Crusaders and Zionists. American armed forces stationed in Saudi Arabia were always going to be a lightning rod to Islamists. Over the decade, the Pentagon quietly pulled out of its Saudi bases and redeployed to other countries throughout the Persian Gulf region.

The U.S. put enormous pressure on Pakistan—the Taliban's sponsor—to break with the militia group. Pakistan's President Pervez Musharraf agreed to support the American efforts, which was a diplomatic coup. The U.S. then delivered an ultimatum to the Taliban: evict al-Qaeda from Afghanistan, shut down the terrorist camps, and hand over bin Laden for trial—or else. The Taliban refused.

On October 7, four weeks after 9/11, the U.S. attacked Afghanistan. The CIA developed an ad hoc plan against the Taliban known as Operation Enduring Freedom that proved remarkably effective and low cost. It sent in a small group of agents and Special Forces, while the U.S. Air Force pummeled Taliban defensive positions. The CIA allied with the Northern Alliance—the strongest anti-Taliban force in the country—and also bought off Afghan warlords, convincing them with briefcases full of money to switch sides. The Taliban soon found itself outnumbered and on the defensive.

The brunt of the fighting was left to the Afghans, who overthrew the Taliban in about two months, then cornered bin Laden at the Tora Bora cave complex near the Pakistani border in December. Bin Laden and his deputy, Ayman al-Zawahiri, slipped away, vanishing for years. At least Afghanistan was now lost as an al-Qaeda haven. Hamid Karzai was installed as head of the interim government, and later elected president of Afghanistan.

Meanwhile security forces began rolling up al-Qaeda's networks, but like the mythical hydra, new terrorist cells popped up to replace the old ones. One cell kidnapped and beheaded Daniel Pearl, a journalist for the *Wall Street Journal*, in Karachi, Pakistan in early 2002. Thus began a spate of al-Qaeda-related beheadings that eventually turned much of the Muslim world against the group for its extreme violence.

After overthrowing the Taliban, the U.S. left 13,000 soldiers in a country the size of Texas. They didn't want to be seen as occupiers, as Afghanistan was still scarred from the Soviet-era occupation. President Bush observed, "This strategy worked well at first. But in retrospect, our rapid success with low troop levels created false comfort, and our desire to maintain a light military footprint left us short of the resources we needed. It would take several years for these shortcomings to become clear." [20]

Most of the Special Forces in Afghanistan, who are so critical for counterinsurgency, were pulled out as the United States prepared to invade Iraq in 2003. Afghanistan was unfinished business, an unstable country that allowed the Taliban to reorganize and renew the fight. The trail of Osama bin Laden went cold. In 2005, Afghanistan turned violent as the Taliban rebounded from its hideouts in Pakistan. The U.S. quietly increased its forces in the county to protect the Afghan government and international development organizations. Afghanistan was destined to become the longest war in American history, a low-level Taliban insurgency funded by opium poppies that seemingly had no end and left the country permanently destabilized.

While the CIA led the effort to overthrow the Taliban, Congress swiftly passed the USA Patriot Act with little discussion, which Bush signed into law on October 26, 2001. The law was a national security act that gave federal agencies like the CIA and FBI broad powers for enhanced surveillance against possible terrorist conspiracies. In addition, it allowed federal agencies to better share information. (This was how Bradley—later Chelsea—Manning got access to so much intelligence that she leaked to WikiLeaks in 2010.) Attorney General John Ashcroft was the father of the Patriot Act, which came under heavy criticism for trouncing civil liberties, and at its reauthorization in 2005 numerous changes were made.

Just days after 9/11, Cheney remarked on television that the Bush administration would have to work on the "dark side." That came to epitomize the vice president as a *Star Wars* villain. He became the driving force behind the unprecedented electronic surveillance that would follow. Bush secretly authorized the National Security Agency to listen in on communications traffic within the United States without a warrant. The program was known as the Terrorist Surveillance Program. The legal justification for TSP came from John Yoo in the Department of Justice's Office of Legal Counsel, who produced eleven memoranda that gave Bush permission to bypass the strenuous court process set up under the Foreign Intelligence Surveillance Act (FISA). This was intended to ferret out future terrorist attacks that might come from within the country. The NSA's charter was to listen in on foreign rather than American communications, but with this broad expansion in surveillance, the NSA collected a huge swath of data from its citizens, far more than was practically useful. In the fight to preserve our freedom, did we yield too much of our own freedom?

When TSP came up for reauthorization in March 2004, Deputy Attorney General James Comey was serving as AG while his boss John Ashcroft was in the hospital. Comey rejected the full reauthorization without some changes to the collection of Internet metadata. White House staff attempted an end run around Comey by visiting Ashcroft in the hospital. Learning about this, Comey rushed to the hospital, with a crew of Department of Justice lawyers and FBI director Bob Mueller, and got there before the White House staff arrived. When the Oval Office replaced the attorney general's name as the approving authority with White House counsel Alberto Gonzales, DOJ's leadership threatened to resign en masse. Bush himself was blindsided by this—the episode revealed that the president had delegated too many critical decisions. The president wisely steered away from this cabinet revolt, agreeing to curtail parts of the surveillance program and to give it better legal standing. [21]

Vice President Dick Cheney had developed the administration's surveillance policies, but he glossed over the mutiny. "Faced with threats of resignation, the president decided to alter the NSA program, even though he and his advisers [e.g., Cheney himself] were confident of his constitutional authority to continue the program unchanged," he wrote. He offered no further explanation, nor how he had kept the president in the dark about the Justice Department's objections until the attorneys threatened to resign. That got the attention of the president, who did not know about the internal machinations behind reauthorization.[22]

The *New York Times* revealed the existence of the warrantless surveillance program in 2005, nearly four years after it started. The Obama administration continued many of the Bush-era surveillance programs. In 2013, Edward Snowden would reveal far more details of how invasive the NSA's surveillance programs actually were.[23]

President Bush reorganized a host of twenty-two federal agencies into the brand-new Department of Homeland Security. Pennsylvania governor Tom Ridge was appointed to lead this huge new 180,000-person bureaucracy. DHS was focused on preventing terrorism, not on responding to natural disasters. Sorting through the new federal bureaucracy took years, as New Orleans discovered when Hurricane Katrina struck in 2005, catching DHS unprepared.[24]

Just two weeks after 9/11, some malcontent began mailing anthrax-contaminated letters from Princeton, New Jersey. These were particularly directed at Capitol Hill and members of the media. Five people died and seventeen were sickened. The Brentwood postal facility, which routed mail for the U.S. Capitol, had to be shut down and decontaminated. Some people stocked up on Cipro, a super-strength prescription antibiotic, just in case. The anthrax scare also fostered a series of copycats who wanted to get even with their exes or childhood bullies. A single anti-abortionist mailed envelopes with white powder to 550 abortion clinics around the country.[25]

There were fears that al-Qaeda had access to biological weapons; however, the FBI soon focused its investigation on Fort Detrick, Maryland, home to the country's anthrax research. The FBI named Steven Hatfill as a person of interest, hounding and investigating him for several years before concluding that he was innocent of mailing anthrax. Hatfill sued, and the FBI settled for $5.8 million. Investigators then closed in on another Fort Detrick scientist, Bruce Ivins, who committed suicide in

July 2008 just before the FBI could bring criminal charges against him. The FBI released its evidence, which was largely circumstantial but taken together quite compelling. It had taken seven years to close the anthrax killer case. [26]

For three weeks in October 2002, the so-called Beltway Sniper terrorized the Washington, D.C. metropolitan area by shooting and killing ten people and wounding three others. John Allen Muhammed, a former army sergeant, and Lee Boyd Malvo randomly picked targets from the inside of the trunk of a blue 1990 Chevrolet Caprice, where they had built a sniper's nest. They shot their victims in parking lots, at craft stores, at bus stops, and gas stations. People grew fearful of doing everyday activities outdoors, and the press coverage was relentless. The shooters left Tarot cards at some of the crime scenes, including the Death card. Investigators finally caught a lead from an earlier armed robbery in Alabama that had left Malvo's fingerprints behind, and in the early hours of October 24 police and state troopers arrested them as they slept in their car at a Maryland rest stop. The two were tried and convicted. Muhammed was sentenced to death and executed in 2009, while Malvo, who was seventeen at the time of the killing spree, was sentenced to six consecutive life sentences.

Few cities were as reconfigured in light of the terrorism threat as the nation's capital. Washington, D.C., was ripped up to hamper terrorist attacks. Temporary concrete jersey barriers were erected everywhere, then gradually replaced with more aesthetically pleasing impediments to protect against truck bombs and other threats. Security experts would have preferred to build a wall around the Capitol building and shut down Ronald Reagan Washington National Airport, which was close to downtown D.C., but these proposals drew much protest. In 2005, the Department of Defense required most of its offices and defense contractors to relocate to secure facilities. This caused some 17,000 jobs to be relocated from Crystal City near the Pentagon to Fort Belvoir and the massive Mark Center in Alexandria, Virginia.

Likewise, American embassies abroad were hardened against terrorist attacks, many of them practically built as bunkers. The most egregious example of this was the U.S. mission to the United Nations in New York, which was constructed as a twenty-six-floor tower. The first seven floors had no windows. This contradicted the image of the U.S. being an open, transparent society and reflected a bunker mentality.

In March 2002, the Department of Homeland Security introduced the Homeland Security Advisory System, a color-coded chart that was like a terror-alert system. Green indicated low risk; blue for general risk; yellow offered significant risk; orange warned of high risk; and red was severe risk (in other words, an attack was imminent). The alert system seemed perpetually stuck in orange, though the general public rarely had an idea what they should be looking out for. The threat was always general, rather than specific, and this made it rather abstract. Like the fable of the boy who cried wolf too many times, after a while people began disregarding the threat and went on with their lives. A country cannot live in a perpetual state of readiness. At some point there will always be a return to normalcy. DHS retired the color-coded system in 2011.[27]

There has not yet been another major terrorist attack in the United States on the scale of 9/11. The FBI thwarted numerous plots, of which we likely only know about a few. Future historians no doubt will fill in the discrete efforts of the CIA and FBI to foil terrorist plots before they happened. Richard Reid carried a bomb in his shoes aboard a Paris-to-Miami flight, but the shoe bomber could not light the fuse and passengers subdued him. The result: everyone had to remove their shoes for inspection at airport security. Six Yemeni-born friends living in upstate New York became known as the Lackawanna Six. They had trained in an al-Qaeda camp in Afghanistan in early 2001, and then the FBI arrested them in 2002. They pleaded guilty to providing material support to al-Qaeda. In June 2006, the FBI arrested a Muslim group that was plotting to blow up the Sears Tower in Chicago; after two mistrials, five of the men were convicted and imprisoned. Another terrorist cell in England sought to blow up transatlantic planes by smuggling aboard concentrated hydrogen peroxide in plastic sports bottles. They planned to detonate these homemade bombs while in flight, but Scotland Yard got wind of the plot and arrested the group in August 2006. The result was that passengers lost nearly all ability to carry liquids on board, reduced to three-ounce containers that could fit into a one-quart, clear plastic bag.

One major change in airline safety was the creation of the Transportation Security Administration (TSA). Private airport screeners became federal employees and adopted the blue shirt of the TSA agent. Going through airport security was never enjoyable, but now it became onerous. Everyone had to take off their shoes, remove laptop computers for separate screening, take off belts and jackets, and place all personal belongings into a plastic bin to run through the X-ray machine, making sure there was no metal in your pockets. You then walked barefoot through another X-ray machine (and later a full-body scanner) and retrieved your belongings. One wondered if the security precautions were as much theater as anything else, demonstrating that we were doing something about the terrorist threat. And yet there wasn't another hijacking or plane-based terrorist attack. The enhanced security must have served as a strong deterrent.

The so-called 9/11 recession had actually started in March 2001 in the aftermath of the dot-com meltdown, six months *before* the terrorist attack, and lasted until November. Unemployment rose from 4.3 percent to 5.5 percent, making this a fairly mild economic downturn. The September 11 terrorist attacks might have made the recession worse, though the Federal Reserve countered by aggressively lowering interest rates, and the federal government spent massively on recovery efforts.

Airlines and hotels experienced severe contractions as businesses and consumers cut back on travel after 9/11. Most of the country's major airlines filed for Chapter 11 bankruptcy protection in 2002 to reorganize. The industry recovered within five years, but by then the travel market had changed. Before, airlines counted on business travelers to buy overpriced fares, and that in turn subsidized low-priced consumers in coach. A plane could fly half-full and still be profitable. But as business travelers dried up, the airlines had to fill the seats with price-sensitive consumers, and the result was very full airplanes, no arm room, shrunken seats, and little ability to travel on standby. Gradually the airlines adopted an *à la carte* model, charging you for every little thing: checking a bag, reserving a seat, buying food, and so on. Airline travel looked deceptively inexpensive. And as airplanes got ever more crowded, traveling became more stressful and unpleasant.

In the Civil War, one out of eight Americans served in the armed forces to restore the Union. In World War II, Franklin Delano Roosevelt called for enormous national sacrifices to win the war, drafting every available person, shifting industrial production entirely over to wartime manufacturing, and calling on people to buy Victory Bonds. But instead of calling the citizens to sacrifice for the War on Terror, George Bush cut taxes and told Americans to continue their normal lives. The result was a wide discrepancy: the military went to war, while the nation went shopping. Bush noted the duality of war and peace for the civilian population:

Later, I would be mocked and criticized for telling Americans to "go shopping" after 9/11. I never actually used that phrase, but that's beside the point. In the threat-filled months after 9/11, traveling on airplanes, visiting tourist destinations, and yes, going shopping, were acts of defiance and patriotism. They helped businesses rebound and hardworking Americans keep their jobs.

In his defense, Bush stated, "This was a different kind of war. We didn't need riveters or victory gardens like we had during World War II. We needed people to deny the enemy the panic they sought to create."[28]

After 9/11, the political center of the country took several steps to the right as security became the main concern, and economics took the back seat. President Dwight Eisenhower warned the country in the 1950s about the lobbying power of the military-industrial complex, which attempted to frighten the country into spending ever more on defense. In the 21st century, he might equally warn us about the homeland-security complex—the let's-spend-anything mode to hire an army of security consultants, largely from the private sector, and do-everything to stop the next terrorist attack—even if that came at the expense of civil liberties.

A Place Called Gitmo

As the United States rounded up al-Qaeda cells and captured high-value combatants, there rose the question of where to imprison them—and equally fundamental, what was their status as prisoners. The War on Terror was no conventional war, but did that mean that the detainees were not prisoners of war?

The Bush administration found a solution in Guantanamo Bay, known to the marines who guarded it as "Gitmo," a U.S. naval base leased from Cuba since 1903. The Guantanamo detention camp opened in January 2002 when the first twenty detainees arrived. Since it was not on American soil, detainees would not have rights to American courts. Combatants could be held indefinitely without trial.

Vice President Dick Cheney led the detention policy during the War of Terror. He ignored decades of international law and the Uniform Code of Military Justice to implement how he wanted to try the captured terrorists.

Rather than leave it to the Department of Justice to try the terrorists in criminal courts, Cheney pushed for the Pentagon to take the lead, believing that military tribunals could swiftly mete out justice. As the first prisoners were brought to Guantanamo Bay, Cheney and Donald Rumsfeld categorically stated that they, the detainees, would not be treated as prisoners of war, but rather as "unlawful combatants." The U.S. disregarded its commitments to international law, such as the Geneva Convention. As it turned out, the wheels of military justice moved far slower than anyone anticipated—but that was the Bush administration's own fault for attempting to circumvent established legal precedence. Trying the terrorists in federal district courts would have likely moved faster. [29]

Within two years, the population of detainees at Guantanamo rose above 650 people. It was an imperfect system, but detainees were well treated. Many of these people were extremely dangerous, and others were not wanted by their home countries, so they stayed in the legal limbo that was Guantanamo. Still, it did not seem like the American way to hold people indefinitely without charging them with a crime. The ancient Roman system known as *habeas corpus*—literally "present the body"—was enshrined in the American legal system, and it ensured that everyone had a right to their day in court. The U.S. was heavily criticized in the global community for the Guantanamo detention camp, as the country ignored international rules of law that governed how prisoners of war are treated. [30]

Khalid Sheikh Mohammed, whom the 9/11 Commission called "the principal architect of the 9/11 attacks," was captured in Pakistan in 2003. A photo of him was released at the moment of his arrest in the middle of the night, roused from bed, disheveled and hairy in a dirty shirt. However, KSM wasn't flown to Guantanamo right away. He was sent to a secret prison for interrogation. [31]

After 9/11, the CIA built secret prisons, also known as black sites, in Afghanistan, Eastern Europe, and Thailand, where terrorism suspects were held and interrogated outside the bounds of the Geneva Convention. The *Washington Post* revealed the existence of these prisons in 2005. The international community denounced the U.S. for using black sites. [32]

Five 9/11 leaders—Khalid Sheik Mohammed, Ramzi bin al-Shibh, Walid Muhammad bin Attash, Ammar al-Baluchi, and Mustafa Ahmed al-Hawsawi—were interrogated at CIA secret prisons before they were transferred to Guantanamo Bay. It was these five whom President Barack

Obama would finally order military trials for in 2011, ten years after the 9/11 attacks.[33]

The CIA's use of secret prisons was not the only thing that undermined the moral high ground for the United States in the War on Terror: there was also the "enhanced interrogation techniques," as they were technically called, some of which were clearly torture. These included sleep deprivation, twenty-four-hour questioning, and most infamously, waterboarding. Waterboarding was the act of holding a person downward on a board, tying a towel to their face, then pouring water on the towel. The person felt like they were drowning, and anyone who has been waterboarded will tell you: it is torture. The CIA used waterboarding, but not the Pentagon.

In his memoir *Decision Points*, George Bush admitted that he authorized waterboarding on three al-Qaeda detainees to extract information. The three were Abu Zubaydah, Khalid Sheikh Mohammed, and Abd al-Rahim al-Nashiri (the mastermind behind the attack on the USS *Cole*). All were interrogated at secret prisons abroad. All broke after they were waterboarded; in fact, KSM was waterboarded 183 times.[34]

The U.S. had longstanding policies forbidding torture, but after 9/11 the White House looked for ways to circumvent these rules. Once again, John Yoo in the Office of Legal Counsel provided legal justification. He authored documents informally known as the "Torture Memos" that said enhanced interrogation techniques were no longer out of bounds for American intelligence services. These were signed in August 2002, and leaked to the *Washington Post* nearly two years later. There was much outcry: again, the United States was flouting the Geneva Convention and trashing its reputation as a humane society.[35]

Vice President Cheney strove to justify the enhanced interrogation techniques as being both necessary for national security and yet somehow not being torture. "For the safety of the nation we needed [Khalid Sheikh Mohammed] to talk, and that happened after we put him through the enhanced interrogation program." He added: "The techniques worked."[36] George Tenet, the Director of Central Intelligence, likewise defended special interrogation of "high-value detainees"—without mentioning the secret prisons that caught the world's attention. The ends justified the means, the Bush administration seemed to argue.[37]

In 2009, Susan Crawford, a retired judge tasked with reviewing Guantanamo Bay detainees and deciding if they should be brought to trial, told journalist Bob Woodward that the United States had tortured Mohammed al-Qahtani. The man was a Saudi national, and probably the twentieth hijacker from 9/11 who had been blocked from entering the country, and was later captured in Afghanistan.[38]

The Bush administration's attempt to circumvent due process for unlawful combatants in the War on Terror did not go unnoticed. The U.S. Supreme Court ultimately ruled four times against the administration regarding detainees. In June 2004, it stated in *Rasul v. Bush* that detainees had the right to petition under habeas corpus, and that same day decided in *Hamdi v. Rumsfeld* that a U.S. citizen held as a detainee was entitled to legal representation and a hearing in court. However, the court supported the right to detain enemy combatants, a win for the Bush administration, but one that opened the question of indefinite detention without due process.

The most significant case came in 2006 with *Hamdan v. Rumsfeld* when the Supreme Court struck down the administration's attempt to set up military tribunals, saying that they would violate the Geneva Convention and the Uniform Code of Military Justice. Congress soon passed the Military Commissions Act that put the military tribunals on sounder legal footing, while also explicitly forbidding torture. However, interrogators could use coercive methods to elicit information.[39]

The fourth case came in 2008. The Department of Justice argued that detainees had no right to challenge their imprisonment in federal court, but the Supreme Court ruled against the government in *Boumediene v. Bush* and *Al Odah v. United States*. This left the Bush administration's policy toward detainees in disorder: they did not want to formally charge these men in federal court, as it would mean presenting secret evidence in public that might threaten national security or reveal America's surveillance techniques. The Supreme Court made clear that the president had no blank check when it came to imprisoned combatants.[40]

About 775 people were held at Guantanamo Bay in total, and the prison population peaked at 680.[41] Only a handful had undergone a military trial by the time Bush left office. A military jury convicted Osama bin Laden's driver, Salim Hamdan, in August 2008 of supporting terrorism, but not of more serious charges. He was sentenced to sixty-six months in prison, which included the sixty-one months he had already spent in Guantanamo. Rather than continuing to hold the man beyond his sentence, the U.S. deported Hamdan to Yemen, his home country. In 2012, his conviction was overturned on appeal.[42]

A second conviction came on November 3, 2008—the day before Election Day. As an aide to bin Laden, Ali Hamza al-Bahlul received a life sentence for providing material support for terrorism. Two weeks later, a federal judge ordered five Algerians held at Guantanamo for seven years released, rejecting the government's contention that they were enemy combatants. The government had initially charged the men with conspiring to blow up the American embassy in Sarajevo, Bosnia, but then dropped those charges.[43]

Dick Cheney's overarching concern was keeping America safe. Concluding the administration's eight years, he wrote, "Finally, terrorists around the world now understand that the United States would strike at those who intended us harm. We had done all these things—and kept the American people safe from another attack." At the same time, this keep-us-safe-at-any-cost attitude—the secret prisons, the torture, the lack of due process—had undermined America's moral authority in the world.[44] In his Pulitzer Prize–winning biography of Dick Cheney, author Barton Gellman wrote:

> With Bush's consent, Cheney unleashed [American] foreign intelligence agencies to spy at home. He gave them legal cover to conduct what he called "robust interrogation" of captured enemies, using calculated cruelty to break their will. At Cheney's initiative, the United States stripped terror suspects of long-established rights under domestic and international law, building a new legal edifice under exclusive White House ownership. Everything from capture and confinement to questioning, trial, and punishment would proceed by rules invented on the fly.[45]

Gellman added that this was done in "near-hermetic secrecy." The public learned about many of these things only after they were leaked to the press.[46]

❖

The 9/11 terrorist attacks forever changed the United States, reminding Americans that this is a dangerous world. The attacks generated enormous sympathy for the country. The nation responded in ways that were noble, but in other ways that undermined our moral standing. The War on Terror could never end with something so simple as a peace treaty, as the enemy was people who followed a flawed, hateful ideology that was determined to murder people.

It was equally important to remember the 2,973 people who lost their lives that horrible day. The three crash sites became impromptu memorials, long before they were officially designated as such. By the spring of 2002, the Tribute in Light created a striking visual monument near Ground Zero: eighty-eight searchlights beamed light straight up into the darkness of night, creating a ghost-like image of the Twin Towers that once proudly stood at the foot of Manhattan.

At the Pentagon, construction workers toiled day and night to repair the damaged building. They raced against the clock, taking pride in completing the repairs before the first anniversary of the terrorist attacks. Soon after that, work began on the Pentagon Memorial. Steel-and-granite cantilevered benches, one for each of the 184 people who died at the Pentagon, were laid out in a park-like setting by the order in which the victims were born. Dedicated on September 11, 2008—seven years after 9/11—it was the first official memorial to open of the three disaster sites.

At the Shanksville, Pennsylvania, crash site, visitors left memorabilia, messages, and photographs. The Flight 93 National Memorial was dedicated on September 10, 2011, to commemorate the forty crew members and passengers who bravely fought back against the terrorists and in their sacrifice probably saved many lives.

The Ground Zero site was the most challenging of all, as the World Trade Center had the greatest amount of damage and human loss. Much of the area surrounding Ground Zero had to be rebuilt, including the impressive One World Trade Center skyscraper that now anchors lower Manhattan. The site of the Twin Towers became the National September 11 Memorial & Museum, where two sunken one-acre pools mark the site of the fallen towers. The memorial was dedicated on May 15, 2014.

4

Scandals of the Decade

n Greek mythology, Icarus took to the sky on wings made of feathers and wax. Elated with his ability to fly, he flew too close to the sun, despite the warnings of his father Daedalus. The wings melted and Icarus plunged into the sea and died. Hubris, as the ancient Greeks called excessive pride, led to his ruin. It was the pride before the fall.[1]

Like a Greek tragedy, two freewheeling American companies—Enron and WorldCom—reached for the sun, then fell back to the earth in disaster. Their sin was fraudulent accounting by leaders who believed they were part of the New Economy and therefore beyond the traditional business cycle. These showed the worst of corporate greed, dishonesty, malfeasance, and moral bankruptcy—in short, the dark side of human nature. Their story reflected the fallout from the dot-com meltdown.

Enron started out as a fairly normal, boring energy company: it owned a gas pipeline network and operated out of the country's energy capital, Houston. But its chief executive officer, Kenneth Lay, had a grand vision for deregulating energy markets and turning Enron into an energy-trading powerhouse. Enron would take advantage of the free market by buying and selling power like a commodity, taking unfathomable risks and implementing cowboy trading to ratchet up its profits. The firm grew so rapidly that it became the country's seventh-largest company. Enron called itself the World's Leading Company. Its corporate symbol was a crooked E, which was apropos for its crooked dealings.

The company's president, Jeff Skilling, was as brilliant as he was arrogant. He was Mr. Big Idea, but he often fumbled execution. He moved the company into energy futures trading—an industry much larger than the natural gas industry. Doing deals and energy trading became core to the company, rather than providing energy. This gave Enron the chance to exploit new markets, especially as states were deregulating electricity. Deregulation turned out to be a foible: when there is only one line into your house, how are you supposed to choose electricity providers? Electrons are electrons. Skilling put a new accounting system in place that rang up all the potential profits in a deal all at once, rather than over its course. This would prove the seeds of Enron's demise. Bethany McLean and Peter Elkind, who covered Enron's fall for *Fortune* magazine and later wrote *The Smartest Guys in the Room*, said of Jeff Skilling: "More than anyone else, Skilling had come to personify the Enron scandal." They added, "Skilling turned it into a place where financial deception became almost inevitable."[2]

Enron was a company so full of hubris that its leaders were convinced they could not fail. It angered the financial gods, and their downfall was certain. Its leadership was competitive and dysfunctional, managers who undercut one another, rather than working together. It was a deal-hungry company that fumbled many of the deals it won. It was brilliant in vision, but terrible in execution. Many of the company's deals and investments went awry. It used creative accounting to cover these up, though one day the bad deals would return to haunt Enron. The company used its stock price as a hedge, which means that it used itself to guarantee itself. This was no hedge at all.

Ken Lay picked the board, and there were many conflicts of interest. The board mostly rubberstamped his ideas. Wall Street historian Roger Lowenstein wrote about the CEO: "Lay was indifferent to the gritty details of management, and his desire for wealth, combined with his aversion to unpleasantness, gave rise to a significant flaw—a permissiveness toward underlings who did the dirty work."[3]

Much of that dirty work was done by chief financial officer Andy Fastow, who created complicated financial systems to move bad investments off the balance sheet, and thus hide Enron's ballooning debt. These off–balance sheet operations had names like Chewco, Jedi, LJM, and the Raptors, and were often registered in the Cayman Islands. Chewco, a company-owned entity named after the *Star Wars* character Chewbacca, kept $600 million in debt off the company's balance sheet. Enron was a publicly traded company, where such things are expected to be reported. It used aggressive accounting methods to juice up the profits, when in fact many of its off–balance sheet operations hemorrhaged money. As the losses were off the books, they remained out of the public eye.[4]

Fastow encouraged dozens of banks to invest in Enron and to loan the company money. He used this money to keep the company afloat from the massive losses it was incurring through trading. The company's independent financial auditors, Arthur Andersen, signed off on Enron's books, certifying them as accurate and upstanding, when in fact Enron was a shell game.[5]

Fastow faced a significant conflict of interest: he was not only the Enron CFO, but also ran a private equity fund, LJM, that buried much of the company's bad investments—and allowed Fastow to charge large fees to Enron for doing so. He spent much of his time running this charade, rather than overseeing Enron's finances. Through LJM, Fastow skimmed off $60.6 million for himself and a few select allies. LJM was a house of cards: not only was it loaded up with all of Enron's deals gone wrong, it was guaranteed with the company's stock. Thus if the stock price ever fell—and it would—the company could collapse.

The company spent extravagantly. Employees did everything first class, carrying with them a sense of entitlement. It thought it would become an electricity retailer, but after hundreds of deals, the retail operation was sinking in red ink. Enron attempted to build a broadband industry to offer on-demand Internet programing, but Enron Broadband was a decade ahead of its time, and turned into a billion-dollar boondoggle. The company eventually killed the project. Enron also built a global energy empire that was a wreck. This cost the company enormously, and it shut Enron International in early 2001. Creative accounting managed to hide these losses for several years while the stock price charged ever higher. Credit-rating agencies gave Enron bonds investment-grade ratings, though they were really junk bonds. With most Wall Street analysts signaling Enron as a Buy, the company's stock rocketed upward, eventually peaking at $90 per share.

Enron even had a sordid part in California's power outages in 2000, better known as the rolling blackouts. The Golden State had deregulated its energy market but had done so in such a hobbled way that Enron took advantage by withholding power from the state to drive up prices. California actually had a large surplus in electricity transmission, but Enron tactically cut off the state's supply, resulting in rolling blackouts. With power rates set by the free market instead of by regulators, the price of electricity skyrocketed whenever Enron and other companies choked off the supply. Enron then could supply the market at this much higher rate—an artificial crisis that it itself created. The man-made emergency began in May 2000 as the price of electricity skyrocketed and continued into summer 2001.

California governor Gray Davis spent billions buying power for the state's residents, as the state's utilities were teetering toward bankruptcy. The state finally implemented price caps and partly reregulated the electricity market, which brought the soaring prices down. Over the year-long energy crisis, California had paid $40 billion—four times its usual energy costs. Enron had profited by commandeering the state's energy market.[6]

In February 2001, president Jeff Skilling was promoted to CEO, replacing Ken Lay. Trouble was just around the corner as the company's stock price began its inexorable fall coinciding with the dot-com meltdown. The company was burning through cash and taking on ever more debt—yet somehow its profits kept growing. Wall Street finally woke up to the obfuscation and began questioning Enron's version of reality. The company's finances, built on a precarious assumption that the stock could only go up, sprung leaks. The stock price fell and fell throughout 2001. By autumn it was clear that the Enron house was collapsing. Skilling resigned as CEO in August after just six months, and Lay took charge of the company again.

Accounting firm Arthur Andersen had signed off on Enron's obfuscations as legitimate accounting practices. As rumors of financial shenanigans surfaced, however, Andersen employees shredded documents and deleted tens of thousands of emails about Enron. This was an ill-advised move. An Enron whistleblower, Sherron Watkins, raised questions internally about the company's finances and possible accounting fraud, even taking it to Ken Lay via an anonymous letter.[7]

Enron dissolved LJM and other off–balance sheet vehicles that Andy Fastow had devised to hide company losses. It also took a huge $1 billion charge against its earnings. CFO Andy Fastow was fired in October 2001. The damage was done, however, and the Securities and Exchange Commission began investigating Enron, while the press dug into the company's finances. Enron's stock price melted down to $.40. The company sank under the weight of costly and underperforming and indebted assets.

Many of the company's employees received their retirement fund investments in company stock, but as the company stock tanked, corporate leaders like Ken Lay reassured them that everything was fine and encouraged them to buy more—even while these leaders dumped their own shares. The employees' retirement funds would be wiped out. Skilling had dumped his own shares, half a million of them, making a $15 million profit.[8]

Desperate, Enron tried to sell itself to Dynegy, but that deal collapsed. The only option left was to file for bankruptcy. On December 2, 2001, Enron filed for Chapter 11 and laid off many employees. It was the largest bankruptcy in American history, though that record would be broken within months.

Enron emerged from bankruptcy three years later considerably smaller and humbler, its prized but costly trading division sold off and large parts of the company shut down. Most of its employees were laid off. The new company, Enron Creditors Recovery Corporation, sold off its remaining assets, and its leaders spent years suing major banks for their role in abetting Enron's finances.

There was extensive political fallout from the Enron bankruptcy. The scandal threw a shadow over the Bush administration for its close ties with the company, as Ken Lay was close to the Bush family. California voters blamed Governor Gray Davis for the rolling blackouts. A recall drive got underway and a special election was held in 2003, which Austrian-born actor and former bodybuilder Arnold Schwarzenegger won. He was nicknamed the Governator for his role in the *Terminator* movie franchise.

Federal prosecutors first went after the accountants who had signed off on Enron's fraud: Arthur Andersen. Rather than cooperate, the company chose to fight the federal charges—and it was convicted on June 15, 2002, of obstruction of justice for its role in abetting Enron's con. The accounting firm immediately went out of business, throwing some 30,000 people out of work. "Anderson had been a corrupt enabler," concluded John Emshwiller and Rebecca Smith, two journalists who covered the Enron collapse.[9]

Enron was a far trickier case than Arthur Anderson, and it took federal prosecutors several years to investigate and build their case. Enron used a tremendous amount of obfuscation with its off–balance sheet partnerships. Prosecutors eventually indicted dozens of executives. Some struck plea deals in return for testifying against Ken Lay, Jeff Skilling, and Andy Fastow.

The first company officer to fall was chief financial officer Andy Fastow, who was indicted in October 2002. He eventually pleaded guilty in early 2004 and was sentenced to up to ten years in prison and forfeited $23.8 million, but he also turned state's witness against other executives, including Ken Lay and Jeff Skilling. He was released from prison in 2011.[10]

In May 2006, former Enron CEOs Ken Lay and Jeffrey Skilling were convicted of conspiracy, fraud, and insider trading. Skilling was ordered to pay $630 million and was sentenced to twenty-four years in prison, later reduced to fourteen years. He was released in 2019. Lay died of a heart attack before sentencing, thus escaping earthly justice.

Such was the rise and fall of Enron. "The Enron scandal was a new century's first entry in a very thick ledger, and it almost certainly wouldn't be the last," wrote *Wall Street Journal* reporters John Emshwiller and Rebecca Smith prophetically. The next scandal was just around the corner.[11]

WorldCom

Hard on the heels of the Enron collapse and Arthur Andersen's conviction in 2002 came another accounting scandal at Jackson, Mississippi–based telecommunications provider WorldCom. It was ironic, as Andersen was the accounting firm for both companies. "WorldCom became Mississippi's Cinderella story," wrote Cynthia Cooper, the vice president of internal audit, noting that in a poor state like Mississippi, a large company like WorldCom had an outsized impact on the local economy. It was her team that uncovered the massive fraud.[12]

The Telecommunications Act of 1996 opened the telecom industry to competition and likewise spawned acquisitions and overinvestment. Local telecom providers could now sell long distance services, and long-distance providers could now offer local telecom services. The act sparked an acquisitions spree as companies tried to extend their capabilities through a huge wave of consolidation. Leading the charge was WorldCom, which had grown voraciously through seventy-five acquisitions, acquiring smaller telcos and casting off redundant parts and laying off people. When you hear the word "synergies" from a corporate merger, the first thing that should come to mind are layoffs of duplicate personnel.

Bernie Ebbers, a Canadian-born former basketball coach, put together a business plan under a company called Long Distance Discount Services (LDDS), the precursor to WorldCom. Ebbers was 6'4" and, unusually for a CEO, preferred cowboy boots and jeans, and he headquartered his company in Mississippi rather than a major metropolitan center. For a man who ran one of the largest technology companies in the world, Ebbers was surprisingly low-tech and folksy. He didn't bother using email. He famously remarked, "I am not a technology dude." Ebbers was an acquisitions guy. He even owned a yacht named the *Aquasition*.[13]

Ebbers was the kind of CEO who would chastise an executive for selling personal stock in the company, whose cost-cutting went after trivial things like taking away company coffee and water coolers, while ignoring larger issues like access line costs or integrating billing, order entry, and trouble-shooting systems. Thanks to its acquisitions, WorldCom had dozens of order entry systems. To the bean counters, every employee was a cost that could potentially be eliminated. To Ebbers, shareholder value was gospel. His entire business model was predicated upon driving the stock price ever higher, which was how he financed his next acquisition. WorldCom always paid in stock, rarely in cash. Employees were showered with stock options—options that would prove worthless.

Thanks to its 1998 purchase of communications company MFS, which had recently acquired Internet access company UUNET, WorldCom became the world's largest Internet service provider. WorldCom then brilliantly out-maneuvered British Telecom to acquire MCI. It was like a shark swallowing a whale: MCI was nearly four times as large. WorldCom was now the nation's second-largest long-distance telephony provider after AT&T.

The company's downfall began in October 1999, when it offered to acquire Sprint, the third-largest long-distance company and growing wire-less provider, for a mind-boggling $129 billion. It had acquired the larger MCI the year before for $40 billion, so offering three times as much for Sprint was ludicrous. Federal and European regulators nixed the merger on competitive grounds in July 2000. The company's slide had begun as the stock market lost faith in its once-shining star. WorldCom's growth stalled, which was perilous to a company whose business model was predicated on a rising stock price.

With the collapse of the dot-com bubble in March 2000, many high-tech companies closed shop, which in turn triggered the collapse of the telecom bubble six months later. Once high-flying telecom stocks sank throughout 2001. A reckoning followed from all of the overbuilt capacity of fiber optical lines and networks. Many smaller telecom providers filed for bankruptcy, including FLAG Telecom, Global Crossing, McLeodUSA, Metromedia

Fiber Networks, Rhythms NetConnections, Winstar Communications, and XO Communications. WorldCom felt the squeeze from falling margins.

Instead of retrenching or consolidating operations to ride out the storm, WorldCom leaders decided to boost the stock with artificial earnings. Rather than write off operational expenses, just as a business would write off gas or travel, chief financial officer Scott Sullivan directed that these be put in the capital expenses column. This meant they would be written off over a number of years, rather than right away as the law required. Turning expenses into capital was a fast and dirty way of hiding the collapse in earnings while keeping profitability up. WorldCom's fraud was simple to understand and easy to uncover.

Ebbers had stacked the board of directors with his cronies. The billionaire made significant purchases using WorldCom stock as collateral, betting that it would keep going up and make him even richer. He purchased a shipbuilding company, a half-million-acre Canadian ranch, a rice farm, and hundreds of thousands of acres of timberland. This worked fine while the stock price was high, but when WorldCom's stock price declined after the telecom bubble burst, the banks came calling for their money. Ebbers turned to the WorldCom board for personal loans to help him through his predicament, as if the company was his personal piggy bank. He borrowed $408.2 million, and the board rubberstamped the loans. [14]

Cost cutting at WorldCom began in earnest in January 2002 when the company canceled pay raises and took away a slew of employee benefits. The federal government began investigating, and the bond rating agencies downgraded its $29 billion in debt to junk status. WorldCom's stock price plummeted from a high of $60 down to $1. The company instituted layoffs in April to cut costs, but not before the board of directors authorized yet another loan to Ebbers. This last loan did not sit well with the public once word got out. On April 29, Ebbers resigned from WorldCom after seventeen years at the helm. His handpicked board had forced him out.

The news kept getting worse. Cynthia Cooper, who led the internal audit team, uncovered the accounting fraud in June 2002. "My team and I began to grow increasingly suspicious of some entries in WorldCom's books," she wrote in her memoir. "The more we investigated, the stranger the reactions from our colleagues became. No one would give us a straight answer." [15] What they had uncovered were inexplicable accounting entries for "prepaid capacity" that went back five quarters to late 2000 when the telecom bubble burst and the company's earnings dried up. It was a coded entry for how CFO Scott Sullivan had bundled various operational expenses and declared them capital costs. Cooper took her team's findings and blew the fraud whistle to the company's audit committee.

Within days, the board fired Sullivan and David Myers, the company's controller, and promoted John Sidgmore from UUNET to run the company. He quickly negotiated for lines of credit with major banks to keep the company from failing altogether. On June 25, WorldCom restated its earnings for the past five quarters, admitting to $3.8 billion in fraud (this would later rise to a jaw-dropping $11 billion). It also announced it would lay off 17,000 people, or twenty percent of its workforce. The company scrambled to conserve cash and credit in order to prevent insolvency. With so much of the Internet riding on WorldCom's backbone, it was vital that the company survive. The only path to survival was Chapter 11.[16]

WorldCom declared bankruptcy on July 21 in the largest Chapter 11 filing in American history. The bankruptcy wiped out $107 billion in equity. That record surpassed Enron's bankruptcy, but would only stand six years before Lehman Brothers and Washington Mutual surpassed it.[17]

After the twin Enron-WorldCom scandals, Congress responded by passing the Sarbanes-Oxley Act, known as SOX or SarbOx, which President Bush signed into law just nine days after the WorldCom bankruptcy filing. This was a direct result of accounting fraud at Enron and WorldCom. The law instituted much stricter corporate reporting requirements. CEOs would now have to sign a pledge that their earnings statements were accurate. No longer could executives use companies as piggy banks; personal loans were now expressly prohibited. Overdue corporate board reforms were instituted in order to reduce cronyism and to protect whistleblowers. Accounting firms could no longer provide consulting services in order to eliminate the blatant conflicts of interest that had wrecked Arthur Andersen. CEOs hated the new law, but Corporate America was in sore need of reform.

As WorldCom melted down, New York's hard-charging state attorney general, Eliot Spitzer, went after Merrill Lynch, home of analyst Henry Blodget. Blodget had left an email trail that showed him privately panning stocks even while he was publicly praising them. Rather than go to trial like Arthur Andersen, Merrill Lynch settled with a $100 million fine and agreed to separate analysis from banking. This led to further federal and state charges against other financial firms, as well as additional settlements.[18]

A month after the WorldCom bankruptcy, cheerleading analyst Jack Grubman was forced out of Citigroup with a $32 million severance package. The collapse of the telecom bubble had cost investors $2 trillion, but Citigroup had made nearly $1 billion in fees thanks to Grubman's promoting telecom stocks. The following year, the Securities and Exchange Commission fined Grubman $15 million and banned him from the financial industry. [19]

Meanwhile, the employee bloodbath continued apace at WorldCom as the company desperately cut costs to stay afloat. The pink slips came in wave after wave. The bankrupt company seemed to have a round of layoffs every three weeks as WorldCom cut its workforce in half, from 90,000 down to 45,000 in about a year.

WorldCom jettisoned its Bernie Ebbers–era leadership and hired Michael Capellas from Compaq, who helmed the company for three years, changing its name back to MCI. Sadly, John Sidgmore, the interim CEO who had done so much to keep the company from going under in the 2002 crisis, died of acute pancreatitis in December 2003.

Free of the disgraced WorldCom name, MCI emerged from bankruptcy in April 2004. It did not remain an independent company for long. After the telecom bubble burst, there was a big squeeze on telecom providers, which resulted in another round of consolidation. SBC Communications acquired AT&T in late 2005, while Verizon acquired MCI in January 2006, thereby ending the era of independent long-distance carriers. Ten years after the Telecommunications Act passed, the national telecom market had consolidated into just a handful of players like AT&T and Verizon.

WorldCom's former chief financial officer Scott Sullivan pleaded guilty to conspiracy and fraud and turned state's witness, as did the former controller, David Myers. The paper trail against Bernie Ebbers was difficult to find: he rarely used email, and most of his interactions were face-to-face or over the phone. It took a slate of witnesses, many of whom had pleaded guilty, to testify against the former CEO. Ebbers was convicted on March 15, 2005, and given a twenty-five-year prison sentence. Sullivan served five years in jail, while Myers received a one-year sentence.

Enron and WorldCom had created a raft of villains, thousands of victims in terms of employees and shareholders, and a handful of heroes. WorldCom's Cynthia Cooper, Enron's Sherron Watkins, and the FBI's Coleen Rowley were named *Time* magazine's Person of the Year in 2002. All three were women whistleblowers.

Despite the shameful Enron and WorldCom scandals, despite the heightened regulations and public outrage, the next corporate scandal was just around the corner. This time it didn't just impact investors, but millions of home owners, as we'll cover in the chapters on the housing bubble and the Great Recession.

Scandals, Large and Small

This was a decade for notable scandals, large and small, financial, political, and personal—or sometimes all three. Many of them will be historical footnotes, forgotten by future generations, but some deserve to be remembered for the anguish and harm they caused.

Samuel Waksal, the founder of ImClone Systems, tipped off family members that federal regulators were going to reject his company's cancer drug in December 2001, and they sold their stock shares before the news got out in a classic case of insider trading. Through a stock broker, Waksal alerted his friend Martha Stewart, the homemaking idol who ran Martha Stewart Living Omnimedia. She too dumped her shares. Stewart went on trial in 2004 for conspiracy, lying to federal investigators, and obstruction for trying to cover her tracks. She was convicted and sentenced to five months in jail. For Stewart, who was both revered but also reviled for her imperious perfectionism, prison did much to resuscitate her public image.

Eliot Spitzer—the ambitious Democratic attorney general of New York State who had investigated the banking industry after Enron and put a muzzle on their analysts and banking operations—ran for governor and was elected in 2006. Just over a year in office, the *New York Times* revealed that Spitzer had been a frequent client of a high-end prostitution ring. He resigned in disgrace, putting an end to the political career of a high-profile reformer.[20]

No humiliation did more to bring down the Republican Party from its position of moral leadership in Congress than the Jack Abramoff influence-peddling scandal. Abramoff was a film producer turned conservative power lobbyist at the Greenberg Traurig law firm. A hard-charging character who billed $750 an hour for his work, Abramoff's attitude was that Washington was made for looting. He offered thousands of dollars in meals and tickets to sporting events and concerts in exchange for helping clients win federal contracts and access to Congress, whose "members swim in a swamp of corruption, and thrive in it," Abramoff declared. [21]

Abramoff had close ties to Washington insiders, especially Republican House Majority Leader Tom DeLay of Houston, Texas. DeLay dreamed of a permanent Republican majority in Congress. The anti-regulation businessman founded the K Street Project, so named after the Washington street where many lobbying firms had their offices. DeLay and others pressured lobbying firms to hire Republicans and fire Democratic lobbyists, or they would not get access to congressmen. This was a hostile takeover of the lobbying industry. Abramoff showered DeLay with free meals and all-expense paid trips—and in return DeLay gave Abramoff access to Republican congressmen, with the added incentive of money. Abramoff likewise sold access to DeLay—and DeLay's political action committees distributed the funds to his priorities. It was a win-win for the two men.

Abramoff's clients included the textile industry in the Mariana Islands, which was using indentured servitude to attract Asian workers to work in sweatshop garment factories. His big gravy train, however, were American Indian tribes that operated casinos. To bilk even more money from the tribes, Abramoff told them they needed grassroots lobbying to prevent other tribes from opening casinos, thus limiting the competition. He brought in his scheming friend Mike Scanlon for these efforts. (Abramoff wrote of the take-no-prisoners Scanlon: "He knew how to bury the hatchet—in his opponent's head."[22]) Scanlon charged enormous fees, and then kicked back a cut of the action to Abramoff. They funneled the casino money through other organizations to cover their tracks, including Grover Norquist's Americans for Tax Reform and Ralph Reed's Century Strategies, the latter of whom was ostensibly opposed to gambling, but was happy to take gambling money. Over three years Abramoff and Scanlon bilked $82 million from six Indian tribes. Abramoff became known as "Casino Jack."[23]

The tribes began questioning the huge sums they were being asked to pay, and dissidents leaked accounting records. Abramoff's scheme began to unravel. The press smelled trouble and pounced. Abramoff and his associates had unwisely left a swath of documents: foul-mouthed, self-congratulatory emails at how much they were extorting from their clients. The *Washington Post* published a detailed investigative report exposing Abramoff and Scanlon's shady lobbing practices in February 2004. The Senate Committee on Indian Affairs opened an investigation, where many of these emails were read in public. The chairman, Senator John McCain, repeatedly excoriated Abramoff.[24]

In November 2005, Scanlon pleaded guilty to a $19.7 million kickback scheme. Abramoff pleaded guilty twice. On January 3, 2006, in a Washington, D.C., courtroom, where he acknowledged he had defrauded four tribes of $25 million, had evaded federal income taxes, and bribed public officials. The next day, he pleaded guilty in Miami in a case involving SunCruz, a fleet of floating casinos. He agreed to testify against his co-conspirators. Abramoff was sentenced to six years in prison, but was released in December 2010 after forty-three months in jail.[25]

The Jack Abramoff scandal sent shock waves through the political lobbying world. Numerous congressional aides and lobbyists were charged and convicted of conspiracy. One of those in trouble was Ohio congressman Bob Ney. Abramoff had taken Ney to Scotland on a junket to golf and to lobby for a bill that would reopen a casino in El Paso, Texas. The bill never made it through Congress, but Ney was charged with corruption. He resigned from Congress, pleaded guilty, and served seventeen months in jail. House Majority Leader Tom DeLay resigned from Congress in June 2006; in 2010, a Texas jury found him guilty of money laundering and campaign finance violations, though on appeal his conviction was thrown out. An ethics cloud hung over California congressman John Doolittle, who left Congress in 2008, for his connections to Abramoff's network. He was never charged.

Money is at the heart of American politics. It panders for policies. It seduces and corrupts. It buys votes with campaign contributions and pay-to-play demands. And it is every politician's first job to be reelected. The American election system was addicted to money to fund the nonstop campaign mode. Instead of staying in Washington to work on the people's business, Congress had four-day workweeks so representatives and senators could fly home to fundraise every weekend. And it raised the question: why didn't the U.S. have publicly financed elections? Mike Lofgren, who spent nearly three decades in Congress as a budget analyst, noted how corrupting the influence of money was on the political system: "Money has overtaken politics so completely that factional interests are now simply competing to buy votes."[26]

By no means is greed confined to Republicans. One of the more curious scandals of the decade seemed like a throwback to Tammany Hall in the 19th century, when patronage and political favors all came with a price tag. After Barack Obama was elected to the presidency in 2008, Illinois's Democratic governor, Rod Blagojevich (pronounced Bluh-GOY-yeh-vitch), was arrested for conspiring to sell Obama's now-vacant Senate seat to the highest bidder. The FBI taped Blagojevich saying, "I've got this thing, and it's fucking golden. I'm just not giving it up for fucking nothing." This capped a multi-year investigation into corruption in the Blagojevich administration.

Blagojevich was impeached and removed from office by the Illinois state legislature. Federal prosecutors brought twenty-four charges against him, but in August 2010 a jury convicted him on just one count, deadlocking on the others. The judge declared a mistrial on the other charges, and prosecutors charged him again, and this time the jury convicted Blagojevich of seventeen counts in June 2011, including attempting to sell Obama's senate seat. He was sentenced to fourteen years in prison.

Billionaire real estate investor Donald Trump starred in a reality television show called *The Apprentice* that first aired in January 2004, where he got to spout his signature line, "You're fired." The show opened with Trump announcing, "My name is Donald Trump and I'm the largest real estate developer in New York." The *New York Times* immediately took exception to Trump's brash statement, pointing out that there were numerous developers who had larger real estate portfolios. One property owner called it "a watershed in self-promotion, coldly and carefully designed as a business strategy to achieve millions in free publicity." Angered by this affront to his celebrity status, Trump threatened a libel lawsuit but never followed through.[27]

A year into *The Apprentice*, Donald Trump was recorded making a lewd statement on a hot microphone while filming for *Access Hollywood*, though the video itself would not surface until October 2016 as he ran for president. In a conversation aboard a bus with Billy Bush, he talked about his power as a celebrity and how he could walk right up and kiss a woman. "I don't even wait," he said. "And when you're a star, they let you do it. You can do anything. Grab them by the pussy. You can do anything." By this point, Trump was married to his third wife.[28]

Trump ran a private real-estate empire. Without shareholders, he had no constituents to satisfy other than himself. And as a private business, Trump made no public disclosures or reported on whom he was doing business with. But far from being a storied and successful businessman, Trump's various business dealings went into bankruptcy four times in the early 1990s when he got financially overextended. His fifth bankruptcy occurred in 2004 when Trump Hotels and Casinos Resorts filed for bankruptcy protection, and his sixth bankruptcy occurred in 2009 when Trump Entertainment Resorts filed for bankruptcy; after emerging from bankruptcy, it refiled in 2014. After these numerous bankruptcies, most banks shut Trump out from lending.

Between 2006 and 2014, Trump acquired fourteen golf courses and other real estate properties for more than $400 million, and he paid entirely in cash. Trump had earlier piled up a mound of debt to finance his purchases, followed by bankruptcies, such that banks would no longer loan to him, other than Deutsche Bank, which loaned him money to renovate the properties.[29]

The Donald (as he was notably called by his first wife Ivana) opened Trump University in 2005 as a for-profit college to educate people in the real estate market. It offered no degrees and triggered a number of lawsuits. The university closed in 2010, and Trump settled three lawsuits against him for defrauding students for $25 million in November 2016, shortly after he was elected president.[30]

Perhaps it's human nature for powerful men to cheat on their spouses—but the consequences can be ruinous, especially in an era when the press and the public no longer turn a blind eye. John Edwards, a former presidential candidate, committed political suicide when he had an affair with a campaign videographer and fathered a child with her—all while his wife Elizabeth was fighting cancer. New Jersey governor Jim McGreevey was married but came out as a gay man after his relationship with an Israeli man on his staff was exposed, leading to the governor's resignation. Senator Larry Craig of Idaho was arrested in a sting in the men's room at the Minneapolis airport, a notorious gay cruising spot. His excuse for bumping the man's foot in the next stall was that he had a "wide stance."

In May 2011, former California governor Arnold Schwarzenegger and his wife Maria Shriver, the niece of John F. Kennedy, separated after he confessed that he had fathered a child with their housekeeper. The following month, South Carolina's governor, Mark Sanford, disappeared for almost a week, and his staff claimed he was hiking the Appalachian Trail. He later confessed that he had flown to Argentina to visit his mistress. "Hiking the Appalachian Trail" became a euphemism for having an affair. This was the second major Republican adultery confession in a week. Just days before, Nevada senator John Ensign admitted to having an affair. This ended his consideration as a presidential candidate.

Football legend O. J. Simpson published a 2007 book called *If I Did It*, describing how he would have killed his wife and her friend Ron Goldman (the two were murdered in 1994). However, much of the public still assumed that O.J. had in fact done it. On October 3, 2008—exactly thirteen years after being found not guilty of murdering the two—Simpson was convicted in Las Vegas of twelve felonies for attempting to kidnap and rob two Simpson memorabilia collectors. He was sentenced to prison for at least nine years of a thirty-three-year term. He was paroled in 2017.

Tiger Woods—the legendary golfer who had a squeaky-clean public reputation—turned out to be not so squeaky. In 2009, more than a dozen women came forward to reveal that they had had affairs with him. He had kept all this secret for a long time, but it eventually caught up with him. His wife filed for divorce, and many of his corporate sponsors dropped him. As they say, there are no secrets—especially not for public figures. David Letterman, the long-serving late-night television host and comedian, admitted in 2009 that he had had sexual relations with a number of women on his staff. This was a full decade before the #MeToo movement that challenged men over sexual harassment. The story came forward when a television producer attempted to extort him.

Pop icon Michael Jackson had sold more albums in history than anyone, including his multiplatinum 1982 album *Thriller*. The man was enormously wealthy, but his behavior was increasingly erratic over the years. Although a breakthrough artist for African Americans and renowned as the King of Pop, he had a succession of plastic surgeries that made him nearly unrecognizable. Jackson built a fairy-tale home near Santa Barbara, California, a child's version of Xanadu called Neverland, complete with amusement park and zoo. It was expensive to operate, and Jackson, though rich, had mortgaged himself to the hilt to support his opulent lifestyle. Then came the charges of child molestation, of which a jury acquitted him in 2005. Jackson had difficulty sleeping and his personal physician prescribed various sleep medications, but when they failed to help Jackson asked for something stronger. On June 25, 2009, Jackson's doctor administered a lethal dose of Propofol. Jackson died at the age of fifty in his rented Los Angeles mansion, leaving behind three children and a financial mess of an estate. His memorial service, broadcast on July 7 on a multitude of television stations, was the most-watched media event since President Barack Obama's inauguration.

Professional cyclist Lance Armstrong staged a storybook comeback that turned out too good to be true. After recovering from cancer, he roared back and won the Tour de France seven times between 1999 and 2005. His Livestrong Foundation made its yellow bracelets ubiquitous for several years—even Senator John Kerry wore one during the 2004 presidential election campaign. Rumors of doping surrounded Armstrong. The rumors proved true in 2012 when Armstrong's teammates testified against him before the United States Anti-Doping Agency. Confronted with the truth, Armstrong admitted that he had in fact cheated, using a long list of performance-enhancing drugs that were illegal to professional athletes, and that he had bullied his fellow teammates into silence. Armstrong was stripped of all seven Tour de France medals and banned from competitive sports.

The most devastating scandal of the decade was not related to the rich and famous, or to the politically powerful. Its victims were thousands of children—mostly schoolboys—who were molested by priests in the Roman Catholic Church. After a lengthy investigation, the *Boston Globe* published a damning series of reports that opened the floodgates in early 2002. (The investigation was portrayed in the Oscar-winning 2015 movie *Spotlight*.) Cardinal Bernard Law, who led the Boston archdiocese, had for years swept the molestation crisis under the rug, reassigning dozens of priests to new parishes rather than firing them, and settled with the families privately. Child molestation, whether by a priest or not, is still a crime, but the church fought to keep this secret and to shield its priests, rather than to protect children. Cardinal Law should have gone to jail.

Once the *Globe*'s Spotlight team began publishing its articles, thousands of people came forward claiming abuse at the hands of priests. Public outrage led the Vatican to reassign Cardinal Law to Rome, which in essence meant the church protected Law from civil prosecution for abetting these crimes. The Boston archdiocese settled with more than five hundred victims for $95 million, closed many parishes, and sold much of its local property to Boston College to fund the restitution. A number of priests were convicted and imprisoned. The most notorious of the priests, John Geoghan, was murdered in his prison cell.[31]

But the church scandal wasn't limited to Boston, nor just to the United States. Further investigations revealed that hundreds of Catholic dioceses around the world had similarly dealt with child molestation by reassigning priests and covering up the problem. The sex abuse scandal left many questioning the church, and financial contributions plummeted. The Catholic

Church had its crisis of faith as many people abandoned it, some never to return.

The human condition tends toward hubris. Perhaps it's a survival mechanism for our species. The idea that we are always right—even when we are wrong—can blind people to injustice, or to only one point of view. The United States would make its single biggest mistake of the decade in 2003, following a false trail of evidence and messianic zeal to overthrow a Middle Eastern dictator. The result was the invasion of Iraq.

5

The Iraq War

"One of the great mysteries to me is exactly when the war in Iraq became inevitable."[1]

—George Tenet, former CIA director, *At the Center of the Storm*

In his January 2002 State of the Union Address, President George Bush called out Iran, Iraq, and North Korea as an "axis of evil, arming to threaten the peace of the world." There was actually no axis—these countries were not allied. Iran and Iraq had been rivals for decades. North Korea was appropriately known as the Hermit Kingdom by being closed off to everyone. The latter two were probably more capable of destabilizing the world order than Iraq. But being the weakest, Iraq was the easiest to go after.[2]

Saddam Hussein had been Iraq's secular dictator since he seized power in 1979. He brutalized his own population to maintain control. He led a high-casualty but inconclusive war against Iran in the 1980s in the wake of the latter's revolution. In August 1990, he invaded Kuwait. Led by President George H. W. Bush and the United States, an international coalition evicted Hussein from Kuwait in a six-week military campaign called Operation Desert Storm in early 1991. The United Nations placed strict impositions on Hussein to destroy his biological, chemical, and nuclear weapons of mass destruction (WMD) capabilities, which he had earlier used against Iran and his own Kurdish-minority population. The U.S. encouraged the Kurds and Shiites to rebel against Hussein, which they did, then stood by as they were slaughtered. The Bill Clinton era of the 1990s focused on containing Iraq through U.N. inspections, an embargo, and no-fly zones.

Iraq was successfully contained. So why, after twelve years, did the Bush administration choose to preemptively invade the country in 2003 and overthrow Saddam Hussein? Was it because Hussein attempted to assassinate Bush's father in 1993? Was it because the administration genuinely believed that Hussein had weapons of mass destruction? Was it to promote democracy in the Middle East? Or was it to secure Saudi Arabia—and thus the oil lifeline to the United States? And what was Dick Cheney's and the neoconservatives' influence in all of this? No clear answer exists yet. Future historians will have access to archival research about the decisions that were made, and why we went to war in Iraq. In the meantime, we have newspaper accounts and the public word of the participants.

There were some in the Bush administration who believed, wrongly, that there was a direct link between al-Qaeda and Saddam Hussein. Deputy Defense Secretary Paul Wolfowitz argued the case to bomb Iraq shortly after 9/11. President Bush approached Richard Clarke, his counterterrorism expert, and told him, "Look into Iraq, Saddam."[3] George Tenet, the director of the CIA, attended a White House meeting the day after 9/11. He bumped into Richard Perle of the Defense Policy Board, who remarked, "Iraq has to pay a price for what happened yesterday. They bear responsibility."[4]

Bush later acknowledged that Paul Wolfowitz wanted to confront Iraq over 9/11. Secretary of State Colin Powell cautioned against it, as Bush recalled him saying, "Going after Iraq now would be viewed as a bait and switch. We would lose the U.S., the Islamic countries, and NATO. If we want to do Iraq, we should do it at a time of our choosing. But we should not do it now, because we don't have linkage to this event."[5]

Like many of the neoconservative policy leaders at the Pentagon, Donald Rumsfeld promoted action against Iraq, and believed it reasonable to investigate the alleged ties between al-Qaeda and Saddam Hussein:

> Much has been written about the Bush administration's focus on Iraq after 9/11. Commentators have suggested that it was strange or obsessive for the President and his advisers to have raised questions about whether Saddam Hussein was somehow behind the attack. I have never understood the controversy. Early on, I had no idea if Iraq was or was not involved, but it would have been irresponsible for any administration not to have asked the question.[6]

George Tenet later wrote, "For many in the Bush administration, Iraq was unfinished business. They seized on the emotional impact of 9/11 and created a psychological connection between the failure to act decisively against al-Qa'ida and the danger posed by Iraq's WMD programs. The message was: We can never afford to be surprised again."[7] In November 2001, shortly after Kabul fell, Bush directed Rumsfeld to draft military plans to invade Iraq and topple Saddam Hussein. Clearly 9/11 made the Iraq War possible.[8]

"Before 9/11, Saddam was a problem America might have been able to manage. Through the lens of the post-9/11 world, my view changed," Bush acknowledged. "The lesson of 9/11 was that if we waited for a danger to fully materialize, we would have waited too long. I reached a decision: We would confront the threat from Iraq, one way or another."[9]

So just when did President Bush make the decision to go to war in Iraq—or, as George Tenet asked, when did war become inevitable? Historians will no doubt be arguing over this for years.[10]

Bush laid out the general case for preemptive war in a June 1, 2002, speech at West Point. "Our security will require all Americans to be forward looking, to be ready for preemptive action when necessary to defend our liberty and to defend our lives," the president argued. This Anticipatory Self-Defense policy, as it was officially called, justified a first-strike against enemies, rather than responding to their attack. This controversial new policy became known as the Bush Doctrine, and pundits immediately recognized its mostly likely target was Iraq.[11]

The following month, Richard Haass, the director of policy planning at the State Department, met informally with National Security Advisor Condoleezza Rice. He asked her if Iraq was really the centerpiece of Bush's foreign policy. She cut him off: "You can save your breath, Richard. The president has already made up his mind on Iraq," and Haass assumed she meant taking the nation to war against Saddam Hussein.[12]

Bush's first major biographer, Robert Draper, believed that Bush had decided on regime change by August, calculating that the military campaign would have to take place during the winter before the summertime heat set in.[13] Another biographer, Jean Edward Smith, pointed out that the British government became convinced in July that Bush was intent on war with Iraq.[14]

Vice President Dick Cheney sent out a trial balloon for a war against Iraq at a speech to the Veterans of Foreign Wars on August 26. "There is no doubt" that Iraq possessed WMDs, and he argued the case for the Bush Doctrine: "We realize that wars are never won on the defensive. We must take the battle to the enemy." Cheney stated that "The risks of inaction are far greater than the risk of action," and concluded that Iraq should be liberated from Saddam Hussein and democracy established. At that point it became increasingly clear that the Bush administration was determined to confront Saddam Hussein.[15]

Cheney's blunt words before the VFW got out ahead of where Bush actually was—the vice president strongly implied that war was inevitable, while the president may in fact have not made up his mind. The Cheney speech outflanked Colin Powell, who was counseling caution and U.N. action. Powell was the odd man out, the only cabinet official in the Bush administration who had actually seen combat. The State Department saw Saddam Hussein "as a nuisance not a mortal threat," according to Richard Haass.[16] Bush assented to Powell's recommendation to follow the U.N. process—as long as it could be concluded before winter ended, when it would be too hot to lead a military campaign in Mesopotamia.[17]

Condoleezza Rice penned in her memoir that "The President had decided on a policy of coercive diplomacy" to put pressure on Saddam Hussein to comply with U.N. orders or face being overthrown. She noted that Bush made the decision for war in September. Rice recalled him saying, "Either he will come clean about his weapons, or there will be war."[18]

Historian Michael Mazarr, who extensively studied the decision-making that led to the Iraq War, believed that war was a foregone conclusion by the time the National Security Council met with the president at Camp David on September 7. But even he couldn't determine exactly when the decision was made. "Our understanding of precisely why and how that choice came to be made remains radically incomplete," he wrote. "We still do not know when or how, precisely, the decision took place."[19]

Journalist Bob Woodward, on the other hand, noted that Bush did not decide on taking the country to war until early January 2003. In the intervening period between when he ordered Rumsfeld to build a military plan in November 2001 and his decision to go to war fourteen months later, Bush pursued both diplomatic and military options against Saddam Hussein. Woodward noted that "war plans and the process of war planning become policy by their own momentum."[20]

Bush was heavily influenced by a group of neoconservative or "neocon" policymakers in the Pentagon. This group of hawks believed that toppling Saddam Hussein would trigger democracy in Iraq and throughout the Middle East. They took Wilsonian diplomacy to the extreme, not just promoting democracy abroad, but willing to topple foreign governments to impose democracy. Rajiv Chandrasekaran, the Baghdad bureau chief for the *Washington Post*, wrote in his National Book Award–winning *Imperial Life in the Emerald City*:

> The neoconservative architects of the war—[Paul] Wolfowitz, [Douglas] Feith, Rumsfeld, and Cheney—regarded wholesale economic change in Iraq as an integral part of the American mission to remake the country. To them, a free economy and a free society went hand in hand. If the United States were serious about having democracy flourish in Iraq, it would have to teach Iraqis a whole new way of doing business—the American way. [21]

Bush's missionary zeal was to plant democracy, but the administration was naïve to believe that democracy could be imposed on Iraq. Few Middle Eastern countries had experience with democracy, nor were their cultures imbued with values of individual liberty and personal rights that had emerged out of the Enlightenment in the 18th century. The Middle East was traditionally tribal and was ruled by kings, sheikhs, and strongmen. Democracy may not be for every country.

Meanwhile, the *New York Times*'s Judith Miller published a series of articles in September 2002 articulating the biological, chemical, and possible nuclear weapons that Saddam Hussein could deploy. Her key sources were Iraqi defectors, including Ahmed Chalabi, as well as the Bush administration itself. Chalabi was an Iraqi exile, a staunch opponent to Hussein who led the Iraqi National Congress, and who fed misinformation to the U.S. The Pentagon in particular embraced Chalabi as a possible new leader for Iraq. [22]

The Bush administration went on a public relations offensive to make the case against Saddam Hussein. Although the intelligence might not be crystal clear, Condoleezza Rice stated on CNN, "We don't want the smoking gun to be a mushroom cloud." President Bush addressed the United Nations on September 12, five days after the Camp David meeting of his national security advisers, noting the threat that Iraq posed to the international community.

His speech was met with near silence. This was a warning that there was little international support for a preemptive move against Iraq.[23]

The CIA was given a very short time frame to prepare a National Intelligence Estimate on Iraq, which it published in October. The NIE turned out to be full of errors about Hussein's supposed weapons of mass destruction. George Tenet, the CIA director, insisted that the Bush administration did not politically lean on his analysts to achieve a certain outcome. "Intelligence professionals did not try to tell policy makers what they wanted to hear, nor did the policy makers lean on us to influence outcomes," he wrote. On the other hand, Tenet freely admitted that some in the Bush administration were predisposed to link Saddam Hussein to al-Qaeda and constantly pushed for more intelligence that would prove their assertion.[24]

Armed with the NIE, the Bush administration went to Congress for a use of force authorization against Iraq. The resolution was designed in part to put Congress on the record shortly before the midterm election. On October 10, the House voted 296–133 in favor of the authorization, while the Senate voted at midnight 77–23 in favor. The vote would later become controversial when the results of the war turned out to be far different than promised, and Democrats especially seemed to wish that they could take back their "aye" votes. This would become a presidential campaign issue in 2004.[25]

The 2002 midterm election four weeks later served as a referendum on Bush's leadership in the War on Terror. Republicans recaptured the Senate and widened their majority in the House by eight seats. It was a resounding ratification for Bush and bucked the historical trend that the president's party loses congressional seats in midterms.

Just days after the election, Bush sought and won a U.N. resolution on Iraq, U.N. Security Council Resolution 1441, which passed unanimously on November 8. It required Saddam Hussein to own up to his WMD capabilities. He was given thirty days to comply, and he responded with a huge document designed for obfuscation, not clarity. While the U.N. dispatched an investigative team under Hans Blix to comb through Iraq for WMDs, American military forces continued their buildup in Kuwait.

After hearing a less-than-convincing CIA presentation about Iraq's WMD evidence on December 21, Bush asked if this was all the agency had. Director George Tenet responded with the most controversial justification for war: "Don't worry, it's a slam dunk."[26] Tenet later denied calling the evidence a "slam dunk," but both Bush and Cheney confirmed that the director did in fact say it. The president himself recognized that the lack of hard evidence was a problem—much of what the CIA had collected was based on assertion or assumption. He was the only person who could apply the brakes to a war that was quickly becoming inevitable, but he did not. No one challenged the assumption that Saddam Hussein had WMDs. [27]

Bush had decided for preemptive war by early January 2003. Hussein was continuing to obfuscate, and the fact that the Hans Blix mission was turning up nothing was evidence, to the Bush administration, that Iraq was hiding and shifting around its WMDs. [28] Blix formally reported to the U.N. on January 27 that, after two months of searching, "Iraq appears not to have come to a genuine acceptance—not even today—of the disarmament which was demanded of it and which it needs to carry out to win the confidence of the world and to live in peace." This fed into the Bush administration narrative that Iraq was continuing to obfuscate its WMD capabilities. [29]

Secretary of State Colin Powell was the most publicly esteemed person in the Bush cabinet, and his skepticism about invading Iraq was well known. He thus became the point man for selling the war not just to the U.N., but also to the American people. On February 5, Powell delivered a seventy-six-minute speech before the U.N., laying out the detailed evidence against Iraq, showing that Saddam Hussein had covertly maintained his weapons of mass destruction labs in violation of international law and U.N. resolutions. Powell's speech largely silenced public opposition to the war. Much of this evidence, as it turns out, was false. Powell would later call it "one of my most momentous failures." [30]

White House press secretary Scott McClellan noted that the president's "advisers decided to pursue a political propaganda campaign to sell the war to the American people." The Bush administration sold the invasion of Iraq as the solution to the nation's and the world's problems, that Iraq would be liberated from tyranny, and claimed that Saddam Hussein was an imminent threat. [31]

The Bush administration had won a major U.N. resolution in fall 2002 to force Hussein to come clean about his WMDs; however, it declined to pursue a second resolution. Bush recognized there was too much opposition from France, Germany, and Russia. He had already decided on war and believed the earlier U.N. resolution, 1441, provided the necessary authorization.

There was a rush to war. The hot summer weather would soon arrive. The Bush administration did not want to gather more evidence or wait for more allies. Bush wanted to overthrow Saddam Hussein now. He built a "coalition of the willing," a hackneyed term that was much derided once people realized that American and British troops would do almost all the work. Allies from thirty-two other countries would contribute soldiers, but most were small contingents. Italy and Spain contributed troops, an unpopular action in their countries, but after elections shifted their governments, the troops went home. The American troops stayed.

Donald Rumsfeld ignited a diplomatic squabble by calling France and Germany part of "old Europe" for opposing American efforts in Iraq. America turned a deaf ear to its allies, and some even called for French fries to be renamed "freedom fries," echoing the anti-German hysteria from World War I. European allies accused the U.S. of cowboy diplomacy: shooting first, asking questions later. It was irresponsible for the world's leading power to act this way. [32]

Rumsfeld wanted the smallest-sized military force possible for the Iraq mission and so understaffed the invasion. The U.S. would invade Iraq with only 125,000 soldiers, plus a 20,000-person British contingent. These were far too few troops to occupy and control the country. The generals had asked for 300,000 troops. But with vastly better and more accurate firepower, the Pentagon reasoned, far fewer troops were needed compared to the Persian Gulf War twelve years earlier. In addition, the U.S. had overthrown the Taliban in Afghanistan with a minuscule force. But Iraq was another animal, with a large standing army and huge weapons caches stored around the country. [33]

The Bush administration believed that only the best could happen and failed to adequately weigh the risks in invading Iraq. The Iraqi people would greet the Americans as liberators, they believed. They maintained an optimism that they could replace Saddam Hussein with a democratic regime and quickly step away. They were completely unprepared for what actually happened. The military force was far too small, and too little planning was conceived for what would happen after Hussein fell. The Iraq War opened a Pandora's Box.

Bush biographer Jean Edward Smith called Bush's decision to invade Iraq "easily the worst foreign policy decision ever made by an American president." [34] It would come to haunt the Bush presidency. And like Lyndon Johnson and Vietnam, Bush would be chiefly remembered for the Iraq War.

Operation Iraqi Freedom

The allied military forces, mostly composed of Americans, continued their buildup in the Kuwaiti desert. With the hot weather approaching and Saddam stonewalling on further transparency about his alleged WMDs, President Bush delivered an ultimatum on March 17, 2003, that Hussein and his son leave Iraq within forty-eight hours—or else.

Before the ultimatum window expired, false intelligence placed Hussein at Dora Farm south of Baghdad, and Bush ordered the air force to bomb the farm on a decapitation strike. Hussein was in fact not there. He had gone into hiding and would not be seen again for nearly nine months.

Military operations known as Operation Iraqi Freedom began on March 19 with massive aerial bombardments and Tomahawk cruise missile strikes against Iraqi communications and military targets. Pentagon planners called it "shock and awe." Operation Desert Storm in 1991 had begun with a monthlong air attack before the armies moved in to liberate Kuwait, but in 2003 the ground offensive began almost immediately. On that first day, allied forces seized most of Iraq's oil fields, and on March 21, American and British armies began the ground offensive from Kuwait.

While British force seized Basra, Iraq's largest southern city, American forces skirted around southern Iraqi cities as they blitzed to Baghdad, the Iraqi capital. The press was embedded with advancing troops and reported live on television as the campaign developed. Like 9/11, the nation was glued to its TV sets.

The Iraqi army did not capitulate or stand aside but fought even in the face of vastly greater American firepower. The elite Republican Guard and Ba'athist insurgents, known as the Fedayeen Saddam, battled the invaders, often adopting insurgent warfare of the ambush and checkpoint. They had stockpiled weapons around Iraq for just such an insurgency. The inability to defeat these guerrillas and later, foreign jihadists, would have consequences.

The highly mechanized American column quickly moved hundreds of miles into the Shiite-dominated area south of Baghdad, where it encountered significant resistance. The U.S. Army had a long supply line back to Kuwait, and had brought along too few military police to secure the route. An army maintenance column got lost and barreled into an Iraqi ambush in Nasiriyah on March 23. Eleven soldiers were killed and PFC Jessica Lynch was severely injured and taken prisoner. Lynch was taken to an Iraqi hospital, where her wounds were treated. A week later, the Pentagon released dramatic video of a daring nighttime raid to rescue her in the hospital, something that played well in the press, until the story broke that she was virtually unguarded.

The following year in Afghanistan, a former National Football League player turned Army Ranger, Pat Tillman, was killed. The Pentagon created a fictional account of how he fell battling the Taliban and even awarded him the Silver Star. The truth finally emerged that he had been killed by friendly fire, not by the enemy. In both cases, the Pentagon painted a false narrative that eroded public trust.

The U.S. Army stormed into Baghdad. The capital fell faster than anyone expected on April 9, and the army symbolically tore down a statue of Saddam Hussein in Firdos Square. The Iraqi army and Hussein's government melted away or went into hiding. The war had lasted just three weeks and the regime was toppled; however, Iraq remained unpacified. Massive looting broke out in Baghdad, and the U.S. did not have enough troops on the ground to control the city. It was the first of many surprises for the Americans, who would soon be deemed as occupiers, not liberators.

Donald Rumsfeld's Pentagon had gone to war with too few troops. In World War II, the Allies occupied Germany with several million soldiers, disarmed the Germans, denazified the political system, and stabilized the country. With the occupation of Iraq in 2003, the U.S. and Britain occupied a 25-million-person country with no more than 150,000 soldiers.

The Pentagon hoped to turn governing Iraq over quickly to the Iraqis. But the Iraqis were incapable—Hussein had been all too efficient at rooting out potential opponents. Rumsfeld shied away from nation-building, eager to turn over security and governing to Afghans and Iraqis, though neither country was ready for the task. Rumsfeld believed that, "Solving corruption in Afghanistan or building a secular democracy in the Middle East are not America's problems to tackle. They are not our broken societies to fix."[35] Nation-building and economic development may have been far less expensive than the endless wars that the U.S. got instead. The U.S. spent a fortune on security in both countries—and a fraction on developing their institutions and economies. The Bush administration seemed blind to this huge cost—and to the opportunity cost of putting all the eggs into the security basket. The cost of keeping an army stationed overseas in two unstable war zones was enormous.

The U.S. administration set up camp in the Green Zone, a seventeen-square-mile area of Baghdad formerly at the center of Saddam Hussein's regime. It was transformed into a massive fortified compound and later, headquarters for the Iraqi government. Rajiv Chandrasekaran, the Baghdad bureau chief of the *Washington Post*, noted that people called it the Emerald City, as in *The Wizard of Oz*. He observed firsthand how out of touch the occupiers were.[36]

With Saddam's regime toppled, the CIA-led Iraq Survey Group hunted through the country to find the hidden weapons of mass destruction. It found no WMDs, as it turned out Saddam Hussein did not have any. The team found evidence of his desire to produce such weapons, but not the stockpiles themselves. David Kay led the team for most of its existence, then he handed it off to Charles Duelfer. The ISG published the three-volume Duelfer Report in September 2004, concluding that Hussein had destroyed his WMDs in 1991 after the Gulf War.[37] Hussein then engaged in a policy of mass deception. He needed his population to believe he still had these weapons, as it was key to keeping the rebellious Kurds and Shiites in check, and especially to deter Iran, whose influence was growing in the region. In essence, Hussein bluffed.[38] Colin Powell observed, "If Saddam wanted us to believe he had WMDs, then he convinced us." He added, "If we had known there were no WMDs, there would have been no war." Powell called this "one of the worst intelligence failures in U.S. history."[39]

The Duelfer Report undermined the case for why the U.S. had invaded Iraq. "This was a war that had been justified by an intelligence judgment, not a strategic one," noted Condoleezza Rice. When the intelligence fell apart, the lack of a strategy became apparent.[40]

Karl Rove, the president's political strategist, asked: "Would the Iraq War have occurred without W.M.D.? I doubt it. Congress was very unlikely to have supported the use-of-force resolution without the W.M.D. threat. The Bush administration itself would probably have sought other ways to constrain Saddam, bring about regime change, and deal with Iraq's horrendous human rights violations." He added in defense of his boss: "So, then, did Bush lie us into war? Absolutely not."[41]

In the backlash against the Iraq War, one saw bumper stickers and protest signs that read, BUSH LIED. PEOPLE DIED. This simply was not true—everyone, including the international community, believed that Saddam Hussein had weapons of mass destruction. Bush wrote in his memoir, "Nobody was lying. We were all wrong."[42] They were misled, and based on this evidence, Bush made a faulty strategic decision.

Confessing that the Bush administration was wrong about intelligence on Iraqi WMD and the reasons for war, Donald Rumsfeld later wrote: "Powell was not duped or misled by anyone, nor did he lie about Saddam's suspected WMD stockpiles. The President did not lie. The Vice President did not lie. Tenet did not lie. Rice did not lie. I did not lie. The Congress did not lie. The far less dramatic truth is that we were wrong."[43]

Bush admitted that the intelligence failure had undermined his case to invade Iraq: "While the world was undoubtedly safer with Saddam gone, the reality was that I had sent American troops into combat based in large part on intelligence that proved false. That was a massive blow to our credibility—my credibility—that would shake the confidence of the American people."[44] Karl Rove added, "The failure to find stockpiles of WMD did great damage to the administration's credibility."[45] Much of the international goodwill that the U.S. earned as a result of 9/11 was squandered when the U.S. blundered into Iraq.

Nevertheless, the Bush White House continued to justify the American invasion of Iraq, clearly as a reaction to 9/11. Condoleezza Rice wrote, "After 9/11, Saddam in possession of WMD in the world's most volatile region was a terrifying prospect; the Middle East would be a less frightening place without him. I still believe that the latter is true. I have many regrets about the run-up to the war, but I'm not sorry that we overthrew Saddam.[46]

Rumsfeld's memoir, *Known and Unknown*, was an apology of sorts for Iraqi regime change. An unfailing supporter of the war, Rumsfeld criticized the administration's sole focus on Iraq's alleged weapons of mass destruction. To his point of view, there were many valid reasons to overthrow Saddam Hussein.

> Intelligence evidence about WMD had a way of taking pride of place in the litany of reasons for going to war. In fact, that should have been only one of the many reasons. There was a long list of other charges against Saddam Hussein's regime—its support of terrorism, its attacks on American pilots in the no-fly zones, its violation of the United Nations Security Council resolutions, its history of aggression, and its crimes against its people.[47]

Dick Cheney likewise had heavily advocated for the U.S. to overthrow Saddam. The vice president continued to believe that the Iraqi dictator had links to al-Qaeda and posed an imminent and direct threat to the U.S., though most of the Bush administration did not, nor did the nation's intelligence agencies.[48] "When we looked around the world in those first months after 9/11, there was no place more likely to be a nexus between terrorism and WMD capability than Saddam Hussein's Iraq," Cheney later wrote. "With the benefit of hindsight—even taking in account that some of the intelligence we received was wrong—that assessment still holds true." Actually nearly all of it was wrong—not just some of the intelligence.[49]

George Tenet, the director of Central Intelligence, wrote definitively: "CIA found absolutely no linkage between Saddam and 9/11."[50] Condoleezza Rice amplified this statement: "There was simply no convincing case to be made for a link between 9/11 and Saddam. The Vice President and his staff, however, were absolutely convinced that Saddam was somehow culpable." It wasn't just Cheney; President Bush likewise continued to push the al-Qaeda/Iraq connection long after the Iraq invasion.[51]

Bush always spoke of the Iraq War as making the U.S. more secure. But did it? And was Saddam Hussein a threat to the United States? No, he was not. Hussein was a thug, but he was a secular dictator, not a terrorist. It made no sense that he would give WMDs to al-Qaeda in the first place, given that the terrorist organization wanted to overthrow him and other Muslim leaders and replace them with an Islamic caliphate. The State Department's Richard Haass concluded, "Yes, Saddam Hussein was a monster, but that did not justify the decision to go to war to oust him"[52]

Invading Iraq was a strategic mistake. It destabilized the Middle East. Saddam Hussein was the glue that held Iraq together, and Iraq was the main bulwark against Iran. And Iran became the main winner when Hussein was overthrown, as its influence in the region grew. Eighty percent of Iraq's population was Shiite Muslim, the same faith as Iran, and thus they were natural allies.

Iraq made the case that it's easy to win a war, but difficult to win the peace. In the runup to the war, Secretary of State Colin Powell warned President Bush: "If you break it, you own it." Some called it the Pottery Barn Rule, named after the homewares store. The U.S. had broken Iraq—and now owned its chaos.[53]

The Iraqi Occupation

On May 1, 2003, as the aircraft carrier USS *Abraham Lincoln* approached San Diego harbor on its return from the Iraq War, President Bush landed in

a Navy jet and stepped out in his flight suit to deliver a prime-time television address. The president announced, "Major combat operations in Iraq have ended. In the battle of Iraq, the United States and our allies have prevailed." A banner reading MISSION ACCOMPLISHED hung over the ship's bridge and served as an unfortunate backdrop that would come back to haunt the president. Bush's speech and the optics of the sign smelled of triumphalism. It soon became clear that the war of occupation was just beginning. The speech would be one of the biggest public relations flops of the administration. Bush later called the Mission Accomplished sign a "big mistake." The mission in Iraq was nowhere close to being finished. [54]

The Bush administration hoped for a quick exit from Iraq, but that quickly became a lost cause. A key problem was that the Iraqi economy was dysfunctional. It was a state-run socialist economy, one that had promised lifetime employment, even if people did no work. An estimated 40 percent of Iraqis were out of work after Hussein was overthrown, but there was no plan to put them to work. There was plenty of disgruntlement, and Americans soon made things worse.

The Americans were woefully unprepared for postwar Iraq. General Jay Garner governed Iraq for two months, then was replaced. President Bush then appointed a former diplomat, Lewis Paul "Jerry" Bremer III, to lead the Coalition Provisional Authority (CPA) in May, essentially becoming the viceroy over Iraq. He made several crucial mistakes that polarized Iraqis and helped launch the resistance against the Americans, who were increasingly seen as occupiers, not liberators.

Bremer's first mistake was de-Ba'athification, which purged the largely Ba'ath Party technocrats from their jobs. This was Saddam Hussein's political party, one that handed out jobs through patronage, but they were also the people who had run the country. The Ba'athists were almost entirely Sunnis (only 20 percent of the country). Now thousands were out of work. They became immediate supporters of the growing insurgency.

Disbanding the Iraqi army and other security forces was Bremer's other major mistake. The army was the one national institution that could have held the country together. With the army and police out of the way, outlaws took over as Iraq descended into chaos with kidnapping, looting, and revenge killing. It was not safe for anyone, least of all for Iraqi citizens.

The Bush administration was ideological on the question of lowering taxes. In earlier wars, there was a sense of shared sacrifice to fund the country's war—a sense that everyone needed to contribute. Instead, Bush refused to budge on his earlier tax cuts and financed the war through deficit spending, and even pushed through yet another tax cut in May 2003, thinking that the Iraq War was over. The expenditures for the Iraq and Afghan wars were not paid for through the usual budget bills, but were forced through Congress as emergency spending bills each year. The cost of this very expensive war was far beyond anyone's prediction, and the nation's budget deficit reached record heights.

In the runup to the Iraq War, the White House had estimated the cost to be only $50 to $60 billion. White House economic adviser Lawrence Lindsey went off the reservation by telling the *Wall Street Journal* that he thought the war might cost $100 to $200 billion. That proved a woeful underestimate. Lindsey and his boss, Treasury Secretary Paul O'Neill, were dismissed in December 2002.[55] In fact, the Iraq War alone would cost about a trillion dollars, plus another trillion for Afghanistan.[56]

Instead of spending billions on reconstructing Iraq, much of the money went to security. Iraq was a vast, endless money pit. The Bush administration had little idea how truly broken the country was. Decades of sanctions had reduced its economy to a shoestring. Saddam Hussein had clung to power through the ruthless application of force on his own people. His strength as a dictator masked how fragile and dysfunctional the Iraqi economy had become. The U.S. could not just decapitate the leadership, install new leaders, and go home. Iraq was broken: it would take a huge effort to fix it.

The hard lesson of history is that, anytime one country topples another's government, they will have to engage in nation building, just as the U.S. rebuilt Germany, Italy, and Japan into viable democracies after World War II at great effort and expense. Once its institutions are dismantled, a country can quickly descend into chaos.

Even Dick Cheney, who never apologized for anything, admitted that the Bush administration had been mistaken: "It is fair to say that we underestimated the difficulty of rebuilding a traumatized and shattered society." His former company, Halliburton, won lucrative no-bid contracts for postwar operations in Iraq. Congress investigated the company in 2004, which resulted in a feud between Cheney and Vermont senator Patrick Leahy. Cheney told Leahy on the Senate floor, "Go fuck yourself."[57]

❖

In making his case for the war, Bush had included in his 2003 State of the Union Address sixteen controversial words about Hussein's supposed intentions to build nuclear weapons: "The British government has learned that Saddam Hussein recently sought significant quantities of uranium from Africa," Bush remarked. This was in fact not the case, yet these sixteen words formed the argument for a preemptive strike against Iraq. The CIA had even sent a mission to Niger under former ambassador Joseph Wilson in early 2002 to learn the truth of whether Hussein had sought to purchase yellowcake uranium, and he discovered that the Iraqi dictator had made no attempt. Wilson was married to a CIA agent, and he was also a fiercely partisan Democrat who sought to undermine Bush's rationale for war. After the *Washington Post* reported that the CIA had not passed along Wilson's findings to the White House, Wilson penned an accusing op-ed in the *New York Times* called "What I Didn't Find in Africa." He opined that the Bush administration had twisted the intelligence to exaggerate the Iraqi threat. Based on his intelligence, the sixteen words should have never been uttered. Wilson faulted the Bush administration for misleading the public.[58]

Shortly after that, conservative *Washington Post* columnist Robert Novak revealed that Joe Wilson's wife, Valerie Plame, worked for the CIA—and that he heard it from two sources high within the Bush administration that she had sent her husband to Niger to investigate the yellowcake uranium claim. Leaking the name of a covert officer such as Plame was a felony. The leak came across as a White House vendetta to punish Plame's husband, Joe Wilson, for his op-ed.[59]

Novak himself insisted that there was no conspiracy or crime intended by publishing Plame's name. One of his sources, Deputy Secretary of State Richard Armitage, was not even in the White House, though other sources were: Ari Fleischer, Karl Rove, and Lewis "Scooter" Libby. Still, the timing of Novak's column was suspicious—right after Wilson had published his own op-ed and gone on the offensive against the White House. A special prosecutor, Patrick Fitzgerald, was appointed to investigate. A dark cloud hung over the White House for the next three years.[60]

In 2005, the special prosecutor charged Scooter Libby with lying to the FBI about Plame's identity, though the prosecutor strongly suspected (as did a federal grand jury) that Libby was covering for his boss Dick Cheney. The Valerie Plame episode was deeply embarrassing to the Bush administration. Libby was convicted in 2007. President Bush commuted Libby's prison time, but not his fine. Cheney asserted that Libby was innocent and tried until the very end to get Bush to pardon him, but Bush never did. Cheney did his best to cast doubt on the entire affair. He, for one, believed that Hussein had in fact intended to buy uranium in Niger. "*The sixteen words were true,*" he championed in his memoir. The Duelfer Report contradicted this assertion, finding no evidence that Hussein had attempted to acquire uranium abroad.[61]

Meanwhile, the *New York Times* conducted an internal investigation of its reporter, Judith Miller, who had widely reported on Saddam Hussein's weapons of mass destruction. It concluded that she had used inaccurate information and forced her to resign in 2005. Miller refused to testify before the grand jury that Scooter Libby was her source for Valerie Plame being a CIA agent and was consequently jailed for contempt of court for nearly three months.

❖

The Iraqi insurrection erupted in summer 2003, largely by alienated Sunnis, and supplemented by foreign volunteers who wanted to fight the U.S. wherever they could. The insurgency detonated a massive truck bomb, destroying the United Nations headquarters in Baghdad. Most of the U.N pulled out of Iraq, as did many international aid groups. Insurgents began attacking the Green Zone with mortars and rockets. Others began using the improvised explosive device, or IED, to target American convoys and patrols. The casualties mounted.

One bit of bright news came on December 13, 2003, when Saddam Hussein was found hiding in a tiny hole near his hometown in northern Iraq. The next day, American military forces suffered their 3,000th casualty since the Iraq War began.

Many of the troops rotated into Iraq were not active duty soldiers, but rather National Guard and Army Reserve units. The Vietnam War was fought by draftees who served two years and then were discharged. But after Vietnam, the country did away with the unpopular draft, replacing it with the all-volunteer force. There were not nearly enough troops for the country's myriad of missions in the post–Cold War world, so troops ended up on twelve- to eighteen-month deployments, then were sent home, then were rotated back to combat zones. Many units went to Iraq three or four times. This was very tough on soldiers and their families. Turnover was high, and many soldiers suffered from post-traumatic stress disorder, or PTSD.

Service members were right to believe that they had gone to war while the nation stayed at peace. As the regular army and reserve units were rotated in and out of Iraq, most Americans did not know any soldiers who fought in the conflict. There was a major societal disconnect. It was difficult for Americans to personally associate with the military's experience in the Iraqi quagmire. Americans responded superficially when they met a soldier, saying a rote "Thank you for your service" or delivering an obligatory standing ovation for service members at the ballpark. Americans might fetishize the military, but they really had no idea what a soldier had gone through, or the real sacrifice that person had made to serve their country in a deeply unpopular war.

The American military was prepared for a conventional war in Iraq, but had forgotten the counterinsurgency lessons from Vietnam. It wasn't about killing the bad guys with deadly force; it was about winning over the population. One area of early success was in northern Iraq, where General David Petraeus's 101st Airborne Division immediately shifted to counterinsurgency operations and was successful in keeping the northern part of the country at peace. But most division commanders used a sledgehammer.

Initial American military tactics in Iraq were aggressive, sweeping up every male suspected of insurgency and sending them to the overcrowded prison at Abu Ghraib. Most were innocent bystanders, but it took months to release a detainee. This did nothing to win the hearts and minds of Iraqis. An innocent detainee, once released, now set his heart on fighting the American occupiers.

In March 2004, the military charged six soldiers with abusing prisoners at Abu Ghraib. It soon became clear why, after photographs of what they had done were leaked, and the television program *60 Minutes* aired a segment on the photos. The photographs were humiliating and sadistic, showing naked prisoners being forced into simulated sexual positions, stacked up into a human pyramid, while another showed a man on a leash being walked by a soldier as if he were a dog. Most sickening was a photo of a hooded man standing on a box with wires attached to his body. The guards told him if he stepped off the box, he would be electrocuted. In many of the photos, American soldiers seemed to be enjoying themselves, as if it were some sick joke. The treatment of the prisoners at Abu Ghraib reflected a breakdown in leadership and moral decency. Any sympathy the Muslim world had for the United States after 9/11 evaporated after Abu Ghraib. [62]

"I share a deep disgust that those prisoners were treated the way they were treated," President Bush stated after the photos were revealed. Secretary of Defense Donald Rumsfeld took responsibility for the photos. He offered to resign, but Bush declined. Rumsfeld later admitted that not leaving the administration then was a mistake. His presence had become a lightning rod for administration critics.[63]

Against this backdrop of American misbehavior, the Iraqi insurgency gained new steam. The city of Fallujah, roughly forty miles west of Baghdad, had become a hotbed for insurgents and jihadists. On March 31, 2004, insurgents ambushed a convoy and killed four Blackwater USA contractors, and mutilated and strung up their bodies over a bridge. Marines soon surrounded the city and over the next several days won a foothold in the city while airstrikes took out enemy positions. Civilian casualties were high, and on April 9 the U.S. declared a unilateral cease fire. Insurgents still controlled most of the city, but rather than attempt to clear them out, block by block, the U.S. attempted to hand the job over to an Iraqi militia brigade. The insurgents were emboldened, and their attacks continued with renewed vigor.

As the First Battle of Fallujah was underway, Shiite militia in Baghdad's Sadr City neighborhood erupted in violence against the Americans. They hated the Sunni minority that had long oppressed them, but they hated the American occupiers more. Sectarian violence increased and attacks against American forces escalated. Entire neighborhoods were ethnically cleansed by rampaging Shiite militia.

The United States found itself increasingly alone and besieged. The "coalition of the willing" splintered as the allies pulled their troops out of Iraq. Al-Qaeda attacked Spain, one of the American allies in Iraq, by detonating bombs on multiple commuter trains on March 11, 2004, killing dozens of people. The attack brought down the Spanish government, and Spain pulled its forces out of Iraq.

The Bush administration continued to shift the goalposts for Iraq: first it was about eliminating Saddam Hussein's WMDs, which turned out not to exist. Then it was the revisionist conjecture that Hussein *would have* given WMDs to terrorists, if he could have developed them, and that is why the U.S. had to invade. Then it changed to stopping terrorism as the Sunni insurgency and its deadly suicide bombers ramped up. Iraq did in fact turn out to be a battleground for terrorism, but one of the U.S.'s own making: it laid out the welcome mat to al-Qaeda, which was spoiling to take on the U.S. again. The Iraq War fed into the al-Qaeda narrative of Islamic victimization.

On June 28, 2004, the U.S. Coalition Provisional Authority handed governing back to the Iraqis, who were ill-prepared for self-governance. Shortly after that, the U.S. remanded Saddam Hussein to Iraqi custody. The Shiite-led government tried and hung Saddam on December 30, 2006.

The 2004 Election

The 2004 presidential election took place against the backdrop of the increasingly unpopular Iraq War. The war had undeniably become a quagmire, yet perhaps surprisingly, this didn't reverberate against the Bush administration in the 2004 election. Bush might have been evicted from the White House like his father in 1992, who won the Persian Gulf War yet did little to counter the postwar recession that followed. When Dubya ran for a second term, he highlighted his bona fides in the War on Terror and in keeping Americans safe. The attacks of 9/11 were still foremost in many people's minds. His strategist Karl Rove drove evangelicals to the polls by stoking their fear of gay marriage.

Democratic senators who had voted for the Iraq War—Joe Biden, Hillary Clinton, John Kerry—later scurried away from their 2002 authorization of force votes. Bush effectively labeled them "flip-floppers." It was a charge that especially stuck against John Kerry of Massachusetts, Bush's opponent in the 2004 presidential campaign. Kerry chose Senator John Edwards of North Carolina as his running mate.

Kerry was a decorated Vietnam War hero who had commanded a Swift Boat in the Mekong Delta. He attempted to position himself as a decisive leader to counter Bush, but there was a weakness in this approach. True, Bush was not a wartime veteran, but he had the upper hand as the commander-in-chief in the War on Terror. Meanwhile, another opposition group known as Swift Boat Veterans for Truth produced a video questioning Kerry's role in combat. It was their word versus his, and Kerry's ineffective response cost him. Kerry was "swift boated."

Bush was also able to run against Kerry's own political record. "My opponent has spent two decades in Washington and he's built up quite a record," he stated. "In fact, Senator Kerry has been in Washington long enough to take both sides on just about every issue."[64] First and foremost was his voting record for the Iraq War. Kerry blundered into a public statement where he said, "I actually did vote for the $87 billion [allocation for the war in Iraq] before I voted against it." Bush noted, "We grabbed the 'flip-flop' theme and ran with it for the rest of the campaign."[65] It was an effective strategy. Besides, was the heartland going to vote for a northeastern liberal who windsurfed and was unquestionably part of the nation's elite? Of course not. This ignored the fact that, despite his folksy twang, Bush was part of a well-educated political dynasty and was as much of the elite as Kerry.

At the Democratic convention in Boston, a virtually unknown state senator from Chicago named Barack Obama was invited to give the keynote address. His wife, Michelle, would call him a "complete nobody." Obama was African American and delivered an electrifying speech about racial reconciliation and national unity, claiming that Blue States and Red States were false choices. Obama had published a largely unnoticed autobiography, *Dreams from My Father*, in 1995. Suddenly everyone wanted to know more about this black man and his soaring rhetoric, and the book became an instant bestseller. The convention keynote immediately raised Obama's national profile and propelled him both into the U.S. Senate that November and into the 2008 presidential campaign.[66]

On election day 2004, Bush narrowly won 51 percent of the popular vote by taking the vast heartland, the South, and the populous states of Florida, Ohio, and Texas. Republicans added five seats to their House majority and also solidified their lead in the Senate, picking up four seats. Congress now tilted more conservatively.[67]

The 2004 reelection proved the high-water mark of the Bush presidency. In 2005, his authority and popularity would significantly diminish with his quixotic quest to reform Social Security, the inept response to Hurricane Katrina, the drifting war in Iraq, and a series of political scandals that tainted the Republican Party. Yet Bush also became a more hands-on president in his second term, trusting less to Dick Cheney and the vice president's advisers.

With the election behind him, Bush shook up his cabinet. Attorney General John Ashcroft departed, replaced by the weaker Alberto Gonzales, a man who would ultimately stir more partisan controversy than Ashcroft's pieties. Secretary of State Colin Powell likewise departed, replaced by Condoleezza Rice, who had proved vital as a presidential sounding board and coalition builder within the cabinet. Bush retained Donald Rumsfeld at the Pentagon, which was likely a mistake, given that Rumsfeld had become a lightning rod for the Iraq War.

The Iraq War Escalates

The American death toll in Iraq rose as the country spun out of control. It passed the symbolically important 1,000-person mark on September 1, 2004. By October 25 of the following year, Iraq War deaths surpassed 2,000, and by March 23, 2008, the total had surpassed 4,000 American deaths. Nearly 5,000 Americans service members died in combat during Bush's presidency—and more than 30,000 were wounded in Iraq.[68]

After the inconsequential First Battle of Fallujah in March 2004, the city in the Sunni heartland became crowded with foreign insurgents eager to fight against American forces. The Iraqi militia tasked with pacifying the city soon sided with the insurgents, prompting the American military to return in November 2004 to finish the job in the Second Battle of Fallujah. The Iraqi government approved the operation. This would become the biggest and most hard-fought battle American forces participated in while in Iraq.

Army, marine, and naval forces surrounded Fallujah while the air force pummeled insurgent positions. The Islamist insurgents had fortified many buildings in the city and most of the civilians had evacuated. American forces began their assault on November 8, six days after the presidential election, and over the next ten days killed or captured many of the insurgents. Though the city was temporarily pacified, Fallujah had suffered major damage. The operation proved to have little impact on the insurgency, which shifted elsewhere throughout the country. And violence would soon return to Fallujah.

Iraq was steadily slipping out of control, and the soldiers chased after insurgents while the insurgents killed Americans with IEDs and terrorized the population. Iraq became very dangerous, and for the Americans, 2005 felt like a treadmill as they killed insurgents, yet more violence kept erupting. There was no end to the vicious cycle.

In the December 2005 national elections in Iraq, the minority Sunnis boycotted the vote, leading to Shiites taking over the country politically, which in turn fueled civil war in spring 2006. Iraq spiraled downward with mass killings and ethnic cleansing of neighborhoods and towns. Shiites largely controlled the army and the national police and were intent on vengeance for years of cruel Sunni rule under Saddam Hussein. The weak government did little to hold the Shiite militias back. The U.S. could also do little to stop it. Secretary Rumsfeld was proving inadequate to the task and prickly to any criticism.

It soon became clear that Iraq was descending into a civil war. On February 22, 2006, Sunni insurgents blew up the gold-domed al-Askari Mosque in Samarra, a holy site to Shiites. The Samara mosque bombing "proved a game changer in Iraq," wrote Donald Rumsfeld. Iraq had been an unstable country since the U.S. invasion in 2003, but now the violence surged as Sunnis attacked Shiites, Shiites retaliated, and al-Qaeda in Iraq attacked everyone. American forces had one brief moment of success when they killed al-Qaeda in Iraq's leader, Abu Musab al-Zarqawi, a Jordanian thug fond of beheading his enemies, but Iraq was spiraling out of control.[69]

The Bush administration was in denial about how bad the situation in Iraq was. There was no strategy to contain the violence. The Pentagon counted on Iraqi forces to defend their own country, but they were proving inadequate, even while the generals were planning to draw down American forces. The American military largely kept to its huge bases in the country, which were ineffective at combating insurgents. American policy in Iraq was bankrupt.

The 2006 midterm election in the United States was a referendum on the Iraq War, which had become deeply unpopular. Iraq was the big issue that drove people to the polls to vote for change. It was a seismic-scale election: Democrats seized control of Congress, gaining thirty-one seats in the House and six Senate seats. Nancy Pelosi, a liberal Democrat from San Francisco, became the first-ever female Speaker of the House. President Bush's approval ratings plummeted and never recovered.

Many blamed Secretary of Defense Donald Rumsfeld for the Iraqi quagmire. He was indeed a liability; however, Bush was ever loyal to his advisers and refused to dismiss Rumsfeld before the election, even while many Republicans called for Rumsfeld to go. The secretary resigned just days after the election, too late to affect a positive outcome for the president. He exited the Pentagon under a cloud. "Rumsfeld had become the most powerful secretary of defense since Robert S. McNamara" in the Vietnam War era, wrote biographer Bradley Graham. He concluded:

> Given his leading role in two wars that have become national sinkholes, his association with some of the most shameful incidents in modern U.S. military history, and his personification of the arrogance and misjudgments of the Bush administration, Rumsfeld is likely to remain a deeply controversial figure for many years, easy to caricature and easy to loathe.[70]

The 2006 midterm election defeat (a "thumping," as Bush called it) forced the White House to reassess its failing strategy for Iraq. Rumsfeld's replacement as secretary of defense was Robert Gates, a widely respected and pragmatic former director of the CIA who stopped the infighting among the nation's top brass. He also led a quiet shakeup of the generals and promoted a group of outsiders who recognized that the key was to fight a counter-insurgency campaign, rather than a conventional war. His leadership was considered so vital that Barack Obama asked Gates to stay on after the new president was sworn into office in 2009.

The government was divided during Bush's last two years as president (2007–2009), as Republicans controlled the White House and Democrats controlled Congress. By this point Bush was deeply unpopular. The housing bubble was collapsing, which led to the Great Recession, and Americans were tired of the Iraq War. Democrats wanted to pull out of Iraq, but were unwilling to confront the White House over it.

The Surge

Four years after the Americans had invaded Iraq, the country was spiraling out of control. The Bush administration needed a new strategy. And remarkably, the Pentagon came up with one with the help of several astute generals: Ray Odierno and David Petraeus. Odierno was a mountain of a man with a bald, bullet-shaped head, while Petraeus was far smaller and a physical fitness nut. Petraeus was hypercompetitive and an intellectual, having earned a PhD from Princeton University in international relations. In addition, Ryan Crocker was nominated as the new ambassador to Iraq. He and Petraeus worked well together to coordinate Iraqi policy, something that had been sorely lacking for the past four years, as Rumsfeld in the Pentagon was territorial and did not work well with the State Department.

General Odierno developed the idea for a "surge." This was a counter-offensive against the lawlessness that had overtaken Iraq. He asked for five additional combat brigades, about 20,000 soldiers, to deploy to Iraq to help calm Baghdad. Gates approved, and even later dispatched a sixth brigade. From pre-surge levels of about 130,000 troops, the U.S. raised troops levels to 168,000 at its peak—and went from 17,000 troops around

Baghdad to 40,000. Soldiers' time in Iraq was extended from twelve to fifteen months. The surge would last eighteen months.

President Bush delivered a nationwide address announcing the surge and shift in strategy on January 10, 2007. It was humbling to admit that Iraq was flailing, but Bush had to seek a new path: "The situation in Iraq is unacceptable to the American people, and it is unacceptable to me. Our troops in Iraq have fought bravely. They have done everything we have asked them to do. Where mistakes have been made, the responsibility rests with me." The combat reinforcements would focus on stabilizing Baghdad, where most of the violence in Iraq was taking place. He set expectations: fighting the insurgents and terrorists "will make the year ahead bloody and violent," and there was no clear goalpost of what victory would look like.[71]

Lessons in Iraq were hard-learned, but they were finally sinking in. One was that American troops had to get out of the safety of their sprawling bases and mingle more with the locals, providing security for Iraqi civilians, not just for themselves. This was a classic counterinsurgency strategy. American military leaders began a dialogue with Sunni insurgents and managed to peel many of them away from al-Qaeda. The insurgents had revolted at the thought of a Shiite-dominated Iraq, and al-Qaeda was an alliance of necessity. But al-Qaeda took things too far for Iraq's largely secular Sunni minority, such as its deadly suicide missions, car bombings, and beheadings. When al-Qaeda began targeting wavering Sunni leaders, that was the last straw: supported by the U.S. administration, the Sunnis formed Awakening Groups that hunted down al-Qaeda with the ruthlessness of the Iraqi Republican Guard.

Odierno concentrated the American reinforcements around Baghdad in spring 2007—home to more than one in five Iraqis—knowing that the war would be won or lost in the capital. Violence immediately erupted as the al-Qaeda insurgents in Iraq and Shiite militias attacked the American outposts in what became known as the Battle of Baghdad.

For months the slaughter continued, but by summer the violence began tapering off as the insurgent power waned. Combined with the increasing effectiveness of trained Iraqi forces and Sunni insurgents who turned against al-Qaeda, the security situation in Iraq improved dramatically. The American presence in the Baghdad neighborhoods was having a positive impact. Normal life returned to city streets as cafes and markets reopened.

The Iraqi capital became safer, and Iraqi refugees began to return to the city. The surge came at a cost of 1,124 American soldiers lost, while another 7,710 were wounded. [72]

By mid-2008 the surge was over and the extra combat brigades were sent home, returning the American force in Iraq to 130,000 troops. The surge had stabilized Iraq but little else. Baghdad was definitely safer for Iraqi civilians, and al-Qaeda in Iraq was in retreat. However, there were no steps taken toward political reconciliation within Iraq. The country still faced political instability between its ethnic and sectarian rivals while Iran stoked tensions from across the border.

Journalist Bob Woodward pointed out that more than just the surge had tamped down the violence in Iraq. U.S. intelligence agencies and the military began using new covert technologies against the insurgents and al-Qaeda and steadily killed their leaders. Second, the Anbar Awakening was vital in that the Sunnis themselves—the faction that was fueling the insurgency—turned against al-Qaeda in Iraq. Third, Shiite leader Muqtada al-Sadr ordered his Mahdi Army militia to stand down and stop opposing Iraqi army incursions. [73]

While the surge was winding down, Iraqi prime minister Nouri al-Maliki asserted his authority to govern his country. In April 2008 he led a hastily improvised campaign to root out the Shiite militias and thugs that had taken over Basra, Iraq's large oil-rich city in the south. His surprise victory in this strengthened al-Maliki's position as head of government.

By the fifth anniversary of the Iraq War in March 2008, Americans stood overwhelmingly against it and blamed Bush for its mishandling. The only thing that overshadowed Iraq was the rapid decline of the economy and the presidential election campaign. The American dead now numbered more than 4,000, yet when confronted with polling data that showed the American public opposed the war in Iraq, Vice President Dick Cheney shrugged and said, "So?" [74]

Before the Bush presidency ended, a number of tell-all books from administration insiders were published, including Scott McClellan (*What Happened*), Douglas Feith (*War and Decision*), George Tenet (*At the Center of the Storm*), Ricardo Sanchez (*Wiser in Battle*), and Paul Bremer (*My Year in Iraq*). All told their version of the story of how the U.S. got into the mess of Iraq—and pointed the finger at who was to blame. It was never the same person, nor was it ever their fault. Ultimately the responsibility rests with

President Bush. Bush will be remembered best for the Iraq War, a war that he justified on humanitarian grounds:

> Many of those who demonstrated against military action in Iraq were devoted advocates of human rights. Yet they condemned me for using force to remove the man who had gassed the Kurds, mowed down the Shia by helicopter gunship, massacred the Marsh Arabs, and sent tens of thousands to mass graves. I understood why people might disagree on the threat Saddam Hussein posed to the United States. But I didn't see how anyone could deny that liberating Iraq advanced the cause of human rights.[75]

Bush convincingly argued that Saddam had to go. But why the relentless focus on this one dictator, when the world was full of bad men, and North Korea was arguably more dangerous? Or what overthrowing Hussein would do to the balance of power in the Middle East? Bush was unapologetic about the Iraq War, believing it necessary. Many Americans came to disagree with him.

The Iraq War figured in the 2008 presidential election, though the main issue was the collapsing economy in the Great Recession. Democratic candidate Barack Obama wanted a timetable for withdrawal, as he had other strategic priorities to focus on in the Middle East, notably Afghanistan. His Republican opponent, John McCain, wanted to strengthen the U.S. presence in Iraq and confront its neighbor Iran, whose military power was rising. Obama won the election.

With less than five months left in his administration, President Bush and Iraqi leaders agreed to remove American forces from the country by the end of 2011. On January 1, 2009, the U.S. turned over the Green Zone in Baghdad to Iraqi authorities. Obama continued the phased withdrawal as American forces were pulled from Iraqi cities. As promised, the last American forces were pulled out of Iraq in 2011, just shy of nine years after the invasion.

The road to Iraqi democracy was bumpy, costly, lengthy, and violent. Only time would tell if these seeds took root in the Middle East, or if they withered. During the first decade, the United States spent nearly $2 trillion on the wars in Afghanistan and Iraq. These were just the military and nation-building costs. The wars were funded on the nation's credit card, meaning that interest on these costs would balloon. In addition, veterans would have medical and psychological treatment for decades afterward. One study estimated the wars' ultimate cost would be $4 to $6 trillion. [76]

Was the Iraq War worth it? The trillion dollars spent to topple a dictator could have helped pay down the national debt, be invested for the pending retirement of the Baby Boom generation, or financed a massive upgrade in the nation's aging infrastructure. The war placed enormous stress on the nation's armed forces, cost thousands of dead and wounded, and took a psychological toll on the veterans. The war squandered American power, lost the world's goodwill earned after 9/11, and unsettled the balance of power of the Middle East in Iran's favor. Ultimately, did the Iraqi venture make the U.S. more secure or advance American interests? The answer is no.

Public dissatisfaction over the Iraq War, combined with the Jack Abramoff influence-peddling scandal, which had tainted Republican congressional leaders with corruption, significantly discredited the Bush administration. But it took Hurricane Katrina, which drowned New Orleans in August 2005, to shatter the dreams for a permanent Republican majority.

6

Katrina

The year 2005 was an especially busy year for hurricanes in the Atlantic Ocean. In the last week of August, a deadly hurricane named Katrina roared through the Caribbean and across southern Florida, killing six people and leaving a swath of destruction before heading west into the Gulf of Mexico. There it gathered strength into a colossal storm. The shallow waters of the gulf were unusually warm that year, giving Katrina even more fuel. It was one of the most powerful storms in recorded history to hit the U.S.—a rare Category 5 hurricane. The storm veered to the northwest, barreling toward New Orleans.

The city of New Orleans sits in a bowl, or saucer, much of it below sea level, and all of it surrounded by water: the Mississippi River to the south and Lake Pontchartrain to the north. The city earned its nickname, Crescent City, for the smiley-face like crescent bend in the river. The original city, the old square or Vieux Carré (better known as the French Quarter) and the Garden District to the west, were wisely built along the narrow strip of high ground along the Mississippi River levees. They usually stayed dry when storms appeared—which was often. But if any barrier failed, the water would flood in.

In the 20th century, New Orleans expanded when the swamps were drained north of the city, between it and Lake Pontchartrain. People moved out of the dense, historic districts in search of more room. Much of the new development was built on lowland, at risk of flood from a storm surge from the lake.

Hurricanes were just part of life in New Orleans, and its citizens held a certain disregard for Mother Nature, believing that the city had weathered almost every storm just fine. Hurricane Betsy in 1965 had flooded parts of New Orleans. In 2004, just a year before Katrina, Hurricane Ivan had served as a wake-up call. Bearing down on New Orleans, it veered to the east instead. Disaster was averted and life continued as usual.

After Betsy, the U.S. Army Corps of Engineers designed an ambitious flood control plan for the Big Easy but never finished it. The Corps built levees, then handed them off to local levee boards to maintain. What held back the waters was 350 miles of levees—an enormous man-made defensive system that, as it turned out, was far from perfect. [1]

One particular weakness was the outfall canals, dug to drain water from the city into Lake Pontchartrain. These had pumping stations to pump water into the lake in a constant battle against nature. Without the pumps, water would seep back into the city. But the pumping stations were put at the tail end of the outfall canals, deep inside neighborhoods, rather than right at the lake's edge. This meant a storm surge would fill the canals with lake water, potentially bringing floodwaters into the city itself if the canal levees ever broke. [2]

As Hurricane Katrina barreled down on New Orleans, the city was largely unprepared—especially for how to deal with the considerable population of the city's poor. Out of 460,000 people who called New Orleans home, 112,000 didn't own an automobile—a quarter of the population. The Big Easy was two-thirds African American. It also had a significant population of elderly who couldn't drive. Many others had survived Hurricane Betsy in 1965 and thought there was no need to evacuate. [3]

Mayor Ray Nagin issued a voluntary evacuation order on the afternoon of Friday, August 26, then turned it into a mandatory evacuation two days later, the first time in the city's history. The Saturday before the storm was a day wasted when people should have evacuated. The evacuation did not truly get underway until Sunday, and by then it was a mess: hundred-mile-long traffic jams on Interstate 10 as people fled to Houston and other cities. Eighty percent of the New Orleans area population of one million people had evacuated. Many would never return. [4]

The nation might call it Hurricane Katrina, but locals simply called it "the storm." Historian Douglas Brinkley, who lived in New Orleans and survived the catastrophe, later wrote: "The name 'Katrina' had conjured whimsical images of a Gaelic ballad or a Vegas cocktail waitress. A close friend of mine, in fact, was named Katrina. There was no menace in the echo. Perhaps if the storm had been named 'Genghis Khan' or 'Attila the Hun' or 'Caligula,' I would have fled."[5]

Brinkley was just one of an estimated 127,000 people who stayed behind in New Orleans. Unable to evacuate all the people, Mayor Nagin opened the Louisiana Superdome as a refuge of last resort on Sunday as Katrina took aim at the city. About 10,000 people crowded into this covered stadium, most of them black. They were protected by 350 Louisiana National Guardsmen.[6] Brinkley noted how the massive hurricane collided with urban poverty, explaining why so many poor people stayed behind when anyone in their right mind would have fled:

> They didn't hear about Katrina on television, for a simple reason: they didn't own a set. Even if they did hear about the storm, they didn't have the money to leave. They had no credit cards with which to rent a car and reserve a motel room in Dallas, Memphis, Little Rock, or Baton Rouge. Poorly educated, and often illiterate, they couldn't figure out what all the evacuation commotion was about. With no driver's license or other form of identification, some were afraid the NOPD would arrest them at city-run shelters or handcuff them for hitchhiking on I-10.[7]

New Orleans is sixty miles inland from the Gulf of Mexico and surrounded by storm-surge-swallowing coastal wetlands and barrier islands, but these were weakened substantially over the years. The Louisiana wetlands of the bayou region were in terrible condition, eroding at the equivalent of a football field each day. More than one thousand square miles or one million acres had been lost since the 1930s, largely because of human activity. There is a reason why the Mississippi River is called the Big Muddy: it's full of silt. The Mississippi brought down tons of sediment that replenished the wetlands, but once engineers started making the Mississippi more navigable, it messed with the hydrology. The levees confined the river to its path, rather than allowing it to meander through the delta. The sediment-rich water was steered out to sea and deposited far offshore, rather than coursing its way through the delta to replenish the islands and wetlands. The oil and natural gas industries had dredged parts of the wetlands over the decades, considerably weakening them. The wetlands had naturally absorbed the shock of many hurricanes, but in their deteriorated state, Katrina's storm surge rose farther than it would have.

Another factor contributed to the catastrophe: a 2,000-foot-wide canal known as the Mississippi River-Gulf Outlet (MRGO, pronounced "Mr. Go" locally) gave ships a faster route to the Gulf of Mexico. Once it was dug, salt water increasingly encroached into the wetlands, causing even more wetland demise. However, the canal was rarely ever used. And most dangerously, MRGO pointed directly at the Industrial Canal in New Orleans.

The Industrial Canal is a shipping canal, complete with levees and locks, that allows ships to navigate into the port of New Orleans. It forms a sideways T intersection, with Lake Pontchartrain and the Mississippi River at either end, and with the Intracoastal Waterway bisecting it. Ivor van Heerden, who helped found the Louisiana State University Hurricane Center, called the intersection of MRGO and the Intracoastal Waterway the "Funnel," a chokepoint that pushed the storm surge even higher as it propelled its way toward New Orleans. He called it "one of the world's best storm-surge delivery systems."[8]

Katrina came ashore the morning of Monday, August 29, 2005, near Biloxi, Mississippi. Although it seemed to aim directly for New Orleans, it suddenly veered to the east. It was soon downgraded to a Category 3 hurricane as it weakened over land. Still, the storm was massive and its surge reached thirty feet. Floodwaters poured into Lake Pontchartrain and surged up MRGO, which funneled the storm surge directly toward the city. The surge demolished the levees in its path and flooded St. Bernard Parish just downriver from New Orleans.

The man-made barriers were not tall enough, nor strong enough to withstand the storm surge from MRGO and Lake Pontchartrain. The levees protecting New Orleans began to fail. The first to break were the levees along the Industrial Canal. Water from the storm surge in the Intercoastal Waterway overtopped the levees, then scoured the supporting soil away until the levees buckled and broke. Soon after, the Seventeenth Street and London Avenue Canals burst. Though Lake Pontchartrain rose seventeen feet, the storm surge never overtopped these outfall canals. Rather, the weight of the water put enormous pressure on the canal walls, fatally undermining the soil under them until the levees gave way in multiple places. Water poured into the bathtub that is New Orleans, flooding eighty percent of the city, all but the narrow band of the historic districts along the Mississippi River. New Orleans was drowned.

The flooding was particularly bad in the Lower Ninth Ward, an area east of the Industrial Canal. The Lower Ninth was mostly black working class. It wasn't a slum, nor was it a ghetto. Most of the families living there owned their homes. This neighborhood was home to rock 'n' roll icon Fats Domino. It was a place the working class could afford to settle down and have a bit of the American dream. And it wasn't exclusively black—no neighborhood in New Orleans was. It was a city that, like a pot of gumbo, had a little of everything mixed in it. At its worst, the floodwaters in the city reached ten feet deep. That was enough to leave only a home's roof sticking out of the water, and that's where the remaining residents fled. More than 100,000 people were now trapped inside the flooded city.

Once the storm passed, people realized they couldn't stay in their flooded houses. A haphazard "Cajun navy" of boats piloted by volunteers and the Louisiana Department of Wildlife and Fisheries evacuated people from the flooded wards. U.S. Coast Guard helicopters rescued people from roofs. Many of them gathered either on Interstate 10 overpasses, where they broiled in the nearly 100° heat, or trudged to the Superdome.

On Tuesday, August 30, the floodwaters continued to rise in the drowned city. People who had been rescued from their houses were put on pockets of dry land and sent to the Superdome, where the population doubled from 10,000 to 20,000, overwhelming the support services there and creating a humanitarian nightmare. Water, food, and medical supplies were in short supply. Many of the residents left behind were poor, and quite a number were diabetics who required regular insulin shots. The lack of insulin became a major health crisis for the survivors. The toilets weren't working, and the humid, hot air was fetid. The Superdome was soon renamed the Sewerdome.[9]

As the Superdome filled up, another 10,000 people broke into and took refuge at the nearby Convention Center. Conditions were inhumane at both places: there was no running water or sewage, and the toilets soon filled up so that, at the Convention Center at least, people gathered on the street outside, unable to stand the stench inside. For several days, federal authorities were unaware that so many people had sought shelter at the Convention Center, so no food was provisioned.

A group of people from the Convention Center, mostly black, tried to cross the Crescent City Connection, the bridge right next to the Convention

Center that crossed the Mississippi. There they were met by a sheriff's posse from the town of Gretna and forced to turn back into the city that was becoming a living nightmare.

Katrina knocked out the power in New Orleans, severing much of the city's communications with the outside world and with first responders. Katrina left everyone scrambling—from the mayor to the governor to the Federal Emergency Management Agency (FEMA) to the president. No one seemed prepared for the disaster, and the rescue operations in the days after were haphazard.

The federal response was agonizingly slow. On Monday, Tuesday, and Wednesday, it was Louisianans who did the rescuing with the help of the Coast Guard. Katrina exposed the dysfunctionality of the Department of Homeland Security, which was geared more toward fighting terrorism than helping people after a natural disaster.

People asked, Where is the government? Where is the cavalry? Where is the Red Cross? The media was ahead of the federal government on the breaking of the levees. It took the feds days to ramp up in response while the situation in New Orleans deteriorated. How to evacuate so many people who now needed to leave the city?

On Wednesday afternoon, two days after the storm hit, President Bush flew over the flooded region in Air Force One, but he didn't land or stop to console the survivors, as Lyndon Johnson had done with Hurricane Betsy in 1965. Bush appeared out of touch and uncaring, caught by surprise and unable to provide leadership in a crisis that had upended so many lives. Where was the decisive man who had reassured the nation in the hours after the 9/11 terrorist attacks? Bush later acknowledged in his memoir, "I prided myself on my ability to make crisp and effective decisions. Yet in the days after Katrina, that didn't happen. The problem was not that I made the wrong decisions. It was that I took too long to decide." Bush never recovered politically after Hurricane Katrina.[10]

The man running the rescue operation was FEMA director Michael Brown. He was a political appointee, a thank-you gift for his political support that helped get Bush elected. Brown had raised thoroughbred horses and had no experience in disaster recovery or relief, yet he was given this important job through patronage. Days passed by, and the federal response was sluggish. It was clear that Brown was ill-informed. Even the news channel CNN had better information than Brown: CNN reporter Soledad O'Brien grilled

Brown live on television. CNN revealed that thousands of people had taken refuge in the Convention Center, but the federal government was apparently unaware of this.

On Friday, four days after Katrina had swamped New Orleans, Bush finally made landfall in the area. With the television cameras running, Bush publicly praised Brown for his efforts: "You're doing a heckuva job, Brownie." Americans who saw this event on TV were stunned. No one was doing a heckuva job—in fact FEMA was doing a downright lousy job of rescuing people and providing comfort and aid.

Infighting among Mayor Ray Nagin and Louisiana governor Kathleen Blanco (both Democrats) and the Bush administration didn't help. Bush was wary of stepping into a fight about states' rights when people were desperate for assistance. He rightfully noted in his memoir, "But after four days of chaos, it was clear the authorities in Louisiana could not lead."[11] However, the states would never have the resources to handle a catastrophe on the scale of Katrina—only the federal government did. Former secretary of homeland security Tom Ridge called it a "bureaucratic disaster."[12]

Help finally came on Thursday when Lieutenant General Russel Honoré, a blunt Creole, arrived in the city to head the military relief effort. Mayor Nagin referred to him as "one John Wayne dude" who finally brought a semblance of order to the chaos. The response to Katrina was never federalized—Honoré simply took command of the Louisiana National Guard and active duty troops and asserted control through the force of his personality.

Things started improving as the federal response finally kicked in. Honoré got the convoys rolling with relief supplies and water for the thousands of embattled residents in the Convention Center and Superdome, and then began the evacuation through hundreds of buses. The exodus was on. People were bused out of the city and relocated to cities far away. The 82nd Airborne Division arrived on Saturday, banishing the lawlessness that had prevailed for the past week.

On September 5—eight days after the levees broke—the Seventeenth Street Canal breach was closed, the last of the levee breaches to be plugged. The pumps kicked on and began draining the city, or "unwatering" it, though that would take more than a month.[13]

Hurricane Katrina was the worst natural disaster that ever struck the United States. Eighty percent of New Orleans was underwater. Some 1,500 people drowned. Hundreds of thousands of people had lost their homes, and property damages were estimated at $75 billion. The 9/11 terrorist attacks in New York were contained to a few blocks at the south end of Manhattan, and the rescue efforts were largely led by local police and the fire department. Katrina, on the other hand, caused the wholesale evacuation of more than a million people and had devastated 90,000 square miles of the Gulf Coast in Alabama, Louisiana, and Mississippi. Most of the residents of New Orleans—a half-million people—lost everything. The U.S. had never experienced anything like this before.[14]

The majority of New Orleanian evacuees fled west to Texas, about 150,000 of them settling in one city, Houston. Thousands of people ended up at the Houston Astrodome. People from throughout the Gulf region evacuated to other cities. Many of them settled in hotels, and months later, FEMA stopped paying their hotel bills.

Bush addressed the nation from Jackson Square two weeks after Katrina, saying that the United States would rebuild New Orleans. The square was flooded by generator-powered lights (power was still out in the city), but as soon as the president left, the power was cut off. Angry over the inept response, rap artist Kanye West remarked on television, "George Bush doesn't care about black people." Bush later wrote in his memoir, "But the suggestion that I as a racist because of the response to Katrina represented an all-time low. I told Laura [his wife] at the time that it was the worst moment of my presidency."[15]

Katrina exposed the deep fault lines of race and poverty that still undercut the United States. Many people had forgotten about the urban poor—people who were too poor even to own a car, people who barely squeezed by, paycheck to paycheck. Images on the nightly news and on the Internet showed flood victims taking shelter on the roofs of their homes—most of them poor blacks—and thousands of people crowding the inhumane conditions at the Convention Center and Louisiana Superdome.

New Orleans sat in stagnant, dirty water for six weeks before the U.S. Army Corps of Engineers finished draining the city. When it did, everything was covered in grey muck, a foul line on every house and building showed just how high the flood waters reached. Orange Xs from spray paint cans marked every house where rescuers had searched, indicating the date and if any bodies were found. The stagnant warm water created a huge mold problem.

Many residents returned to New Orleans to collect what possessions they could salvage, and then most left again. Many doubted they could ever rebuild: insurance companies denied billions in claims, claiming that the damage to their homes was flood, rather than hurricane-related. But how could insurers decouple the two? Hurricane Katrina clearly caused the flooding. As a result, hundreds of thousands of people who thought they were insured weren't. Many of them had lost everything and wouldn't be compensated.

To add to the problem of rebuilding New Orleans, property insurers dramatically raised insurance premiums, even after dodging the billions-of-dollars payout from Katrina. And not just in Louisiana, but along the Gulf Coast and Florida. Many people discovered they could no longer afford insurance, and that was another reason why they decided not to rebuild. This was a double insult: insurance companies denied claims, then raised rates.

Still, New Orleans was home to many people, and despite the insurance fiasco and risk of another hurricane, residents were determined to return home and rebuild their lives. Progress was measured in the piles of mildewed sheetrock, mucky carpet, and wrecked furniture that stacked up in front of houses as people sorted through what remained of their lives. Among the piles of rubble and debris in front of every house (or what used to be a house) was a taped-up refrigerator. When the power went out, the food spoiled inside, and colonies of flies descended on the city to devour the food. Residents described the stench of rotting food as unbearable, and so they put the refrigerators out on the sidewalk.

The New Orleans diaspora appeared to be permanent. A year after Katrina, only 170,000 people had returned. The storm caused a huge displacement of urban poor. Many would never return: they rebuilt their lives and found jobs in other cities. Their former lives were buried under a pile of mildewed rubble that used to be their houses.

FEMA continued to bungle the relief. It hurriedly bought 145,000 trailers on no-bid contracts, then ended up storing most of these at storage facilities and airfields. It took months for people to get a trailer to live in while they rebuilt their homes. The FEMA trailers cost $75,000 each and were so hazardously built that people were warned not to live in them. That amount could have quickly rebuilt many houses instead. There were also the famously expensive blue tarps to cover houses that FEMA purchased.[16]

The major question after the storm was: should the city rebuild itself exactly where it was? Or given the fact that New Orleans's population had contracted for decades, and that major parts of the city would remain at risk of flood (such as Eastern New Orleans and the Lower Ninth Ward), should it not contract to a smaller, more defensible perimeter of levees? The topic was hotly debated, and Mayor Nagin's own citizens commission recommended a contraction, but he then disowned the plan when the residents of those neighborhoods decried any buyout. Ultimately Nagin allowed redevelopment across the entire city in its existing boundaries, yielding to political necessity, but in the long term, it may have been an unwise decision.

Mayor Nagin further opened his mouth and made a rather impolitic remark: "I don't care what people are saying in Uptown or wherever they are. This city will be chocolate at the end of the day. This city will be a majority African American city. It's the way God wants it to be."[17] His remark fell flat among the many who were committed to seeing New Orleans restored as a multicultural city. And if Nagin was speaking for God, could God really have intended for New Orleans to concentrate so much poverty, to maintain a failing school system, and to lack economic opportunities for its citizens?

Katrina showed that the federal government was inept at protecting, rescuing, and sheltering its own citizens, especially those with the greatest need. John McQuaid and Mark Schleifstein concluded in their book *Path of Destruction*:

> At the peak of its technological versatility and military strength, the U.S. government had failed to protect one of its own cities, then stumbled all over itself trying to rescue the victims of its neglect and incompetence. And for many around the world, the question of whether the Bush administration's profound failure was the result of incompetence or indifference only added to increasing doubts about American leadership at home and abroad.[18]

On June 1, 2006, the U.S. Army Corps of Engineers released a candid 6,000-page report on why the levees around New Orleans had failed. It admitted that it had inadequately built the levees to withstand a storm surge on the magnitude of Katina. The corps acknowledged human error in designing an inadequate flood control system.

A massive lawsuit against the corps was dismissed in federal court. Though the judges were sympathetic to the plaintiffs, they ruled that the Flood Control Act of 1928 made the corps exempt from prosecution in the event that flood control projects failed. In other words, the corps couldn't be held accountable, nor would the federal government cover the massive property losses endured along the Gulf Coast.

Before the storm, New Orleans had an estimated 460,000 people; by the end of the decade, barely two-thirds of its population had returned. Many neighborhoods remained vacant, and many houses remained boarded up or were in ruins. Locals called it the "jack-o-lantern" effect, with a home here and another there being rebuilt, while others remained boarded up. On the other hand, reconstruction continued apace, and the city experienced a small boom of its own that continued despite the Great Recession. Merchants implored visitors to tell their friends to come, that the city whose chief business was tourism urgently needed more tourists. The city was clean and safe, and big crowds returned for Mardi Gras.

The U.S. Army Corps of Engineers developed a new plan to protect New Orleans. It patched the canal walls, shifted the pumping stations, built new levees, and significantly upgraded the city's flood defenses. Congress authorized the closure of MRGO. The corps also developed a plan to restore the wetlands by releasing silty Mississippi River water into the bayous, rather than sending it out into the Gulf of Mexico. It remains to be seen if this new system can protect the city in time for a future hurricane. For there would be more hurricanes. Another storm like Katrina could turn the city into a shadow of itself, a museum city that only tourists visit.

Hurricane Gustav struck the Gulf Coast on September 1, 2008—three years after Katrina. New Orleans was much better prepared, the citizens heeded a mandatory evacuation, and FEMA and state first responders were well positioned in advance of the storm. Fortunately, the hurricane came ashore to the west of the city, the partially repaired levees held, and the Big Easy dodged another bullet. The Republican National Convention was occurring in Minneapolis at the same time, but it was suspended during the day Gustav came ashore: the party couldn't afford another hurricane that made them look out of touch.

Although a long-declining city, New Orleans was one of the country's oldest and certainly one of the most important culturally. Its Cajuns and Creoles had made the city a culinary destination, and its natives had invented jazz while its bartenders had perfected the cocktail. New Orleans had fostered many a musical prodigy. It was a city where the good times rolled, a Caribbean outpost that provided a home to waves of immigrants—French traders, American businessmen, Haitian Creoles,

Germans, Greeks, Italians, Irish, Spanish royalists, and above all African slaves—all of whom added their flavor to the gumbo pot. It was also one of the country's largest ports, as the products from the heartland flowed down the Mississippi River to the city, destined for foreign markets. New Orleans may have been known as the city that care forgot, but it was still a great and vital American city. The survival of New Orleans meant that Americans would not turn the back on their past.

7

A Nation of Minorities

The island nation of Cuba lies just ninety miles south of the U.S. and was led by communist dictator Fidel Castro. By U.S. policy, Cubans who could reach American soil could stay—but if they were intercepted at sea, they would be sent back. In the decades after Castro seized power in 1959, thousands of Cubans attempted to escape on boats and makeshift rafts. One such raft full of Cuban refugees sank off the Florida coast in November 1999. Clinging to the detritus were just three survivors, including a six-year-old boy named Elián González, whose mother had drowned. Elián was brought to relatives in Miami. His presence led to an international incident that took seven months to resolve and created a rift between mainstream Americans and the stridently anti-Castro Cuban-American community in Miami.

Elián's father flew to the U.S., insisting that his son return to Cuba. By family law, the surviving parent had the right to determine the boy's fate. However, the Cuban-American community, particularly in Florida, was incensed, insisting that the boy must not be returned to Cuba. Attorney General Janet Reno decided González belonged with his father. When the family refused to return the boy, the Border Patrol raided the Miami house on April 22, 2000. A Pulitzer Prize–winning photograph was taken during the raid, showing a federal agent holding an assault weapon while finding Elián and Donato Dalrymple, the fisherman who'd rescued him, in the closet of the house.

González was whisked to Washington, D.C., where he was reunited with his father. They resided in the city for two months while a custody battle waged that went to the U.S. Supreme Court. The father was finally granted legal custody of his son, which was in line with what most Americans wanted, and the two returned to Cuba in June.

For many Americans, the Elián González incident was a wake-up call for how much the Cuban community in Florida determined U.S. foreign policy toward Cuba. The first generation of Cubans, many who had fled Cuba after Castro came to power, were vehemently anti-Castro. Many of them were prop-ertied families who lost everything when Castro nationalized industries and confiscated lands. It was this community that largely dictated a hard-line policy toward Cuba: for decades the U.S. maintained an economic blockade against the island nation, including preventing tourists from visiting. The blockade seemed to have little impact on Castro, and certainly did nothing to undermine his regime. The second generation of Cuban-Americans did not nearly have the blood-boiling passion of their parents, and as the 2000s wore on, they advocated loosening restrictions against Cuba, particularly as Castro aged and his brother Raul began running the country.

The debate over Elián González was a microcosm over the debate of immigration in the United States, a divisive issue between those who wanted to greet newcomers with open arms, and others who felt that the country had enough people, or that immigrants were changing the country too rapidly. And the González case asked a fascinating question: with so many people risking their lives to get to the U.S., why would someone want to leave?

For most of America's history, the country was dominated by people of white European descent. But during the first decade of the 21st century, a new reality emerged: the United States was becoming ever browner. The country's demographic trajectory was toward becoming a nation of minorities.

The country's population continued to grow during the first decade, largely because of immigration, surpassing 300 million people in October 2006 (it had leapt past 200 million in 1967).[1] In 1990, the American popula-tion was 75.6 percent white—but that shrank to only 63 percent by the time of the 2010 U.S. Census. White people were having fewer children, while the Hispanic population in particular was youthful and growing rapidly, as were Asians, the country's fourth-largest minority after African Americans.[2]

During the first decade, Hispanics surpassed blacks as the largest minority group. According to the Census Bureau, Hispanics reached 42.7 million people in 2006 (64 percent of whom were of Mexican origin), forecast to top 100 million by 2050.[3]

In 2008, the Census Bureau released a report forecasting that the United States would become a nation of minorities by 2042 as the white population slipped under 50 percent of the total population. This caused deep anxiety as some whites grew concerned with one day losing their status as the dominant group in American society, stemming from a belief that it was a zero-sum game: one group's gain was another group's loss. It led to harsh feelings against immigrants, who were largely brown-skinned, particularly among working-class whites. What none of this accounted for, however, was mixed-race births, which were becoming increasingly common in the four decades since the U.S. Supreme Court struck down bans on interracial marriage in 1967 in *Loving v. Virginia*.[4]

In 2011, the Census Bureau reported that, for the first time in American history, a majority (50.4 percent) of children one year old or younger were nonwhite. Some states were already majority-minority, including California, Hawaii, New Mexico, and Texas. The *Washington Post* called it "the browning of America." But ultimately, did it matter? What was more important was that these young children, regardless of their ethnic heritage or skin color, embraced the country's democratic traditions and engaged in civil society. And every signpost indicated that these kids were becoming good Americans.[5]

America's demographics have always been evolving. Hatred and scorn were heaped upon the poverty-stricken Irish who came to the U.S. in the 1840s. And where are they today? Fully assimilated and a vital part of the American fabric. And the Italians and the Eastern European Jews, or the Chinese who built the Transcontinental Railroad? Same thing. These immigrant groups went from being outsiders to being fully embraced as Americans. We are a nation of immigrants.

The nation's attitude toward immigrants swung back and forth like a pendulum. Our borders were essentially open to European immigrants in the Ellis Island era until 1924, when an updated immigration law slammed the gates shut to Eastern and Southern Europeans and Asians while giving preferred status to white Europeans. Initial immigrants could sponsor family members for citizenship in what became known as chain migration. This law stayed in effect until 1965, when the national quotas were ended and Asian exclusions repealed. President Reagan exercised an amnesty for Hispanics in the 1980s, but by the 21st century the country was overdue for more immigration reform, although there was no consensus on how to address it.

Sinclair Lewis published his satirical novel *Babbitt* in 1922, which won the Nobel Prize for literature. He aimed his spotlight on the contradictions and hypocrisies of American society. In the novel, a character with the Polish name of Koplinsky denounced immigrants: "Another thing we got to do is to keep these damn foreigners out of the country. Thank the Lord, we're putting a limit on immigration. These Dagoes and Hunkies have got to learn that this is a white man's country, and they ain't wanted here. When we've assimilated the foreigners we got here now and learned 'em the principles of Americanism and turned 'em into regular folks, why then maybe we'll let in a few more." Lewis was satirizing American society of the 1920s, but his criticism and sharp wit seemed equally relevant a century later, especially if you replaced the ethnic slurs with *Hispanics*. [6]

The 1993 North American Free Trade Agreement (NAFTA) between Mexico and the U.S. led to a labor surplus in Mexico that would take about two decades to rebalance. Small Mexican farms were no longer competitive against larger, more efficient American farms, and cheaper American corn flooded into the Mexican market, which was disruptive. Free trade was a powerful economic driver for Mexico. The country witnessed a rising middle class, more opportunities for women, and family size stabilized, which eventually curtailed the country's labor surplus. However, many of the economically displaced Mexicans headed north to find work in the U.S., essentially becoming economic refugees seeking a better life.

The influx of immigrants—especially Hispanics—was indeed reshaping the United States. An estimated twelve million of them were here illegally. Smugglers, known as coyotes, brought them over the border for a price, sometimes abandoning them in harsh conditions in Arizona's Sonoran Desert with little or no water. They arrived with neither English language skills nor education, which put them at the bottom rung economically: they often found work in agriculture, housekeeping, restaurants, or retirement homes, though the more fortunate found better-paying jobs in construction. They worked labor-intensive, low-wage work that most Americans didn't want to do.

America developed a symbiotic relationship with immigrants, needing this cheap source of labor, but also stressing over the cost of providing services, education, and medical care to a large number of poor people with large families. At the same time, these hard-working Hispanics had to support their families back home through remittances. The Inter-American Development

Bank estimated in 2006 that immigrants sent $45 billion in remittances home to their families to pay for basic living expenses like food and shelter. [7]

Many Home Depots and Lowe's outlets became day-laborer sites, places where undocumented workers gathered to find work for the day, whether for construction, landscaping, or painting. These home improvement stores posted their signs in both English and Spanish. While some might protest, "Speak English, dammit!," you wanted the contractor who was fixing your home to find the right supplies and tools.

Despite the prevalence of Spanish, there was little to no chance that the U.S. would become a bilingual culture. The fact is, you have to speak English to function in American society. The rate of English adoption among Hispanic immigrants mirrored other immigrant cultures that came to the U.S.: the first generation learns bits and pieces of English, their kids speak English as their primary language (it's what they learn in school, plus that's what their friends speak—an example of positive peer pressure), but speak their parents' language at home. By the third generation, the grandkids are Americans in every conceivable way, and often speak as much of their grandparents' language as their grandparents speak English. This is a de facto assimilation model that has worked quite well in the U.S. for four hundred years.

Many Hispanic parents brought their children across the border, and these kids in turn grew up culturally as Americans, learning English as their primary language. The U.S. was the only country they knew, though technically their presence here was illegal. They became known as the Dreamers, after the proposed Development, Relief, and Education for Alien Minors (DREAM) Act. It was a dilemma about what to do with these 750,000 or so people, who grew up in the States, went to school, and ran businesses. Should the Dreamers be granted citizenship, or sent back to their parents' country?

Immigration shouldn't be considered a zero-sum game. Adding an immigrant to the economy doesn't subtract a white person's job. Rather, it expands the pie by adding another person to the workforce who will contribute to the economy. Consider as well that immigrants are taxpayers, and without immigrants our population would flatten or even shrink, given that American families were having fewer children. Who is to pay taxes for aging Americans?

The United States itself is an immigrant culture, as everyone came from somewhere else. The immigrants become Americans, and Americans in turn are changed in ways both great and small by the newcomers. Food is a classic example: immigrants often open restaurants as the first step to joining the middle class. For a century, Italian food was America's favorite "ethnic" food, but one that is now considered mainstream. Mexican food overtook Italian as the country's favorite cuisine, bolstered by the adoption of the margarita as a beloved cocktail.

American culinary habits became even more international and with a myriad of choices. It branched out to include just about every ethnic group that was stirred into the American melting pot—Vietnamese pho soup, Thai chicken satay, Bolivian salteñas, Peruvian ceviche, and the ever-popular tacos, no doubt influenced by a huge wave of Mexican immigrants. Regional cooking saw a resurgence as well, as chefs rediscovered old favorites and gave them modern twists. Meat and potatoes hadn't disappeared from American tables—it had just transferred to the nearby Argentinean steakhouse or Brazilian *churrascaria*.

In the half century after World War II, white flight to the suburbs left the central cities to minorities, creating a white demographic ring around a black or brown core. But that model upended itself during the first decade as immigrants, predominantly Hispanics, settled in outlying suburbs where they could find affordable housing. And central cities were no longer just for minorities as affluent young whites moved downtown in search of the many amenities and excitement of city life, rather than the monoculture of suburban neighborhoods.

Hispanic families often came to the States poor, and so to survive financially, they pooled their resources. An extended, multigenerational family might pile into a single house—often a dozen people or more, representing moms and dads, grandparents, children, aunts and uncles, and children. Because they were working-class and lived in the suburbs, each person needed a car to get to their job (and often they had several jobs each). This meant a single house might have a dozen cars parked out front, often used jalopies. This caused consternation and parking problems in many neighborhoods.

There was a backlash against illegal immigrants, particularly from law-and-order people, who wanted the government to do more to stem the flow of people entering the country. In 2006, Congress attempted to pass heavy-handed laws to curtail illegal immigrants and to punish people who supported them. Hispanic communities rallied in cities around the country, holding major public demonstrations against the proposed laws. These bills withered on the vine.

Congress came up with an alternative. Mexico and the U.S. share a 2,000-mile border, much of which is rural and porous, but which also has many natural obstacles that limit humans from crossing it. Building a fence or wall along the entire Mexican border wasn't feasible, but it could be built along stretches where large numbers of people crossed into the country. In 2006, Congress appropriated $4 billion to build a nearly 700-mile fence along the areas where most of the illegal border crossings occurred, while greatly increasing the size of the Border Patrol. The fence stretched, with some gaps, between San Diego to just beyond El Paso, largely built on federal land.

The Border Patrol noted that the number of people apprehended crossing the border illegally peaked in 2000 with 1.67 million apprehensions. The rate then fell noticeably as enforcement efforts stepped up and the border fence provided more of a deterrent to illegal crossings. As the economy soured in 2007, many immigrants could not find work, and that too was a reason why fewer people tried to cross into the U.S. By 2018, just 403,479 people were apprehended. [8]

President George W. Bush recognized that the U.S. is an immigrant society and was fond of saying, "Family values don't stop at the Rio Grande." He attempted to get a much-needed immigration reform bill passed in 2007, but could not get Congress to go along, especially his own party. The Republican working-class base wanted no more immigrants in the country, who saw immigrants as taking their jobs and demanding services.

However, the immigration issue failed to resonate at the polls in the first decade. Nativists might rail about the flood of illegals coming in, yet this was not on the priority list for most voters, and as we've seen, many businesses relied on this low-cost source of labor. Voters did not give Republicans points for voting for the seven-hundred-mile fence in 2006: instead, they handed control of Congress back to the Democrats. The election issue that year was the flailing Iraq War.

One victim of his own mouth that year was Virginia senator George Allen, who ran for reelection in 2006. His Democratic challenger, Jim Webb, dispatched a Virginia-born college student of Indian descent named S. R. Sidarth to track Allen's stump speeches. During one of the speeches, Allen pointed out Sidarth to the audience: "This fellow here, over here with the yellow shirt, macaca, or whatever his name is." He added, "Let's give a welcome to macaca here. Welcome to America and the real world of Virginia." Allen's comments hinted that the only real Americans were white, that somehow an American-born, brown-skinned person must be a foreigner. The day had passed when someone could make such a presumptuous (and possibly racist) comment and get away with it. Allen, a popular Republican senator, subsequently lost the election to Jim Webb, who had little chance until Allen's "macaca" moment. [9]

Illegal immigration plummeted during the Great Recession of 2008 and 2009. When jobs disappeared, immigrants remained in Mexico, not risking the treacherous border crossing for jobs that no longer existed. In 2000, some 1.67 million illegals were arrested crossing the border; in 2011, only 327,577 were arrested, according to the Department of Homeland Security. This was not only because of stepped-up enforcement by the Border Patrol, but also because fewer Mexicans were attempting to get into the U.S. Likewise, the amount of money Mexicans remitted home peaked at $24 billion in 2007, then dropped to $21 billion in 2011 because of the Great Recession. [10]

Once Barack Obama entered the White House, his administration enacted a Secure Communities program to crack down on illegal immigration. This required local law enforcement to fingerprint and report people arrested for criminal violations to be crosschecked in the federal database for immigrants. Anyone deemed to be an illegal could be detained and deported. It also stepped up audits on companies known to hire illegals. The program deported more than 392,000 people in 2010, most of them Hispanic. During the Obama years, Obama deported far more people than George W. Bush had. [11]

The 2010 census revealed just how strong the Hispanic population was growing in the country. In Arizona, a state with high population growth with the nation's toughest anti-immigrant laws, the Hispanic population grew to 30 percent of the population from a quarter the decade before. Arizona had a reputation as a state full of white retirees, but it was getting younger and browner. [12]

California's population grew 10 percent over the first decade to 37 million people. More than one in ten Americans was now a Californian. The one-time boom state had stabilized, no longer experiencing rapid growth, in part because of economic turmoil from the housing market fallout. It was still by far the most populous state. Though its population hadn't grown that much, the ratio of Hispanics had soared to 38 percent of the population, compared to 40 percent whites. This was a trend that had been underway for years. It was only a question of time before Hispanics became the majority in California. [13]

The Hispanic surge posed a long-term threat to the Republican Party. Other than Cuban-Americans, who congregated in South Florida and still blamed Democrats and John F. Kennedy for failing to stop Fidel Castro, the country's Hispanic population voted Democratic. This made sense in that the Democrats had become a multiethnic political party that championed minority rights.

❖

One of the more relevant novels of the early 21st century was Junot Díaz's *The Brief Wondrous Life of Oscar Wao*, published in 2007. It offered multiple characters, shifts across the space-time continuum, and incessant quoting of J.R.R. Tolkien, comic books like *The Fantastic Four*, and science fiction. And at the heart of its story was Oscar de León, a nerdy Dominican immigrant who, like all immigrant kids, struggled to fit in.

At a crowded book-signing event, Díaz explained how he came to the states from the Dominican Republic when he was six and grew up in New Jersey. There he learned to write about the people he knew best: Dominicans in the Garden State. The characters in *Oscar Wao* were entirely fictional, though the setting was real. Díaz noted that New Jersey lived in the shadow of New York, and that it gave the residents an inferiority complex. (New Yorkers, especially Manhattanites, did not help one bit, referring to people in New Jersey as the "bridge and tunnel" crowd, or worse, "bridge, tunnel, and trash.") People pretended they were from New York, or they embraced where they came from. And that is what Díaz did.

Oscar Wao is about the Dominican diaspora in the United States who fled the brutal dictatorship of Rafael Trujillo. Dominicans are both black and Latino, what some call "Blatino." Christopher Columbus first landed on the island in 1492. Díaz wrote that the Admiral's name was taboo and was not to be uttered aloud, or it would draw a *fukú*, a curse. [14]

Though written in English, Díaz weaved Spanish phrases throughout the novel. Like the hero, nerd-boy Oscar, Díaz knew plenty of nerds growing up (he admitted he was one of them)—not street smart, but the kind who read comic books and science fiction and who went off to college. Díaz won the Pulitzer Prize for fiction for *Oscar Wao*. It was, at heart, the story of immigrants in a new land. [15]

For many immigrants, the U.S. was a place to start over. You read about them in Willa Cather's 1918 novel *My Ántonia*, which celebrated the immigrants who came to Nebraska. Or the many Russian Jews who came to this country, fleeing pogroms and the czar's army that conscripted their boys. Or the southern Italians who came to the U.S. looking for work in a great wave after Italian unification in 1861. Or the "boat people" who arrived after South Vietnam collapsed in 1975. The U.S. has long been a place of refuge. The Statue of Liberty has long stood as a beacon of hope to the newcomer and the refugee. And most people arrive poor. They quickly learn that the streets aren't paved with gold, but that they have to work hard to get ahead. And they do.

❖

The United States had a small population of 2.5 million Muslims, of whom about a quarter lived around New York City. In 2010, as the ninth anniversary of 9/11 approached, controversy arose over a proposed Muslim community center in lower Manhattan. An existing community center had grown overcrowded, and its trustees sought to build a new thirteen-story building on private property. The city of New York approved it, and Mayor Michael Bloomberg, himself a Jew, weighed in on the importance of religious tolerance as one of the fundamental values in American society.

But the 9/11 terrorist attacks were still too fresh for many, and the Muslim community center was branded the "Ground Zero mosque." Ground Zero was considered hallowed ground, though the community center was to be built two blocks to the north in a dense, bustling downtown neighborhood. Some thought that a Muslim community center would be like erecting a victory arch for the 9/11 terrorists. Others declared that putting a mosque so close to Ground Zero would be an insult to the families of the 9/11 victims; in fact, the families were split over the question.[16]

Much of this debate was not in New York City, but rather in the nation's heartland, which actively distrusted Islam, and where many people would object to a mosque opening in their neighborhood, claiming that it would foster terrorism. It was also an election year, and suddenly everyone weighed in with their opinion—President Obama, the blogosphere, the national newspapers, and talk shows. This debate would not have happened if it were over a Christian church or a Jewish synagogue. It showed that Americans still had a sharp distrust of Islam, that many equated the religion with terrorism and hate for America.

In June 2015, Donald Trump announced his presidential campaign, coming down the escalator in the gold-plated tackiness of Trump Tower to speak to reporters and demagogue against immigrants. "When Mexico sends its people, they're not sending their best," he stated. "They're sending people that have lots of problems and they're bringing those problems with us. They're bringing drugs. They're bringing crime. They're rapists. And some, I assume, are good people." He would later promise to build a "big, beautiful wall" to keep Hispanic immigrants out (perhaps he forgot that we already had a large fence). This demagoguery was well designed to agitate white working-class people, who had angst about the browning of America and viewed immigrants as a threat to their way of life.[17]

The U.S. was well on its way to becoming a nation made up of minorities, no longer dominated by whites, but one where whites are simply the largest minority. This was likely demographic destiny, no matter the quixotic nativist protest against immigrants. The future of the country did not belong to aging, insecure white folks; it belonged to the young. And the young were increasingly pluralistic, multicultural, and multiracial.

A democratic society is judged on how it treats minorities. The United States is rapidly becoming a country where minorities are the majority, whether ethnic, religious, or sexual. A just society is one where everyone has a fair stake and a seat at the table, and where tolerance is more than skin deep.

8
Gay in America

I n 1998, a young gay man named Matthew Shepard was tied to a rural fence post near Laramie, Wyoming, and pistol-whipped and tortured nearly to death by two men. They left him bleeding and unconscious, his skull fractured, his face covered with blood save for where his tears had washed the blood away. The following day, a cyclist passing by found what he thought was a scarecrow before realizing it was a person and called the police. Shepard never regained consciousness, and he died in a hospital six days later with his parents, Dennis and Judy, at his bedside. It was a savage hate crime, one that galvanized the nation's growing gay community. The two perpetrators were convicted and sent to prison.

Few social changes were as dramatic over the course of the first decade as American society's decisive shift in its acceptance of the gay community. It had taken a century after the Civil War to finally extend civil rights to African Americans. It had taken more than seven decades for women to win the right to vote. But the struggle for gay rights—as represented by marriage equality—happened with remarkable speed as states legalized gay marriage like falling dominoes. In this short period of time, gays went from fringe to mainstream.*

---

* For the purpose of keeping it simple, I will refer to this broad, diverse movement as the gay community. In this case I'm not using "gay" as a reference to homosexual men, to which I count myself, but to the broader community. The term "queer" is probably more accurate to describe the broader umbrella of sexual and identity minorities, but to some it is pejorative. All this sounds rather academic, I know, but words do matter.

Modern gay political activism symbolically charts its origin at the Stone-wall riots in New York's Greenwich Village in June of 1969, though there were certainly other protests around the same time, and police raids and riots had been going on for decades. Stonewall, however, triggered gay liberation as a national movement for legal equality. The annual Pride celebrations took place in cities and towns around the country near the anniversary of Stonewall, with the rainbow flag proudly displayed as the community symbol.

When uninformed straight people asked what was the point of Pride, a common response became, "Be thankful you don't need one." Every day of the year was straight Pride, as heterosexuals flaunted pictures of their children at work and nonchalantly held hands or kissed in public, while such behavior might get a gay person beaten up, fired from their job, or cast a judgey look of disapproval. Pride was about finding community and experiencing that you weren't alone. Nor was the fight for recognition about special rights, as some asserted, but rather about equal rights. Gays simply wanted a seat at the table and to be treated with dignity.

By the 1990s people came up with letters to identify the various subgroups of the gay community. LGBT was the most prevalent, standing for lesbian, gay, bisexual, and transgender. The first three were about sexual orientation (in other words, who you were attracted to), while being transgender was about sexual identity. By the mid-2000s, Q (for queer or questioning) was added to incorporate the myriad sexual identity groups that were emerging. In the following decade, many more initials were added to this alphabet soup, including QIAA2S, which stood for questioning, intersex, allied, asexual, and two-spirit. One could also add P for pansexual, or GNC for gender nonconforming. This was a big tent and wasn't so much a community as a coalition.[1]

A Brief History of Gay Rights

One can trace the presence of LGBT people as far back as history is recorded. Alexander the Great and Frederick the Great, playwrights William Shake-speare, Oscar Wilde, Lorraine Hansberry, Tennessee Williams, and James Baldwin, authors Truman Capote, Willa Cather, Gertrude Stein and Gore Vidal, poets Allen Ginsberg, Mary Oliver and Walt Whitman, blues singer Ma Rainey, civil rights activists Bayard Rustin and Frank Kameny, tennis stars Billie Jean King and Martina Navratilova, rock stars Elton John and

Freddie Mercury, comedians Ellen DeGeneres, Rosie O'Donnell and Wanda Sykes, reporters Anderson Cooper and Don Lemon, drag empress RuPaul, flamboyant pianist Liberace, and possibly even President James Buchanan and FBI director J. Edgar Hoover, were all sexual minorities, to name just a few.

Four years after the Stonewall riots, the American Psychiatric Association declared that homosexuality was not a mental illness. Being gay was no longer a medical diagnosis. Most Americans were still fairly intolerant toward the gay rights movement. The movement itself was long marked by its outsider status, left-wing and even Marxist counter-culturalism, and insurgence against heterosexual norms. Gays had often fought against traditional institutions such as marriage; they were rebellious and anti-assimilationist. They wanted sexual freedom and liberation from societal traditions.

The HIV/AIDS crisis of the 1980s devastated the gay community, especially among men. But it brought new activism and visibility from people like Larry Kramer and the grass-roots political movement ACT UP (which stands for AIDS Coalition To Unleash Power), as families were forced to deal with the loss of so many brothers, fathers, and sons. People began to recognize those with AIDS not as sinners who deserved death but beloved family members whose lives were tragically cut short. Family and friends created panels of lost loved ones for the AIDS Memorial Quilt, which traveled the country and brought home the tragedy of this disease. In 1996, the quilt returned to Washington, D.C., and covered the entire National Mall. It was breathtaking and heartbreaking to see, each panel representing an individual loss, while the enormous quilt evoked the national tragedy that was AIDS.

Public perception dramatically changed when beloved public figures began dying of the disease. Actor Rock Hudson died of AIDS in 1985, followed by Freddie Mercury, the lead singer of the rock band Queen, in 1991. Basketball legend Magic Johnson announced that same year that he had HIV. Tennis legend Arthur Ashe died of AIDS in 1993 contracted from a blood transfusion. Pedro Zamora, a character on MTV's reality program *The Real World*, unflinchingly documented how his health declined as a person living with HIV. He died in 1994. These public figures with HIV forced the public to reexamine their attitudes about the disease and the people infected by it. It was clear that not just gay people could contract HIV—both Ashe and Johnson were heterosexual. AIDS was a public health threat to everyone. Though no cure for HIV has as of yet been found, a cocktail of antiretrovirals was developed in the 1990s to keep the virus in check, and the death rate plummeted.

Because gays had long existed in the shadows, some considered them a national security threat, as they could be blackmailed. But what about those who were open and honest about their sexual orientation? They were still forbidden to serve in the American armed forces, which forbade homosexual conduct. When Bill Clinton ran for the presidency in 1992, he enlisted gay support with the promise that he would allow gays to openly serve in the military. He greatly overpromised, and in 1993 reached an awkward compromise with Congress known as "Don't ask, don't tell" (DADT). Gays could serve, but they couldn't be open about it. This essentially meant that many soldiers had to lie to serve their country.

When the Hawaii Supreme Court in 1993 deemed that the state discriminated against gay couples by forbidding them to marry, this seemed to open the door to gay marriage (the state would shut the door five years later). Gay marriage suddenly became a national bogeyman, whooped up by religious conservatives as a threat to society that would undermine traditional marriage and mark the veritable decline of Western Civilization itself. This defied millennia of Judeo-Christian teachings—never mind that wives were treated as property, husbands could have multiple wives, and that our concept of marrying for love is only a couple centuries old. As they were fond of saying, God created Adam and Eve, not Adam and Steve. They believed being gay was a sinful lifestyle choice promoted by promiscuous libertines who wanted to corrupt and recruit the nation's youth. Some evangelicals even pushed conversion therapy, a quack science that was psychologically damaging to its participants as it attempted (and overwhelmingly failed) to turn its subjects straight.

Gay rights advocates countered that marriage is a legal, civil institution, and that even with gay marriage, churches would still have the right not to perform gay weddings. The legal nature of marriage gives spouses tremendous benefits in such areas as taxes, property, Social Security, pensions, and inheritance rights. Marriage was a good thing, and gays wanted in. Besides, gays had shown that they could provide stable households for raising children. In any case, with adoption, artificial insemination, foster parenting or surrogacy, gays were seizing control of their reproductive rights and parenting children. There was a strong conservative case for gay marriage, as marriage is fundamental to a stable society.

And why did the gay community want marriage equality so badly? The debate over gay rights during the 1990s and early 2000s was largely fought over this single issue. The answer was that marriage is the ultimate form of equality. Whatever you think about marriage—whether it's a holy covenant before God or a legal agreement between consenting adults—marriage is recognized as a legal contract at the federal and state level. To deny gays the right to marry was to deny them full equality before the laws of the United States.

In 1996, the U.S. Supreme Court made the first of four key rulings over the next nineteen years that would profoundly elevate the cause of LGBT equality. Four years earlier, Colorado voters had approved Amendment 2 to deny legal protection to gays as a class—in effect legalizing discrimination. The court overturned the state amendment by a 6–3 vote, arguing that no one could be denied the protection of the law. Associate Justice Anthony Kennedy wrote the majority opinion, noting that "the amendment seems inexplicable by anything but animus"—that is to say, by sheer homophobia, and there was no state rationalization for this. Kennedy would write the majority opinions in all four significant cases affecting gay rights—and was joined in every one of them by Stephen Breyer and Ruth Bader Ginsburg.[2]

That same year, President Bill Clinton signed the Defense of Marriage Act (DOMA), recognizing marriage as only between a man and a woman, and giving the states the right not to recognize gay marriages conducted in other states. It was a presidential election year, and gay marriage had become a wedge issue. Clinton couldn't afford to further alienate conservatives. Though he had been a key supporter for gay rights, congressional Republicans forced him to throw the gay community under the bus.

Many gays had long asserted that 10 percent of the population was homosexual ("one in ten" was the popular refrain). This was based on Dr. Alfred Kinsey's studies in the 1940s. Yet the actual size of the gay community was much smaller. A study by the Williams Institute at UCLA's law school noted that 3.5 percent of Americans self-identified as gay, lesbian, or bisexual. In 2010, this was equivalent to 9 million people.[3] Similarly, Gallup surveyed that 3.5 percent of Americans identified as LGBT in 2012. That rose to 4.5 percent five years later. Gays were always going to be a small minority.[4]

American society came around significantly on the question of gay rights over the first decade of the 21st century. Most people realized that gays were most likely born that way. Homosexuality was simply innate, like being left- or right-handed, or near or farsighted. But there are still no easy answers as to why most people are straight, while a minority are gay. And what explains attraction, whether you fall for someone tall or short, dark-haired or fair, slender or stout, or of the same or opposite sex?

The threat of gay marriage was fairly abstract, but over time as people began to witness gay relationships and as more people came out, the opposition softened. Many conservatives shed their overtly hostile antigay language while remaining committed to heterosexual-only marriage. There was really no societal threat from marriage equality, though it was difficult for many to see it that way initially. Ultimately it took an army of straight allies to support full equality. Gay civil rights could never be earned on their own, given the small size of the gay community.

Gallup tracked American attitudes about gays for decades by asking, "Do you think marriages between same-sex couples should or should not be recognized by the law as valid, with the same rights as traditional marriage?" The "should nots" spiked to 59 percent in 2005, just after George Bush was reelected in a campaign that stoked fear of gay marriage, then gradually declined to 37 percent a decade later. Similarly, the "shoulds" saw a steady rise in support from 37 percent in 2005 to 60 percent in 2015, the year that the U.S. Supreme Court declared that gay marriage was a constitutional right. This was a stunning mirror-image reversal. The number in support continued to rise in subsequent years as more Americans embraced the idea that gays deserved equal rights.[5]

Vermont became the first state to establish legal recognition for gay couples. In the year 2000, the state Supreme Court ruled that gay relationships deserved legal recognition and directed the legislature to address the issue. The legislature chose the route of civil unions rather than marriage, essentially creating a separate-but-equal state-sanctioned institution. Vermont stood alone on the issue for several years. That same year, California voters approved the Knight Initiative, a state law declaring marriage to be only between a man and a woman, by 65 percent to 35 percent. The law was similar to the federal Defense of Marriage Act.

In neighboring New Hampshire, Episcopal priest Gene Robinson was elected as the first-ever openly gay bishop in the United States in June 2003. It was a prophetic moment in American history. Just three weeks later, the U.S. Supreme Court provided a significant victory for gay rights in *Lawrence v. Texas*. Texas had outlawed sodomy for homosexuals, but not for heterosexuals, creating a separate-and-unequal treatment before the law. The court struck down sodomy bans nationwide. Justice Anthony Kennedy, a conservative Catholic who nonetheless supported gay rights, wrote in the 6–3 majority opinion that "the state cannot demean their existence or control their destiny by making their private sexual conduct a crime." The *Lawrence* decision overturned a 1986 decision known as *Bowers v. Hardwick* that upheld sodomy as a criminal act. *Lawrence* largely reflected where most Americans were on the question of sex: that the state had no business regulating people's bedroom behavior, that gays and lesbians should be treated equally before the law, and that the gay community had reached a point of social acceptance where majorities now believed discrimination was wrong.

Not everyone was happy with this decision. Justice Antonin Scalia read a scathing dissent from the bench, denouncing that "the court has largely signed on to the so-called homosexual agenda." He worried that "this reasoning leaves on shaky, pretty shaky, grounds state laws limiting marriage to opposite-sex couples." He was right about that. The *Lawrence* decision emboldened gay activists to demand equal treatment, including the right to get married. [6]

Conservatives often accused liberal justices of engaging in judicial activism, pushing their favored policies onto the country. Yet it was clear that conservatives were equally activist and had their own pet policies. Scalia's policy preference was abundantly clear in his *Lawrence* dissent: he was downright opposed to gay marriage. He was a devout Catholic and frankly viewed gays as immoral, an opinion held by many evangelicals.

Five months later, the Massachusetts Supreme Court went even further than Vermont in declaring that gays had a right to marry—not just civil unions. It gave the state legislature six months to act. Massachusetts became the first state to legalize same-sex marriage on May 17, 2004. It was a considerable but fragile victory, one that would nearly be undone as the legislature attempted but failed to reverse the court decision. Governor Mitt Romney, who was Mormon, was opposed to extending marital rights. Though he couldn't block gay marriages altogether, he invoked a 1913 law that prevented out-of-state residents from marrying within the commonwealth, a law originally intended to prevent interracial marriage.

In February 2004, San Francisco Mayor Gavin Newsom, a straight ally, ordered city clerks to provide marriage licenses to same-sex couples. Thousands of couples flocked to City Hall to get married. The State Supreme

Court soon voided these marriages on the grounds that it had yet to decide whether gay marriage was even legal. Newsom's action was legally dubious and it stoked political opposition.

With the actions of Massachusetts and San Francisco clearly in mind, President George Bush called for a constitutional amendment to define marriage as being between a man and a woman on February 24, 2004. He denounced "activist judges" who had made gay marriage equal and stated unequivocally, "the preservation of marriages rises to this level of national importance." This was more symbolic than anything, as the amendment had little if any chance of winning the necessary two-thirds vote in Congress. Three days after Bush's statement, Mayor Jason West of tiny New Paltz, New York began issuing marriage licenses, though a judge soon halted his actions.[7]

Gay marriage as a national issue had been on a low simmer since the passage of DOMA in 1996, but with the *Lawrence* decision, Massachusetts legalizing marriage equality, and the San Francisco and New Paltz weddings, conservatives grew alarmed. Gay marriage was propelled into the national spotlight during the 2004 presidential campaign. Karl Rove, President Bush's political strategist, admitted that "gay marriage was an ugly fight we had not asked for but could win if we handled it with care," meaning opposing same-sex unions. A fierce partisan at heart, Rove believed the issue "revealed the nuttiness of the Left, which never saw how persistent America's traditionalism really was." Bush capitalized on this political blowback in the campaign, and it helped drive conservatives to the polls that November.[8]

Rove penned a non-denial denial of his role in the election. He denied that he had "single-handedly injected gay marriage into the 2004 election," but he certainly took advantage of it and stoked public fear that gay marriage might become a reality. "But I saw up close how it benefited my candidate: gay rights activists bent on defeating George W. Bush helped reelect him by overreaching on same-sex marriage. Bush's views were shared by most Americans." This was Rove's view in 2010 when he published his memoir, and as we've seen, most Americans changed their minds on the question.[9]

During a presidential election debate, Democratic candidate John Kerry mentioned that Vice President Dick Cheney's daughter Mary was a lesbian. The right called foul, as they believed that a candidate's children were off-limits. Cheney's wife Lynne called it a "cheap and tawdry political trick." But Mary's orientation was public knowledge, and she was an adult, not a child.

Kerry was certainly trying to score points with the left, especially with the gay community (which overwhelmingly voted for him), while pointing out the hypocrisy of the right.[10]

Gay marriage was a powerful wedge issue in the 2004 election. Eleven states placed initiatives on the ballot that limited marriage to a man and woman, and every one of these states passed it. Karl Rove had neatly politicized this issue, tying the Bush reelection to the state constitutional amendments, and thus ensuring high evangelical turnout for the president. This was particularly important in Ohio, the swing state that gave Bush the presidency. After Bush's reelection in 2004, he effectively dropped the issue of gay marriage. It had served its political purpose and helped get him reelected. He had other goals for 2005, notably Social Security reform.

Meanwhile, "Don't ask, don't tell" continued as an official policy in the armed forces, but with the wars in Afghanistan and Iraq, the military quietly suspended its discharges. Every person was deemed vital for the war effort, whether gay or straight. It sent a hypocritical message to gay soldiers: it was acceptable to serve in wartime, but in peace, your military service is not welcome.

Donald Rumsfeld, Bush's secretary of defense, did not mention DADT once in his memoir. He simply sidestepped the question by choosing not to address it. His friend, Vice President Dick Cheney, was more outspoken in his support for gay rights, in part because of his lesbian daughter Mary. During the 2000 vice presidential debate with Joe Lieberman, he answered a question about whether gays should have the same constitutional rights as straight people: "I think we ought to do everything we can to tolerate and accommodate whatever kind of relationships people want to enter into."[11]

The Changing Culture

The ballot losses of 2004 were demoralizing and a huge setback for the LGBTQ community. George Bush had been reelected and showed no desire to support gay rights. However, the movement would reemerge. It was already winning the cultural argument.

Gays and lesbians began making more positive appearances in movies and television as the closet door gradually opened. Comedian Ellen DeGeneres came out in real life and also on her fictional *Ellen* television show in

1997. This aired just three weeks after a hilarious episode of the subversive cartoon comedy *The Simpsons*, featuring gay raconteur and film director John Waters. Homer Simpson becomes fearful that his son Bart is "turning gay" and decides to butch him up, including taking him to a steel mill that turns out to be entirely gay—and which turns into a nightclub called The Anvil. It was a brilliant spoof of parental fear.

In 1998, the television comedy *Will & Grace* debuted, which was a huge hit. The show revolved around the friendship of Will Truman, a successful gay lawyer in New York, and his best straight friend, Grace Adler. Campy, hilarious, and always positive, *Will & Grace* allowed society to be in on the joke. Will was so likeable that he couldn't help but disarm hostility. Similarly, the television series *Modern Family* a decade later introduced a gay couple that was part of a broader, complex family.

People saw themselves mirrored in these television shows. They humanized rather than demeaned gays, and made the clear point that gays were part of the family. True, most of these situations showed whites rather than people of color, but there were notable exceptions, such as *The Wire*, which had both a lesbian police detective, Kima Greggs, and a particularly compelling gay stick-up man named Omar.

There was admittedly a delicious sense of irony when National Association of Evangelicals president, Ted Haggard, resigned in 2006 after a male prostitute revealed that Haggard had hired him a number of times for sex and drugs. It was a reminder that just because someone is married that does not mean they are heterosexual.

Former boy-band member Lance Bass of NSYNC outed himself over the July 4 holiday party in Provincetown, Massachusetts, in 2006. By the end of the weekend, it seemed every gay person in the country had received the news by text, and within days, Bass admitted publicly that he was gay. During Bass's publicity storm, actor Neil Patrick Harris quietly issued a press release that he too was gay. When high-profile people like this came out, people cheered and overwhelmingly supported them.

Visibility and positive associations of gay people rose. Gays were no longer some abstraction, but real people, and that significantly altered how society perceived them. And people began to realize that gay relationships, just like straight relationships, weren't just about sex, but were about love. Gay people are as multidimensional as everyone else, and gay relations just as complex as straight relationships.

And then there was the movie *Brokeback Mountain*.

No other movie in the decade expressed the complexity and nuance of gay relationships as did the 2005 Academy Award–winning *Brokeback Mountain*, based on a novel by Annie Proulx. In the story, two young men—Ennis Del Mar (played by Heath Ledger) and Jack Twist (Jake Gyllenhaal) were hired to tend sheep in the Rocky Mountains, and this began a twenty-year love affair. Both men married women and had families, yet would return each year to the mountain to be together. They could only be themselves in isolation, as the fear of getting caught—particularly for the closeted Ennis—was debilitating. Ennis suffered from acute internalized homophobia.

When Jack was killed in an accident in Texas, Ennis visited Jack's dirt-poor father and mother. The venomous father denied Jack's wishes to be buried on Brokeback. "I know where Brokeback Mountain is," he practically spat at Ennis, hinting that he knew of their relationship. The kindly mother showed Jack's childhood room to Ennis, and it was there that Ennis found something that left audiences in tears. Searching through Jack's closet, he found a shirt that Jack was fond of wearing—and tucked inside of it was one of Ennis's old shirts he thought he had lost. Jack had hung the shirts together on a single hanger, symbolizing their devotion.

In the movie's final scene, Ennis had reversed the shirts so his shirt was outside Jack's as if to embrace and protect him. With teary eyes he whispered, "Jack, I swear." But what was it he swore? I'll never forget you? I wish I'd done things different? I wish we had built that cabin? That I'd come out and we could live together? That I'll dig up your ashes and scatter them on Brokeback Mountain like you wanted?

Ennis lived an unhappy life of might-have-beens. Would he ever come out to another person again? Or was he exiled from both the gay and straight worlds, living in his trailer with his picture of Brokeback Mountain, his two shirts, and his memories of Jack? And would Jack ever be able to be himself? The story gave no answer, but it left audiences brokenhearted for Ennis.

The actor who played Ennis, Heath Ledger, was a remarkably talented straight Australian artist. He portrayed Ennis as cautious, mumbling and repressed. He died in his New York apartment from an accidental overdose after taking a lethal combination of prescription medication in January 2008. He was just twenty-eight.

The Legal Case for Marriage Equality

The "homosexual agenda," as conservatives asserted, simply never existed, nor was there a "monolithic movement working to push toward a single, shared goal," wrote historian Nathaniel Frank, who chronicled the struggle for marriage equality.[12] Rather, the gay community was often at odds as to its goals, whether for liberation (whatever that meant) or traditional marriage that essentially mirrored the heterosexual institution. Gay thought leaders like Randy Lloyd and Andrew Sullivan had long argued the conservative case for marriage equality.

Fighting for marriage equality was something that the LGBTQ coalition gradually evolved to support. A host of organizations, including the Gay & Lesbian Advocates and Defenders, the Human Rights Campaign, Lambda Legal, the American Civil Liberties Union, Freedom to Marry, the Gill Action Fund, and many others would fight the battle. Unable to secure marriage equality through Congress or most states, they turned to the courts to essentially make the case that banning gay marriage was discrimination.

President Bush's political strategist Karl Rove made an astute observation: "The gay rights movement had turned to the courts because it wasn't able to make any headway in the state legislatures." That is mostly correct: a minority of states would in fact advance marriage through the legislature. But for the remaining states, the question was, how is a small minority expected to win its rights when the majority is indifferent or downright opposed? They turn to the courts. And it would be largely through the courts that marriage equality would ultimately be won as it gradually unwound the election defeat from 2004.[13]

This court-based strategy first bore fruit in California in 2008. Four years after nullifying the marriages that San Francisco Mayor Gavin Newsom had allowed, the California Supreme Court changed its mind. By a vote of 4–3, it ruled that gays had the same right to marry as straight people.

Gay marriage became legal in California on June 16, 2008. Amid great excitement and the flash of paparazzi, Mayor Newsom officiated at the wedding of Del Martin and Phyllis Lyon, lesbians in their eighties who had been together for more than five decades. The next day, hundreds more married at county clerk offices, city halls, churches, and synagogues throughout the state. *Star Trek* actor George Takei applied for a marriage license with his partner of two decades, Brad Altman; the couple married in September.

Ellen DeGeneres and girlfriend Portia de Rossi married in August. Seeing popular public figures getting happily married had a positive influence. After all, who doesn't like weddings?

Washington Post columnist Harold Meyerson noted the significant shift in how society viewed homosexuals just a week after the California Supreme Court decision: "This shift is being driven by the young: Overwhelmingly, young people favor gay unions and, increasingly, gay marriage. Opposition rises in direct relation to the age of the poll respondents. In 20 or 30 years, I suspect gay marriage will be legal—and no big deal—throughout most, if not all, of the nation." As it turned out, it only took seven years for Meyerson's prediction to come true.[14]

California had no stipulation that only in-state gays could marry. Fearing that the Golden State would capture all of the wedding dollars, Massachusetts governor Deval Patrick announced that his state would no longer enforce its 1913 law banning out-of-state marriages, giving gays two state choices for marriage. People began recognizing the economic argument for supporting marriage equality.

Antigay forces struck back in California, led by the Catholic and Mormon churches. They placed an initiative known as Proposition 8 on the November 2008 ballot, a state constitutional amendment that defined marriage as being only between a man and a woman. The same day that the nation elected Barack Obama president with California's support, the Golden State endorsed Proposition 8 by a narrow margin, 52 to 48 percent. Two key pillars of the coalition that elected Obama, gays and minorities, had splintered over the issue. Although the black community voted overwhelmingly for Obama, it was also socially conservative, and black ministers preached against gay marriage. There was widespread belief in the black community that gay rights were not a civil rights issue. The result was that more than 70 percent of black voters in California voted for Proposition 8, as did the majority of Hispanics.[15]

Voter-approved Proposition 8 halted gay marriage in California, which was a major setback. There was widespread anger in the gay community, particularly directed at Mormons, for bankrolling the ballot initiative. There was a huge inflow of money and volunteers from Utah into California in the months before the November election, and this had a significant impact on voter opinion, who were swayed that gay marriage would somehow undermine traditional marriage.

California voters simultaneously approved another referendum that called for more humane treatment of farm-raised chickens, even as voters narrowly voted down gay marriage, causing some to quip that people cared more about chickens than people. Yet it is also astonishing to see how quickly the public was changing its mind about gay marriage. California had passed the Knight Initiative in 2000 by 65 percent, while just eight years later it barely overturned gay marriage by a narrow 2 percentage point margin.

There were only three antigay marriage amendments on state ballots in 2008 (Arizona, California, and Florida), compared to eleven in 2004. Gay marriage was not the wedge issue it had been four years earlier. The economy was in bad shape with the Great Recession, and voters were far more vexed over the soaring cost of health care and the collapse of their retirement plans than they were over Mr. and Mr. Smith's wedding plans.

In the 2008 presidential campaign, both Democratic and Republican presidential candidates, Barack Obama and John McCain, opposed gay marriage. However, as the decade unfolded, the Democratic Party evolved from sitting on the fence to throwing its political weight behind gay rights. The Republican Party, which had successfully leveraged the fear of gay marriage in 2004, increasingly fell silent on the issue, as the party had grown cautious about opposing gay rights for fear of being accused of bigotry. Republicans rarely mentioned it in 2008.

Incensed at California's vote on Proposition 8, a new generation of activists emerged, many of them young people who had never been politically involved before. They called it "Stonewall 2.0" after the Stonewall riots and for their heavy use of the Internet and social networking. Many activists were inspired by the message of change that Barack Obama had campaigned on. They also took insight from the movie *Milk*, which came out just weeks after the 2008 election. Actor Sean Penn played Harvey Milk, the gay activist and political organizer who became the country's first openly gay elected official in the 1970s. After ten months in office, he and Mayor George Moscone were assassinated by a former city supervisor, Dan White. Milk had helped convince California voters to reject Proposition 6, the 1978 "Save Our Children" ballot measure that would have fired any public-school teacher for being homosexual, along with anyone who supported them. It was a mean-spirited proposal that linked homosexuality with pedophilia (an issue that had been widely debunked). Proposition 6 sounded like a witch hunt, yet it came dangerously close to passing. [16]

Against the backdrop of the 2008 election, the Connecticut Supreme Court overturned the state ban on same-sex marriage, making it the third state to legalize gay marriage. Connecticut already offered civil unions, but the court ruled these were separate-but-equal. The first marriages in Connecticut took place on November 12—just eight days after the presidential election. The following month, the Episcopal Church splintered over the ordination of its first gay bishop, Gene Robinson, five years earlier. A small group of conservatives split off into their own denomination, severing themselves from the larger church body.

In April 2009, a victory came from an unexpected place: Iowa. The state Supreme Court ruled unanimously that a state law limiting marriage to only a man and woman was unconstitutional, as it denied equal protection. Unlike many other states, Iowa had never changed its constitution to ban gay marriage. "If gay and lesbian people must submit to different treatment without an exceedingly persuasive justification, they are deprived of the benefits of the principle of equal protection upon which the rule of law is founded," the court ruled. Iowa became the third state to legalize gay marriage after Massachusetts and Connecticut. [17]

Just days later, on April 7, the Vermont legislature overrode the governor's veto of a bill permitting gay marriage. This was the state that had initiated civil unions nine years earlier, and gay relationships had become widely accepted since then. Vermont was now the fourth state to support marriage equality—and the first that had done so via the legislature, rather than the courts.

Next up was Maine, the fifth state to legalize gay marriage when the legislature passed the measure, and which Governor John Baldacci signed into law on May 6. The city council of the District of Columbia soon voted to recognize gay marriages performed elsewhere, though the vote was met with a firestorm from some black ministers.

On May 26, the same day that President Obama appointed Sonia Sotomayor to the U.S. Supreme Court, the California State Supreme Court ruled in favor of letting Proposition 8 stand. The court was reluctant to overturn the vote of the people. It declared that the marriages of the 18,000 couples who had wed were legal, but that henceforth gays could only be recognized through civil unions, not marriage. This put a damper on the momentum gained that spring in Iowa and the Northeast.

Still, the momentum continued. New Hampshire's legislature voted for gay marriage, which Governor John Lynch signed into law on June 3. Six states now permitted gay marriage—including all of New England except Rhode Island. This had happened quickly, in large part because of the decimation of the Republican Party in the region, the party that had traditionally opposed marriage equality.

President Obama, who took office in January 2009, was initially on the fence politically on the question of marriage equality, saying it was a states' rights issue, which is what presidents often say when they don't want to spend their political capital. Although the LGBTQ community was a vital part of the Democratic coalition, he tended to trail public opinion concerning gay rights, rather than lead.

After five months in the Oval Office, Obama had not yet acted on his promise to reexamine "Don't ask, don't tell" and the Defense of Marriage Act. A number of prominent gays threatened to pull out of a major fundraiser for the president, which prompted him to act to shore up the base. He announced benefits for same-sex partners of federal employees, such as sick leave to take care of a partner. He likewise held an event at the White House commemorating the fortieth anniversary of the Stonewall riots. Throughout the year, Obama reiterated his pledge to end DADT and DOMA, and he signed a long-debated hate crimes law known as the Matthew Shepard Act. While the gay community was still infatuated with the president, there was no timetable for repeal.

In the November 2009 election, voters in Maine narrowly overturned the state law allowing gay marriage. Maine had become the thirty-first state to block gay marriage by public referendum. The New York state legislature voted down a bill to allow gay marriage in the state, and similarly New Jersey opted against a bill. Compounded by California's loss, gay marriage advocates had suffered significant setbacks to their cause.[18]

Meanwhile the city council of the District of Columbia voted in favor of gay marriage in December 2009. Congress had thirty business days to review any legislation passed by the district; the Democratic-controlled Congress declined to review, though Republicans attempted to author bills calling for a public vote. In March 2010, gay marriage became legal in the nation's capital.

After a full year in office, President Obama was finally ready to move against "Don't ask, don't tell." In his State of the Union address in January 2010, President Obama called for Congress to repeal the 1993 law. A week later, Admiral Mike Mullen, chairman of the Joint Chiefs of Staff, spoke before the Senate Armed Services Committee to discuss his views on the issue. "Speaking for myself and myself only, it is my personal belief that allowing gays and lesbians to serve openly would be the right thing to do." He added, "No matter how I look at the issue, I cannot escape being troubled by the fact that we have in place a policy which forces young men and women to lie about who they are in order to defend their fellow citizens. For me personally, it comes down to integrity—theirs as individuals, and ours as an institution." Defense Secretary Robert Gates echoed these words as well and began laying the groundwork for how the Pentagon would implement repeal once Congress acted. [19]

The next day, Colin Powell, the former chairman who had opposed allowing gays and lesbians to openly serve in 1993, threw his support behind Gates and Mullen. He noted that most NATO countries allowed gays and lesbians to serve without any apparent negative impact on morale or unit readiness. He stated, "If the chiefs and commanders are comfortable with moving to change the policy, then I support it." Powell noted how far society had moved toward accepting gays, and it was this same society that supplies soldiers for the armed forces. [20]

Indeed, a week later, a *Washington Post*-ABC News poll revealed that 75 percent of Americans believed it was time for "Don't ask, don't tell" to end. When the poll was first taken in 1993, only 44 percent said that gays should be allowed to serve openly. [21] Pollster John Zogby noted in a 2006 survey that nearly three-quarters of men and women in uniform were comfortable having gays and lesbians serve. It was clear that DADT's days were numbered. The public and the military no longer supported it. [22]

Several gay plaintiffs who had married in California during the 2008 window sued the state in federal court. It was a remarkable and risky case in which two unusual advocates served as counsel for the plaintiffs: conservative Ted Olson and liberal trial lawyer David Boies. Both men had been on opposing sides when they argued *Bush v. Gore* before the U.S. Supreme Court in 2000, and Olson had later served as Bush's solicitor general. They both recognized that marriage equality was a civil right and would champion the issue all the way to the Supreme Court. The case became known as *Hollingsworth v. Perry*. The federal judge overseeing the case, Vaughn Walker, held a twelve-day trial in his San Francisco district court in January 2010. The trial drew national attention, and that in turn helped favorably shape public opinion when the public saw a lesbian couple, Kris Perry and Sandy

Stier, who were simply asking for marriage to cement their bonds as parents to four children.

On August 4, Judge Walker published his ruling. It was a decisive victory for gay marriage, striking down Proposition 8 for violating the Equal Protection Clause of the Fourteenth Amendment of the U.S. Constitution. Walker's meticulous 138-page decision in *Hollingsworth v. Perry* established legal precedence, clearly with an eye to it being appealed to the Supreme Court. The facts that he established in his decision would be difficult to overturn. He wrote:

> Proposition 8 fails to advance any rational basis in singling out gay men and lesbians for denial of a marriage license. Indeed, the evidence shows Proposition 8 does nothing more than enshrine in the California Constitution the notion that opposite-sex couples are superior to same-sex couples. Because California has no interest in discriminating against gay men and lesbians, and because Proposition 8 prevents California from fulfilling its constitutional obligations to provide marriages on an equal basis, the court concludes that Proposition 8 is unconstitutional.

In other words, Walker struck down the separate-but-equal notion that gays could have domestic partnerships but not be married. He also wrote that it did not matter what the majority of voters wanted—marriage was a constitutional right for everyone, and civil rights should not be put up for vote. In undermining the argument that marriage had always been between a man and a woman, Walker noted how much the institution had evolved as the role of sexes changed:

> The evidence shows that the movement of marriage away from a gendered institution and toward an institution free from state-mandated gender roles reflects an evolution in the understanding of gender rather than a change in marriage. The evidence did not show any historical purpose for excluding same-sex couples from marriage, as states have never required spouses to have an ability or willingness to procreate in order to marry. . . . Rather, the exclusion exists as an artifact of a time when the genders were seen as having distinct roles in society and in marriage. That time has passed.

Walker concluded, "Gender no longer forms an essential part of marriage; marriage under law is a union of equals." Walker's decision in *Hollingsworth v. Perry* would be widely cited in future state challenges. He had provided the framework to undermine state laws and state constitutional amendments that prevented gays from marrying. His decision was appealed to the U.S. Supreme Court, meaning that gay marriage in California remained suspended.[23]

By 2010, five states allowed gay marriage: Massachusetts, Vermont, New Hampshire, Iowa, and Connecticut, plus the District of Columbia. Seven states recognized out-of-state same-sex marriages (the same states above, plus Maryland and New York). And fifteen states offered some recognition for same-sex domestic partnerships. Legal marriage was largely confined to New England, while recognition was across the Northeast and Pacific coast. The vast Midwest and Deep South were holdouts, states where social conservatism resisted extending rights to gays. Meanwhile, thirty-one states had constitutionally defined marriage as between a man and a woman. There was clearly a showdown brewing over whether states had the right to discriminate on the basis of what the majority voted.

A wave of gay teen suicides, largely stemming from cyberbullying, reminded people that gays could still be singled out, and that not everyone was comfortable with the new normal. The most egregious case was a gay Rutgers University student, Tyler Clementi, whose roommate live-streamed him hooking up with another man in their dorm room onto the Internet. After learning what his roommate had done, Clementi jumped to his death from the George Washington Bridge on September 22, 2010.

Obama had asked Congress to repeal "Don't ask, don't tell" in early 2010, and the House of Representatives passed the measure in May; however, the Senate held up the issue. Republicans waited for a key implementation report from the Pentagon, due to be published December 1. The window for repeal dramatically narrowed after Republicans seized control of the House of Representatives in the midterm elections, giving the lame duck Congress minimal time to act. Democrats seized their last opportunity, knowing that Republicans were not likely to support repeal, especially given that many new congressmen were Tea Party conservatives who opposed compromise.

As predicted, the Pentagon published its report in December about the impact of repeal on the armed services, and concluded that there was low risk. The Pentagon also released a troop survey that revealed 70 percent of soldiers weren't concerned about repeal.[24] After President Obama reached an agreement with Republicans over extending the Bush-era tax cuts, Republicans tacitly allowed the vote to come up. Shortly before Congress adjourned, the Senate voted 65 to 31 in favor of repeal, with eight Republicans joining Democrats. The bill was sent to the president, who signed it into law on December 22. At the signing ceremony, Obama stated:

> No longer will our country be denied the service of thousands of patriotic Americans who were forced to leave the military—regardless of their skills, no matter their bravery or their zeal, no matter their years of exemplary performance—because they happen to be gay. No longer will tens of thousands of Americans in uniform be asked to live a lie, or look over their shoulder, in order to serve the country that they love.[25]

Seventeen years and 13,000 discharges later, "Don't ask, don't tell" was over. It was the most significant federal legislative accomplishment for the gay community in the decade. DADT officially ended on September 20, 2011, after the Pentagon certified that it could implement new policies and had undergone training for all soldiers and sailors.

Barney Frank was the first openly gay congressman—the first of many. A Jewish Democrat from Newton, Massachusetts, Frank had a quick wit but always seemed a little feisty and grumpy. He had worked diligently to repeal "Don't ask, don't tell" during his career in the House of Representatives. "The repeal of DADT was an exhilarating conclusion to an extraordinarily productive two years" in Congress, Frank wrote.[26]

With the repeal of DADT successfully behind him, Obama shifted his political weight, as he was under heavy pressure from the gay community to act. In February 2011, the Obama administration stated that it would no longer uphold the Defense of Marriage Act, holding that the law was unconstitutional. The public was swinging in favor of gay marriage, and three legal cases challenging DOMA were making their way through federal courts.

Four months later, on June 24, New York Governor Andrew Cuomo signed a statute legalizing marriage equality, making it by far the most populous state where same-sex marriage was now legal. This came on the eve of the forty-second anniversary of the Stonewall riots and New York's annual Pride event, and the Empire State Building was lit up in the rainbow colors of the Pride flag. There were now six states that had legalized gay marriage—and it should be noted that New York's action was done through the legislature, not the courts.

In spring 2012, Maryland became the third state to legalize same-sex marriage via the legislature. It was promptly challenged and sent to the voters in an attempt to overturn the law. In such cases, gay rights advocates cried foul: civil rights should never be voted on by the electorate. A popular gay protest sign of the time was, "When do I get to vote on *your* marriage?" Gays knew they would generally lose in popular referendums on marriage equality.

A case in point was North Carolina. Despite pockets of progressivism around its cities, much of the state was dominated by Christian and social conservatives, including its large black population. The state placed Amendment One on the ballot, a state constitutional amendment to declare marriage to be only between a man and a woman. It passed with more than 60 percent of the vote in May 2012. Every Southern state had now banned same-sex marriage by constitutional amendment.

Obama's political base was angry over the outcome in North Carolina, which finally forced the cautious president's hand. The day after the state election, May 9, Obama declared that his position on same-sex marriage had evolved. He stated in a television interview, "I think same-sex couples should be able to get married." Days before, both Vice President Joe Biden and Education Secretary Arne Duncan had stated publicly that they were in favor of marriage equality. There were risks to this: it could further alienate Obama from social conservatives (who were unlikely to vote for him anyway), and there was the potential that Republicans would make gay marriage an election year issue to rally around as they had in 2004. On the other hand, it would motivate younger voters, who were highly in favor of marriage equality.[27]

We can look to polling to see how much the public shifted its stance on gay marriage over the decade. A *Washington Post*-ABC News poll in May 2011 revealed for the first time that a majority of Americans supported marriage equality. The trend continued a year later, when 53 percent of respondents favored same-sex marriage, while 39 percent opposed it. The poll results virtually flipped those from 2004. The survey also revealed that 71 percent of Americans had a friend, family member, or acquaintance who was gay.[28]

The November 2012 balloting that reelected President Obama showed how much the public tide had turned in support of gay marriage. Four states—Maine, Maryland, Minnesota, and Washington—put gay marriage on the ballot, and all four upheld gay rights. In addition, Tammy Baldwin of Wisconsin was elected as the first lesbian to serve in the U.S. Senate. The Catholic and Mormon churches, which had heavily funded the fight for Proposition 8 in California two years before, largely stayed out of the debate. This was a dramatic reversal from just eight years before when anti–gay marriage sentiment drove conservatives to the polls. By the end of 2012, nine states and the District of Columbia had legalized marriage equality. The tide was clearly turning.

A month after the 2012 presidential election, the U.S. Supreme Court agreed to hear the challenges to the Defense of Marriage Act and California's Proposition 8. The cases would be heard in March 2013 and decided the following June. By the time the court decided the case, four more states had added their names to the lists where gays could marry, now totaling thirteen states plus the District of Columbia.

On June 26, 2013, the Supreme Court struck down the Defense of Marriage Act by a vote of 5–4 in *U.S. v. Windsor*. It was not a sweeping decision declaring a universal right for gay marriage, but it declared that those who had legally married had every right to federal benefits and recognition as heterosexual couples. Marriage is marriage, the court declared in essence, and should be recognized as such. Justice Anthony Kennedy provided the key swing vote, just as he did earlier in *Romer v. Evans* (1996) and *Lawrence v. Texas* (2003), two earlier landmark gay rights cases. He concluded, "DOMA writes inequality into the entire United States Code." In addition, the court declined to rule on the constitutionality of California's Proposition 8, and thus Judge Walker's ruling stood. Marriage equality was reinstated in California.[29]

After the Supreme Court's decision in *Windsor*, more states adopted gay marriage, some by democratic action, but most through court challenges, often by citing Judge Walker's decision in *Hollingsworth v. Perry* and the Supreme Court's ruling in *U.S. v. Windsor*. One by one, the state constitutional amendments were shown to be discriminatory and were overturned. By the time the Supreme Court addressed the question again just two years later, only thirteen states had not legalized marriage equality. Legalization had moved with astonishing speed.

The decisive case *Obergefell v. Hodges* came before the Supreme Court in 2015. The court's decision was announced on June 26, fittingly just two days before the anniversary of the Stonewall riots. Once again, Justice Anthony Kennedy wrote the majority opinion in the 5–4 decision, siding with the court's four liberals. *Obergefell* established that gays and lesbians had a constitutional right to marry, based on the Due Process Clause and Equal Protection Clause of the Fourteenth Amendment. "Under the Constitution, same-sex couples seek in marriage the same legal treatment as opposite sex-couples, and it would disparage their choices and diminish their personhood to deny them this right," Kennedy wrote, calling marriage a "keystone of our social order." Gay marriage was now legal nationwide. [30]

The *Obergefell* decision came just eleven years after Massachusetts became the first state to legalize same-sex marriage. Most Americans had come around on the question and now supported gay unions, and there were widespread celebrations around the country. Overjoyed people took to the streets while others met with their wedding planners, and the exterior of the White House was lit with the rainbow colors of the Pride flag. Just hours after the decision, President Obama commented: "Sometimes there are days like this when that slow and steady effort is rewarded with justice that arrives like a thunderbolt." The rapid transformation of gays from outcasts to public acceptance and legal equality was one of the most stunning and unexpected reversals in American history. [31]

There was little if any backlash against the *Obergefell* decision, certainly not in the 2016 election seventeen months later, where gay marriage was hardly mentioned. There were those who still opposed gay marriage, but most of the country embraced it and moved on. Gays and lesbians who had earlier referred to their spouses as partners now identified them as husbands and wives. Gender was removed from the institution of marriage, but the institution survived. Peter Hart-Brinson, who studied marriage equality and public opinion, wrote, "Paradoxically, gay marriage may hasten the revitalization, not the demise, of marriage." [32]

The gay rights movement had achieved an enormous victory in the fight for marriage equality, but in doing so the LGBTQ+ movement was fundamentally altered. It was no longer about flouting social norms, but rather about upholding traditions. Gays were still overwhelmingly left-wing and voted Democratic, but they had joined traditionalists in embracing marriage as a vital foundation of American society. One wonders if conservatives will someday fathom the extent of their own victory. It cost them nothing but their pride to widen the tent just a smidge. Gay liberation, which was once about freeing oneself from society's constraints, now ended—and began anew—at the marriage altar.

With the legalization of same-sex marriage, Corporate America embraced Pride to demonstrate its commitment to diversity. Mayors and politicians of all stripes passed resolutions and marched in parades while businesses and communities hung the rainbow Pride flag everywhere in June. "Pride parades around the U.S. are a celebration of gay assimilation," observed Richard Schneider, editor of the *Gay & Lesbian Review*. This spawned its own backlash from further leftists in the LGBTQ+ community who were anti-capitalist and anti-corporatist, or who still wanted to continue the liberation theme. Others criticized the achievement as privileging white gays, often to the exclusion of people of color and transgenders. But there was no doubt: gays were now part of mainstream America. As activist Frank Kameny said in the 1960s, gay is good. To which one might add, being gay is normal.[33]

The cremated remains of Matthew Shepard—the young gay man who was mortally beaten in Laramie in 1998—were interred in the crypt at the Washington National Cathedral in November 2018, two decades after his death. Gene Robinson, the gay Episcopal priest who was promoted to bishop in 2003, led the service as Matthew's parents, Dennis and Judy Shepard, finally laid their son to rest.

9

The National Pastime

Baseball was once considered the country's national pastime. Not anymore. As broadband access proliferated at homes, offices, and on mobile phones, surfing the Internet became the new national pastime during the first decade.

The Internet fundamentally changed how Americans conducted business, socialized, and spent their free time. The bursting of the dot-com bubble in 2000 didn't put a damper on the public's enthusiasm for technology. In fact, the technology changes were downright dizzying in what we might call the Digital Decade. Consumers went from dial-up Internet access to broadband. Flat screen televisions replaced cathode ray tube TVs. People began communicating through social networking sites like Facebook, shopped on Amazon, went mobile through Apple, streamed movies on Netflix, and searched for content on Google. By the end of the first decade, not only did everyone including your grandparents have a mobile phone, but people were upgrading to the smartphone, thanks in part to the most revolutionary device of the decade: the iPhone. Mobility was now a part of everything.

During the first decade, digital replaced analog in every possible way. At the beginning of the decade, most people had dial-up Internet access; ten years later, dial-up was as dead as a dinosaur, as people had converted to high-speed Internet access, usually over DSL (copper telephone lines), cable television lines, or even fiber optic lines to the home.

Analog television broadcasts went digital in 2009. People ditched their film-using cameras and went digital. Instead of having your pictures developed at a lab, you simply downloaded them to your computer. At the start of the decade, few people had mobile phones, and the ones available were mostly analog. By 2010, it seemed everyone had a mobile phone and every phone was a digital device. Some people walked around with a Bluetooth device permanently attached to their ear, signaling their self-importance as they waited for that all-important call to come in any second now.

This great new digital toy was also fiercely disruptive. The Internet was a double-edged sword for many business models. With the Internet, a company or a rock band could reach an entirely new audience at very low cost. On the other hand, many people seemed to expect that, since content was online, it should be free. Witness how sales of the venerable compact disc, around since the 1980s, plummeted as people shifted to downloading music—often by pirating it—without finding any new way of raising revenue.

Similarly, published content shifted from print to electronic, drastically reducing newspaper subscriptions and books sold. Wikipedia, an online encyclopedia, debuted in January 2001. Actual encyclopedias, multiple volume editions that were updated each year, were sent to the dustbin. The world's knowledge could now be updated online and in real time. Anyone could be a contributor. And it was all right there at your fingertips. Why pay for content, consumers reasoned, when you can get it for free?

As the decade opened, one consumer technology seemed to dominate all others: America Online (AOL), a private network that used a dial-up telephone line to access. A friendly voice would announce, "You've got mail" as you logged in. AOL was superbly well positioned, yet it was also derisively referred to as the "Internet on training wheels."

To use AOL's email, you had to subscribe to the service, and that became its chief drawback as a slew of free, Web-based email services—Hotmail, MSN, Yahoo, Google's Gmail—made it so anyone could check email from any computer or mobile device. Email addresses emerged as status symbols. As the decade progressed, being stuck with an AOL address was akin to declaring that you were a 19th century Luddite and unable or unwilling to keep up with the times. AOL was slow to respond, not offering free email until 2006, and by then it was far too late. Someone had built a better mousetrap.

On January 10, 2000—just ten days into the new decade—AOL announced it would merge with entertainment giant Time Warner. This was just two months before the dot-com bubble burst. AOL's value was double that of Time Warner's, but that was in part driven up by a supercharged stock market high on Internet stocks.

Once the bubble burst, AOL's ad-driven sales shrank and its stock price tanked. The market shifted toward broadband as consumers ditched dial-up for dedicated Internet connections and free email, and that meant they canceled their AOL accounts. The business model collapsed. The two cultures—an upstart technology and content provider and an old-line media company—never quite gelled. It did not take long for people to realize that the AOL–Time Warner merger was a spectacularly expensive mistake, and it was widely considered to be the most disastrous large merger in corporate history. Together the two companies were once worth $350 billion, but a decade later, after the merger came undone (Time Warner spun off the AOL brand in December 2009), their combined value was less than a seventh of that.[1]

The first wave of the Internet was known as Web 1.0. That crested with the dot-com meltdown in 2000, and soon after Web 2.0 was born. This supported the ability of the user-generated content to develop their own content for the Internet. User-generated content democratized the Internet, as now anyone with a computer and rudimentary skills could write their own weblog (better known as a "blog"), post a homemade video to YouTube, or edit a Wikipedia page. Before, publishing content meant working with a major corporation and signing contracts and turning over the rights to the content; now the point of entry had become very low, as anybody could self-publish. This was revolutionary. Of course, the old guard wailed about this: how would they make money if people didn't buy their books, newspapers, or CDs? Social media became a classic model for user-generated content: it was the end-user who provided all of the content for Facebook, Instagram, and so on. The media company simply played host.

The Internet made so many things easier. No longer did you need to mail out invitations to a party, or call people up individually. You could just send them an Evite, where they could RSVP online. With the Internet and a mobile wireless connection, the world's information could follow you anywhere. You had a library at your fingertips.

Starting in the 1990s, many Americans had a laptop or personal computer at home and another at work. They replaced and upgraded them every four or five years, and every computer was connected to the Internet. The desktop computer didn't disappear altogether, but it significantly declined as people and businesses bought laptops instead, designed to support people on the go. They connected their computers to the Internet not through a cable, but through a short-range wireless Wi-Fi connection. The first question anyone would ask when visiting you was, "What's your Wi-Fi password?" so they could join your home network.

A crucial piece of technology that saw widespread adoption in the first decade was the mobile phone. People hilariously recalled slimy financier Gordon Gekko (played by actor Michael Douglas) using a shoebox-sized phone in the 1987 movie *Wall Street*. By the 2000s, mobile phones had shrunk down to pocket size, and could easily fit inside a purse instead of a suitcase. Initially these were telephone call–only phones, but quickly text (SMS) capabilities were added. And near the end of the decade, a mobile Internet connection was added, transforming the mobile phone into a smartphone.

The Millennials Come of Age

No generation in American history has been so associated with technology as the Millennial Generation. Born between 1981 and 1996 and so-named because they came of age at the millennium in 2000, they numbered more than 80 million people. This was the largest generation in American history. They were the children of the Baby Boom.

Pollster John Zogby referred to Millennials as "First Globals" because they saw themselves first as global citizens. "This is in fact the most outward-looking and accepting generation in American history," Zogby wrote. "These new global citizens are far more likely than their elders to accept gays and lesbians. For all practical purposes, they're the first color-blind Americans and the first to bring a consistently global perspective to everything from foreign policy to environmental issues to the coffee they buy, the music they listen to and the clothes they wear."[2]

Millennials were digital natives, seemingly born with a mobile phone or video game controller in their hands. Technology was part of their lives from the beginning. The rest of us were digital immigrants, people who adapted to technology, yet it always felt a little foreign. Millennials received their first mobile phones in high school or even earlier, and they simply never bought a landline telephone. They carried their mobile phones like a child carries a favorite blanket: they took it everywhere. And pretty soon, so did everyone else.

If Millennials had a favorite activity, it was texting. Texting had its root in handheld pagers and instant messaging, a computer-based chat program popularized in the late 1990s. Texting simply shifted that capability over to the mobile phone. The younger you were, the more likely you were to text—although parents soon adopted texting habits, as they found it an efficient way to keep track of their little ones. And pretty soon, everyone else adopted texting.

Millennials might be nicknamed Generation Text. It could be disconcerting to be around one of these young adults: their mobile phones were going off every two or three minutes. Millennials didn't just text one person; it was a constant, ongoing conversation with dozens of their friends, all thanks to the unlimited mobile phone plan and Qwerty keyboard. Communications were instant. If a person didn't receive a text response back in a minute or two, they'd text back, asking what was the problem. In a world of instant communications, you were expected to be available 24/7. Who had time to sleep when there were important messages to answer, such as: sup? how r u doing? l8r and thx? u up? cu soon. NBD (no big deal), LOL (laugh out loud), and best of all: LMAO (laughing my ass off).

Texting could also be rude. It interrupted conversations between actual people. "Just a sec," a person might say as they reached for their mobile phone, as if the text message was more important than the person right in front of them. Many Millennials preferred to text rather than make phone calls—in fact, hardly anyone called anymore. In this sense, the mobile phone was more like a mobile computer rather than a telephone. They quickly became an important part of people's lives—most people kept their mobile phones within arm's reach.

While there was much concern that so many devices and time on the Internet would take away from people's ability to build relationships, in fact the opposite seemed to happen. Texting kept families in touch. Many parents realized they could keep up with their children—and summon them to dinner—by texting them. On the other hand, a family could sit at the dinner table, each person busily texting away with someone else.[3]

The downside to texting was "sexting." That is, taking a risqué photograph of oneself, then sending it via text message. But once it was sent, the person who originated the photo lost control of it, and it could be distributed anywhere—including posting on the Internet. A sexting photo could come back to haunt a person years later.

Some might think that Millennials lived along a different space-time continuum. True, life in the early 21st century was fast-paced for everyone and certainly not slowing down, but Millennials lived at hyper speed, trying to take honors courses, volunteer, go to three parties in one evening, text with fifty people all while trying to change the world. There was a social phenomenon for this called FOMO, or fear of missing out. It's no wonder they adopted the caffeine-spiked Red Bull energy drink and vodka as one of their favorite club drinks: even a young adult only has so much energy.

Distractions!

The first decade brought a plethora of digital devices and digital distractions. "Amid the glittering promise of our new technologies and the wondrous potentials of our scientific gains, we are nurturing a culture of social diffusion, intellectual fragmentation, sensory detachment," wrote Maggie Jackson in *Distracted*. "In this new world, something is amiss. And that something is attention."[4] Americans were becoming a people with a serious attention deficit. It became difficult for many to sit still and concentrate on one task, like read a book, when so many things were whizzing past and demanding attention.

American society was driven to distraction, increasingly having difficulty filtering what was most important, or even to achieve intimacy. You were sitting with your significant other at dinner, enjoying each other's company, when your mobile phone alerts you to something. "Let me just see what this is," you announced as you virtually left the room, allowing another person or an application to intrude on your private space. We willingly surrendered. We allowed our devices to control us. We forgot that the devices existed to serve us, not the other way around.

A popular way to combat this at restaurants was for friends to stack their mobile phones in the middle of the table. The first person to reach for their phone before dinner concluded got to pay the bill. It was an incentive to be present, rather than be off in the ether.

Americans were becoming a nation of multitaskers, even though multitasking itself is a myth. The human brain is wired to concentrate on one subject at a time, yet people insisted on multitasking—like chatting on a mobile phone while driving, or doing email while listening to a conference call.

Elected president in 2000, Republican George W. Bush served two terms during the tumultuous first decade. Here he speaks to the nation on the evening after the September 11, 2001 terrorist attacks. *National Archives & Records Administration*

The World Trade Center in Manhattan two months before the 9/11 terrorist attacks. *Carol M. Highsmith's America, Library of Congress, Prints & Photographs Division.*

The Twin Towers of the World Trade Center on fire after being struck by two hijacked airplanes on September 11, 2001. Both towers soon collapsed. *Dan Howell, Shutterstock*

Firefighters and journalists observe the smoking wreckage of the World Trade Center on 9/11. The site soon became known as Ground Zero. *Anthony Correia, Shutterstock*

ABOVE: A temporary memorial to the 9/11 victims on United Flight 93 at Shanksville, Pennsylvania. Permanent memorials were later built in Manhattan, at the Pentagon, and in Shanksville. *Carol M. Highsmith Archive, Library of Congress, Prints & Photographs Division.* BELOW: Vice President Dick Cheney on 9/11, the powerful behind-the-scenes mandarin who engineered many of the controversial policies during the War on Terror and pushed for the Iraq War. *National Archives & Records Administration.*

ABOVE: American forces toppled the statue of Iraqi dictator Saddam Hussein in Baghdad's Firdos Square on April 9, 2003. *Jerome Delay, Associated Press.* BELOW: President George W. Bush announced the end of major combat operations in Iraq on May 1, 2003 aboard the aircraft carrier USS *Abraham Lincoln*. The Mission Accomplished banner would come to haunt him. *J. Scott Applewhite, Associated Press.*

The Iraq War was far from over as insurgents counterattacked against the American occupying forces, and Iraq soon found itself in a civil war. *Shutterstock.*

A demolished barber shop in New Orleans' Ninth Ward from Hurricane Katrina in August 2005. The powerful storm destroyed much of the city and trapped more than 100,000 people who could not evacuate. *Carol M. Highsmith's America, Library of Congress, Prints & Photographs Division.*

Americans in the early 21st century were living decades longer than the previous century, but retirement was fraught with the fear of running out of money before running out of life. *Shutterstock.*

ABOVE: Part of the southern border fence in Nogales, Arizona between the U.S. and Mexico that Congress authorized in 2006 to prevent Hispanic immigrants from entering the country illegally. *Shutterstock.* BELOW: Polar bears became an endangered species because of global warming, which reduced the Arctic ice pack that the bears depended on to hunt. *Shutterstock.*

When the housing bubble burst in 2007, millions of homes went into foreclosure, which in turn prompted the Great Recession. *Shutterstock.*

ABOVE: Federal Reserve chair Alan Greenspan, testifying before Congress on February 16, 2005, believed that markets were self-correcting, and thus did little to prevent the housing bubble. *Rob Crandall, Shutterstock.* BELOW: Greenspan's successor at the Federal Reserve, Ben Bernanke, had studied the Great Depression and teamed with Treasury Secretary Hank Paulson and New York Fed President Tim Geithner in an unprecedented rescue of the American banking system in fall 2008. Here Bernanke speaks at the National Press Club on February 3, 2011. *Albert H. Teich, Shutterstock.*

Democrat Barack Obama, elected the nation's first African American president in 2008 as the nation plummeted into the Great Recession. *Pete Souza, Library of Congress, Prints & Photographs Division.*

The conservative, populist Tea Party movement arose in the wake of the financial bailout to protest government intervention in the market. Seen here is a tax day protest in Pensacola, Florida on April 15, 2009. *Cheryl Casey, Shutterstock*

The leftist Occupy Wall Street movement demonstrated against the rising economic inequality of the country, pitting the 1 percent against everyone else, as seen at this December 12, 2011 protest against Goldman Sachs in Manhattan. *Daryl L., Shutterstock*

A crowd gathered at the U.S. Supreme Court in Washington, D.C. to celebrate its decision affirming gay marriage on June 26, 2015. *Rena Schild, Shutterstock.*

Donald Trump briefly ran for the presidency in 2000 as a Reform Party candidate, then tried again in 2012. He was elected president in 2016 as a Republican populist. Trump proved the ultimate disrupter in American politics. *Library of Congress, Prints & Photographs Division.*

Instead of doing one thing well, you do two or three things half-way—and ultimately it takes longer to accomplish them than if you did one at a time.

Distracted driving was becoming more and more of a problem. While everyone universally panned texting while driving, an incredibly high number of people still texted while behind the wheel of a car. You might say, I would never text while driving, yet it would only take one quick glance down at your mobile phone to see who just texted you and you'd completely miss the brake lights ahead. WHAM! You rear-ended a car.

People were reading fewer books during the decade, even as self-published titles exploded, thanks to the Internet. But it wasn't the case that people were reading less; rather, they were reading more than ever before, and much of that content was online. Books now had to compete for reader's eyes. Their size had a definite disadvantage in a culture that increasingly valued brevity. And the cost of a book was high compared to free content online.

Video games were another major distraction and source of entertainment for Americans. Whether one played Nintendo, PlayStation, or Xbox, all of these platforms offered a plethora of fun—but it also meant you might never leave the house as you spent hours trying to reach the next level. Some worried that video games were dumbing down Americans and making people anti-social, but that was generally overblown. In fact, Steven Johnson stipulated in *Everything Bad is Good for You* that the opposite was true: "The culture is getting more intellectually demanding, not less." Johnson argued that video games make people brighter, as does television, the Internet, and even violent movies. Johnson concluded: "Today's popular culture may not be showing us the righteous path. But it is making us smarter."[5]

Video games—including the first-person shooter action—got increasingly violent, even while the graphics and storylines improved noticeably. Were we creating a generation of antisocial misfits, good only for slaughtering zombies? No. The kids were alright, remarkably well adjusted. Video games involved developing complex problem-solving skills, and that was a societal benefit. We as a culture weren't dumbing down, but actually getting smarter. The skill set young people learned through technology put many adults to shame.

There was a stunning proliferation of device choices for consumers. Young people in particular, who viewed themselves as keen multitaskers, had a bewildering number of options to pursue in their free time. Video games,

Internet, iPods, texting, social media websites like Facebook, Internet and satellite radio, a bewildering choice of television stations, not to mention shows that could be downloaded and watched online and on demand. Other than television, little of this existed a decade before. There once was a mass market, but now there were so many choices that the mass market seemed to drown.

A widely read book from the decade was Chris Anderson's *The Long Tail*. He observed, "The era of one-size-fits-all is ending, and in its place is something new, a market of multitudes. . . . Increasingly, the mass market is turning into a mass of niches." His point was that mass culture had previously created a handful of winners—the "head"—while niche products were the "tail." As the head shrank, the tail got longer. "When mass culture breaks apart, it doesn't re-form into a different mass," Anderson wrote. "Instead, it turns into millions of microcultures, which coexist and interact in a baffling array of ways." Everything was becoming part of a niche. One might argue that there was only one mass culture point left in America: the Super Bowl, the last television event that almost everyone watched, at least for the creative commercials and halftime show.[6]

Even television was part of the long tail. Fifty years earlier, there were only three TV networks, and at work or on the playground, pretty much everyone discussed the same programs. With the proliferation of cable and Internet programming, however, mass consumer culture had blown apart. Your coworkers or friends on Facebook might be all abuzz about *The Sopranos* or *The Wire*, but you were watching a Netflix movie or catching up on *Lost* or *The Office*. And Lord knows your DVR (digital video recorder) was already jammed with programming that you hadn't gotten around to watching yet. There was simply far too much content for anyone to digest.

The Knowledge Worker

For much of the 20th century, America was an industrial society, but it began the transition toward a services-based economy late in the century. Work shifted out of the factory and into the office. People worked less with their hands and more with their minds and on computers. The knowledge worker emerged, a person whose specialty was what he or she knew.

The knowledge worker could work from anywhere. Armed with a laptop computer with a high-speed VPN connection, mobile phone, instant messenger program, and teleconference bridge meant you could have a virtual workplace and never actually commute to an office. Technology had advanced so far that people could work from home. The idea of teleworking (or sometimes telecommuting) came to fore. This rose to prominence during the decade, both after 9/11 when many firms realized they had to have a Plan B in case an office was closed, and later in the decade when fuel prices rose above $4.00 a gallon, as management gave their workers a break from the horrors and expense of commuting.

Early in the decade, corporations issued the BlackBerry, a wireless email device, to executives and managers. It became known as the "CrackBerry" because people were addicted to checking their email. A running joke was how people engaged in the "BlackBerry prayer" at meetings: they looked like they had bowed their heads to pray, but were really looking down into their laps to check email.

The BlackBerry gave people greater freedom to go on the road—but it also kept them tethered to work at all hours. An executive could fire off an email Saturday evening and expect an immediate response. Work life seriously encroached upon private life. There was no more this-can-wait-till Monday discretion.

The BlackBerry lost its way when the company that made them, Research in Motion, failed to adapt to the market. The company was an early mover into smartphones, but it underestimated the pull of consumer smartphones. The Apple iPhone and Google Android were introduced as consumer devices, but like all persistent technology, workers brought their smartphones to their IT departments and demanded support. By the end of the decade, the iPhone and Android devices had captured most of the smartphone market.

Once the dot-com meltdown of 2000 subsided, a clear group of survivors emerged that had solid business plans and a path to profitability. Five Internet-based companies in particular reshaped consumer technology during the decade: Facebook, Amazon, Apple, Netflix, and Google—the FAANG companies, as they became known. They were the proof that Silicon Valley (and Seattle, in the case of Amazon) was a hub of innovation, whose mantra was "fail fast, fail often"—and that someone was always looking to build a better mousetrap. These companies proved disruptive to many older business models.

Apple

Apple was the oldest of the FAANG companies, dating back to 1976 in what seemed like ancient days to Silicon Valley historians. It was based in Cupertino, California. The company had always been a niche for computer geeks who wanted something more intuitive than Microsoft's clunkier Windows-based personal computers.

The company floundered in the 1990s, then brought back one of its founders, Steve Jobs, in 1997. He was an amazing choice to revitalize the company. From a tiny share of the computer market, Apple soon began turning out hit after hit. In 1998, Apple rolled out the iMac with a line of candy colors and a curved translucent shell. Design rather than engineering was put at the center. No one was making attractive computing products like this, and the iMac was an instant hit.

Steve Jobs was brilliantly intuitive but argumentative. He was a demanding, feisty, temper-prone, and uncompromising control freak, but also a genius. He was the Albert Einstein or Henry Ford of his generation. He had an unusual understanding of aesthetics, and how technology should be intuitive, not just a beige box that housed software. Under his leadership, Apple evolved into a remarkably innovative company.

Apple was one of the great business stories of the decade—a blend of consumer appeal, savvy, and style. One by one, Apple built beautiful products that solved earlier problems. With the rise of the Internet, consumers were buying fewer music albums on compact discs and began to listen to music digitally. They carried around portable music devices known as MP3 players, which were often poorly designed. The problem facing consumers was that they couldn't buy digital music, so they pirated it for free through peer-to-peer websites like Napster. The problem facing the music industry was that it was stuck in its old model of selling physical albums, angrily braying at customers who were pirating its music. And tens of millions were.

Jobs came up with a new model that solved both the consumer and music industry's problems. In 2001, Apple launched a revolutionary portable digital music player called the iPod, a brilliant, translucent white device with an intuitive click wheel. It was about more than just technology: it was easy to use and sexy as all hell. Apple annually revamped the iPod, giving it new flavors, styles, and shapes like the iPod Mini, iPod Shuffle, and iPod Nano. Jobs biographer Walter Isaacson wrote, "The iPod became the essence of everything Apple was destined to be: poetry connected to engineering, arts and creativity intersecting with technology, design that's bold and simple." The iPod quickly became the dominant portable music player.[7]

To solve the piracy issue, Apple introduced a digital music store called iTunes where people could buy music to play on their iPods. Jobs had achieved his vision of a digital hub. Consumers no longer had to buy an entire album, but could purchase an individual song for $.99, buying exactly the music they wanted. Consumers could now buy a song for, well, a song. Digital music nailed the coffin shut on the compact disc. iTunes also helped put bootleg music websites out of business, along with retail music stores. This was creative destruction in action.

Late in the decade, streaming music services such as Pandora and Spotify emerged as customized online radio stations. Consumers soon realized they could get away without paying anything to listen to music—it was all free, supported by online advertising. Bands and musicians, who formerly made their living on album sales, now had to rely on concert tickets. They found themselves constantly on the road to make a living. Over time, these streaming websites developed subscription-based plans where for a few dollars a month you could skip advertisements and listen to all the music you wanted. The shift to streaming undermined album and even individual song sales. The iTunes model became obsolete and Apple shut down the platform in 2019.[8]

As Americans widely took to mobile phones in the early 2000s, they were stuck with cheaply built models, phones that you threw away after a year or two and traded up to something else. Smartphones that included Internet access began appearing, largely for business people who used BlackBerries. Apple decided to tackle this market by developing a device that was nothing short of revolutionary: the iPhone.

The iPhone was the consumer appliance of the decade. Introduced in June 2007, just as the last *Harry Potter* novel was being published, it was a digital hub that combined a mobile phone with music, a camera for photography, Internet access, and much more. It had a multi-touch screen and no keyboard. A year later, the much faster iPhone 3G was released. When Apple released a software development kit, third-party vendors developed hundreds of thousands of applications ("apps") for the iPhone, many of them free, which drove even more customers to buy the device. An app was simply a website culled down to a special piece of software that was installed on your smartphone.

For example, you could check in for a flight on your airline's app, download a digital boarding pass, and skip paper altogether.

A smartphone like the iPhone was essentially a computer in your pocket that could handle not just phone calls, but email, texting, playing music, driving directions and mapping, accessing social media, locating restaurants and making reservations, and countless other activities including playing games like the hugely popular Angry Birds or Words with Friends. Despite the Great Recession, consumers kept buying smartphones—they had become a necessity, even for job searching—and socially, people were more and more expected to be instantly available.[9]

In 2009, Apple released its third iPhone, the iPhone 3GS. The smartphone market finally witnessed its most significant challenger when Google released its Android operating system that year. That company simply gave the software away, licensing it to any mobile handset maker. Android devices quickly proliferated and actually surpassed iPhone sales within several years, as they were less expensive.

At the beginning of the decade, BlackBerry, Nokia, and Windows had dominated mobile phones, but they had lost their way in the forest. By the end of the decade, Apple iOS and Google Android were the dominant mobile operating systems. Consumers drove smartphone adoption—and once they had them, they demanded to use their phones in the office. In a very short period, Apple and Android smartphones eclipsed the BlackBerry. BlackBerry didn't have a touch screen interface or the myriad applications that iPhone lovers used. Once a status symbol, it became positively uncool to be seen with a BlackBerry. This is how quickly culture and technology change.[10]

Apple continued the annual tradition of releasing updated iPhones. In 2010, out came the iPhone 4. In 2011, the iPhone 4S and a new operating system that included the Siri voice recognition software. And in 2012, Apple released the iPhone 5, based on super-fast LTE wireless technology (ten times the speed of the 3G iPhones). And so on.

Apple didn't invent the smartphone—it just perfected the device with its touch screen and easy-to-use applications. It was intuitive to use and simply brilliant. Likewise, Apple didn't invent the tablet market—there were already e-readers and other devices, but Apple perfected it by releasing the touch screen iPad in 2010. The name immediately raised eyebrows; it sounded vaguely like a feminine hygiene product. Why not call it an iTab? It was a tablet, after all. While many scoffed at the product, it quickly caught on, not least among business executives who could now leave their laptops at the office when they traveled. "Whenever teenage girls and corporate CEOs covet the same new technology, something extraordinary is happening," noted Michael Saylor, CEO of MicroStrategy.[11]

The iPad was a game changer, one that redefined the tablet market. It had a much larger screen than the iPhone, making it easier to read content. Competitors were slow to market with their versions, giving Apple a solid lead for a number of years.

By the end of the decade, Apple had a lineup of beautiful products that ranged the gamut of personal computing needs. It produced gorgeous computers and laptops for people who wanted to create content; the iPad for content consumption; and the iPhone for communication. It had opened Apple Stores to directly sell its products, giving people a place to camp outside the night before a new product was sold. Apple fans were nothing if not fanatics.

Steve Jobs was more of an innovator than an entrepreneur—and he was notably different in Silicon Valley culture, where many entrepreneurs created businesses then sold them off to start others. He was at Apple for the long haul, building a company that made some of the most beautiful and innovative technology products ever.[12] *Fortune* magazine named Jobs the CEO of the decade in 2009.[13]

Steve Jobs died of pancreatic cancer on October 5, 2011. Apple was the most valuable company in the world with a stock price in the stratosphere. Tim Cook was promoted to be Jobs's successor. He was now the most high-profile gay CEO in the country.

Walter Isaacson published the definitive biography of Jobs shortly after his death. He wrote, "At a time when the United States is seeking ways to sustain its innovative edge, and when societies around the world are trying to build creative digital-age economies, Jobs stands as the ultimate icon of inventiveness, imagination, and sustained innovation."[14]

Amazon

Amazon was founded in 1994 by Jeff Bezos and was based in Seattle, Washington. The Internet was just getting started, and the commercial potential of selling stuff online was vast. It was an idea whose time had come. Amazon initially focused on being an online bookstore. Customers could order books from the comfort of their computer and without having to run to a retail outlet—or interact with anyone at all. And the prices were quite attractive, marked just above the wholesale cost. This was a less expensive business model, as it didn't require the brick-and-mortar of a regular store—only vast distribution warehouses. It soon undermined many bookstores with its low prices and selection. [15]

Amazon grew by acquisitions and by extending to new retail areas far beyond books. Jeff Bezos's goal was to "get big fast"—in other words, to scale up. That meant Amazon eschewed profits for rapid growth based on low prices and high volume. The company weathered the dot-com meltdown in 2000 with barely a hitch. [16]

By the end of the decade, Amazon was offering far more than just discounted books—it was an entire virtual shopping mall. Pet care products. Linens. Sporting goods. Toys. Video games. Streaming movies. Watches and mobile phones. Electronics. An entire partner ecosystem. And for far cheaper than just about anywhere else. The website was easy and intuitive to browse: you could find anything quickly. The company branched out into cloud-based services with Amazon Web Services, which came to dominate Web hosting.

Consumers particularly loved free shipping, and in 2005 Amazon introduced an addictive service called Prime: for $79 a year, you could get unlimited free two-day shipping. Prime expanded to cover streaming video services. Consumers were cutting the cord from cable television packages, and Amazon seized the opportunity, creating Amazon Studios to produce content to rival the Hollywood studios and Netflix. It was yet another service it could offer through Amazon Prime. The company also expanded its presence to dozens of warehouses nationwide to move products closer to customers, who increasingly expected fast delivery.

Amazon had another advantage that it leveraged for years: it often didn't collect state sales taxes, giving it an even greater price advantage when shipping to states where it didn't have a physical presence. Many states called for online retailers like Amazon to change their ways, and by the end of the decade Amazon stopped fighting federal and state laws targeted at closing this tax loophole.

Amazon introduced the first e-reader, the Kindle, in 2007. It later enabled self-publishing, meaning that authors could bypass the traditional publishing house route and instead publish online instantly—and keep most of the price of the book. Electronic publishing and audio books gave consumers more choices for how to read books while providing an additional way for the publishing industry to weather the storm.

Amazon came to dominate the retail industry, which was hit hard by the Great Recession and in many ways never recovered. Americans shifted their shopping habits to online, getting everything delivered to their homes. Many a shopping mall or boutique store went out of business, as they had higher brick-and-mortar costs and were unable to match Amazon's prices.

National bookstore chains like Barnes & Noble and Borders often became a gallery for consumers to browse through, then run home and order a book on Amazon for far less. Economists call this freeloading. Barnes & Noble barely held on, while Borders went bankrupt in 2011 and countless independent bookstores closed in the wake of the Great Recession. Amazon squeezed competitors with its lower prices and endless selection. Those independent bookstores that survived the shakeout, such as Politics and Prose in Washington, D.C., lived on because of customer service, dedicated fans, and unique programs that drew customers in, such as author talks, classes and tours, story time for children, and of course, excellent coffee. Successful bookstores had evolved into a community gathering place.

Amazon grew into such a retail behemoth that it created an affordable housing crisis in Seattle, its hometown. The company was growing so rapidly that it decided to open a second headquarters known as HQ2 in another city that would host 50,000 high-paying jobs. In November 2018, Amazon announced it had split HQ2 into two cities: Arlington, Virginia, and Queens, New York, but after local opposition surfaced in New York, Amazon quickly revoked its Empire State decision. Lest anyone question the importance of Amazon, Jeff Bezos that year became the richest man in modern history, wealthier than Microsoft founder Bill Gates or investor Warren Buffett. [17]

Netflix

Marc Randolph founded Netflix in 1997. He brought in Reed Hastings as an early investor. They operated as co-CEOs for a period before the more intense Hastings elbowed out Randolph. The company was a classic technology startup that, amazingly, was never acquired.

Based in Los Gatos, California, at the southern end of Silicon Valley, Netflix was founded on the idea of disrupting the traditional video rental market. People had to go to retail outlets like Blockbuster or Hollywood Video to pick up a VHS movie rental, a clunky magnetic tape. The in-store selection was iffy, and customers complained about being hit by late fees if they failed to return a movie on time.

Netflix built a better mousetrap. It embraced the DVD format, which looked identical to the compact disc (CD), only holding vastly more information. The slim DVD made Netflix's business model possible: the company would mail you a DVD rental in a thin red envelope, which ingeniously doubled as the return envelope. There were no late fees, and Netflix would send you the next movie in your online queue once you returned it. Netflix soon had a vast selection of movies and above all: monthly subscribers that gave the company a growing stream of revenue. You no longer had to go to Blockbuster to pick up a movie when the movie would come to you.

Technology enabled Netflix's success. American consumers were just starting to buy DVD players to replace VHS, and Hollywood quickly embraced the format. Flat screen televisions were becoming affordable, and Americans turned their living rooms into home entertainment centers. It became more difficult to lure people to expensive movie theaters when they could watch movies at home for a fraction of the cost. If anything, the Great Recession aided Netflix, as consumers shifted to inexpensive entertainment.

"In the pursuit of elegant software and intuitive user interfaces, [Netflix] created a tastemaker to rival Apple, an innovator on the order of Google, and a brand power equal to Starbucks," noted Gina Keating in *Netflixed*.[18] The company's name gave rise to the phrase "Netflix and chill," a euphemism for hooking up. When the action in the movie began, the real action was on the couch.

Netflix postponed its initial public offering to May 2002 because of the dot-com meltdown, but it steadily gained customers and had high customer retention. After the IPO, founder Marc Randolph exited the company. By 2003, Netflix reached one million subscribers.

The competition wasn't standing still. Blockbuster Video in particular launched its own online movie rental platform and undercut Netflix pricing. This trade war lasted four years before Blockbuster surrendered in 2007: it was hemorrhaging money. Blockbuster filed for bankruptcy in 2010, but there was no saving this doomed ship. The last Blockbuster outlets closed in 2013. Walmart attempted to launch a similar service, but retreated within a year.

Reed Hastings had ambitions to take Netflix beyond DVDs and beyond the United States. He recognized that the DVD was an interim technology, and that streaming video over the Internet would take hold as consumers deployed broadband to their homes. He envisioned that Netflix would even provide content one day.

In 2007, Netflix launched its streaming service. DVDs began their long decline, but they had had a good ten-year run. Netflix cut deals with game console providers like Xbox to deploy its app for streaming, meaning that the console would serve as a set-top box. Netflix deployed its app on smartphones and tablets for streaming on the go. Soon Internet-enabled "smart" TVs came preloaded with Netflix and other apps, obviating the need for a set-top box. You only needed an Internet connection. By the end of the decade, most Netflix content was streamed over the Internet, rather than mailed in its signature red envelopes.

Streaming likewise undercut the cable television bundle, which came with hundreds of unwatched TV channels and high prices. Younger consumers in particular started to pick and choose streamable content from Amazon Prime, Hulu, and Netflix and bypassing the cable bundle. All they needed was a broadband Internet connection and they could watch all-you-can-eat content on demand. And all this was because of Netflix.

Fortune magazine named Reed Hastings as businessperson of the year in 2010, the same year that the company expanded internationally.[19] By the following year, Netflix had over twenty-five million customers worldwide and continued its heady growth.[20]

Netflix made one major misstep in 2011 when it raised prices and announced it was spinning off its DVD business into a service called Qwikster. Customers who were using both DVD and streaming would have to pay separately, infuriating many people. Netflix ended up backtracking, canceling Qwikster, but the company temporarily experienced numerous customer cancellations before it returned to growth. It was also clear that DVDs were not long for this world—or for only as long as Hollywood held out, believing that it could squeeze the last penny from the dying format. Netflix had clearly moved on.

Google

One company more than any other came to personify the Internet: Google. In fact, during the decade, when you searched online for information, you "googled" it, which turned the company into a verb. The American Dialect Society named *Google* the word of the decade.[21]

This Mountain View, California, company was founded in 1998 by Larry Page and Sergey Brin. Google entered a crowded field of Internet search engines and quickly eclipsed them by making searching better. It built a better mousetrap by indexing the entire Internet and inventing an artificial intelligence system to intuitively know what a user wanted to find. It was also one of the few companies that had learned to monetize the Internet through cost-per-click advertising. And it did this without charging consumers a cent. Within six years of its founding, Google's revenue exceeded $1 billion.[22]

Google was a remarkable company staffed by gifted young engineers and offered employee benefits rarely seen: free meals, shuttle buses from around the Bay Area, bicycles to get employees around its campus (the Googleplex), massages, and personal trainers. Employees were allowed to spend a fifth of their time working on any project they wanted—it was the company's way of fostering innovation. Google continually added new products, such as Gmail and Google News, and acquired video platform YouTube, while still offering all these tools for free. Online advertising paid for it all. It was impossible not to be impressed by Google.

"Don't be evil" was the company's motto, though Google removed this from its code of conduct in 2018. Google was highly disruptive to many old media companies as it siphoned off so much advertising, business, and consumer attention, essentially offering it all for free. Ken Auletta, author of *Googled*, came up with the title of his book as a way to describe what happened to a company whose business model was shattered by Google. How were businesses to survive if consumers learned to expect everything at no cost, though there were still significant costs in producing it?[23]

Google came out of nowhere and vaulted past every other Internet search engine. It was such a threat, and established such dominance in online search, that it challenged the king itself, Microsoft. Microsoft rose to the challenge, launching a hostile bid to buy second-ranked Internet search engine Yahoo in 2008 for $44.6 billion. This reflected the transition of the Internet from startup to big business. Google controlled much of the text-driven ad searches, while Yahoo controlled much of the pop-up ad market. Yahoo had no interest in being acquired, and there was strong public opposition to the merger, and eventually Microsoft withdrew its offer. However, the two companies eventually teamed up their search operations to launch the Bing search engine in

2009 to challenge Google, ten years late to the search party. Google had an enormous lead in the market, even though Bing and Google search results were similar.

As consumers were watching ever more content online, including videos, Google bought YouTube in 2006. This budding free video sharing website soon dominated online video, again, paid for through online advertising. YouTube offered anyone with a few basic tools (computer, digital camera, and Internet access) a place to upload videos that might be shared with billions of people worldwide. The cost of entry to instant stardom was low.

The rock band OK Go made a name for itself by posting music videos to YouTube of themselves, including their song "Here It Goes Again" featuring them dancing on gym treadmills. It was one of those things you just *had* to see, that people forwarded to their office mates and relatives. Or Susan Boyle's electrifying performance on *Britain's Got Talent* that made her an instant global star. With YouTube, a video could go viral, hitting a wide audience in a matter of minutes. The broadcast industry responded to the Google threat by creating its own video broadcast platform called Hulu for viewing television shows.

Google also began a project to digitize every book ever published. This ran into headlong resistance from authors and publishers who were concerned that their content would be given away for free if everyone could simply look it up online. The various interests eventually reached an agreement in 2008 whereby Google would pay $125 million for copyright infringement. They agreed to allow Google to post some book content—up to 20 percent of a title—and came up with a payment method. The books would not be free online.[24]

As consumers were wholesale adopting mobile devices, Google read the tea leaves and acquired Android in 2005, an open-source mobile operating system. Android-powered smartphones directly challenged the iPhone, as open sourcing meant developers could build myriad applications that consumers could use on mobile devices.

Thanks to its enormous lead in online advertising, Google's mousetrap had helped create an expectation among consumers that all digital content was free. The company upended so many traditional businesses models that it collected considerable opposition. Yet Google was largely deaf to its critics. Google historian Ken Auletta wrote that its founders Brin and Page "displayed an inability to imagine why anyone would question their motives and a deafness to fears that can't easily be quantified." As an author himself who wondered if consumers would still buy books, Auletta asked tellingly, "a central question that will profoundly shape the future of old and new media is this: Will users who have grown up with the Web pay for content they now get free?"[25]

Facebook and the Rise of Social Media

Technology has a short half-life. Google may have led the traditional Internet, but it was Facebook that became the leading website by the end of the decade, with more than a half-billion members—an astonishing accomplishment, given that the company was only founded in 2004. Of the five FAANG companies, Facebook was the youngest. It represented the success of an emergent technology and cultural medium: social media.

The social media first mover was Friendster, a company launched in 2003. It rapidly grew, but the company couldn't keep up with so many users as its servers slowed. It turned people off from using the platform. Plus there were so many fake profiles mimicking celebrities, and women from the Philippines or Russia who would suspiciously message you, saying they wanted to be friends. Friendster didn't adapt to the way consumers wanted to use applications and share content, so Americans abandoned the platform.

MySpace launched later that year with highly customizable pages; you could be whoever you wanted and be anyone's friend. People collected thousands of friends. MySpace commanded an early lead in social networking, but Facebook surpassed it within a few years. MySpace was viewed as something for young people, not adults. A multinational corporation, News Corp, acquired the social media site in 2005 for $580 million, and there it stagnated: the large corporation wasn't sure what to do with the platform, or how to let it continue growing organically. MySpace shrank into an entertainment and music portal as people quit in droves for Facebook, and ultimately it became irrelevant. News Corp sold off MySpace for a mere $35 million in 2011.

Mark Zuckerberg and Eduardo Saverin founded Facebook in 2004 at Harvard University. The social media platform was initially targeted at college students, and it soon became so indispensable that other colleges demanded access to the portal. Like Microsoft's Bill Gates, Zuckerberg dropped out of Harvard. He moved to Silicon Valley, where he sensed

Facebook could thrive in an innovative culture. Facebook grew quickly and organically, even virally. It was careful to avoid the mistakes that Friendster and MySpace had made that had alienated users.

Zuckerberg was the subject of a riveting 2010 movie, *The Social Network*, based on Ben Mezrich's book *The Accidental Billionaires*, one that was heavily critical of the company founder, like Orson Welles's skewering of William Randolph Hearst in *Citizen Kane*. The movie portrayed Zuckerberg as uncaring, unfeeling, duplicitous, even sociopathic. The book made the case that Zuckerberg had gotten the Facebook idea from Harvard twins Cameron and Tyler Winkelvoss. They later settled out of court in 2008 for $65 million.[26]

For Zuckerberg, Facebook wasn't about money, but about opening the world and sharing ideas transparently. Facebook was a platform—the content was provided by the users themselves. Zuckerberg said, "We're a utility."[27]

Facebook became *the* place to hang out online. You could update your status, join an online conversation, post vacation photos and tag your friends in them, share online articles, or check if a romantic interest was single. As camera-equipped smartphones proliferated, people could share photos with their friends instantly. Facebook was also hugely addictive. "You didn't just visit the site once," wrote Ben Mezrich. "You visited it every day. You came back again and again, adding to your site, your profile, changing your pictures, your interests, and most of all, updating your friends." With Facebook people could remotely check in with each other throughout the day and have small interactions, no matter how far away they were.[28]

Katherine Losse, Facebook's fifty-first employee, quit the company in 2010 and wrote about her experience in *The Boy Kings*. She was fairly critical toward the social media phenomenon and how users broadcast everything about themselves all the time as a way to seek attention. "The televising and digitization of private life was the new colonialism: without any continents left to explore and own, private life had become the last frontier," she wrote. "To own not the physical map of the world but the map of human life was, I began to think, the goal."[29]

Social media came to be synonymous with Facebook. It was the company that seemed to get it right. Unlike MySpace, Facebook required that you use your real name. You couldn't hide behind a fake screen name. This held people accountable for anything they posted online. You controlled your profile and who saw it; you only added the friends you wanted to add.

At the same time, fake profiles proliferated, often by copying real profiles in a case of virtual identity theft. There were hundreds of millions of fake profiles used to scam people. Like a game of whack-a-mole, if one got shut down, the scammer simply set up another one.

One of the problems with Web 2.0 functionality was that people could hide behind a made-up screen name on blogs, online newspapers, and some social media sites, and then post the most horrible things. This was called trolling: the art of saying something controversial to generate a reaction from someone. You would never say such a nasty thing to another person's face, but with a screen name that hid your identity, you could call people all sorts of terrible things and get away with it. Social media was rife with such cyberbullying.

At the heart of Facebook was the News Feed, where you could broadcast your thoughts to your network, and see what your friends were up to. An artificial intelligence algorithm spoon-fed users information, rather than allowing them to curate their own content. It led to people only seeing opinions they agreed with, and reinforced the bubble-nature of social media. Everyone lived in a bubble of confirmation bias. People's opinions or world-views were seldom challenged, as you simply didn't see the posts that you might disagree with.

Zuckerberg kept the company private, and even though he had venture capital investors, he was solidly in control. No corporation could derail his vision for the site. He effectively played off the two leading search engine companies, Google and Microsoft, and took a $240 million investment from Microsoft that valued Facebook at $15 billion (giving Microsoft 1.6 percent ownership in the portal). But was this really what the company was worth? Who knew?[30]

Social media became a powerful platform to transmit ideas. After the arguably fixed presidential elections in Iran in 2009, hundreds of thousands of Iranian youth took to the streets in protest, coordinating their actions through Facebook and Twitter. In early 2011, Tunisians, Egyptians, and Libyans overthrew their dictatorial regimes in the so-called Arab Spring, revolutions that were started in part by activists using social media.

The main emergent rival to Facebook was Twitter, founded in 2006. It likewise served as a forum to transmit ideas—but without the features of Facebook. You could simply broadcast 140 characters and attach a link or a photo. Marketers loved it, as they could constantly broadcast information about their products, while likewise monitoring what people said about them. Journalists loved it, as they could use it as a source of information and broadcast the latest news. Some referred it as a nonstop cocktail party. Twitter momentarily threatened Facebook, so Facebook adapted its News Feed to resemble Twitter's. Facebook continued to get the most social media traffic worldwide.

Google launched its own social media website called Google+, but it never gained traction. People were already up to their eyeballs in social media with Facebook and Twitter. Just how many sites did one need to track and use? The company finally shut down Google+ in 2018.

Facebook acquired Instagram in 2012, a photo-oriented platform favored by Millennials. *New York Times* columnist David Brooks wrote: "The internet has become a place where people communicate out of their competitive ego: I'm more fabulous than you (a lot of Instagram). You're dumber than me (much of Twitter). It's not a place where people share from their hearts and souls." Social media was terrible for children's self-esteem, as kids could perceive that everyone else was having a more fabulous life, even though the smiling duck-lipped photo on Instagram might be hiding crushing depression or suicidal thoughts. You had to remind yourself: what you saw or read on social media wasn't always real. People could present a mythology of themselves, something that bore little resemblance to reality.[31]

Facebook went public in May 2012. Its stock was valued at $104 billion—the largest initial public offering in history. At that point, the platform had 901 million users, making it by far the largest social media network. Mark Zuckerberg controlled 55.8 percent of the company, meaning that he alone would decide its destiny. The twenty-eight-year-old billionaire continued to wear his hoodie with jeans, signaling that he was not about to yield to Wall Street or the world.[32]

Whatever Happened to Privacy?

The Internet was largely unregulated, and Congress had kept it at arm's length since the 1990s so it could flourish without interference. The Internet was a success beyond anyone's wildest dreams; however, while everyone pursued the gold rush, there was no one home watching the farm.

The worry about the government becoming Big Brother like in George Orwell's dystopian novel *1984* was overblown. If anyone was like Big Brother, it was the private sector, which was gathering enormous data about every consumer so they could sell it to you in the form of advertising or market products that matched your profile.

Facebook and Google were the two highest-trafficked websites on the Internet and commanded most of the online advertising revenue. They built digital avatars to predict our behavior and then sold those to advertisers. Both platforms tracked massive amounts of data on each user by surveilling their Internet usage. When you looked at a pair of shoes at L.L. Bean or Nordstrom, then logged onto Facebook, there was a targeted ad for those shoes directed at you. You were being tracked. End users had effectively surrendered their privacy to these platforms, and these companies had no compunction about selling your data.[33]

Just what is privacy in the age of the Internet? Everyone leaves a huge electronic trail from purchasing stuff online, surfing the Web, and posting on social media. Many concluded that there was no such thing as privacy anymore as every aspect of their lives—childhood photos, drunken college parties, vacation photos—was posted online and subject to scrutiny and "likes." Privacy as we knew it was a thing of the distant past.

As the Internet matured, others questioned if some regulations around privacy may be necessary. Who owns your personal data—you, or the company collecting and selling it to others? Many spoke of data as the new oil, a valuable commodity that could be traded on the market. The Onion, a satirical website, posted a headline in 2011 that read, "CIA's 'Facebook' Program Dramatically Cuts Agency's Costs," meaning that people were willingly handing over their personal and private information for the spy agency to track.[34]

Facebook's Mark Zuckerberg initially disregarded privacy concerns, not quite grasping that not everyone wanted to put themselves out there for the entire world to see, nor that many were unhappy with Facebook selling their personal data to advertisers. President Barack Obama even warned students that whatever they posted to social media would be part of their permanent record. "I want everybody here to be careful about what you post on Facebook, because in the YouTube age, whatever you do will be pulled up later somewhere in your life. And when you're young, you make mistakes and you do some stupid stuff," the president said. If someone tagged a photo of you making a drunken fool of yourself or rudely flipping the bird to the camera, a future employer might see that and decide not to hire you.[35]

So much personal data was available online that people were vulnerable to identity theft. That is, someone could literally steal your identity, raid your financial accounts, and set up credit cards in your name. All it took was some basic information like your birthday, Social Security number, and mother's maiden name, information that could be found online or in hacked databases, and they'd be in business making a mess of your life.

Surfing the Web meant maintaining a high bullshit meter, as there was so much unreliable information online, some of it downright false. Just because you read it online didn't make it true. Propagandists quickly realized the potential for spinning new realities and alternative facts to steer public opinion, such as spreading pseudoscience that vaccines cause autism (they do not). The Internet, a platform that many believed would bring the world together into an online utopia, masked a very dark side. Hackers with malicious intent sent out supposedly trustworthy social engineering emails to get you to click on links that would then install software viruses or ransomware on your computer. Conspiracy theorists gathered in the dark web to air their racist beliefs and plot the next mass shooting of ethnic minorities, immigrants, and schoolchildren.

Then there was the strange and hubris-filled story of WikiLeaks. Australian activist and hacker Julian Assange founded the website in 2006 in order to leak governmental secrets to the world. Believing that all information should be available to the public, WikiLeaks published a video in early 2010 of a U.S. Army helicopter gunning down a group of people in Iraq that included two Reuters reporters. The organization followed this with nearly 80,000 classified documents about the war in Afghanistan—followed by another trove of documents about the war in Iraq.

In November 2010, WikiLeaks released tens of thousands of U.S. State Department diplomatic cables. The source of much of this information came from Bradley Manning, an army intelligence analyst stationed near Baghdad (she later changed her name and identity to Chelsea Manning). She was soon arrested. In the years after 9/11, government agencies opened their electronic databases to other departments, and thus a lowly private first class with a security clearance like Manning could access wide swaths of classified information. Having this enormous number of secret documents leaked was a serious embarrassment to the U.S. government and impacted its foreign relations. And it raised serious ethical questions. Where were the bounds of privacy? Was everything—every email, every text message you sent—meant for public consumption?

WikiLeaks would later receive and publish a trove of hacked emails from the Democratic National Party in 2016. The source was Russian intelligence operatives, who wanted to aid Republican presidential candidate Donald Trump and undermine Democratic candidate Hillary Clinton. Russia put its thumb on the scale of the 2016 American presidential election.

Whither the Newspaper?

The Internet delivered a crushing blow to the nation's magazines and newspapers. Print journalism had long counted on both advertisers and subscribers to make them profitable. But subscription rates were in long-term decline as eyeballs shifted to the Internet, and the Great Recession witnessed an advertising nosedive. Many magazines simply folded, unable to pay their bills.

Newspapers had once printed extensive Help Wanted sections, but even that shifted to the Internet, in particular to a free service known as Craigslist. Craigslist was a company largely composed of a website and run by only about two-dozen people. The end-user provided the website content—say, if you wanted to sell your sofa or were looking for a house painter. Economists often spoke about how creative destruction in free-market economies destroys older jobs while creating newer, higher paying ones, but it wasn't clear with free Internet-based services if this would be the case. Craigslist simply eviscerated newspaper want ads and destroyed the old model. Consumers certainly got a benefit—they no longer had to buy an expensive advertisement, and a Craigslist ad could be updated in real-time. And why pay for something when you can get it for free? Craigslist built a better mousetrap.

The publishing industry was in a seismic shift from hard copy to online viewing. Earlier generations had purchased the daily newspaper and bought books, but Millennials now expected to get these things for free online and often read the news on their mobile devices. Some newspapers attempted to reinvent themselves for the digital age, building mobile phone-friendly applications.

Just as blogging for a living wasn't a sustainable business model, neither was online advertising for newspapers. Online advertising simply did not compensate for the loss of print advertising. As struggling newspapers sent out distress signals, some investors, infatuated with print-form journalism, rushed in to buy companies, only to be burned when advertising plummeted as readers canceled their subscriptions. Investor Sam Zell purchased the Tribune Company, owner of the *Los Angeles Times*, then filed for bankruptcy to reorganize. Brian Tierney, who purchased Philadelphia Newspapers in 2006 and owned the *Philadelphia Inquirer* and *Daily News*, likewise filed for Chapter 11. So did the *Chicago Sun-Times*. The *Boston Globe*, owned by the *New York Times*, had eliminated so many reporters through numerous rounds of layoffs that the newsroom was effectively gutted. The *Times* sold the *Globe* to an investor in 2013.

In 2008, *The Christian Science Monitor* became the first national newspaper to fold its print edition and only publish online. Two Detroit dailies soon followed, cutting home delivery to three days a week. Many dailies and weeklies went out of business. The *Baltimore Examiner*, *Cincinnati Post*, and *Rocky Mountain News* folded. The *Seattle Post-Intelligencer* threatened to shut down, but instead shifted to online-only, though it laid off most of its employees. In 2012, the *New Orleans Times-Picayune*, which had won Pulitzers for its coverage of Hurricane Katrina, laid off many staff members and shifted to a print edition only three days each week. Free online content had shattered these old media business models. Consumers no longer seemed willing to pay to subscribe to the paper, but expected to get it online at no cost. In the long term, this was a business model that simply would not work.

Australian media mogul Rupert Murdoch's News Corp. acquired the *Wall Street Journal* in 2007, only to learn that even prestigious business journalism was in the same downward spiral. With the Great Recession in 2008, ever more readers canceled their print subscriptions and chose to read their content online. The *Journal* was a pioneer at building a paywall, meaning if you wanted to read its articles online, you had to pay up. The *Financial Times* and the *New York Times* likewise erected paywalls, and other papers soon followed.

The Washington Post, arguably the country's second newspaper after the *New York Times*, trimmed its sails substantially. Gone was the venerable Book World section. It outsourced more of the reporting to the Associated Press and Bloomberg. Most newspapers likewise cut their newsroom staffs as advertising revenues shrank, which meant the newspapers could now cover fewer topics. Their quality was definitely affected, and this in turn drove more people to cancel their subscriptions. Amazon founder Jeff Bezos purchased the *Washington Post* in 2013 for $250 million.

The pace of technological change accelerated over the first decade and became ever more disruptive. People wanted innovation all the time—and then complained that they couldn't keep up. Five years after Apple rolled out the iPhone—and with annual updates that added many new features—technologists complained that Apple wasn't being innovative enough. Google's Android mobile operating system was offering more gizmos and whizbangs—and was doing so at a lower price. Technology has a short half-life, and in the blink of an eye, someone can build a better mousetrap. Your prime invention can become instantly obsolete.

10

A Smaller World

Americans have long considered themselves exceptional, a special part of God's creation, fostered in part by two broad oceans that isolated the country in our own hemisphere. But America is not an island, nor does it stand alone or apart from other nations. Globalization has altered the way Americans think and the work that we do. Pollster John Zogby observed: "Americans want to live in a world *with* other people, not in a walled empire surrounded by enemies." We are living in a smaller world. [1]

Even while the U.S. was the only remaining superpower and the largest economy, the country was no longer the single, dominant power of the post–Cold War world. Other countries were stepping forward, notably China. Even more tragic was the decline of American moral leadership. As the leader of the West, America was the leading democracy in the world. The Iraq War squandered that authority.

America lost its way after 9/11 and no longer seemed to lead as it focused on keeping itself safe. *New York Times* foreign affairs columnist Thomas Friedman noted that, "America has shifted from a country that always exported its hopes (and so imported the hopes of millions of others) to one that is seen as exporting its fears." [2]

The country was still far too dependent on oil for its automobiles and burning coal for electricity, even as it debated the challenge of global warming. The scientific evidence was in, yet there were those who insisted it was just a hoax. Can the U.S. and other countries slow carbon emissions enough to stave off a potential environmental disaster to our planet? That is the greatest global challenge for the 21st century. Despite being the world's only remaining superpower, the U.S. refused to lead on the issue of climate change nor invest in new technologies that would take us off fossil fuels.

During World War I, President Woodrow Wilson included free trade in his Fourteen Points, which were America's wartime goals. Before the war, he had significantly cut tariffs. Tariffs serve as a tax on working people, as it makes the products they buy more expensive, so cutting tariffs was like a massive tax cut. Harry Truman carried the free trade mantra forward after World War II, and it became a crucial part of American foreign policy. Simply by trading with other countries, we helped lift billions of people out of poverty, as it gave them an opportunity to participate in the global market.

Globalization, then, was a force for overall economic well-being. Globalization brought less costly products and far greater choice to American consumers and helped keep inflation in check, but it also had a downside. Producers were always on the lookout for the cheapest labor market and so shifted manufacturing jobs overseas to China, Mexico, Vietnam, and other places. The worker who lost his job when his factory closed in Indiana and reopened in Mexico soured on globalization. This effectively meant that wages for working- and middle-class Americans stagnated over the first decade, or even shrank once the escalating cost of health care was factored in. This was one of the factors that made this a lost decade.

There were few jobs that were safe from offshoring—save being a hair stylist, police officer, fireman, or a chef or waiter at a restaurant. The service industry created many jobs, albeit fairly low-wage ones that young adults usually take at the onset of their careers, then jettison once they find something better paying.

But the blame for American job losses can't rest entirely on China and Mexico, free trade, and globalization. Automation was the single biggest job destroyer, as improved processes and computers took over the low-skill work that humans once did. Many of these jobs would have disappeared with or without China and global trade. Capitalism and technology have the habit of both creating and destroying jobs, what economists call creative destruction. The telephone switchboard operator has long since gone extinct, as have the buggy whip manufacturer and the whale oil producer. Farming had once been the mainstay of the American economy, but now a tiny fraction of people grew the food for a vast population. A steel mill might have once employed 50,000 workers, but now it only needed a few hundred, all thanks to automation. Someone built a better mousetrap.

Many jobs disappeared forever because of automation in the wake of the Great Recession. Who needed someone to deliver the newspaper to your front door if you now got it digitally on your tablet? Poof, another job vanished. Now that everyone had Microsoft Outlook on their work computers, they could schedule their own appointments and meetings. Who needed secretaries (or administrative assistants, as they were known professionally) anymore? Poof, another job vanished. Who needed to rent a video at a Blockbuster outlet when you could simply stream a far greater selection of movies from your living room couch? Poof, Blockbuster and a host of video rental stores went out of business. Why should an electricity or gas company send out someone monthly to check your usage when the meter could radio this in automatically? Poof, another job vanished.

Small-town America hollowed out. Where Main Street was once the retail hub, the arrival of Walmart with its massive scale and low prices meant small businesses had difficulty competing. Small towns in rural American had few jobs for young people, who moved to cities and suburbs for their careers. They left behind dying towns populated by aging people. The movies *The Last Picture Show* (1971) and *Nebraska* (2013) reflected dying small town America.

Global trade led to the expansion of the middle class worldwide, but also demand for more things like air conditioning, cars, fine wine, steak, and televisions. The global population continued to rise, especially in the developing world, and this put a strain on the planet's resources. If the entire world lived at the standard of living as Americans, the world's resources would quickly be used up and we would have to find several more planets to inhabit. Thomas Friedman observed that the world "is getting *hot, flat, and crowded*. That is, global warming, the stunning rise of middle classes all over the world, and rapid population growth have converged in a way that could make our planet dangerously unstable."[3]

China, India, and the Global Supply Chain

With a population exceeding a billion people, India was the world's most populous democracy and one whose economy was growing at a steady clip.

Thanks to once being the crown jewel of the British Empire, India had many English speakers and had developed numerous high-tech hubs like Mumbai and Bengaluru (Bangalore) to attract global business. Transoceanic fiber optic cables linked the country to the world, and this enabled it to become a key player in global outsourcing.

American businesses often outsourced back-office computer systems, call centers, help desks, and software development to India for a fraction of the cost of hiring American workers. Everyone had humorous stories of calling a company's help line and having the call routed to an Indian call center, where invariably the customer service rep had an anglicized name like Brett or Sally and a heavy Indian accent.

After the Cold War ended in 1989, capitalism emerged triumphant. There was no ideological challenger to the free market. Even communist China, while remaining a one-party state, adopted state-run capitalism that rapidly modernized the economy from a low-tech, farming economy to a heavyweight in the global supply chain. It developed an export-driven industrial economy to lift its 1.3 billion people out of poverty. China became the manufacturer to the world.

China joined the World Trade Organization in 2001 and seized the opportunity provided by global trade to transform its economy. It heavily subsidized state-owned companies, demanded high-tech transfers from multinational investors, engaged in espionage to steal technology, rather than develop it on its own, all while protecting its economy and citizenry from Western competition and technology that would potentially open its society to such outside ideas as Facebook, Google, and Wikipedia. China was still ruled by the Communist Party, an illiberal regime that viewed technology, such as facial-recognition software, as a way to control its citizens. Yet the communists had also taken on distinctly capitalist tendencies.[4]

China and the United States had a rather lopsided trade arrangement. American-based multinationals rushed to invest in China, transferring enormous swaths of American-made technology to the Middle Kingdom and taking advantage of a vastly cheaper labor force. The U.S. then imported much of our consumer goods from China, resulting in a large trade deficit. The Chinese reinvested a good portion of its earnings into U.S. Treasury bonds to ensure their largest customer could still purchase its goods. This kept American interest rates low and helped provide cheap financing for the housing boom of 2003–2006.

The purchasing power of Walmart, the largest retailer in the United States, put heavy pressure on its suppliers to lower costs, with the result that much of the country's manufacturing base left the U.S. for cheaper markets such as China. "Walmart's global supply chain is really a China supply chain," noted journalist Fareed Zakaria. Americans got cheap consumer goods while losing well-paying manufacturing jobs, multinationals like Walmart greatly increased their profits, and China advanced into the 21st century. It was just a question of time before the Chinese economy surpassed the American economy in size. [5]

China's population was four times that of the U.S. Its economy was growing by leaps and bounds, but that was from a very low point: China in fact remained a poor country. It was undergoing a rapid transformation from agrarian to manufacturing, such as the U.S. had done in the early 20th century. Millions of workers were moving off tiny farms to work in factories in cities.

As China's economy roared ahead, it helped spur inflation worldwide. China's appetite for raw materials—concrete, copper, iron, and steel, not to mention food and energy—was voracious. Its newly wealthy citizens demanded automobiles and consumer products. Tight gas supplies worldwide ratcheted up gas prices, and up, up, up they went. Even as Americans cut back on gasoline use, worldwide demand was so high that prices continued to climb through 2008—until the gas bubble finally burst that summer.

The 2008 Summer Olympics in Beijing announced that China had arrived on the world's stage. A *Dilbert* comic strip showed Dogbert the consultant explaining that there were only three types of companies: China, Facebook, and Irrelevant. [6]

"One way to think about India and China is as two great global deflating machines, pumping out goods (China) and services (India) for a fraction of what they would cost to produce in the West," observed journalist Zakaria. Global labor markets had shifted toward specialization. [7]

Addicted to Oil

In his State of the Union address in 2006, President Bush acknowledged that the United States was "addicted to oil," and he was right. After World War II, the U.S. had heavily subsidized suburban development with roads and by keeping gas prices low. Cheap gas was part of the equation that made the suburbs work: you couldn't live there without a car. But when gas prices rose dramatically from increased global demand, that changed the economics of suburbia. As a result, when the housing bubble burst in 2007, the outer suburbs and exurbs took the brunt of falling property values, while the core cities and inner suburbs better retained their values.

Cheap oil was the lubricant for the global economy. It was obviously necessary to transport goods from one country to another and from market to market. It also carried people back and forth, whether for business, vacation, or emigration. But oil was also essential to so many plastic products: shampoo and water bottles, Styrofoam containers for take-out food, and fertilizers necessary for growing ever larger amounts of corn that could, in turn, produce ethanol to replace fossil fuels.

Even before Hurricane Katrina knocked out the oil platforms and refineries in the Gulf of Mexico in 2005, the price of oil had shot up. This was a result of tight supplies worldwide, as millions of Chinese and Indians were entering the middle class and buying their first automobiles. The result was a classic case of rising demand—and rising prices—on the global market. Energy analyst Daniel Yergin called it the "globalization of demand" of oil as developing countries wanted cars and electricity. Energy demand was poised to grow exponentially as millions were lifted out of poverty. [8]

Some analysts spoke of "peak oil"—that is, when oil production worldwide would reach its highest rate, and after that inexorably decline. The U.S. had once been the largest producer of oil, but domestic production peaked in the 1970s. The country's key oil supplier to the south, Mexico, rapidly declined in oil production during the first decade.

The U.S. consumed about a quarter of all gasoline produced worldwide each year. By 2005, the country consumed about 20.7 million barrels of oil per day, of which only 5.1 million were domestically produced, and that was declining. The other 15.6 million were imported. Consumption stayed at this peak and only began to decline once fuel prices surpassed $4 a gallon in 2008. [9]

Some believed that the world's oil supply peaked in 2005. Others countered that new technology would be able to extract more crude oil, though that extraction would be far more expensive. No one really knew when oil would peak, though with rising global demand, it was frightening to think we would run out. [10]

America's gas problems of the first decade were partly rooted in the previous decade. Economic crises swept through Russia and much of Asia in 1997 and 1998, tamping down on global fuel demand. Gas prices in the U.S. fell to around a dollar per gallon, and Americans responded by upsizing their cars. Who needed to conserve fuel when gas was so inexpensive?

The Big Three Detroit automobile manufacturers (Chrysler, Ford, and General Motors) made a big bet on $1 a gallon gas, a decision that would haunt them. They focused on building light trucks and sport utility vehicles (SUVs) that were often targeted at suburbanites who had big garages and long commutes. SUVs were big, heavy, gas-guzzling vehicles that embodied American ideals of rugged individualism and the great outdoors—even though most SUVs never went off-road, but were used for commuting to the office and picking up the kids. Their names cleverly evoked the outdoors: 4Runner. Blazer. Cherokee. Denali. Durango. Excursion. Expedition. Pathfinder. Suburban. Tahoe. Xterra. Yukon.

The most extravagant of the SUVs was GM's Hummer, a consumer-oriented version of the military's Humvee. It was driven by people who really didn't care about the gas mileage: they were rich or status-conscious enough. They could flaunt their in-your-face consumption, driving a car that practically shouted, I don't care what my car does to the environment—I'm entitled to this!

General Motors' business model was based on the SUV: the company had very high health care and retiree costs. SUVs were more profitable than small passenger vehicles, and GM needed the cash flow to pay for all the benefits. Meanwhile, other automobile makers started shifting toward smaller cars and hybrids. GM kept plugging along as if nothing had changed, even as fuel prices crept upward.

As China's economy boomed, the country's new middle class headed for the car dealership and purchased the largest vehicles they could afford, as large cars conveyed status. The country's demand for gas exploded. This rising demand was a key reason why global fuel prices increased so much in the first decade.[11]

The price of gas hit the stratosphere. From the beginning of 2007 until the middle of 2008, gas prices nearly doubled, while crude oil had quadrupled in just four years to $110 per barrel. Gasoline had hit an all-time, inflation-adjusted peak in May 2007 of $3.23 per gallon, but then prices continued climbing over the next year. San Francisco became the first city with $4 a gallon gas, and the rest of the nation soon followed. In May 2008, a barrel of crude surpassed $135, then $140 a month later. It hit a new record on July 11, 2008, at $147.27 per barrel, and that same day gas reached its all-time high of $4.11 per gallon in the U.S., just two months before Lehman Brothers collapsed, triggering the financial panic of the Great Recession. Gas prices then tumbled as global growth slowed. [12]

Even at their peak, American gas prices were low relative to European countries, which were even more reliant on foreign oil, but chose to heavily tax gas to limit consumption and subsidize transit. England, France, and Germany paid about $8 per gallon—twice that of the U.S.—while the Netherlands paid $10 per gallon. Most of the difference was in taxes. As a result, European countries organized their societies less around the automobile, and more around transit. Europeans also drove much more fuel-efficient cars, while Americans loved their big gas hogs.

The airline industry, which had barely recovered from the 9/11 recession, went into another tailspin with these high gas prices. Gas was their single largest expense, and when it nearly doubled in the course of a year, the airlines couldn't raise airfares fast enough to cover the difference. The result was significant losses, reduction in routes, retirement of older, less fuel-efficient planes like the McDonnell Douglas MD-80, and canceled flights to entire destinations, particularly small, regional markets.

Sales of American-made cars plummeted: they were too big, and their gas mileage too low. The love affair with the SUV and truck was over, at least for now. People joked that SUV now stood for Suddenly Unwanted Vehicle. Detroit began closing or retooling plants for small cars and hybrids. In 2007, President Bush signed off on higher car mileage standards to reduce the nation's consumption of oil, and President Obama would later do the same.

The collapse of SUV and truck sales really shouldn't have been a surprise to Detroit. They had been through this before with the oil shocks of the 1970s when the price for oil skyrocketed. Back then, Americans responded by shifting to smaller cars, and that's when Honda, Toyota, and other Japanese car manufacturers made their big move into the American market. But once oil prices stabilized in the 1980s, Detroit and Americans went back to their big car and gas-guzzling ways. They yielded the compact car market to foreign imports. Car makers were experimenting with rechargeable batteries and even hydrogen, but they were a long way off from eliminating the internal combustion engine.

Luckily peak oil never happened. New technologies led to new methods of oil and natural gas extraction. High oil prices incented wildcat entrepreneurs to try hydraulic fracturing, better known as fracking, which injected high-pressure liquid into underground shale formations to crack them, which in turn released its hidden treasure of gas and oil. North Dakota of all places became the epicenter of the fracking revolution. Appalachia and West Texas also became key centers of shale gas and shale oil production. By the century's second decade, the U.S. was far closer to energy independence than anyone could have imagined. The country once again vaulted to the top of the oil producers list, and even began exporting oil. The global price of gas plummeted. Furthermore, the world's known reserves of oil continued to expand.

With the fracking boom came an unexpected glut of natural gas. American power-generating companies shifted out of coal, which was no longer competitive in the free market, and toward natural gas, which was cheaper, cleaner to burn, and had much lower greenhouse gas emissions. The country's energy mix shifted toward natural gas and budding renewables like geothermal, solar, and wind. The world had a long, long way to go, however, before it could wean itself off fossil fuels. But doing so was vital to combat man-made climate change.

Climate Change: A Decade of Procrastination

By the mid-1990s, the scientific community had reached consensus that our hydrocarbon-fueled society was damaging the environment through greenhouse gas emissions. Man-made climate change was rapidly warming the planet, and scientists warned that we had to take constructive steps to curb carbon emissions. A global framework was mapped out in 1997 called the Kyoto Protocol, but the United States largely ignored it.

In 2001, climate scientists charted how the world's climate had evolved from 1000 C.E. on, noting the Medieval Warm Period and the Little Ice Age. The temperature fluctuated slightly but was largely stable. And then the Industrial Revolution began in the 1800s, fueled by burning coal. The world's temperature rose steeply in the 20th century. Climate scientists called it the "hockey stick," a graphic representation of the warming climate.[13]

Former vice president and presidential candidate Al Gore had long fought to raise public awareness about climate change. Gore produced and starred in an influential 2006 documentary called *An Inconvenient Truth*, which noted the scientific evidence behind climate change and called for action. So much of what he noted was political procrastination: climate change was happening, an observable event to many people, yet slow enough that people were adjusting to it. It was far down the list of issues for politicians to tackle.

The following year, the United Nations' Intergovernmental Panel on Climate Change published its fourth assessment. It stated that the scientific evidence that human actions were warming the planet was "unequivocal." The IPCC report, signed off by delegates from more than one hundred countries, called for the world to wean itself off fossil fuels if it hoped to mitigate climate change. The clock was ticking, and action was needed. For their work fighting climate change, Al Gore and the IPCC were jointly awarded the Nobel Peace Prize in 2007.[14]

Eric Pooley, who published the landmark book *The Climate War*, noted how difficult the obstacles were in confronting climate change, as Americans tended only to react when an emergency was thrust upon them. "The obstacles weren't only political. They were psychological," he wrote. "Human beings didn't respond well to big, slow-moving, seemingly abstract future threats, even if signs of impending doom were visible. We weren't good at paying now to stave off catastrophe later."[15]

Climate change could be observed in the United States during the first decade. The tule fog that once engulfed California's Central Valley virtually disappeared as winter days grew warmer. The snowpack upon which the state depends for its summer water supply melted quicker, or fell as rain instead of snow. The Rocky Mountains were similarly seeing their snowcaps disappear. The glaciers of Glacier National Park in Montana retreated to a fraction of themselves. Seven states of the desert Southwest depend on the Colorado River for their water needs, a river that was drying up, creating a long-term water crisis. The greater heat parched forests nationwide, leading to ever-greater wildfires. Vast tracts of trees died from beetle infestations, as the beetles could now survive at warmer, higher altitudes. Parasites like ticks, which normally die off in cold winter, exploded in number and vastly increased their geography, spreading diseases like Lyme and Rocky Mountain Spotted Fever. Spring was coming ever earlier, and fall arrived later, while winter seemed ever more abbreviated. Warmer oceans provided fuel for storms like Hurricane Katrina, and hurricanes grew larger, more powerful, and ever more destructive. Even regular thunderstorms dropped more rainfall than before, causing greater flooding. Insurance companies saw it in their escalating payouts for property damage claims.

Climate change was proving disruptive to farmers, who found themselves facing shifting growing seasons, more pests, and even having to change their crops. Some farmers' fields were parched from drought, while others were drowned under floodwaters. Thus far the oceans had not risen much, as the oceans had largely absorbed much of the carbon dioxide, but even that would eventually reach a saturation point. As the oceans captured carbon, they turned more acidic, killing the ocean's reefs and shellfish. Already cities at sea level like Miami, Florida, and Norfolk, Virginia, were beginning to see sunny-day flooding from rising oceans.

In November 2006, the U.S. Supreme Court heard arguments for the case *Massachusetts v. Environmental Protection Agency*. Twelve states sued the EPA to demand that it regulate carbon dioxide as a pollutant under the Clean Air Act. Justice Antonin Scalia remarked with some humor, "I told you before I'm not a scientist. That's why I don't want to deal with global warming."[16] In April 2007 the court decided in a 5–4 ruling that the EPA had to regulate carbon dioxide as a pollutant, as the evidence was clear that it was warming the planet.[17]

❖

For the 10,000 years before the Industrial Revolution, the earth's atmosphere registered carbon dioxide levels of about 280 parts per million. Carbon emissions greatly accelerated during the 20th century, such that by 2007, CO_2 in the atmosphere stood at 384 ppm. Scientists called for a cap of no more than 450 ppm, with the goal to limit atmospheric warming to 2° Celsius (3.6° Fahrenheit). If the globe warmed by more than this, the consequences for the planet would be disastrous.[18]

In summer 2007, for the first time in recorded history, the ice cap in the Arctic Ocean melted so much that it opened sea lanes through the Arctic. The fabled Northwest Passage became a reality. It was now possible to steer a ship through the Arctic, just as Henry Hudson and other explorers had tried and failed to do hundreds of years before. Though the Arctic refroze in winter, the ice sheet melted faster than any climatologist had forecast. The next year, the polar bear was placed on the Endangered Species list, with forecasts showing it would be on the brink of extinction within forty years, all because of the shrinking polar ice cap.

The Arctic was the canary in the coalmine. Melting sea ice does not cause oceans to rise, as the ice comes directly from ocean freezing. But without the Arctic ice cap, the ocean water around the North Pole would warm by several degrees, causing the Greenland ice sheet to melt faster and possibly shifting the Atlantic Ocean's currents. Melting glaciers were far more worrisome, as this aboveground ice can add significantly more water to the oceans. Some 90 percent of the world's ice is locked up in Antarctica, and if that ever melts, experts forecast under worst-case scenarios that the world's oceans could rise by up to forty feet. That would destroy vast segments of coastline: Delaware, eastern Maryland, a huge swath of Florida and the Gulf Coast, New Orleans, New York City, Boston. And that's just in the U.S.

Rising oceans would cause even more harm to developing countries like Bangladesh, which largely lies at sea level and is densely populated. This could set off a massive refugee crisis as displaced people search for shelter. The glaciers of the Himalayas provide drinking water to a huge population, and if this water source disappears, what then? The vast permafrost of Siberia was beginning to thaw, and that had to potential to release immense amounts of greenhouse gases that were stored in the soil. The effects of climate change would have a negative impact on the global economy. Persistent droughts could devastate parts of the world, make entire regions uninhabitable, and lead to food shortages and starvation.

As the oceans warmed, fish shifted from their traditional waters toward the North and South Poles where the water was colder. This would have a pronounced effect on societies that depended on fish to feed their population. A major scientific study revealed that this fish migration had been underway for decades.[19]

By the end of the first decade, climate change loomed as one of the world's leading issues, something that would take decades or even centuries to counteract, but there was great pessimism about whether we were stemming the tide fast enough. While industrial nations looked to reduce their greenhouse gas emissions, the developing world was rapidly pumping carbon into the atmosphere, largely by burning coal, which offset the cuts made by others. These countries, places like China and India, said it was unfair for the West to blame them, as they needed to grow economically to support their large populations. They argued that the world's poor should not be burdened with paying for climate change that the West had largely produced since the Industrial Revolution. Energy analyst Daniel Yergin noted: "The world's appetite for energy in the years ahead will grow enormously. The absolute numbers are staggering. Whatever the mix in the years ahead, energy and its challenges will be defining for our future."[20]

China overtook the U.S. as the largest greenhouse gas emitter in 2008. As China added more coal-burning power plants to fuel its booming economy, its power-related carbon dioxide emissions grew to 3.1 billion tons. The U.S. was stable at 2.8 billion tons and soon on the decline as the country shifted from coal to natural gas and renewables to produce energy. If the world wanted to survive, it had to stop burning coal, by far the largest greenhouse-gas producer and source of pollution.[21]

In 2009, researchers at the U.S. National Oceanic and Atmospheric Administration warned that, if carbon concentrations rose from the current 385 parts per million to the forecast 550 ppm by 2035, the damage would be irreversible. Even if the world sharply curtailed its CO_2 emissions, the damage would last a thousand years. Thus climate scientists warned that carbon should not go above 450 ppm if the planet wanted to avoid the worst effects from global warming.[22]

The year 2009 was the second-warmest year since global temperatures began to be recorded in 1880—the warmest year being 2005. Scientists at NASA announced that the first decade was the warmest ever. Since 1880, average global temperatures had risen by 1.5° Fahrenheit, or 0.8° Celsius. We were getting steadily closer to the 3.6° Fahrenheit mark scientists had warned about.[23]

❖

Despite the abundant scientific evidence of manmade climate change, climate change deniers argued that it wasn't real. Other skeptics argued that, even if the planet was warming, it was part of a natural cycle and couldn't be stopped. Therefore, people didn't need to do anything. The leading denier was Republican Senator James Inhofe of Oklahoma, who declared on the Senate floor in July 2003 that "manmade global warming is the greatest hoax ever perpetrated on the American people."

In 2010, Naomi Oreskes and Erik Conway published their book *Merchants of Doubt*, later released as a documentary film by the same name. These "merchants" were lobbyists largely paid by the fossil fuels industry whose job was to sow doubt about whether climate change was real. The propaganda they published was remarkably effective.

The deniers took their cues from the tobacco industry, which fought a five-decade-long struggle to question the addictiveness and deadliness of tobacco, even though the science was settled fact—all while the industry continued selling its deadly products. This was called the Tobacco Strategy. The deniers would often argue that there was no scientific consensus around manmade climate change, when in fact the scientific community had reached consensus in the mid-1990s. The deniers attacked scientists, rather than the science itself, saying that scientists were using their data for political purposes. It was all about casting doubt in the public's mind.[24]

The deniers framed their crusade in terms of freedom: if the government could drive down greenhouse gas emissions through regulation, it could harm the fossil fuels industry or even drive it out of business. So they obfuscated and argued that fighting climate change was a threat to Americans' personal freedom—because who doesn't like freedom? The more extreme propaganda positioned global warming as a hoax designed to vastly increase the power of the federal government.

The deniers' goal was simple: political gridlock, to simply stop action from being taken that might harm the hydrocarbon industry. With climate-change Luddites like Senator Inhofe throwing a wrench into the political machine, the result was a lost decade as the U.S. procrastinated on taking action against global warming.

New York Times columnist Thomas Friedman quipped, "Climate-change deniers are like the person who goes to the doctor for a diagnosis, and when the doctor tells him, 'If you don't stop smoking, there is a 90 percent chance you will die of lung cancer,' the patient replies: 'Oh, doctor, you mean you are not 100 percent sure? Then I will keep on smoking.'"[25]

In December 2009, the U.N. Climate Change Conference met in Copenhagen, Denmark, to build a framework for reducing carbon emissions globally. President Barack Obama attended, making a brief jaunt to Oslo to collect his Nobel Prize. Just weeks before the Copenhagen summit, the climate change deniers pounced. They hacked emails from the climate research center at the University of East Anglia in England, then cherry-picked statements from the emails and released them onto the Internet out of context. The denialists claimed that the scientists had cooked the books to lie about the truth of climate change and to quash dissenting opinion. The deniers pushed their own bizarre claim that the world was actually *cooling*. Climate scientists found themselves on the defensive in the face of a massive disinformation campaign by climate change denialists, who called the affair "Climategate." This shady effort was done to discredit climate scientists and forestall action that might reduce fossil fuel consumption in the international community as well as at home, where the Senate was weighing taking up the House-passed cap-and-trade bill. The climate scientists were cleared of malfeasance by an independent review.[26]

What you believed about climate change depended in part on where you got your news. The mainstream media covered it as a fact, but right-wing media outlets treated climate change as questionable or even a hoax. Thus you saw Democrats overwhelmingly support action to combat climate change, while many Republicans were still questioning whether the science was real. "This divergence between the state of the science and how it was presented in the major media helped make it easy for our government to do nothing about global warming," wrote Conway and Oreskes in *Merchants of Doubt*. "Scientifically, global warming was an established fact. Politically, global warming was dead." But even Republicans began to come around as everyone could see firsthand the impact of a warming planet. It was unmistakable.[27]

"Each year that emissions reductions are delayed, it becomes increasingly difficult to stabilize CO_2 concentrations below safe levels," wrote climate scientist Michael Mann. "This is the so-called 'procrastination penalty' of delayed action." Even if CO_2 emissions had stabilized at the end of the first decade, some climate change effects were already locked in, including at least a one foot higher sea level. "That means that we have already, in all likelihood, ensured the obliteration of some low-lying island nations and the extinction of many animal species, among other impacts."[28]

Corporate America began to take the risk of climate change seriously and began discussing sustainability. Companies realized that rising extreme weather was a threat to their business. For example, a company with a call center in Tampa Bay, Florida, had to plan for the inevitable hurricane that might knock their operation offline for days. They couldn't afford to be in denial about the science. Many companies created environmental officers to find ways to cut energy usage, enacted green energy programs, all while hardening their infrastructure against weather-related events.

The Bush administration avoided taking action to deal with climate change during its eight years in the White House. When President Obama was sworn in in 2009, he made climate change legislation a priority, but even that turned out to be wishful thinking. Dealing with climate change led to political paralysis in Congress.

The Obama administration wanted to address greenhouse gas emissions by creating a market-based solution called cap-and-trade. Under this system, the government would set a price for carbon and a scaling-down cap for how much pollutants can be emitted. Companies that produce fewer greenhouse gas emissions can sell credits to those that produce more, thus providing a profit to the former, and a financial incentive to the latter to stop polluting. Over time, as the cap shrinks and the cost of carbon rises, companies are incented to stop burning fossil fuels. This had been successfully used in 1990, when President George H. W. Bush created a cap-and-trade system to deal with acid raid from coal plants. The government simply provides the goalposts and leaves it to the market to decide how best to get there.

The House of Representatives passed a complicated cap-and-trade bill in 2009, but the right ignited a political firestorm in protest, claiming it would significantly raise taxes and costs jobs in the sputtering economic recovery in the wake of the Great Recession. In particular, Congress ran into wholesale opposition from Americans for Prosperity, a conservative advocacy group funded by Charles and David Koch (better known as the Koch brothers) whose business was deeply wedded to fossil fuels. A cap-and-trade bill would be costly to them, and their goal was the status quo. Obama left the policy details to Congress on an issue that could have benefited from his leadership and bully pulpit. His focus was on health care reform. The Senate never passed the climate bill.

Without Congressional legislation, the fallback position was to use the EPA to regulate carbon emissions, a position rooted in the 2007 Supreme Court decision that confirmed CO_2 as a pollutant and thus in need of regulation. Turning this authority over to regulators would never be as strong as having the full force of the law, as any bureaucratic rules could be challenged in court (and they were). But lacking other options, the Obama administration adopted a clean energy program that mandated lower carbon emissions at the state level.

The United States was finally investing in alternative energy sources, especially natural gas, solar, and wind. The 2009 economic stimulus package strongly pushed green infrastructure. By the end of the first decade, enough wind farm capacity had come online to power 2 percent of the country, and many more wind farms were planned. Solar farms were beginning to sprout, and many families installed solar panels on their homes—some to help the planet, others for personal energy independence. [29]

By 2012, the U.S. had cut its oil imports significantly because of the hydraulic fracking revolution, which released vast amounts of oil and natural gas that was previously unobtainable. Natural gas prices sank in the glut, and power plants ditched their old, dirty coal plants for natural gas. Natural gas released far fewer greenhouse gas emissions than coal or gasoline, meaning that the country reduced its carbon footprint and imported oil dependency at the same time. [30]

Global warming meant that the planet wasn't just getting warmer; it also meant an onset of more extreme weather, from extreme drought to extreme cold and heat to extreme storms. The year 2012 was the warmest year on record in the United States and set heat records around the world. In late October, a monster hurricane named Sandy swept ashore in New Jersey, flooding much of the mid-Atlantic and New England coasts (as it hit right before Halloween, it was nicknamed "Frankenstorm"). Atlantic City was flooded and its famed Boardwalk drowned. Floodwaters burst into the New York City subway and the streets of lower Manhattan were under several feet of water. Power was knocked out to millions. Although a once-in-a-century storm, Sandy was a presage to future floods and storm surges that would become all too frequent. [31]

Human actions are undoubtedly warming the planet. What does it say about us for not taking action against climate change? How will future generations judge us for procrastinating and pontificating on the issue, rather than making some simple changes in our lifestyles and shifting away from burning fossil fuels? The world will suffer for generations for our selfishness. Our stubborn refusal to act in the face of scientific facts has fated our planet to at least some rising temperatures, rising sea levels, and rising numbers of climate refugees. The only question now is: how bad will it be?

11

The New Retirement

In the 2002 movie *About Schmidt*, actor Jack Nicholson plays an old man facing retirement, and asks the question, what now? He spent his career at an insurance company, retiring as a vice president, but once he retires he senses no purpose in life. His generation, which weathered the Great Depression and World War II, placed much of its self-identity in work. A few weeks after retirement, he goes back to the office to help out, and there finds all his records—his lifetime of work—out by the dumpster. His wife dies. His daughter is getting married and wants nothing to do with him except funding for the wedding. And as an actuary, he knows how much longer he can expect to live. It was an understated, nuanced role for Nicholson, who for decades had been one of Hollywood's bad boys. And it left the viewer with a sad, empty feeling: What do you do when your purpose has run out, but your life continues on?

These were the vital questions aging Americans asked themselves as they neared the end of their working years, but realized they possibly had several more decades to live. Americans in the early 21st century had to reconsider what retirement meant, what with greater longevity, the cost of living, and health care. And there was always that awkward but vital question: How do you feel about the end of life? How do you want to go?

An immediate challenge confronting the United States in the first decade was its graying population. Much of the industrialized world was aging, including Germany, Italy, and especially Japan, whose populations were actually shrinking. The population of the U.S. continued to grow, but only because of immigration. Young Americans were marrying later and having fewer children. This meant that the over-65s were the fastest-growing demographic.

The very idea of retirement was made possible in the 1930s with the creation of Social Security. Beforehand, Americans just kept working until they no longer could. Life spans were shorter; if a man reached age sixty-five and could retire, he would likely die within a few years.

By the mid–20th century, Americans experienced unprecedented growth in longevity, as more advanced medical care could treat all sorts of life's ailments. Things that would have killed people earlier were now treated with medication and procedures that could extend life for years, even decades. This included high blood pressure medication and cholesterol-lowering statins; better cancer detection and treatment; heart valve replacement surgery; stents to keep arteries open; hip and knee replacement surgery; outpatient surgery to remove cataracts; and hearing aids to maintain social engagement. People were aging differently and indeed living longer. It helped that smoking had gone way down, people were eating healthier diets and exercising, and they were more likely to wear sunscreen. Modern medicine could extend and improve quality of life for the aging.

American life expectancy had been improving for decades, and the first decade was no exception. In 2006, a survey found that the average life expectancy for Americans was 78.1 years (80.7 years for women, and 75.4 years for men). Thanks to modern medicine, we earned three more decades of life compared to people just a century earlier. [1]

America has always been a youthful country—and its people thought of themselves as young. Americans maintained an attitude of, "You're not old till you're dead." Marketers advertised a message of eternal youth, that we, like Peter Pan, need never grow up. That came face-to-face with reality in 2008, when the first Baby Boomers reached sixty-two, meaning they could qualify for Social Security and effectively retire. Yes, even the Baby Boom generation was growing older. Three years later, 10,000 Baby Boomers were turning sixty-five each day.

Baby Boomers were born 1946–1964 and were a huge cohort of 76 million people. These children of the Greatest Generation (so-called because they fought in World War II) grew up in a time of unprecedented postwar prosperity. There were so many of them, and their cultural watershed was Woodstock, where they celebrated, protested the Vietnam War, and demanded things they felt were their due.

Boomers were reaching retirement age far healthier than earlier generations. But they were such a large cohort that when they left the workforce, the size of the job market actually shrank. The retirement of the Boomers provided an economic headwind that served as a brake on economic growth. People stopped working and started drawing on government entitlements. Plus there were more retirees but fewer workers to subsidize those retirees.

Eternally young Boomers challenged the very concept of old age. Society had to rethink: What is middle age? When does someone become old? No one alive wanted to think of themselves as old, though there certainly were plenty of people who were aging. It was politically incorrect to call someone "old"—that would hurt their feelings (even if it were true). Rather, they were *aging*, *maturing*, or *getting older*.

The concept of retirement began to shift, in particular for Baby Boomers. What was one supposed to do with potentially twenty or thirty years out to pasture? The old days of moving to Florida and playing golf while reaping a juicy pension were long gone. Even immortal Baby Boomers had to reassess their ambitions as they reinvented retirement. Many imagined their golden years as a time of leisure, but suddenly there are so many hours to fill. Without work, people too often get bored and listless—and boredom leads to social disengagement and decline. Perhaps "retirement" was an outdated notion. They began considering it instead as the next chapter of life, not just filled with activity but with fulfillment and purpose.

In her book *Never Say Die*, Susan Jacoby stresses the importance of staying engaged after retirement—or yes, even continuing to work: "Retirement is undoubtedly a cherished and much-needed goal for people whose bodies are marked by decades of hard physical labor or for white-collar workers who have always hated their jobs, but it is a passport to boredom and purposelessness for many old men and women who like to work and are healthy enough to do so. Work, both paid and volunteer, makes people feel useful."[2]

Some older Americans saw their gray years as a second childhood, years for adventure travel and exploring the globe. This may have been true for recent retirees, but once people get into their eighties, health problems mount as bodies decline, and travel becomes ever more challenging.

As the Millennials, the children of Baby Boomers, moved out of their parents' home, many Boomers began downsizing to smaller digs. Many Boomers sold their large homes and moved to apartments, smaller homes, or even to active senior communities. Places like Del Webb communities (Arizona's Sun City is one), generally built in the exurbs, offered community living for people aged fifty-five and older. Others chose independent living communities that allowed people to transition to different levels of care as they aged.

Aging can also lead to loss of independence. You can get so frail that you need full-time care, sometimes in a retirement home or assisted living facility, though increasingly people were aging in place in their own homes, retrofitted to meet the needs of older folks. That meant hiring caregivers at considerable expense—or finding a family member who was willing to commit their finances and time. They could also enroll in local elder villages that provided cooperative care among its members and keep people engaged.

The Economics of Aging

The big scary monster of aging was running out of money before you ran out of life. This was especially consequential for women: they lived longer on average than men and yet earned less in their careers, which made them more economically vulnerable as they aged.

As longevity increased in the 20th century, President Franklin Delano Roosevelt created the Social Security program in 1935 to protect seniors from destitution in their later years. President Lyndon Baines Johnson added Medicare in 1965 so that adults aged sixty-five and older could have health care.

Pensions peaked after World War II, coinciding with the zenith of labor unions. These served to bolster economic security for retirees, who could now count on a three-legged stool of a pension, personal savings, and Social Security. By the late 1960s, six in ten Americans were covered by pensions. Workers often didn't have to save—their pension was their savings. It was possible to earn a pension after working thirty years, meaning you could retire in your fifties, then spend the rest of your life collecting inflation-adjusted checks.

With people living longer, Corporate America grasped how expensive these long-term obligations were becoming, as they may have to pay out a pension for thirty years to a retiree and surviving spouse. Entire industries—airlines, railroads, and steel—had foundered on pension obligations, especially as the industries themselves shrank. They froze pension plans by the 1990s. Governments, however, held onto pensions as a way to keep firemen, police, soldiers, and teachers employed, trading lower pay for promised future benefits.[3]

Pension funding crises struck hardest in regions where unions were the strongest and had negotiated the biggest promises—California, Illinois, Michigan, and the Northeast—even though many realized that there was too little capacity to meet these obligations. It was no coincidence as well that these states had higher tax burdens, as the social safety net was more extensive—and expensive.

In the 1980s, Corporate America embraced a retirement investment alternative: the 401(k). They saw it as a way to get out of the pension business and shift the risk to the workers. The 401(k) was a personal account of retirement money; once the worker left the company, they took their retirement savings with them, and the company removed that employee from their accounting books. Baby Boomers and following generations were heavily reliant on the 401(k) for their retirement.

Employees were now responsible for funding their own retirement. The message became: if you want a comfortable retirement—or if you want to retire at all—you had better start saving early. Americans have never been good savers, but were always happy to spend. With defined benefit plans like pensions shifting over to defined contribution plans, individuals had to become their own retirement plan owners. How you lived in retirement directly correlated to how much you saved—and keeping your spending in check. Most Americans had poor financial literacy, and many lacked the skills to manage retirement accounts on their own.

As pensions went extinct in the private sector, the three-legged stool for retirement collapsed into a two-legged stool (personal savings and Social Security), or more likely a one-legged pogo stick (Social Security). Most Americans had little if any savings. This meant that people had only meager Social Security benefits to rely on, and that also explains why many continued working after they reached retirement age. They just couldn't afford to retire. The official age of retirement for Social Security may have been sixty-seven, but the de facto retirement age was well past seventy. Many people drawing Social Security continued to work.

Medicare and Social Security, the twin federal government programs designed to help the retired in their golden years, represented a massive transfer of wealth from the young and working to the old and non-working. Not that anyone got rich off these entitlements; it was the nation's wealth that shifted. The alternative was to ask the nation's young adults, many of whom were raising families, to bring in their aging parents and grandparents and be caregivers. Few were equipped or wanted to do that. By the end of the first decade, the federal government was spending nearly a quarter of the nation's GDP, and a large proportion of that went toward supporting old folks. The financial cost of caring for an older person is significantly higher than raising a child. Spending on healthcare, Social Security, and retirement communities vastly eclipsed spending on children.[4]

Just a day after winning reelection in 2004, President George W. Bush stated, "I earned capital in the campaign, political capital, and now I intend to spend it." His intention was to reform Social Security, long a goal for conservatives. He launched an ambitious program to sell the nation on "personal accounts" (the same thing as a private account). It was politically dead on arrival. The country didn't have the stomach to change this near-sacred entitlement, nor risk their future benefits to the whims of the stock market. Many adults already had a private account in a 401(k). Few had desire for even more exposure, and events in 2008 during the Great Recession would ring true about the dangers of putting all of one's eggs into the stock market. Bush admitted in his memoir, "On Social Security, I may have misread the electoral mandate by pushing for an issue on which there had been little bipartisan agreement in the first place."[5]

Compounding the American savings problem was the one-two punch of the bursting housing bubble followed by the Great Recession. For most Americans, their main source of wealth was their home, which took a beating when the housing market collapsed in 2007. The average house price declined 35 percent nationwide. It was a reminder that real estate values do not always go up.[6]

Equally devastating was the stock market meltdown in 2008. The S&P 500 declined 56 percent from peak to trough. Many people wondered how they could afford to retire after that. For people close to retirement age, it meant they would have to continue working to make up the shortfall. The congressional Financial Crisis Inquiry Commission estimated that the country had lost $17 trillion in wealth during the Great Recession: about $5.6 trillion in housing wealth, and the remainder in lost financial assets. (Compare that to the dot-com meltdown of 2000, which lost $6.5 trillion, about a third of the Great Recession.) This was a huge hit to future and present retirees.[7]

That said, putting off retirement wasn't necessarily a bad thing. Work keeps people active and engaged. As the American economy deindustrialized and became increasingly automated, work became less physically taxing. People could work longer, as their bodies were not worn out. That said, age discrimination in the workforce was real: workers older than fifty were more likely to be laid off because of their higher salaries and cost of benefits, and afterward they struggled to find equivalent work. Some became entrepreneurs, starting new businesses. A key barrier to entry was the lack of health care options for middle-aged entrepreneurs. "Job lock" became widespread as people stayed at jobs that no longer interested them just so they could have health insurance.

A key to longevity was keeping both mentally and physically fit. The brain is a muscle, and it needs to be exercised or it will degrade. It was no coincidence that people swiftly declined after they retired. It wasn't just that their bodies were aging; they were no longer exercising their minds, and they didn't have the challenges and stress anymore of a working life that kept them mentally fit.

Journalist Chris Farrell wrote about how older Americans were returning to the workforce. "The dire jeremiads aimed at an aging America are wrong and deeply misplaced. The graying of America is terrific news. Living longer is good. Embrace the realization that boomers on average are healthier and better educated than previous generations." Graying people who had left the workforce were reentering it, sometimes because they needed the money, but often because they had a dream or a passion they wanted to follow. Farrell called this "unretirement." He wrote, "If the popular images of retirement are the golf course and the RV, the defining institutions of unretirement are the workplace and the entrepreneurial start-up." Older workers had a lifetime of experiences, proven adaptability, and contrary to popular belief, were not technophobic. Retirees returning to work appreciated flexible working arrangements or reduced working hours, such as part-time—but that also meant workplaces had to adapt and make room for them, just as they did for the Millennials.[8]

Living & Dying

Americans have long worshipped a youth culture, as if some magical elixir could provide a way to live forever. There is not. People claimed that age sixty is the new thirty, and eighty is the new sixty. The American capacity for denial that we are aging is legion. If there is one certainty, it is that everybody dies. None of us are getting off this planet alive. You too, dear reader, will someday board that elven ship and sail off into the West.

The reality is, getting old isn't for wimps. For many, old age didn't mean a swift death, but rather a long, slow, drawn out decline into decrepitude. It could literally be depressing to still be alive when so many friends and relatives had already passed on. If you declined enough to need full-time care, you might lose your independence and be institutionalized in a nursing home at great cost. "The American way of death costs a fortune," observed Susan Jacoby in *Never Say Die*. "Whether they die at home or in an institution, the oldest old usually die after a long period of suffering from chronic, incurable conditions that finally become unmanageable."[9]

If there was one certainty in old age, it was that health care costs were continuing to rise. Hospitalizations and prescription drugs especially pushed the cost curve higher. And since people were living longer, they faced a host of new medical problems that earlier generations seldom experienced: dementia and its terrifying cousin, Alzheimer's disease. Alzheimer's devastates bodies, lives, and minds, and it particularly impacts women, who live longer than men. There is no cure.

For earlier generations, a heart attack was the big widow-maker, especially for men. However, with statins and blood pressure medication, people were now less likely to die suddenly or in their sleep; instead, they would linger for years on a gentle downward slide that resulted in decrepitude, frailty, and the loss of dignity that comes with enfeeblement and sickness. Our bodies will wear out, and they will fail us.

Dr. Samuel Harrington, a gastroenterologist who spent his career counseling people about the end stages of life, asked a series of strikingly pointed questions in his book *At Peace*:

> How do you want to die? Do you want to suffer? Do you want your last conscious sensations to be the chest compressions of an emergency medical technician (EMT) separating your sternum from your ribs? Do you want your last sight to be the specter of a tracheal intubation blade approaching your mouth followed immediately thereafter by the insertion of a tube into your lungs? Do you want people rushing to stab large-bore needles into your neck and groin to access big, reliable veins?

Do you want to die in an ICU, on a ventilator, unconscious, unrecognizably bloated, oozing from sores and pores, every orifice violated with a tube, and unable to communicate with family and friends? This is not hyperbole. This is what saving people from near death looks like. [10]

What Harrington described was the aggressive medical intervention so often employed at the end of a person's life, regardless of cost or the will of the patient. Americans use excessive medical care, especially in their final years, when palliative care might be more effective and beneficial to the patient. But the American way is to throw more health care at the problem, as if we could prolong a person's life indefinitely. "Harsh treatments toward the end of life might help a few patients live a little longer, but these same treatments have no effect (except side effects) for mostly elderly people, and they kill many people sooner than the disease itself," noted Dr. Harrington. [11]

Modern medicine can keep people alive much longer, but is it *worth* extending life just for the sake of extending life? Quality of life has to be the benchmark, rather than extending life at any cost. No one ever said, "I'd like to die in a hospital." And yet that was where most people died. Most prefer to die a natural death at home in familiar surroundings and hopefully with loved ones to say goodbye. That means accepting the inevitable and making the dying comfortable and letting them depart without pain.

Many were too polite or embarrassed to talk about their wishes should they become terminally ill—until Terri Schiavo (pronounced SHY-vo). No death in recent memory was so politicized. In 1990, she collapsed in her St. Petersburg, Florida, home, went into cardiac arrest and stopped breathing. Paramedics managed to restart her heart and rushed her to the hospital. Because she was deprived of oxygen for so long, she suffered massive brain damage. Schiavo was hooked up to a feeding tube and remained in a persistent vegetative state for the next fifteen years.

Schiavo had no advance medical directive to indicate how she wanted to be treated if hospitalized. Her husband Michael insisted that keeping her alive indefinitely was against her stated wishes, but this was at odds with her parents, who were pro-life Catholics and believed their daughter could recover through therapy. As Terri's legal guardian, Michael ordered the feeding tube removed in 2001, but the parents went to court, which ordered the tube reinserted.

Michael Schiavo returned to court in 2003 to allow his wife to die and won approval. At this point Terri's right to die was politicized as the religious right attempted to intervene through state law. Governor Jeb Bush, a pro-life Republican and brother to the president, ordered a special legislative session to pass "Terri's Law" to override the courts. The feeding tube was reinserted. The following year, however, the Florida Supreme Court ruled that this intervention was unconstitutional.

Governor Bush appealed to Congress. Congressional Republicans quickly passed a law authorizing federal courts to take on the issue. President Bush was at his Crawford, Texas, ranch, but quickly flew back to Washington to sign the bill. However, the federal judge overseeing the case refused to buckle. He sided with Michael Schiavo's decision to remove his wife's feeding tube. Terri Schiavo died on March 31, 2005. [12]

The fact is, Schiavo was effectively brain-dead—dozens of doctors had examined her over a decade, and all concluded that she was in a persistent vegetative state. The autopsy confirmed this. Yet her parents and religious conservatives insisted that she be kept alive. The political intervention to save Schiavo's life misfired. Americans overwhelmingly supported Schiavo's right to die, seeing the politicians' efforts as intruding on a very personal decision.

The personal and public debates over Terri Schiavo were fascinating. People discussed this over the dinner table and with their coworkers. Many discovered they had something in common: with increasing longevity and medical care, so many families had already made an end-of-life decision for a relative. That's why the public came down so decisively on the side of Schiavo's husband Michael: few people wanted their lives to be extended unnecessarily, especially when hooked up to a ventilator or a feeding tube. More people began discussing what kind of medical care they wanted in their final days, and put this in writing through advance medical directives, but also a host of legal documents like a medical power of attorney, a do not resuscitate order, a living will, and of course an estate plan for the inevitable. No one wanted to be another Terri Schiavo.

Another more controversial discussion quietly emerged during the first decade: assisted suicide for terminally ill patients. Proponents argued that since pets are commonly euthanized, why can't people be as well if they are deathly ill? But assisted suicide had not yet gained widespread acceptance, though no doubt it took place. Oregon became the first state to legalize assisted suicide in 1997, followed by Washington in 2008, and Montana a year later. More states were added in the following decade. It was called the Death with Dignity movement.

Barring a sudden death or death in a hospital, more Americans were dying in hospices, which first opened in the United States in 1971. They are a place to make the terminally ill comfortable while their bodies shut down. No medical treatments are offered, only pain relief and anxiety medication. It is the last stop in your life before death. Ann Neumann, who volunteered at hospices for years and published *The Good Death: An Exploration of Dying in America*, addressed the myth of the good death.

> There is no good death, I now know. It always hurts, both the dying and the left behind. But there is a good enough death. It is possible to look it in the face, to know how it will come, to accept its inevitability. Knowing death makes facing it bearable. There are many kinds of good enough death, each specific to the person dying. As they wish, as best they can. And there is really one kind of bad death, characterized by the same bad facts: pain, denial, prolongation, loneliness. [13]

Knowing that you will die someday gives one pause. Death is the universal leveler, and we are all equal before it. But perhaps the question we should all ask is not just, *How do you want to die?* but rather, *How do you want to live?*

12

The New Urbanism and the Housing Bubble

I f there was one thing that united Americans, it was worsening traffic. Besides the rising cost of health care, it was the biggest issue on people's minds. Traffic was the start of every dinner party conversation when guests complained about how long it took them to arrive. It was mind-numbing and relentless. Tom Vanderbilt wrote in his widely read book *Traffic*: "As an American in the early 21st century, I live in the most auto-dependent, car-adapted, mileage-happy society in the history of the planet."[1]

Rush hours were once over in an hour; now they kept extending later into the evening, and started earlier in the afternoon. It was common for rush hour to begin at 3:00 P.M. and end five hours later.

Often there was no rationale behind the traffic. One day, your commute would be fifteen minutes, the next day it could be twice that without explanation. In some cities not accustomed to snow, such as in the South, the mere hint of ice or snow sent people into their cars to stock up on bread, eggs, milk, and toilet paper for the inevitable snowdrifts that would trap them inside their houses for weeks at a time (sarcasm intended). Your presence was required at the supermarket.

Why was traffic in the U.S. so freaking horrible?

The traffic was in part rooted in the American Dream, in part in how we built our cities, and in part in the economic success of a country that could afford as many cars as it had drivers. After World War II, city-dwelling

Americans flocked to the suburbs in search of more space, enabled by the wide-spread availability of the automobile. Newer American cities were built with the car in mind. Atlanta, Dallas, and Sacramento all felt like the same city with the same traffic. If you lived in one of these cities, you might ask—*how can you ever live without a car?* The answer is, you can't.

Everyone wanted to own a house, preferably with a little piece of nature for the kids to play in. American tastes shifted toward larger homes—the "keeping up with the Joneses" effect meant you couldn't be satisfied with 2,500 square feet when your neighbor had 4,000 square feet—you needed at least that much to be happy. Schools were part of the traffic problem as well: parents would bid up the prices of houses to be in a good school district, even though that might not be anywhere close to where they worked. The result was a longer commute.

With the two-income family, both parents now worked, so they shopped on Saturday and Sunday, increasing weekend traffic. Rush hour lasted all day, especially on Saturdays. Although women had joined the workforce, they still did most of the family chores, and it was women who largely ran the errands. They become known as soccer moms for shuttling their kids around to school and sports. Few children walked or rode their bikes to school anymore. That meant more cars on the road.

American metropolitan areas were taken over by sprawl, the relentless drive outward from a city center, converting ever more farmland and wilderness to create subdivisions and office parks, all of them connected by a roadway network that struggled to keep up. The more roads they built, the more it induced demand to build houses along that road ("build it and they will come"). A once-open road quickly filled up with cars. People who moved out to the country to escape the city simply brought their city problems with them. Traffic in the car-reliant suburbs and exurbs could be as bad if not worse than in downtowns.

In many cities, the roads were at capacity, and there was no leeway for accidents or bad weather. One traffic accident, a thunderstorm at rush hour, or even a police car flashing its lights could cause rubber-necking, and the effects would be felt miles away as the traffic backed up in response. It was maddening how a road could be open one day, and completely clogged the next. Traffic could even be fierce in rural areas, especially along interstate highways where convoys of trucks hauled goods between cities.

Some people commuted astonishing distances to work, largely based on where they could afford to buy or rent. When the Bay Area of California got too expensive for many middle- and working-class families, some moved to the San Joaquin Valley or Sacramento, then commuted three hours or longer each day. In the Maryland suburbs of Washington, D.C., working-class people moved all the way out to Hagerstown (about seventy-file miles from the district) and then drove in. The Center for Housing Policy released a study finding that the costs of commuting—gas, car payments, insurance, wear and tear, not to mention lost time—canceled out the savings from buying a less expensive house in the suburbs.[2]

As traffic worsened, cities and states worked to find transportation alternatives. People overwhelmingly commuted by car, but even a small shift to bikes, buses, or subway lines could have a huge impact. Cities adopted the smart-growth model, confining development to where the infrastructure could support it and promoting density (housing, jobs, retail) so people could have a walkable lifestyle, rather than be car-dependent.

Many Asian and European countries had substantial bike cultures that promoted biking for commuting and running errands. The U.S. was slow to wake up to this environmentally friendly form of transportation, but it was making strides in building bike trails, sometimes out of former railroad rights-of-way, better bike lanes on city streets, and places to park bikes. Some cities deployed bicycle sharing, where you rented a bike just for the time that you needed it, such as for a commute, then returned it to a dock for the next person. Similarly, car sharing came about with the firm Zipcar that allowed people to skip car ownership and use a car only when they needed it. In the 2010s, ride-sharing companies like Lyft and Uber emerged, but we are getting ahead of ourselves. These actually worsened traffic in cities, as they put more cars on the road and took riders away from public transit.

The reality is that the car is with us from here on out. Even if society one day shifts from gasoline to another energy source, the car will remain. The automobile provides tremendous convenience, and while expensive to drive, one can't take public transportation for everything (like taking one's kids to after-school activities, or buying a case of wine). The challenge for cities is how to get people to drive less, to build denser neighborhoods centered around transit and services within walking distance, and to create more transit alternatives to the car.

The New Urbanism

American suburbs exploded after World War II. People abandoned crowded downtowns for more space and easy commutes by automobile. The low-density suburbs were built completely around the car. "White flight" became common as white people left for the suburbs, leaving the urban poor behind in decaying central cities. Urban renewal of the 1950s and 1960s meant knocking over the decay and putting up sterile office buildings and elevated expressways in once organic neighborhoods. When the workers left their offices at 5:00 P.M. to return to their suburban homes, the downtown business district became a ghost town.

The suburbs were built around several key assumptions: that one had a car, and that gas prices were affordable, as you needed to drive the great distance between the school, the grocery store, the shopping center, and work, as most of these weren't within walking distance. The suburbs became the new population center. Low taxes on gasoline meant Americans could drive all they wanted. European countries heavily taxed gas and consequently Europeans drove less, had denser cities, and owned smaller cars. Most European cities don't have sprawling American-style suburbs nor the gridlock traffic that so often epitomizes American cities.

Over the years, many American families had shifted from small houses in cities or the close-in suburbs for much larger houses in the growing exurbs. These were called McMansions, as they resembled small castles that took up most of the plot of land the house was built on. The term "ginormous" entered the vocabulary. These houses were energy hogs in more ways than one: a larger house took more to heat and cool it, and the owners had a larger distance to drive to work, using more gasoline.

American suburban homes in the first decade ballooned in size like a bodybuilder on steroids. They included a great room, walk-in closets, and massive kitchens, uniformly designed with granite countertops, light brown wooden cabinets, stainless steel appliances (all the better to pick up fingerprints), and a separate wine storage refrigerator. Kitchens often came equipped with an island, where guests at every cocktail and dinner party gathered while they watched the host show off skills learned on the Food Network cable channel. The "foodie" had emerged, a new breed of consumer who was especially interested in eating well, shopped at farmers markets, watched cooking shows, made novelty dishes, and ate at better restaurants. Appreciating better food became a national activity.

This suburban model remained unchallenged for five decades after World War II, but by the turn of the 21st century, a new urbanism had set in. People had tired of the suburbs, which were seen as conformist, soulless, and car-dependent. They headed back downtown. The Millennial generation was a key driver behind this, a generation that skewed toward rejecting the giant suburban house for the small apartment in the city in a walkable neighborhood.

The new urbanism called for transit-friendly neighborhoods and mix-used development that combined living with work, play, and services, all within walking distance. Neighborhoods would become dense and diverse. And to achieve that density, it meant developing upward in high-rises, rather than outward into farm country.

Young adults began moving back into cities, deciding that the public playground was just as good to raise one's children as a quarter-acre yard. People became recommitted to the idea of living close to one's neighbors, that an urban neighborhood can be like a village—in fact, they called it the "urban village." Cities like New York and Washington, D.C. transformed themselves with mayors who fixed infrastructure problems, making them desirable places to live and be part of the urban scene. Property values in those cities soared, which in turn drove gentrification, squeezing the poor and often people of color out of newly revitalized neighborhoods.

The new urbanists were generally college educated and had the means to afford city life, which is usually more expensive than the suburbs. Urban studies professor Richard Florida published an influential book in 2002 called *The Rise of the Creative Class*. People in the creative class, as he defined it, included "people in science and engineering, architecture and design, education, arts, music, and entertainment whose economic function is to create new ideas, new technology, and new creative content." There were also creative careers in "business and finance, law, health care, and related fields." About a third of the American workforce was part of this new creative class. It was growing quickly, as was the service class. This was in stark contrast to the working class, which was on a decades-long decline.[3] Some criticized Florida's ideas, but a decade after he published *The Rise of the Creative Class*, he reexamined the question.

My ideas that the talented were beginning to favor cities over suburbs, that urban centers were challenging suburban industrial park
nerdistans as locations for talent and high-tech industry, that older
cities were starting to regain some of the ground they'd lost to Sun
Belt boomtowns—were widely derided as ludicrous when I first began
to write about them. Ten years later, they aren't even controversial.[4]

There was also a downside. The creative class became part of the timeless
debate of the haves versus the have-nots. That is, those who were succeeding in
the new digital economy, and those who were falling behind. In his 2012 update,
Florida noted that the old working-class order was coming down fast. "Our
increasingly unequal society has become deeply divided, sorted, and segmented
by level of education, the kinds of work we do, and where we live, and this in turn
shapes ever more divisive culture wars and politics. One of the most significant
fault lines of our age is the growing geographic segregation of the Creative
Class and the other classes." As people self-segregated to be with their own
kind, this led to further cultural and economic separation of American society.
Corporations chose to locate in a city where the high-skill workers already live—a
win for that community, but a loss for the nation, as it made inequality worse,
especially for those cities that don't attract high-paying companies.[5]

The rejuvenation of the cities gave rise to the urban hipster. A hipster
might wear too-tight jeans while sporting a cashmere cardigan and bow tie,
his face bedecked with quirky facial hair and a loud set of nerd glasses. She
might humble-brag about her bicycle-only, car-free lifestyle as she walked
to the farmers market after her hot yoga class. He drank Pabst Blue Ribbon
for the irony factor, since many regarded PBR as swill. But hey, it had hipster
cred. Real hipsters worshipped at the altar of locally sourced, artisan-crafted
products, whether it was gin or moustache wax.

Tattoos seemed to be everywhere. Long a staple for enlisted soldiers, getting inked begat a wave of tribal armbands, Japanese calligraphy (even though
most people did not read Japanese), and arm sleeves. Lord knows what they
would look like in several decades after the ink fades and once-hard bodies
sag. But who cared? This was for now. Laser tattoo removal services also
became a thing, giving people the chance to erase the mistakes of their past.

The term *metrosexual* emerged in the early part of the decade, which
described an urban straight man whom you suspected was gay but in fact
wasn't. He dressed fashionably, got a decent haircut, had a gym-sculpted

body, and lived with his girlfriend. The line between gay and straight men became very blurry. It was so confusing!

Until the 1950s, people married before they had sex—and thus they married early, often right out of high school or immediately after college. That ideal had long since vanished. In the early 2000s, the average age for marrying pushed toward thirty. Many couples cohabitated first, and yes, that meant they were "living in sin," as it had traditionally been called, but people did it anyway. There was a societal consensus that it was best to live together first to determine if a couple really was compatible: after all, with today's longevity, a couple might spend five or six decades together. Many young people had seen their parents divorce (half of all married relationships fail, and the social stigma of divorce had worn off in the 1970s), so young adults were more careful about choosing a life partner. When Millennials finally married, they had small families, often just one or two children, and sometimes none.

Women were increasingly demanding that men make room for them in the workforce and also at home; men were expected to help raise the children, not just bring home the bacon as in the past. Parenting had shifted into a collaborative model. The stay-at-home-mom was becoming a thing of the distant past.

Another reason Millennials were marrying later was because of their enormous student loans. The price of a college education skyrocketed as universities invested heavily in upgrading their facilities—and many students took out loans to pay for their education. Having a degree generally secured a better-paying job, but at what cost? George Washington University, the most expensive college in the nation, was the first to raise annual tuition above $50,000 in 2007, which in turn prompted others to follow suit.

When the Great Recession hit in 2008, states scaled back their financial support for public colleges and universities, and students paid the difference. Many college graduates made the economically wise decision to move back in with their parents, giving rise to the term "boomerang generation." But before we can discuss the Great Recession, we have to explore its origins in the housing bubble of the early 2000s.[6]

Roots of the Housing Bubble

Housing prices nationwide tumbled in the early 1990s after the recession that followed the first Gulf War. They remained flat for much of the decade, but values began to rise again in 1997, and what followed was a nine-year boom in housing prices fueled by speculation. The housing boom between 1997 and 2006 was the largest expansion in home prices ever seen in American history. Home prices rose 74 percent during this period.[7] Robert Shiller, professor of economics at Yale University and co-creator of the Case-Shiller Home Price Index, called the housing bubble an "epidemic of irrational public enthusiasm."[8]

American salaries barely budged over the first decade, which makes the housing bubble all the more inexplicable. Instead, people used cheap credit to finance their larger-than-they-could-afford dreams. Americans were terrible savers: their debts were too high, and those Prada shoes were just too enticing. People treated their homes like piggy banks to borrow against and spend. A widespread rant was that America had become a nation of consumers instead of citizens. We existed to amass more stuff and to shop until we dropped. Economist Tyler Cowen noted sardonically, "We thought we were richer than we were."[9]

The shine wore off the stock market after the dot-com meltdown and the subsequent 9/11 recession. Many investors shifted their attention to real estate. People bought and flipped houses, treating homes as if they were stocks. Like a gambler on a winning streak, speculators kept rolling the dice, bidding up property, buying it, then flipping it to the next person for an inflated amount. The problem was, the last person owning the overappreciated house was left holding the bag. This also drove up the cost of housing to the point where first-time home buyers could no longer afford to buy. "When the music stops . . . things will be complicated," Citigroup CEO Charles Prince admitted. "But as long as the music is playing, you've got to get up and dance. We're still dancing." Housing was becoming a game of musical chairs.[10]

Financial institutions likewise looked around for the next big investment. They found it in financial obligations that funded mortgages. Mortgage-backed securities were created three decades earlier to bundle mortgages and sell these to investors. This in turn led to subprime loans. Historically, 7 percent of American houses were bought with subprime mortgages, but by 2005, about 20 percent of loans were subprime. Regulators did too little to regulate subprime, and the problem quickly got out of hand.[11]

The housing boom was built upon the shaky foundation of subprime mortgages. An entire lending industry arose to offer subprime mortgages to people who could not otherwise afford to buy, and the major banks followed suit. Subprime offered exotic mortgages, such as interest-only (you paid no principal, only interest), or an adjustable rate mortgage (ARM) that started with low rates for two to three years, then ballooned once the initial period was over. Companies like Countrywide, New Century Financial, and Washington Mutual issued obscene amounts of subprime mortgages. A mortgage broker offering a subprime mortgage was equivalent to a snake oil salesman.

The country gorged on easy credit. Eager to sell new loans, banks lifted long-existing credit standards that only offered loans to people with a proven ability to pay it back. Lenders stopped checking income statements, long a requirement for credit. Many mortgages required no money down, quite different from a generation earlier, when a 10 or 20 percent down payment was the norm. Many were loaned more than their house was actually worth. Huge amounts of fraud took place: loan officers and mortgage brokers reworked loan applications to make the numbers work and to get their commission, aided and abetted by real estate agents, closing attorneys, and the lending firms. This was a vast, unindicted crime that took advantage of the economically most vulnerable in order to earn bonuses and short-term profits.[12]

Banks had bundled together subprime mortgages into massive bond investment vehicles called collateralized debt obligations, or CDOs, then sold these on the open market and earned large fees. Many CDOs were sold internationally, which spread the subprime contagion overseas. "The CDO was, in effect, a credit laundering service for the residents of Lower Middle Class America," wrote Michael Lewis in *The Big Short*. "For Wall Street it was a machine that turned lead into gold"—and then into raw sewage. The banks flooded the market with CDOs between 2005 and 2007, until the bursting housing bubble finally pulled the plug. Subprime was a $2 trillion market. In 2005 alone, the financial industry offered $625 billion in subprime mortgages—of which more than a half trillion dollars were packed into bonds.[13] The nation's credit rating agencies (Fitch, Moody's, S&P) fumbled when they gave these investment-grade ratings, even though they were effectively junk bonds. When the bonds' value plummeted, banks had to write down the difference—and it was massive. The beginning of the end came in July 2007 when investment bank Bear Stearns closed two hedge funds that had invested heavily in CDOs.[14]

The housing boom most impacted the coastal states of California and Florida, along with Arizona and Nevada. The worst speculative boom was in Las Vegas, Phoenix, and southern Florida. These areas would witness the worst of the fallout when the bubble collapsed. Yet much of the country never witnessed the real estate boom. The heartland and Texas were passed by, and houses there barely appreciated with the rate of inflation.

Though the housing bubble was overwhelmingly pushed by the private sector, the boom was in part encouraged by federal policies intended to promote home ownership: low interest rates, tax write-offs for mortgages, and implicit federal backing for Fannie Mae and Freddie Mac, two government-sponsored enterprises, or GSEs. These two organizations bought up mortgages to recapitalize banks, thus enabling banks to loan more money. During the Clinton administration, Fannie and Freddie came under political pressure to extend home ownership to working-class and working poor people who had been excluded from credit markets, and thus they began buying subprime mortgages. Home ownership peaked above 70 percent in the mid-2000s, but then tumbled down as the housing bubble burst and several million people lost their homes.

Everyone needs a home, but not everyone needs to *own* a home. "Home-ownership, for all its advantages, is not the ideal housing arrangement for all people in all circumstances," observed Robert Shiller. Part of the market is better served by renting. And pushing people to buy homes drove development ever further out into the countryside, rather than concentrating it in urban centers in apartments and condominiums.[15]

The Housing Bubble Bursts

After the 9/11 terrorist attacks, the Federal Reserve cut interest rates to 1 percent as a means of staving off deflation. The Fed began raising rates in June 2004, taking two years to lift interest rates to 5.25 percent, a quarter point at a time. During this era of gradual tightening, Alan Greenspan retired in February 2006 after serving as Fed chairman for eighteen years. He had assumed markets were efficient and self-correcting.

The Fed hoped for a steady return to historically normal interest rates, one that would not roil the financial or housing markets. It took the steam out of the heady housing growth, and exotic subprime mortgages seemed to dry up as they became too expensive. The rampant bidding wars for a single house or condominium calmed down by 2006. But that was not the end of it.

Rising interest rates reset subprime mortgages, which proved a ticking time bomb. Adjustable-rate mortgages would reset at much higher interest rates, meaning that the buyer's monthly payments would balloon. Many families could barely afford the inflated home payments with the mortgage before it adjusted; after the balloon kicked in, they were toast. Their payments reset to the market-prevailing rate, which was often 4 percentage points or more higher. This meant their mortgage payments went up 30, 40, 50 percent, or sometimes even higher. Interest-only mortgages were even more severe: they were based on the assessed value of the home during the boom. But when housing prices declined, the banks demanded that the buyer pay the difference between the purchase and reduced value of the house, and added that into their mortgage payments. These homeowners got walloped. It's no wonder that so many people simply walked away.

The housing market peaked in April 2006. Soon prices settled back down as rising interest rates and resetting variable interest rate mortgages took their toll, but the plummet downward did not hit until the following year as subprime homeowners began to foreclose. The canary in the coalmine became New Century Financial, which restated its earnings in February 2007 to take a significant write-down of subprime mortgages. The company went out of business two months later, the first in a slew of subprime lenders to collapse.

"This precarious structure was fated to collapse as soon as the underlying card—the nonstop growth of housing prices—was pulled out," wrote President George Bush in his memoir. "That was clear in retrospect. But very few saw it at the time, including me."[16]

Nationwide, new home sales fell 26.4 percent in 2007 from the year before—the steepest drop on record, according to the U.S. Commerce Department. Foreclosures that same year rose 75 percent. This signaled that the nation's housing stock was way overbuilt, and that there were few buyers for the thousands of recently completed houses, particularly in large, manufactured developments. Including foreclosures, several million houses now sat vacant. New construction faltered.[17]

As housing became ever more expensive during the boom, many working- and middle-class families were pushed out of reach of buying without moving far out into the exurbs, or taking on an exotic mortgage. Or in many cases, both. It was the suburbs and exurbs that were hit hardest—you could draw a ring around many cities, and it was that outer ring where foreclosures were highest.

No city was hit harder by foreclosures than Stockton, California. As Silicon Valley and Bay Area housing prices skyrocketed, many working-class and service-economy people moved to that San Joaquin Valley city, where they could afford to buy, then commuted great distances to their jobs. They were doubly hit when gas prices rose; wealthier people have the disposable income to absorb the extra expense, but not the working poor. They were offered exotic loans with balloon payments, and many of them bought houses they could never otherwise afford. When the balloon payments hit in earnest in 2007, foreclosures went through the roof. Many people simply walked away from their homes, mailing the keys to the bank. It was now the bank's problem—but soon it became the nation's.

The Case-Shiller Home Price Index revealed that average home prices nationwide had dropped 18 percent between October 2007 and October 2008. Phoenix was hit hardest (a decline of 32.7 percent), followed by Las Vegas (-31.7 percent). San Francisco fell by −31 percent. Nationally, homes had fallen to their March 2004 prices, and consumer confidence, as measured by nonprofit group The Conference Board since 1967, hit an all-time low of 38.6 in December, largely explaining why retail sales for Christmas 2008 were so horrible.[18] The twenty cities in the index had fallen 23.4 percent off their peak in July 2006.[19] The news worsened in early 2009, just as Barack Obama came to the presidency. Property values in Phoenix had now fallen 51 percent from their peak. Las Vegas was not far behind at 48 percent, while Los Angeles and San Diego had each fallen 40 percent.[20]

Paradoxically, real estate in Manhattan skyrocketed after the 9/11 recession and showed little sign of abating, even after the housing bubble finally burst in 2007. Part of this was the influx of foreign property buyers into the island borough, lured by the falling dollar. Once the Great Recession hit in 2008, Manhattan finally had its turn to deflate.

The largest real estate deal in history fell apart as a result of the housing market collapse. MetLife had built 11,000 affordable, rent-controlled apartment units in Manhattan's Stuyvesant Town and Peter Cooper Village after World War II. With Manhattan property values skyrocketing, the company put the two giant complexes on the market. Tishman Speyer Properties and Black Rock Realty bought them in 2006 for $5.4 billion, intending to renovate the buildings and raise rents to market rates. A court ruled that the rents were inappropriately deregulated, and when the market value of the complexes collapsed to $2 billion, the two real estate companies simply walked away, handing the properties over to their investors to deal with.[21]

What may be surprising is that most families had traditional mortgages and were not directly impacted by the subprime foreclosures. The middle, upper-middle, and wealthy were shielded from the mortgage resetting mess—but not from the fallout. The subprime market was always a niche, albeit a large one. However, as the decline in home values rippled through the broader economy, consumers could no longer use their homes as cash machines. As home values fell, many people owed more on their mortgage than their homes were worth.

According to Robert Shiller, home valuations fell 35 percent nationwide after the housing bubble burst. Cities and counties were hit hard by falling property values. School districts are usually paid for through property taxes, and during the boom, cash was flush and schools could expand their programs, particularly to meet federal requirements behind the No Child Left Behind Act. But when property values plummeted, tax collections fell, putting a serious crimp on local spending.[22]

"We may well experience several years of a bad economy," Shiller predicted in 2008 in what was the understatement of the decade. For economic Armageddon was at hand in the Great Recession.[23]

13

The Great Recession

I n September 1998, the Long-Term Capital Management (LTCM) hedge fund collapsed after global economic crises in Korea, Russia, and elsewhere. Concerned about the repercussions for the broader financial industry, the Federal Reserve Bank of New York intervened to recapitalize the company for $3.6 billion so it could conduct an orderly liquidation. This was a pittance compared to the bailouts the Fed would hastily organize exactly ten years later. The notion of "too big to fail" was set.[1]

The dot-com meltdown in 2000 was about the bursting of the high-tech bubble, a subset of the overall market. The 2008 collapse, known as the Great Recession, was far, far worse, as it threatened to take down the entire financial system, especially those banks that had taken large positions in subprime mortgages. As the housing market was the foundation for much of the American economy, many worried that this was a house of cards.

Much of the cause of the 2008 meltdown can be attributed to the financial market deregulation of the preceding three decades, which in turn allowed the housing bubble to form. Former Federal Reserve chair Alan Greenspan had believed the market would regulate itself. Greenspan "was, shall we say, a less-than-enthusiastic regulator," wrote economist Alan Blinder. In fact, the greed of the finance industry nearly wrecked the economy—and the taxpayers had to bail them out while suffering egregious losses in their home values.[2]

Simultaneous with the housing bubble collapse came the burst of the bond bubble, an often-overlooked event that contributed to further decay of the fragile banking system. Banks, consumers, and investors were vastly overleveraged. Alan Blinder noted, "A financial system that is highly leveraged and betting massively on the continuation of bubbles is a two-pronged accident waiting to happen."[3]

Financial markets were globalized and interconnected. The U.S. financial sector had grown into a behemoth, holding $36 trillion in debt and accounting for 27 percent of American corporate profits in 2006. The banks took ever greater risks in chasing profits while regulators looked the other way. Alan Greenspan's faith in self-regulating financial markets was mistaken. All of this was avoidable had regulators—especially the Federal Reserve, which regulates financial institutions—done their job.[4]

The financial crisis was rooted in the housing bust. Credit markets had made one key assumption: American house prices would continue to rise, and thus investors could get a rising return on their investments. But when home prices fell, it proved the market's assumptions wrong, and the ripple effect was catastrophic. Far too much was built upon this shaky foundation.

The resulting Great Recession was not just an American crisis. So many Asian and European banks had bought American mortgage bonds, and when the house of cards collapsed, the financial crisis went global. The U.S. exported its financial crisis like a spreading contagion.

A very small number of people recognized what was going on—just ten or twenty people, according to Michael Lewis in *The Big Short*—and they bet against subprime. Hedge fund manager John Paulson made $20 billion for his fund by shorting the market. Private equity and hedge fund managers called themselves the Masters of the Universe for their power to make deals and bet on markets.[5]

The credit crunch began in July 2007 as the subprime party ended. Mortgage foreclosures skyrocketed as people could not meet their ballooning payments. Banks were now in deep trouble—many were way overexposed to subprime mortgages. The stock market went on a wild ride of volatility, falling one or two percent one day, then bouncing back the next. But mostly it fell.

The deterioration in underwriting and lending standards was a significant cause of the housing bubble. With the credit crunch, one crisis fueled the next like falling dominoes: housing foreclosures, then credit tightening, then enormous write-downs at financial institutions, then fear of recession, then meltdowns on exchanges worldwide. Banks had a huge amount of toxic debt on their balance sheets. It was a logjam of debt that threatened to overthrow the market.

Legendary investment sage Warren Buffet remarked to a business conference in Toronto, "It's sort of a little poetic justice, in that the people that
brewed this toxic Kool-Aid found themselves drinking a lot of it in the end."
He explained how risk had been repriced—returning to a more rational time
when lenders finally started looking at whether people had the ability to pay
back the money they were lent. The credit crunch was not about a shortage
of money—it was just that the banks had stopped lending to each other and
to businesses out of fear that they would not be paid back. "I wouldn't quite
call it a credit crunch. Funds are available," Buffett said. "Money is available, and it's really quite cheap because of the lowering of rates that has taken
place." Even a sage like Buffett is wrong now and then. Even he couldn't
foresee how bad it was about to get.[6]

Throughout 2007 and 2008, the U.S. economy experienced a severe,
even violent repricing of assets. Commodities were repriced in line with high
global demand; housing prices fell after the bubble burst; high-risk bonds
were repriced to demand a premium; gas prices went through the roof; airline
tickets got a lot more expensive; and food costs rose. The dollar lost value
against the euro as the U.S. economy revalued itself in line with its actual
worth. All of this was painful, but it was also necessary for a functioning
market economy. Most Americans just held on and weathered the storm. Like
a ship passing through a storm, the storm would eventually pass, one hoped.

In a global market, capital can be easily transferred to another location.
With severely tightened credit markets, some companies had to take foreign
bailouts. Sovereign wealth funds from wealthy Middle East and Asian
countries saw an opportunity to invest in the U.S. on the cheap and pumped
money into ailing financial firms. Bear Stearns, Citigroup, Merrill Lynch,
Morgan Stanley, and UBS all received substantial investments. Banks were
not the only ones affected: the private equity firm Carlyle Group took a
capital infusion from the Emirate of Abu Dhabi, selling 7.5 percent of itself
for $1.35 billion.

Citigroup was formed in 1998 to become a financial supermarket—a
one-stop shop for all the financial needs of a business or consumer—after the
Depression-era Glass-Steagall Act was repealed in the 1990s. Glass-Steagall
had mandated that financial companies could either be consumer lenders or
investment banks, but not both. The merger combined the Citicorp bank
with Travelers insurance, and it also owned a retail brokerage, Smith Barney.
But the concept never worked. The company had massive exposure to the

subprime market, and as the housing bubble burst, foreclosures skyrocketed. The banking giant was left with a huge portfolio of worthless CDOs, all of which were now a liability.

In the third quarter of 2007, after writing down a $17 billion loss, Citigroup sold a 4.9 percent stake to the Abu Dhabi Investment Authority, the Arab country's sovereign wealth fund to recapitalize after its massive mortgage-related losses. The bank began massive write-downs, forcing its CEO Charles Prince to resign (the same man who admitted he was dancing to subprime). In the fourth quarter, Citigroup took another $18 billion write-down and a $14.5 billion injection from the Singapore and Kuwaiti governments, Saudi Prince Alwaleed bin Talal, the state of New Jersey, and others. It sliced its dividend. Likewise, Merrill Lynch sold $6.6 billion to the Korean and Kuwaiti governments and took a $14.6 billion write-down.

Hundreds of smaller shops that specialized in subprime mortgages went bankrupt, throwing thousands of people out of work. Even large, established firms like Countrywide Financial were in deep trouble. In fact, Bank of America picked up Countrywide for $4 billion—a steal at one-quarter its book value—but it took a larger company to finally help stabilize the credit markets.

Banks had to write down billions in worthless CDOs caused by foreclosures. The credit markets responded by drying up: banks simply couldn't get money, and those that had it weren't willing to loan it for anything. This hung like a dark cloud over the market, as no one would know the full extent of the mortgage write-downs until the banks finally accounted for all their losses.

By the end of 2007, American consumers were tapped out. The economy was teetering on the edge from the housing bust and credit crunch, while the cost of living kept rising. Gas surpassed $100 a barrel in January 2008 and headed higher. Both prices and unemployment were rising. After remaining low throughout the decade, the Consumer Price Index shot up to 4.1 percent in 2007—the highest rate since 1990. The fear of stagflation was in the air. This created a dilemma for the Federal Reserve, which would normally raise interest rates to ward off inflation. The economy officially went into recession in December 2007.

The stock market plunged in January 2008 as Wall Street bet that the economy was turning down. By January 19, the S&P 500 had fallen 15.3 percent from its October 2007 peak. That news hit hard, and the world's stock markets plunged as a result. The Fed cut interest rates by 75 basis points (the largest cut in its history) on January 22, and then another half point a week later, lowering interest rates to 3 percent. The stock market briefly rebounded, then fell even more in February as the market concluded that a recession was at hand. This was just the beginning of one of the worst years on record for the stock market.

Three crucial figures now enter our story as the economy took a nosedive: Treasury Secretary Hank Paulson, Federal Reserve chair Ben Bernanke, and Federal Reserve of New York president Timothy Geithner. Paulson was the CEO of investment bank Goldman Sachs when President Bush appointed him in 2006 as treasury secretary. That same year, Alan Greenspan retired as chairman of the Federal Reserve, and Bush nominated Bernanke to replace him. Bernanke was an academic who had studied the Great Depression and how central banks had failed to effectively respond to the crisis. Lastly, Geithner had the crucial position at the Federal Reserve Bank of New York, which watched over Wall Street. These three men would take point as the banking system teetered on collapse.

In March 2008, investment bank Bear Stearns signaled it was near failure. The company had made enormous bets on subprime mortgages and lost. Lenders were no longer willing to lend to the company. There was a classic run on the bank as investors demanded their money back. JPMorgan Chase and Tim Geithner at the New York Fed came to its rescue—one of the first times in years that the Fed intervened to prop up a company. Nor would it be the last. JPMorgan acquired Bear Stearns for an astonishingly low $2 per share—though it soon raised the bid to $10 a share. (Bear Stearns had traded at $170 a share a year earlier.) The Federal Reserve loaned $30 billion to JPMorgan to assist the acquisition. Their thinking was that, if this one company failed, the impact would disastrously reverberate across the market.[7]

There was a groundswell of opposition to the rescue of Bear Stearns. Economists spoke of moral hazard: rewarding risky behavior, such as providing low health insurance rates for people who smoke, building a vacation house on a hurricane-prone beach, pushing underfunded pension obligations onto following generations, or expecting a governmental bailout after taking on a mortgage far larger than you could afford. The key thing was that someone would be there to clean up the mess you made. Many opponents to the rescue screamed as loud as they could: *Let them fail!* Ben Bernanke, chairman of the Federal Reserve, addressed the dilemma of moral hazard in his memoir:

Some of the critics were ideologues (the free market is always right) or uninformed (the economy will be just fine if a few Wall Street firms get their just deserts). Some simply railed against the unfairness of bailing out Wall Street giants but not the little guy on Main Street. Personally, I felt considerable sympathy for this last argument. (I would wince every time I saw a bumper sticker reading "Where's my bailout?") But it was in everyone's interest, whether or not they realized it, to protect the economy from the consequences of a catastrophic failure of the financial system.[8]

Tim Geithner, president of the New York Fed, likewise took on the moral-hazard argument:

The obvious objection to government help for troubled firms was that it rewarded the arsonists who set the system on fire. This objection took two forms. One was a moral argument about justice, what I called the "Old Testament view." The venal should be punished. The irresponsible shouldn't be bailed out. The other was an economic argument about incentives, the "moral hazard" critique. If you protect risk-takers from losses today, they'll take too many risks tomorrow, creating new crises in the future. If you rescue pyromaniacs, you'll end up with more fires.[9]

Despite its unpopularity, Bear Stearns was rescued and sold to JPMorgan. The rescue calmed the markets for several months, but it was just a question of time before the next crisis arose. The Federal Reserve cut interest rates by another .75 percent down to 2.25 percent to shore up an economy that everyone viewed as falling rapidly into recession. It then cut rates again to 2 percent, but below that it did not have much room to maneuver. Congress responded with a $168 billion economic stimulus package in spring 2008, putting cash directly into the hands of middle-class families. This provided a small economic uptick, but consumers largely used the stimulus checks to fill their gas tanks, as fuel peaked in July at $4.11 per gallon. The stock market moved sideways, rather than continuing its downward spiral. But by June, the shock of $140-per-barrel gas hit, and the stock market tanked once again into bear territory, down 20 percent from its October 2007 high.

It got worse. A year after the credit crunch began, the credit markets were still in turmoil, finally unraveling to the point of threatening Fannie Mae and Freddie Mac, the congressionally chartered mortgage giants that purchased more than half of all mortgages in the country. Many feared the federal government would have to bail out the two companies. In July 2008, Treasury Secretary Henry Paulson requested that Congress give him a "bazooka," authorizing the Treasury Department to save the two government-sponsored enterprises. That same month, the Federal Deposit Insurance Corporation seized IndyMac Bank, another mortgage originator, and liquidated its assets in order to stave off further financial disaster. IndyMac was just one of many banks the FDIC seized that year.

August is traditionally a quiet month on markets as traders are away on vacation. It was only a lull in the crisis. The Department of Labor reported that the unemployment rate rose to 6.1 percent, the highest level in five years. Companies had been laying off employees throughout the year to cut costs. A number of industries, such as airlines and construction, were in recession.

President Bush largely stayed out of sight during the 2008 financial crisis and let the Treasury and Federal Reserve handle the response. He believed in free markets and was not disposed toward intervening, as companies that had taken undue risks should pay the price, but he soon realized that this could undermine the entire financial system. Bush remarked, "If we're really looking at another Great Depression, you can be damn sure I'm going to be Roosevelt, not Hoover."[10]

Once Labor Day had passed, the markets trembled from a violent earthquake brought on by a loss of investor confidence. It started with Fannie Mae and Freddie Mac, and shook its way through the market in a matter of weeks, leaving carnage in its wake. When the market lost faith in the two companies, which together guaranteed $5 trillion in mortgages, Hank Paulson used his bazooka. He placed Fannie and Freddie in federal conservatorship on Sunday, September 7, just six months after the Federal Reserve engineered the rescue of Bear Stearns. That is, the government put the two companies under bankruptcy-like protection so they could reorganize their finances. Paulson nationalized the two companies. The Treasury Department promised to inject necessary capital into them, a bailout that could potentially cost the taxpayers $200 billion. They argued that this was necessary to stabilize the housing market, which continued its downward spiral.[11]

As the crisis deepened, the federal government took an interventionist role in the private lending market, all to reestablish faith in the credit markets that were so crucial to the American economy. Fannie and Freddie went from *implied* to *de facto* federal backing with the government rescue. The bailout of Fannie and Freddie was deeply unpopular as critics screamed "Socialism!"

But that was not the end of the crisis. The day after Fannie Mae and Freddie Mac were put under conservatorship, Lehman Brothers—one of the big five investment banks on Wall Street—signaled it was near the end of its rope. Lehman had more exposure than most investment banks to the subprime market. It recorded a $3.9 billion loss in mortgage-backed securities and desperately attempted to split off its real estate portfolio. Its stock priced plunged. The Treasury Department stepped in to help find a buyer for the company, but this time Paulson was unwilling to guarantee a purchase with taxpayer dollars. He didn't believe the public had the appetite to bail out Lehman. The secretary drew the line: the federal government would not continue bailing out Wall Street firms that had gambled on subprime mortgages. Treasury signaled that it would let companies fail for their sins, and that the market would have to absorb the losses. Populist fury opposed bailouts, and Paulson recognized it was a presidential election year. He also believed, like with the Bear Stearns rescue in March, that more solvent companies could rescue Lehman.

Unfortunately, Paulson and Geithner could not find a buyer for Lehman Brothers. After a weekend of brinksmanship—the same weekend that Galveston, Texas, took a direct hit from Hurricane Ike—Lehman Brothers filed for bankruptcy on September 15. The Dow Jones fell 504 points on the news. Later that week, the British investment bank Barclays purchased Lehman's U.S. operations for a meager $1.75 billion.

Thus began the Great Recession, the most significant economic crisis since the Great Depression of the 1930s. Hyperbole aside, the collapse of Lehman Brothers was a catastrophe. The recession had actually started nine months earlier, but Lehman was its biggest casualty, and its collapse triggered the financial terror that followed. Wall Street historian Roger Lowenstein wrote, "The trouble was not that so much followed Lehman, but that so much had preceded it."[12] If the subprime mess hadn't poisoned the financial system, the market might well have absorbed the collapse of Lehman. Instead it inspired panic. "Perhaps the economy could have crumbled anyway," wrote

Aaron Ross Sorkin in his landmark book *Too Big to Fail*, "but Lehman's failure clearly hastened its collapse."[13]

Just a day after Lehman Brothers filed for bankruptcy, insurer American International Group (AIG) warned that it would also need an infusion of cash to survive after credit rating agencies downgraded its debt. The company had a trillion-dollar balance sheet. It had insured sub-prime mortgages, and banks were demanding payment on these policies. The Federal Reserve initially said it would not help, but when the other bankers could not provide financing in time, and after realizing that the effects of Lehman's collapse were rippling across the system, the Fed made an astonishing deal: it injected $85 billion into AIG in exchange for 79.9 percent of the company. This step effectively nationalized the company and transferred AIG's liabilities to the taxpayers. The Fed reasoned that the consequences for the global financial market would be too dire if AIG went bankrupt—the company was indeed too big to fail. AIG burned through this loan in a matter of weeks, and the Fed injected another $38 billion into the company. The company soon burned through most of that as it tried to pay off its bad debts. At the end of October, AIG came back to the well for another $21 billion, raising the federal line of credit to the company to $144 billion. Eventually the loan would reach $180 billion.

"Lehman weekend, which ultimately became Lehman-AIG week, trans-formed a year-old crisis, already exceptionally severe, into the worst financial panic in our nation's history," observed Federal Reserve chair Ben Bernanke.[14]

Meanwhile, Bank of America agreed to purchase investment bank Merrill Lynch for $50 billion; the latter company put itself up for sale when it realized it could be damaged by fallout from Lehman. Merrill Lynch had $55 billion in subprime mortgages on its books, and would end up writing off nearly all of this. This would have sunk the company, had it not sold itself to Bank of America. (Seven months later, it was revealed that Bank of America wanted to pull out of the merger, but Bernanke and Paulson threatened to remove the board if they did not go through with it.) At the same time, the Federal Reserve pumped hundreds of billions of dollars into the banking system to maintain liquidity so that the credit markets would not freeze up.[15]

The stock market plummeted. A huge question loomed: Who's next to fail? Investing began to feel like a blood sport. Even money market funds froze up. These funds provide much of the short-term lending for companies in their day-to-day operations. The collapse of Lehman Brothers made every banker fearful that they would not get their money back, and so they simply stopped loaning it.

Wall Street was fundamentally changed with the disappearance in one weekend of two independent investment banks, Lehman and Merrill Lynch, leaving just two standing: Goldman Sachs and Morgan Stanley. Within days, both companies ended their tenure as the last surviving independent investment banks. They transformed themselves into bank holding companies, which also meant they were now subject to much more regulation than before. But the two companies saw this as necessary to survive.

The self-proclaimed Masters of the Universe turned out only to be full of hubris. Through the massive intervention, the American taxpayer was on the hook for Wall Street's devastating losses. "The world's most powerful and most highly paid financiers had been entirely discredited; without government intervention every single one of them would have lost his job; and yet those same financiers were using the government to enrich themselves," wrote Michael Lewis in *The Big Short*. [16]

Treasury Secretary Hank Paulson had formerly been a believer in hands-off regulation, but the market meltdown of late summer 2008 changed his mind. The Treasury staged an extraordinary market intervention to avert another Great Depression. It had all unraveled remarkably fast. After the Lehman Brothers collapse stunned the market, the secretary used every tool at his disposal to right the overturned ox cart. When it was over, everything had changed. [17]

"The strategy was a breathtaking intervention in the free market. It flew against all my instincts," noted President Bush afterward. "But it was necessary to pull the country out of the panic. I decided that the only way to preserve the free market in the long run was to intervene in the short run." [18]

Laissez-faire capitalism had failed. Greed nearly destroyed the system, and the global economy faced collapse. There was no option for the federal government but to intervene, though this was unpopular and came at a steep political price. Why should greedy bankers be bailed out for their own malfeasance, many wondered? Meanwhile, the five million households who had lost their homes had no rescue package of their own.

Financial historian Roger Lowenstein wrote in *The End of Wall Street*: "Less than a generation after the fall of the Berlin Wall, when prevailing orthodoxy held that the free market could govern itself, and when financial regulation seemed destined for near irrelevancy, the United States was compelled to socialize lending and mortgage risk, and even the ownership of banks, on a scale that would have made Lenin smile."[19]

Trying to get ahead of the next banking failure, Ben Bernanke and Hank Paulson proposed a systemic solution: the federal government would buy up all the toxic debt, allowing corporations to remove the bad debt from their balance sheets, and thus restore order in the credit markets. They called it the Troubled Asset Relief Program, or TARP. It meant all this debt would be shifted to the taxpayers at an estimated cost of $700 billion. This was the largest corporate rescue plan in history, though others called it a bailout.

On September 18—just a day after the AIG rescue and three days after the collapse of Lehman Brothers—Bernanke and Paulson met with congressional leaders to discuss the rescue package. "We need to buy hundreds of billions of dollars of assets," Paulson said, shying away from saying *trillion*. He warned that they needed this new authority within days. What would happen if Congress declined, he was asked? "May God help us all," he replied.[20]

TARP created a massive backlash, especially on the political right as Republican populists demagogued against bailing out wealthy bankers. Many called it socialism and corporate welfare. Economics historian Adam Tooze wrote, "In the response to the financial crisis of 2008–2009 there was a clear logic operating. It was a class logic, admittedly—'Protect Wall Street first, worry about Main Street later.'"[21]

There was an estimated $2 trillion in toxic assets on corporate balance sheets, but no one really knew if the TARP amount was too high or too low. All they knew was that corporations, financial firms in particular, were awash in bad investments, and the news just got grimmer and grimmer, quarter after quarter, as these companies made multi-billion dollar write-downs. And as the housing market continued to deflate, mortgage-backed securities got ever more toxic. As the recession deepened and unemployment rose, the value of these bonds kept sinking.

The federal government seized the assets of failing mortgage giant Washington Mutual on September 25, then immediately sold part of the company to JPMorgan. The Lehman Brothers and Washington Mutual bankruptcies now topped WorldCom as the largest bankruptcies in history. The failure of Washington Mutual triggered a run on Wachovia, seen as the next vulnerable bank.

The last week of September 2008 proved momentous, a week that would make or break the banking system. On Monday, September 29, the House of Representatives rejected TARP, the Bush administration's $700 billion bailout package. Lawmakers had heard from their constituents, and many were angry: they did not want a bailout for corporate malfeasance. The Dow Jones tanked by 778 points, or nearly 7 percent, to close at 10,365.45, the largest one-day point decline in its history. An estimated $1.2 trillion in market value vanished in one day.[22]

Congress rethought its stance on the bailout package, and on Friday, October 3, voted and passed the bailout. President Bush signed the bill, the Emergency Economic Stabilization Act, into law. Voters were highly displeased with the bailout, and this impacted how they voted, not just in the upcoming presidential election a month later, but for years afterward. Populism emerged against the TARP bailout, the feeling that the system was rigged against them, that the rich were getting bailed out for their misbehavior.

Even with TARP's passage, the markets were not yet out of the woods. The following Monday, October 6, investors decided that the bailout was not enough and continued the rout. The Dow closed down 370 points to end at 9955.50. It was the first time it had closed below 10,000 in four years. The meltdown spilled over into global markets as a worldwide panic ensued. Everything was falling at once—stocks, bonds, real estate, commodities—as investors fled to safety, especially to U.S. Treasury bonds. Global credit markets froze, and central banks injected billions in cash and short-term loans into the system, but to little avail. The market had voted: it was clear that a global recession was at hand.

On October 7, the Dow Jones fell another 5.1 percent, or 508 points, to 9447.11. Early the next morning, the Federal Reserve ordered an emergency interest rate cut of a half point, down to 1.5 percent, and central bankers worldwide likewise lowered their interest rates. The following day, the Dow fell 2 percent, or 189.01 points, to 9258.10. On October 9, the Dow swooned 678.91 or 7.3 percent, down to 8579.19. Remarkably, this was the one-year anniversary of its all-time high of 14,198. On Friday, October 10, buyers finally showed up in a whipsaw market where trading ranged over a thousand points. Sellers finally won the day, driving the market down 1.5 percent, or 128 points, to 8451.19. The market had lost 18 percent in one week. It was the worst week in Wall Street history. The market had fallen 40 percent in one year.

On Monday, October 13—Columbus Day—the stock market finally jolted back to life. The Treasury announced that it would take equity shares in nine major banks that needed recapitalization, investing $250 billion in the institutions, and partly nationalizing them in an unprecedented step. Banks would be expected to pay the government a dividend, and they could eventually buy out the government stake once the crisis passed. Some 650 banks would use TARP funds to recapitalize. Central bankers overseas took similar steps to shore up their banks. In addition, the Federal Reserve offered to produce as many greenbacks as the global economy needed. Since the credit crisis had spilled over to global markets, and many transactions such as oil were priced only in dollars, the credit freeze meant there was a shortage of currency. The stock market loved the Fed's plan, and it soared 936.42 points, or 11 percent, to 9387.61.

The party was short-lived. Consumers had throttled back their spending in September as the financial crisis unfolded. October retail sales were even worse. The stock market on Wednesday gave up most of the ground it had gained on Monday, falling 733.08 points, or 7.87 percent, to 8577.91. Stocks in Asia and Europe tanked as well, as economic activity withered. Even China, the manufacturer to the world, experienced decelerating growth. Its economy had grown at double-digit rates for years, but the global recession acted as a giant brake.

The meltdown continued the following week as fears of a global recession mounted. Layoffs persisted, and it was clear that Corporate America was cutting back its spending, just as consumers had. As earnings season commenced in late October, the market realized that corporate earnings were in a tailspin. The bank Wachovia, which Wells Fargo had recently won in a bidding war with Citigroup, posted the largest quarterly loss ever at $23.7 billion. On October 22, the market fell another 514.45 points (5.69 percent) to close at 8519.21.

If there was any upside to the financial panic, it was that oil prices tumbled to $50 per barrel just four months after its July peak of $140 as traders implicitly knew the fallout from Wall Street would mean a slower economy. Oil prices fell as fast in the fall as they had risen in the spring.

Former Federal Reserve chairman Alan Greenspan had failed to grasp how deep the housing market implosion would impact the broader economy. He testified before the House Oversight and Government Reform Committee in October that he was mistaken in earlier opposing regulations for the financial markets. Greenspan told the committee, "I made a mistake in presuming that the self-interests of organizations, specifically banks and others, were such as that they were best capable of protecting their own shareholders and their equity in the firms." He championed financial deregulation in his years overseeing the Federal Reserve, which led to lax banking regulations and questionable lending practices, such as subprime.[23]

On October 24, the Dow Jones fell 3.59 percent to 8378.95, down 312.30 points, its lowest level since April 2003. International exchanges fared even worse. Since September 1, an estimated $16.3 trillion worth of equities had evaporated on global stock markets. Hedge fund managers who had once considered themselves Masters of the Universe saw their wealthy clients run for the doors, selling their stakes in funds and contributing even further to the market meltdown.[24]

The Treasury realized that the meltdown was reaching into the insurance companies, many of whom had insured the bonds that backed subprime mortgages, and so decided to widen the bailout by taking ownership stakes in a number of insurers. It also provided $7.7 billion in funding to PNC Financial Services Group of Pittsburgh to buy out troubled lender National City Bank of Cleveland, a city that was hit hard by subprime foreclosures.

American consumers watched the meltdown happen before their eyes. Retirement accounts seemed to evaporate. In fifteen months, an estimated $2 trillion in retirement savings had disappeared.[25] Consumers saw the mounting layoffs at corporations and witnessed their retirement portfolios fall 40 percent. People felt much poorer—and it's true, they were. The Conference Board's consumer confidence index fell 23 points in October to 38, the lowest record for the index since it began in 1967.[26]

Consumer spending accounted for about 70 percent of the American economy. With the markets in free fall, consumer fears of recession became a self-fulfilling prophecy. The economy was the hot topic on every blog, newspaper, radio show, and website. Once consumers saw their home values and savings disappear, and witnessed the unemployment rate rise above 7 percent, they ratcheted back their spending, which slowed the economy even more.

On October 28, the stock market staged a remarkable rally. Central bankers around the world signaled interest rate cuts, including the Federal Reserve, and the credit markets finally seemed to thaw as the Treasury's massive investment kicked in. The Dow Jones rose nearly 11 percent, rising 889.35 points to 9065.12, the second-largest gain on record. The Fed did not disappoint, cutting interest rates a half point down to 1 percent, just two weeks after its last cut—and now the same rate as five years before that had helped fuel the housing bubble.

It was astonishing how long the financial crisis had lasted. The housing market bubble had burst in mid-2007, and the credit crunch had already lasted fourteen months before the stunning market meltdown in September and October 2008. Even more stunning was the government's response. "Frankly we had no choice but to fly by the seat of our pants, making it up as we went along," noted Treasury Secretary Hank Paulson afterward. Only the government had the resources to rescue the markets. By the end of the crisis, federal power in the finance industry had been transformed.[27]

The Great Recession was devastating. Four million homes had foreclosed, while another 4.5 million were in the process of foreclosing or were late for a mortgage payment. The recession destroyed nearly nine million jobs. Unemployment peaked at 10.2 percent in October 2009. African Americans were especially hit hard with a jobless rate of 16 percent, followed by Hispanics at 13.2 percent. Some 26 million people were unemployed, underemployed, or had left the workforce altogether. The Great Recession wiped out $17 trillion in household wealth—about three times as much as the dot-com meltdown in 2000.[28]

"This, the most wrenching financial crisis since the Great Depression, caused a terrible recession in the U.S. and severe harm around the world," wrote Hank Paulson afterward. "Yet it could have been so much worse. Had it not been for unprecedented interventions by the U.S. and other governments, many more financial institutions would have gone under—and economic damage would have been far greater and longer lasting." During the Great Depression, unemployment reached 25 percent and the American economy shrank by a third. Compared to that historic event, the Great Recession could indeed have been far worse.[29]

The market meltdown of fall 2008 had consequences that reverberated for years afterward. The Tea Party would rise out of opposition to the bailouts, while the Millennial generation was heavily traumatized just as it entered the workforce. Even as the federal government was staging its massive intervention to save the economy, voters were considering whom to vote for in the 2008 presidential election.

14
The 2008 Election

The Great Recession formed the backdrop for the 2008 presidential election. It felt like an earthquake as the economy melted down. The public desperately wanted change after eight years of the Bush administration and its many wars, and they looked to new leadership to rescue the economy. Change was what the country demanded. Dan Balz and Haynes Johnson, who published a detailed history of the 2008 election, called it "nothing less than a battle for America."[1]

Democrats had an advantage in that President Bush was deeply unpopular and that there was no incumbent. Dick Cheney was not running for office. A large number of Democratic senators threw their hat in the ring, including Joe Biden, Hillary Clinton, Chris Dodd, John Edwards (John Kerry's 2004 running mate), and Barack Obama, along with New Mexico Governor Bill Richardson. Hillary Clinton was the presumed frontrunner because of her presidential husband Bill and her decades of experience in public service, but it quickly became a Clinton-Obama showdown.

The 2008 presidential campaign proved both exceptional and historic. This was the first time that both a woman (Clinton) and a black candidate (Obama) ran for the highest office of the land. Clinton ran on a platform of experience, while Obama stressed change, but otherwise there was little ideological difference between the two. The Clintons were very popular within the black community, which initially sided with her, rather than Obama. Young voters in particular lined up behind Obama: they wanted change from the eight years of George Bush.

But was America ready for a woman or a black man to be president? Pollster John Zogby affirmed that the country was. In June 2007, he measured that 72 percent of 18–27-year-olds agreed that the country was ready for an African American president; 64 percent of 28–41-year-olds, 61 percent of 42–61-year-olds, and 55 percent of 62–80-year-olds agreed. He also showed that nearly identical numbers believed the country was ready for a woman president: 76 percent of 18–27-year-olds; 64 percent of 28–41-year-olds, 62 percent of 42–61-year-olds, and 60 percent of 62–80-year-olds. [2]

Obama was a fairly fresh face to voters. Those who tuned in saw his riveting keynote at the 2004 Democratic convention which rocketed him to national prominence and a seat in the U.S. Senate. They were entranced by the man, but they knew little of him.

Obama had published his autobiography in 1995, *Dreams from My Father*, two years before he entered the world of politics. Obama grappled with racial identity, as his father was born in Kenya and was black, while his mother was white. His father abandoned him at an early age. Obama's mother took him to live in Indonesia, then sent him back to Hawaii, where he was largely raised by his grandparents. Growing up, he was known as Barry.

Obama had a compelling biography. He was a lawyer and the first black editor of the *Harvard Law Review*. He taught at the University of Chicago Law School and worked as a community organizer. Obama married Michelle Robinson in 1992, and the couple had two daughters. He was elected to the Illinois state senate in 1997. Obama was biracial, and his Chicago district was diverse. He never pandered toward black issues, but always understood there was a coalition of constituent interests he had to support. Obama published *The Audacity of Hope* in 2006, a common strategy for presidential candidates to lay out their political philosophies in detail.

Obama was cool and supremely confident. He was bookish, cerebral, and an intellectual who had contempt for how Washington worked. He remained unruffled, thoughtful, unsentimental, and was not prone to outbursts or excessive passion, lending him the nickname "No Drama Obama." He was empirical, his decision-making driven by facts, rather than by gut. He was a gifted orator, and people responded well to his presidential demeanor. Obama had the temperament of Woodrow Wilson. He was attractive, fit, and youthful like John F. Kennedy. He painted a great narrative for his campaign—an American success story, the son of a Kenyan immigrant father and white American mother. People found Obama an embodiment of the

American dream, and they found his story inspiring. It was easy to see why voters fell in love with the man.

Biographer David Maraniss described Obama as cautious and remote, always thinking ahead to avoid life's traps. Obama was "a double outsider, both as a biracial kid and a cross-cultural kid, living in a foreign country, often on the move, tending toward contradictory feelings of inclusiveness and rootlessness," Maraniss wrote. "He stands not alone but apart, with the self-awareness of a skeptical witness to everything around him, including his own career."[3]

Unlike much of the country's African American population, Obama was not descended from slaves. Some argued that he was "not black enough," that he couldn't know what it was like to be black.[4] Obama himself played down his identity as a black person. His surrogates often proclaimed, "Obama is not a black man running for president, but a presidential candidate who happens to be black." This statement was intended to broaden his appeal beyond his political base in the African American community—and it was also a promise that he wouldn't focus just on black issues as president.[5]

"As a candidate for the presidency of the United States, he did not decry the United States for its unfair treatment of black people in both the past and the present," noted Professor Fredrick Harris, who was a keen observer of politics and race and an Obama critic. "He instead proclaimed the failure of blacks themselves to hold up their end of the bargain as citizens in a nation full of freedom and opportunity."[6]

Obama offended rural whites when he discussed their bitterness during a California fundraiser. He meant it as a point of empathy by acknowledging their ordeal during the Bush years and the economic recession, but it was taken as anything but: "So it's not surprising then that they get bitter, they cling to guns or religion or antipathy to people who aren't like them or anti-immigrant sentiment or anti-trade sentiment as a way to explain their frustrations."[7] Journalist Tim Alberta noted that "Obama was a perfect villain for the forgotten masses of flyover country."[8]

Obama organized a sophisticated political operation that targeted younger voters, many of whom had never voted before. He focused on reaching these voters through both grassroots and Internet campaigning. During the campaign, Obama was vocally critical of the Iraq War. He was elected to the Senate in 2004, and thus didn't have the tainted authorization of force vote on his record, unlike Biden and Clinton.

In the initial primaries, Obama took Iowa, while Clinton took New Hampshire. Senator Edward Kennedy, scion of the Kennedy dynasty, younger brother to JFK, and leader of the liberal wing of the Democratic Party, endorsed Obama, as did Caroline Kennedy, JFK's daughter, at the time of the South Carolina primary in February 2008, which Obama won. Senator Kennedy had extracted a promise from Obama to pursue health care reform.

Clinton and Obama raced neck and neck through the primaries before Obama finally clinched the Democratic nomination to be potentially the first black president in American history. It demonstrated how far Americans had come. Many were relieved that the Bush-Clinton dynastic struggles were broken, as if the War of the Roses had come to an end. Americans have no need for aristocracy or oligarchs, we believed, and anytime one family stays in power too long, we grow restless and resentful.

Obama chose Senator Joe Biden of Delaware as his vice president. "Uncle Joe," as everyone called him, was a well-liked six-term senator, having been first elected in 1972. He was known for his occasional verbal gaffes and profanity, but that was also what made him relatable. Biden never pretended to be perfect. He coupled strong working-class appeal with foreign policy experience and bipartisan credentials.

❖

On the Republican side, former New York mayor Rudy Giuliani, Arkansas governor Mike Huckabee, Senator John McCain, and Massachusetts governor Mitt Romney competed for the nomination. None of these were strong candidates, and none of them could match the Republican Party's sainted leader, Ronald Reagan. John McCain edged out the other candidates. The feisty Vietnam War hero had survived as a prisoner of war for more than five years and was a self-described maverick who often bucked his own party. McCain had been a major supporter of the Iraq War, and that hindered his popularity. He was also fighting the receding tide of the Bush years and the collapsing economy. When House Republicans voted down the TARP rescue plan on September 29, 2008, they doomed McCain's candidacy.

John McCain's key campaign message was that Barack Obama lacked experience—but then he picked Alaska governor Sarah Palin as his running mate, who was completely inexperienced on the national level. McCain selected Palin with minimal vetting, believing it would improve his support among women (it didn't). She instantly became a celebrity. Palin was the first Republican woman to run for vice president, and only the second woman in history (the first was Geraldine Ferraro in 1984, Walter Mondale's choice for VP). She was also an evangelical, so selecting her was a way of reaching out to both evangelical and female voters. Most people had never heard of Sarah Palin before, but they soon found out about her. Choosing Palin was a costly mistake.

Sarah Palin should have been a historical footnote. She was an unelectable vanity candidate. Palin was ambitious for the sake of ambition, but she didn't actually have much to offer, beyond being mayor of a small town and governor of Alaska for two years before abruptly resigning. Her foreign policy experience comprised of her statement, "I can see Russia from my house." In media interviews, her lack of experience and knowledge quickly became obvious. Right-wing populists loved her, as she seemed like one of the regular people, however willfully misinformed. In part because McCain chose the inexperienced Palin as his vice president, former secretary of state Colin Powell, who was a Republican, endorsed Obama for the presidency in October.

Race was an unavoidable backdrop of the 2008 presidential campaign. There were some on the right who had obvious trepidations about the prospect of a black president; at a town hall in Minnesota, John McCain faced down hostility from attendees who were frightened of an Obama presidency. One woman even accused Obama of being an Arab. McCain took the microphone back and reproached her, saying that the campaign was about the issues. He defended Obama as a decent family man.

Right-wing conspiracy theorists known as "birthers" insisted that Obama was not born in the U.S., that he was Muslim, and that he was a socialist. This was a form of not-so-subtle racism designed to discredit the black candidate. Michelle Obama and her husband largely ignored the racist attacks, at least in public, choosing the high road instead. "When they go low, we go high," she would later famously say.[9]

When an inflammatory 2003 video emerged of a sermon by Reverend Jeremiah Wright, Obama's pastor, Obama denounced the remarks in a landmark speech in Philadelphia that was as important to his campaign as Abraham Lincoln's at Cooper Union. "And for as long as I live, I will never forget that, in no other country on Earth is my story even possible," he stated. "It's a story that hasn't made me the most conventional candidate. But it is a story that has seared into my genetic makeup the idea that this nation is more than the sum of its parts—that out of many, we are truly one." This was the Obama who appealed to a broad range of people by in part playing down his blackness.[10]

The civil rights generation, led by such icons as Al Sharpton, Jesse Jackson, and John Lewis, was getting on in years. These leaders had been instrumental in winning fundamental rights for the black community. There was, however, a limitation in their broader appeal in that they framed every question in terms of the black experience. The generation that came after had a broader agenda: access to education and health care, and reduction in crime and incarceration. Many of them brought significant experience from corporate America and major law firms. There was an intergenerational conflict between older blacks who led the civil rights movement, and younger blacks, educated and ambitious, who did not want to be told to wait their turn to lead. In essence Obama jumped to the head of the line, in more ways than one.[11]

The torch continued to pass between generations as younger blacks were elected to be mayors, city councilmen, and to Congress. Eliot Spitzer, the white, steamrolling governor of New York who had served as the state's attorney general and had taken on Wall Street after the dot-com meltdown, resigned in March 2008 after he was exposed as a frequent customer of a prostitution ring. He was replaced by the lieutenant governor, David Paterson, the first African American governor of New York. Paterson, who was blind and had to memorize his speeches, was the son of a long-term New York politician, Basil Paterson.

While the 2006 election was a referendum on Iraq, the central issue in 2008 was the economic meltdown that had accelerated in September after Lehman Brothers collapsed. McCain and Obama were fairly close in the polls until the meltdown occurred. After that, the economy became the single issue that drove voters to the polls, and they voted for change. This heavily favored Barack Obama.

Obama found a simple, compelling theme for his campaign: "Change We Can Believe In," often shortened just to "Change." Voters found Obama inspiring. At rallies, people chanted, "Yes we can!" or in Spanish: "Si se puede!" Artist Shepard Fairey created a famous campaign poster of Obama's face over the word *Hope*. Opponents pilloried it with "Nope."

Helen Thomas, a White House reporter since the Kennedy years, noted how keenly the country wanted that change. She wrote, "An overwhelming desire for change, combined with Obama's uniqueness as a presidential prospect, allowed him to keep his vision of change somewhat vague in the campaign. Voters were so desperate for something different that Obama simply was not pressed for specifics. And the news media were so enamored of him that they too did not push for details about how he would govern." [12]

❖

Tuesday, November 4, 2008, was Election Day.

Barack Obama decisively defeated John McCain at the polls. He won 53 percent of the popular vote, nearly ten million votes more than McCain, and won the electoral college by 365 to 173. Virginia, once the capital of the Confederacy, voted for Obama, the first time that the state had voted for a Democratic presidential candidate since Lyndon Johnson in 1964. The traditionally Republican states of Indiana and North Carolina likewise voted for the Democrat. [13]

The United States elected its first African American president. It showed that America remained true to its values: that the country was the land of opportunity, and that anyone could grow up to become president. It felt like the American promise was fulfilled on that historic day. David Plouffe, Obama's campaign manager, called the president-elect a "once-in-a-generation candidate." [14]

Dan Balz and Haynes Johnson called 2008 "the election of a lifetime, one that will be studied for years for its shattering of historical barriers and its long-term consequences for the United States. In the decades we have spent chronicling American politics, nothing has equaled this election for the richness of its characters, for the light it sheds on questions of race, gender, religion, class, and generational changes, and for the stakes it raises for the future." [15]

African Americans spoke of finally being able to "unpack the suitcase." Obama's election gave the clear message that America was their home, they as freeborn people who were a vital part of the country and were welcome to stay. It had taken a long journey to get to this point since African slaves were first brought to Virginia in 1619. For much of the country's history, blacks were marginalized, their votes suppressed, and their communities terrorized. Even after the Supreme Court's landmark ruling in *Brown v. Board of Education* in 1954, it had taken the civil rights movement more than a decade to force the South to recognize black civil rights.

Every political party is a coalition of interests. Obama's political machine built an effective coalition based on traditional Democratic voters—unions, urban dwellers, and minorities like African Americans, gays, and Hispanics—and expanded it to seize a significant part of young voters (the Millennial generation) and highly educated whites in the suburbs. Here was proof that white people would vote for a black man.[16]

The shift among young voters was a considerable factor. This was a generation that came of age with 9/11, but they rejected the more traditional America-first attitude of the Republican Party. Theirs was a global generation. A fifth of the electorate were 18–29-year-olds, and these voted overwhelmingly in favor of Obama (66 percent versus 32 percent for McCain). Obama likewise earned 96 percent of the African American vote and won 67 percent of the Hispanic vote.[17]

Obama had his mandate. Democrats not only owned the White House, but they were firmly in control of both houses of Congress. The 2008 election had increased Democratic seats to 255 congress members and 59 senators initially; in April 2009, Republican senator Arlen Specter switched parties, giving the Democrats sixty senators and a filibuster-proof majority.

The Republican Party was repudiated. The GOP retreated to the margins of aging, conservative, white voters in Appalachia, the Deep South, and the Midwest. Their message of conservative social values and low taxes was increasingly lost on an electorate that demanded government action to solve global problems. The Republicans would lose their relevance if they didn't change with the shifting demographics and values of the country. What they did, instead, was entrench against change.

Obama promised to heal the divide between Blue and Red. That didn't happen, in part because his opponents were not open to reconciliation, and Obama was not the personage who could woo opponents. Conservative opposition to Obama would in fact fuel a populist insurgency against him.

The Meltdown Continues

The presidential election served as a temporary distraction from the financial meltdown. There was even an Election Day stock market rally. But the day after, the downturn continued. On Wednesday, November 6, the Dow Jones fell 5 percent, or 486.01 points. The next day, it fell another 443.48 points, closing at 8695.79. The October unemployment rate rose to 6.5 percent—the highest in fourteen years—as companies slashed workers from their payroll.

On November 12, Treasury Secretary Hank Paulson announced a change for the $700 billion bailout that Congress had authorized. TARP would not buy troubled assets from institutions as he originally intended, but instead focus on recapitalizing banks to restore confidence in the market. He had spent only half of the $700 billion, choosing to leave the other half for the incoming Obama administration. The Dow Jones fell 411.30 points (4.7 percent) that day to 8282.66.

The news about the economy continued to worsen as economists realized we were in a much deeper recession. The consumer price index fell by 1 percent in October, both from lower fuel costs, as well as dried-up demand for goods. Consumers were worried about layoffs and stopped spending on anything but necessities. On November 19, the stock market fell 427.47 points, or 5 percent, to close at 7997.28. It was the first time it had closed below 8,000 points since 2003. The next day, the Dow Jones tumbled another 5.56 percent, or 444.99 points, closing the day at 7552.29. The S&P 500 index fell 6.71 percent to 752.44; the last time it had been this low was April 1997. Nearly twelve years of equity gains were wiped out.

The stocks that fared the worst were in the financial industry, particularly Citigroup, as investors fled, fearing that the financial news would get even worse. The company's third quarter loss was more than $20 billion, and it announced 53,000 layoffs—one of the largest layoffs in corporate history—but that did little to assuage the market's fear. The stock was pummeled: it declined 60 percent in one week, down to $3.77 per share. The market feared that Citi would be another Lehman Brothers; however, Citi had $2 trillion in assets on its books, making it many times larger than the failed investment bank. This was indeed a company too big to fail.

After a weekend of negotiations, the federal government came to Citigroup's rescue. On Sunday, November 23, the Treasury Department, Federal Reserve, and Federal Deposit Insurance Corporation announced a combined bailout for Citigroup. It was unprecedented. The company would absorb up to $29 billion in troubled mortgage-related assets, while the government would cover the remainder, estimated to be $306 billion. The taxpayers were issued, in return, $7 billion worth of preferred shares in Citigroup, and the federal government purchased another $20 billion in preferred shares to bolster the company's capital—again, with taxpayer dollars. The stock market rallied on the news, reclaiming most of the previous week's losses.[18]

Just two days later, the Federal Reserve and Treasury launched a new round of intervention designed to provide credit to consumers and small businesses. This package was budgeted at $800 billion. The lion's share, $500 billion, was to buy up mortgage-backed securities. Another $100 billion went to buy debt owned by Freddie Mac and Fannie Mae, which would then allow them to extend new loans. And $200 billion secured high-rated securities for car, credit card, student, and small business loans. These types of loans were heavily impacted by the credit freeze, as small business credit had dried up, and this threatened the day-to-day operations of many businesses. This was yet another attempt to thaw the frozen credit markets—by having the federal government provide the financing, rather than just the private sector.

On December 1, the bad news that everyone was expecting finally sunk in. A panel of economists from the National Bureau of Economic Research declared that the recession had started in December 2007—a year earlier. The S&P 500 and NASDAQ indices fell nearly 9 percent that day, while the Dow closed down 7.7 percent (679.95 points) to 8149.09.[19] Investors plowed their money into U.S. Treasury bonds, driving the yield for three-month bonds down to zero, while two-year bonds yielded less than 1 percent for the first time ever as people sought a safe haven. People began calling it the Great Recession, which was destined to become the longest post–World War II recession to date.[20]

Right on cue, the Labor Department reported that the economy had lost 584,000 jobs in November, the most monthly job losses since 1974. Unemployment rose from 6.5 percent to 6.8 percent. The price of oil fell to $41 a barrel, less than five months after its all-time peak.[21] As consumers ramped back their spending, the Consumer Price Index fell by a record 1.7 percent that month. The Federal Reserve played its last interest rate card, dropping the federal funds rate from 1 percent down to a target range of 0 percent to 0.25 percent. This was the lowest rate in its history. The Fed would hold interest rates there for the next seven years to assist the sluggish economic recovery.[22]

The unemployment rate continued to rise. In December, employers shed 524,000 jobs, sending unemployment up to 7.2 percent. Throughout 2008, the economy had lost 2.45 million jobs, and more than 11 million people were unemployed.[23]

Just as things seemed to go from bad to worse, a new scandal emerged. A veteran investor for the wealthy, Bernard Madoff, had built a $50 billion Ponzi scheme that unraveled in December 2008. This particularly affected nonprofit groups serving the Jewish community that had invested their money with the man. Madoff was sentenced to 150 years in prison.

The crash of 2008 had wiped out $6.9 trillion in investment. The Dow Jones lost 34 percent of its value in one year, while the S&P 500 sank 38 percent. The NASDAQ had its worst year ever, losing 41 percent. There was simply nowhere to hide: virtually every investment category—stocks, bonds, emerging markets—sank. Six years of investment gains had been wiped out. Americans felt like they were in the crossfire from the stock market drop and ricocheting oil prices: oil had surged to $147.27 per barrel in July, then fell 70 percent to close the year at $44.60. It was clear to all now that the economy was in serious trouble, and that the recession would be deeper and longer-lasting than anyone imagined. Americans bid a not-so-fond adieu to 2008.[24]

❖

The federal government had started the first decade with a budget surplus, but the Bush tax cuts and wars had driven the deficit up to $413 billion in 2004, though it dropped to $162 billion in 2007 as the economy grew. With the federal government spending prodigious amounts of money to shore up the declining economy, the deficit ballooned to $455 billion in 2008. The incoming Obama administration estimated that the deficit would soar to $1.2 trillion in 2009. That, as it turned out, would be a major understatement.[25]

New York Times columnist David Leonhardt wrote how Americans had spent well beyond their means for years, and that behavior had finally caught up to them. "As a country we have been spending too much on the present and not enough on the future. We have been consuming rather than investing. We're suffering from investment-deficit disorder." He concluded, "The norms of the last two decades or so—consume before invest; worry about the short term, not the long term—have been more than just a reflection of the economy. They have also *affected* the economy."[26]

Americans not only were *not* saving—we had a negative savings rate, meaning that consumers were living beyond their means in unsustainable lifestyles. We were an instant gratification society, one not accustomed to saving up to achieve one's goals or making sacrifices for future gains. Our conspicuous consumption habit was out of hand. It wasn't just about buying things that you needed to live, but buying things so you could show them off to others, like buying a fur coat when a wool coat was just as warm, a Rolex watch when a Timex would do, or putting five televisions in a house when one sufficed. Conspicuous consumption defined citizens by what they bought.

The bursting of the housing bubble and the Great Recession forced Americans to reassess how they spent and paid for things. So much of consumer spending was built upon borrowed money, rather than pay-as-you-go. Americans had become addicted to living beyond their means. The Great Recession proved the great reckoning.

Assessing the Bush Presidency

Before we depart 2008 and enter into the Obama years, we must take one last look at George W. Bush. The left-leaning *Rolling Stone* magazine called him "the very worst president in all of American history" in 2006.[27] Jean Edward Smith, author of a highly critical biography of the president, wrote: "Rarely in the history of the United States has the nation been so ill-served as during the presidency of George W. Bush."[28]

But are these judgments accurate? And are they fair? It is too early to name any president to the best or worst list while they are still in office and political bias floats heavily through the air. But now time has passed and the passions of the first decade have receded. Partisanship yields to rational assessment.

By the end of his second term, Bush was deeply unpopular with the American public. This coincided with the Great Recession, and the public was angry over the Iraq War and the direction of the country. He left the Oval Office in January 2009 with a 30 percent approval rating, according to a *Washington Post*-ABC News Poll.[29]

"The shrill debate never affected my decisions," Bush stated in his memoir as he took the long view. "I read a lot of history, and I was struck by how many presidents had endured harsh criticism. The measure of their character, and often their success, was how they responded. Those who based decisions on principle, not some snapshot of public opinion, were often vindicated over time."[30]

Presidents often were judged for just one or two things they did. Abraham Lincoln for the Civil War. FDR for combating the Great Depression and World War II. Truman for the Cold War and Korea. But that overly simplifies what is a deeply complicated job—and doubly so if a president serves two terms. We may shudder at the memory of Lyndon Johnson and Vietnam, but that risks overlooking his astonishing record on civil rights legislation and implementing the Great Society.

So it is with George W. Bush. He may be solely remembered for the Iraq War, but there was much more to his presidency. Yes, Iraq was a terrible strategic mistake, but Dubya accomplished significant things that should not be overlooked—and likewise, he made other mistakes. Let's take a look at what he did.

Bush's main accomplishment of his presidency centered not around his domestic agenda, which was his original intention, but around national security, in particular in the fight against the terrorist organization al-Qaeda in the wake of 9/11. Though the worst terrorist strike against the United States happened toward the opening of his eight years in office, Bush ensured that the U.S. wasn't attacked again. American forces helped overthrow the Taliban and evicted al-Qaeda from Afghanistan with remarkable speed. Bush was bold and decisive. The country was indeed safer, thanks to Bush. There was not another major terrorist attack on American soil. He proudly wrote, "If I had to summarize my most meaningful accomplishment as president in one sentence, that would be it."[31]

Al-Qaeda was on the run, but despite the extensive manhunt Osama bin Laden hadn't been brought to justice. Bush knew this was "unfinished business," as he wrote in his memoir:

> I wanted badly to bring bin Laden to justice. The fact that we did not ranks among my great regrets. It certainly wasn't for lack of effort. For seven years, we kept the pressure on. While we never found the al Qaeda leader, we did force him to change the way he traveled, communicated, and operated. That helped us deny him his greatest wish after 9/11: to see America attacked again.[32]

After 9/11, Bush took important steps to ensure that the nation's small Muslim population was not blamed, marginalized, or shunned. He publicly stated that Islam is a religion of peace, and that Americans should not direct their anger toward their Muslim neighbors, but rather toward the terrorists who had perverted Islam to commit murder. As a result, there was little if any violence directed toward the Muslim community.

Bush had a good record of bipartisanship as governor of Texas, but once in the White House he tacked sharply to the right. This was probably from the influence of Vice President Dick Cheney and the need to satisfy the conservative base. The Bush presidency was too ideological in its approach to decision-making, and too immune to criticism. Republicans were becoming a party less prone to compromise—they had replaced flexible pragmatism with ideological purity and power grasping. Bush was less likely to reach comity or compromise with political opponents, though he had a number of bipartisan successes, including the No Child Left Behind Act. He did little to chart a centrist course until Democrats seized control of Congress in the 2006 midterm election.

Contrary to critics who alleged that Cheney was the actor pulling the strings, Bush was clearly in charge in the White House. Nor was he the dimwit his critics made him out to be. Cheney was distrusting and secretive. He was arguably the most powerful vice president in American history, a man who carved out a special policy-making role for himself, who never wanted to be president, and who really didn't care about public opinion. Over time, Cheney's power within the office waned as Bush made more decisions that contradicted Cheney's advice.

President Bush was quick to make decisions and prided himself on being "the decider." On the downside, sometimes it would have paid to wait to get more information. He could have been more flexible in seeking other options, such as in the run-up to the Iraq War, or making corrections midcourse. His decisive 9/11 leadership failed with Hurricane Katrina, as he hesitated to step in when the local authorities were in fact overwhelmed. He recognized that he had taken too long to decide.

Bush had a stubbornness that resisted self-assessment or self-reflection, at least while in the White House bubble. He would rarely admit to mistakes, but always insisted the path he was on was the correct one. He was no flip-flopper, an effective accusation he made against John Kerry in the 2004 presidential campaign, but one would have hoped he would change directions in light of new evidence. The Iraq War drifted for far too long before the 2007 surge.

Bush didn't quite grasp how deeply corruption and cronyism were endemic to Wall Street, and thus resisted financial reforms until after the Enron and WorldCom scandals. On the upside, his administration prosecuted executives for fraud and malfeasance and secured prison time for those convicted of wrongdoing.

While Bush did not make Israeli-Palestinian peace a major diplomatic initiative like Bill Clinton or his own father, he did quietly push for peace, in particular for getting Palestinians to reform their economy and institute democratic reforms in preparation for future statehood. These efforts were largely overshadowed by the War on Terror. The unresolved question of Palestinian independence and statehood was still the single largest issue across the Middle East. Settling it may have brought peace and recognition to Israel and greater stability in the region of the world that controlled much of the world's oil.

One of the most remarkable successes of the Bush administration was the diplomatic coup against Libyan dictator Muammar Gaddafi. Good intelligence and merciless negotiations convinced the Libyan strongman to give up his weapons of mass destruction—especially after he had been caught trying to purchase capabilities to build nuclear weapons. Gaddafi feared being targeted like Saddam Hussein. He surrendered his capabilities without firing a shot.

Bush took an interest in Africa, a continent long ignored by the West, whose countries were often ruled by strongmen and whose populations were ravaged by HIV/AIDS. Bush championed the fight against global AIDS, especially in Africa and Haiti. In some sub-Saharan African countries, a quarter of the population was infected with HIV. The disease would cripple societies and leave nothing behind but a continent of orphans. Over Bush's two terms, he dramatically increased spending on assistance to Africa and Haiti for HIV/AIDS, as well as for malaria. It was a profound humanitarian gesture that saved millions of lives.

The president acknowledged that the United States was long overdue for immigration reform, and he worked hard to develop a solution, though Congress never would pass it. Bush came up against entrenched nativists who feared demographic change. He made a poignant observation:

> The failure of immigration reform points out larger concerns
> about the direction of our politics. The blend of isolationism,

protectionism, and nativism that affected the immigration debate also led Congress to block free trade agreements with Colombia, Panama, and South Korea. I recognize the genuine anxiety that people feel about foreign competition. But our economy, our security, and our culture would all be weakened by an attempt to wall ourselves off from the world. Americans should never fear competition. Our country has always thrived when we've engaged the world with confidence in our values and ourselves.[33]

Bush called himself a "compassionate conservative," which he indeed was, but he was also a big-government conservative. The Medicare prescription drug benefit was a nice addition for seniors struggling with medication costs, but he created no mechanism to pay for this entitlement. This added to the nation's growing tab for caring for the elderly.

The Bush tax cuts may have been a good short-term solution for a recession, when it is necessary to get more money into the hands of consumers, but as long-term policy, it was a mistake to keep tax rates so low. While everyone had seen their taxes go down some, the rich overwhelmingly benefited, and the country suffered massive fiscal deficits. Combined with the cost of two wars and rising entitlements for seniors, the tax cuts threatened to saddle future American prosperity with crippling debt. His 2005 effort to reform Social Security was dead on arrival.

Every modern Republican president since Ronald Reagan seemed to run into this financial dilemma. Supply-siders called for cutting taxes and reducing government, but the country still demanded services. There was no political will to cut entitlements, especially for the elderly, who were a powerful and vocal constituency. The result was deficit spending, rather than true fiscal conservatism, which meant balancing the budget by trimming expenses and raising taxes if necessary to keep the financial house in order. Bush's father disparagingly called supply-side "voodoo economics." Conservative economist Tyler Cowen wrote critically: "The idea that unfunded tax cuts will significantly raise our real incomes and thus pay for themselves is one of the illusions of our age."[34]

Bush recognized that the nation was "addicted to oil"—as had every president since Richard Nixon—but he did little about the problem beyond raising car mileage standards and agreeing to more energy efficient lightbulbs. He recognized that our burning fossil fuels was harming the planet. Yet the country made few strides in reducing greenhouse gas emissions during his eight years. It was a lost decade for the planet.

Bush's record on gay rights was mixed. In the 2004 presidential campaign, Bush used the gay marriage debate as a wedge issue, and he capitalized on fear to boost Republican votes. He called for a constitutional amendment to define marriage as between a man and a woman, though that was politically dead and he knew it. This may have been good politics, but it alienated a large swath of people and painted Republicans as intolerant.

On the other hand, Bush did little to oppose efforts by gays to achieve greater civil rights. He appointed more LGBT officials to his administration than any before. Vice President Dick Cheney had a lesbian daughter and was in favor of greater gay rights—and Bush's own wife, Laura, later came out in favor of gay marriage. You suspected that Bush was actually sympathetic toward the gay cause, and would have done more for it but for the conservatism of the Republican base who feared any concession toward legal equality. Americans would quickly come around on gay marriage over the next decade.

Bush should be remembered for his leadership after 9/11; instead, his administration will be forever associated with the Iraq War, a strategic and costly mistake for the United States. Bush biographer Jean Edward Smith summarized Bush's chief foreign policy error: "Unaware of the strictures of international law, unwilling to master the details of complex issues, prone to see the world in black-and-white terms, and convinced he was the instrument of God's will, George W. Bush led the nation into disaster."[35]

Despite the accusations, Bush did not lie about the Iraq War; however, his administration registered a major intelligence failure that led to an unnecessary war. Iraq squandered the moral high ground and international goodwill that the U.S. had earned after 9/11. We attacked and occupied an Arabic country and overthrew its government. This reminded many Arabs of the colonial era, which they were rightfully unhappy about. It also seriously divided Americans, who were so recently unified after the 9/11 attacks.

Bush seemed intent on going after Saddam Hussein from early on, though the dictator was in fact contained. Bush did not lean in with the more moderate State Department under Colin Powell. He lent his ear too much to the neoconservatives in the Pentagon and vice president's office, when the State Department provided more prudent counsel. Diplomacy is vastly cheaper than war.

After Saddam Hussein was overthrown in April 2003 but no weapons of mass destruction could be found, the Bush administration stuck to its narrative that Hussein was responsible for 9/11, long after this myth was debunked. Americans were promised a quick in-and-out, and instead got bogged down for years in a volatile country. Shifting goalposts in Iraq left the American public jaded about the war effort. The Bush administration was completely unprepared for the nation building necessary to set Iraq on its feet.

Once the U.S. occupied Iraq—and there was a major difference between being a liberator and an occupier—Bush allowed the situation to deteriorate. There was no strategy. He kept Donald Rumsfeld on too long after he became a political liability. After the 2006 midterm "thumping," the president was shocked into action, and the result was the surge. It was politically unpopular, but it was a brave decision and probably the right one. The U.S. couldn't just walk away from Iraq and somehow expect the country to stabilize itself. We had helped make this mess, and now we had to fix it.

The Iraq War inadvertently turned that country into a battleground for terror, and it also took the administration's eye off the ball in Afghanistan and Pakistan, where the real terrorist threat lay: the al-Qaeda leadership. The insurgency in Afghanistan continued for years with little attention from the Bush administration.

Like Bill Clinton before him, President Bush operated in continual campaign mode. His press secretary, Scott McClellan, penned an especially poignant observation about Bush, governance, and Iraq:

> The president had promised himself that he would accomplish what his father had failed to do by winning a second term in office. And that meant operating continually in campaign mode: never explaining, never apologizing, never retreating. Unfortunately, that strategy also had less justifiable repercussions: never reflecting, never reconsidering, never compromising. Especially not where Iraq was concerned.
>
> The first grave mistake of Bush's presidency was rushing toward military confrontation with Iraq. It took his presidency off course and greatly damaged his standing with the public. His second grave mistake was his virtual blindness about his first mistake, and his unwillingness to sustain a bipartisan spirit during a time of war and change course when events demanded it.[36]

His preemptive war doctrine—the Bush Doctrine—was discredited. Whatever plans Bush had for remaking the Middle East along the lines of democracy were shelved with the Iraq fiasco. Iraq would be the one preemptive strike; the nation had no appetite for another. The Bush Doctrine was one-and-done.

The War on Terror was seemingly endless, and to win it Americans engaged in questionable tactics. Warrantless wiretapping, unprecedented electronic surveillance, and the Patriot Act may have helped prevent another major attack, but at what cost to our civil liberties?

The Bush administration's detainee policies were justifiably criticized. The Guantanamo Bay detention facility was established with the intention to hold "unlawful combatants" indefinitely, which stripped detainees of Geneva Convention protections, much to the dismay of the nation's military leadership. The administration botched the trials of terrorist detainees by attempting an end-run around the established civilian court process. Military tribunals proceeded far too slowly, and Bush policies were successfully and repeatedly challenged at the Supreme Court. This unfinished business was passed on to the Obama and Trump administrations.

And then there were secret CIA prisons overseas that undermined the moral authority of the United States. Bush ordered three al-Qaeda members to be waterboarded at these black sites. This was torture, plain and simple.

The last two years of Bush's presidency (2007–2008) was really where he came into his own. Despite his low approval ratings and the fact that Republicans had lost control of Congress, Bush asserted his leadership in gaining support for the surge in Iraq, which helped stabilize the country. The financial meltdown of 2008 was fueled by private sector greed and a lack of regulatory oversight on the part of the Federal Reserve. This wasn't Bush's fault, but he gave the green light to gifted leaders—Sheila Bair, Ben Bernanke, Tim Geithner, and especially Hank Paulson—to do what was necessary to rescue the economy from disaster. He did indeed prove to be more like FDR than Hoover.

Though bailing out Wall Street and the Detroit automakers was deeply unpopular, it was necessary and it worked. The intervention effectively staved off another Great Depression. TARP recapitalized the financial institutions and restored confidence in the banking system, and at a profit to the taxpayers. And it was the right thing to do to save the economy from going over the proverbial cliff, which would have happened had the federal government not intervened. "Putting a world-class investment banker [Paulson] and an expert on the Great Depression [Bernanke] in the nation's top two economic positions were among the most important decisions of my presidency," Bush wrote.[37]

So was George W. Bush the worst president ever?

No, not even close. Bush certainly had his share of both mistakes and successes. But he would have had to be far worse to eclipse Warren Harding's incompetence and numerous scandals, or Richard Nixon's corruption and undermining of the Constitution, or James Buchanan's inept leadership in the widening gulf between North and South just before the Civil War, or Andrew Johnson's demagoguery and obstruction to rebuilding the nation afterward. Bush was a decent and honest man who proved himself an effective wartime leader, despite the intelligence failure that led to the Iraq War.

15
Obama

Just five days before the 2009 presidential inauguration, US Airways flight 1549 took off from New York's LaGuardia Airport bound for Charlotte, North Carolina. It immediately struck a flock of geese, which disabled both engines. The plane's captain, Chesley "Sully" Sullenberger, ditched the craft in the Hudson River in a perfect gliding landing. Ferries and tugboats swarmed around the floating plane and rescued all of the 155 people on board. It was a historical fascination that plane crashes in New York provided bookends to George W. Bush's time in office—the terrorist attacks on 9/11 and the miraculous landing in the Hudson River.

Tuesday, January 20, 2009, dawned as Inauguration Day. The day before was a national holiday commemorating Martin Luther King Jr.'s birthday. It was a sunny day, briskly cold, in the twenties but it felt colder with a light breeze. The Potomac River was partly frozen over from weeks of single-digit temperatures.

All bridges between Virginia and the District of Columbia were closed and significant parts of downtown D.C. were shut to traffic. The masses arrived by foot, bike, subway, and bus, but they did not drive. The subway system was swamped, the city as crowded as Manhattan during the Christmas rush. Security was tight and very visible: some 30,000 men and women in uniform were out in force, but there were no incidents, and not a single person was arrested.

An estimated 1.8 million people swarmed the National Mall, the first time that the entire Mall was open for a public event. It surpassed the earlier record for an inauguration: 1.2 million people for Lyndon B. Johnson in 1965. Jumbotrons beamed the swearing-in ceremony to the crowd; unless you had tickets to be on the Capitol grounds, you could not see anything. At the moment of the inauguration, hundreds of thousands of digital cameras were held aloft. Every witness seemed to have one, and everyone had become a historian.

All of these people had come to witness history: the swearing in of Barack Obama as the forty-fourth president and first African American to hold the nation's highest office. His wife Michelle would become the first black First Lady.

Obama took the oath of office at the U.S. Capitol, a building constructed by slaves, and then paraded to the White House, another edifice built by slaves. There was just one small hitch: Chief Justice John Roberts fumbled delivering the oath of office to Obama, so he came to the White House that evening for a do-over.

The new president was an exceptional public speaker, though he toned down the soaring rhetoric in his inaugural address. The economy was in crisis, and Obama had to reassure the country of the crucial work ahead to repair the damage. "Today I say to you that the challenges we face are real, they are serious and they are many," he stated. "They will not be met easily or in a short span of time. But know this America: They will be met." Obama continued on: "Starting today, we must pick ourselves up, dust ourselves off, and begin again the work of remaking America."[1]

❖

Barack Obama positioned himself as a transformational leader who would change Washington and bridge the divide between Blue and Red. He was largely an outsider to the establishment, a man who hadn't even completed his first term in the Senate. He was also inexperienced, having never led a major organization and seldom managed people. The public had high, even inflated expectations of Obama. They treated him as if he was a rock star or a superhero. Journalist Jonathan Alter, who extensively covered the Obama administration, wrote, "Never before have we known so little about someone so intensely observed."[2]

Every politician elected to national office swears that they are going to change Washington, but they inevitably fail. The political culture of what some call the "swamp" never changes. This is largely because the framers of the Constitution designed a system for political gridlock through checks and balances, so distrusting were they of power. This is in contrast to most democratic societies worldwide, which adopted the British parliamentary model instead, which is far more efficient. Not many countries adopted the American democratic republic model.

There remained the open question of how Obama would govern. He had campaigned as a centrist Democrat, reaching out to his ideological opposites in order to hear their opinions. Obama had read presidential historian Doris Kearns Goodwin's *Team of Rivals*, a book that revealed how Abraham Lincoln had appointed political rivals to his cabinet to gather the best minds and to foster debate. Obama nominated his political rival Hillary Clinton as secretary of state. It wasn't all change, however: Obama asked Bush-appointee Robert Gates to stay on at the Pentagon.

Much was made of Obama's fulfilling the dream of the civil rights movement and his being a latter-day successor to Abraham Lincoln. Two days before the inauguration, Obama spoke at a concert held at the Lincoln Memorial near where Martin Luther King Jr. had delivered his "I have a dream" speech in 1963, and where Marian Anderson had performed on Easter 1939 before a crowd of 75,000 people after Constitution Hall (owned by the Daughters of the American Revolution) turned her away because of the color of her skin. It was a symbolically significant site.

The nation commemorated the bicentennial of Lincoln's birth on February 12, 2009, just weeks after Obama's swearing-in. The historical echoes continued: Lincoln was from Illinois, as was Obama. Yet the economic situation seemed more like the Great Depression than the Civil War, and perhaps the best historical comparison for Obama was Franklin Delano Roosevelt, just as he was for President Bush at the end. The crisis of the day was the economy.

Obama's network of Washington insiders was small. And as president, he largely kept to a core group of advisers in the White House bubble. Obama was an introvert who felt more comfortable with policy than how to sell it to Congress. Michael Grunwald of *Time* wrote that Obama was "a data-oriented, left-of-center technocrat who is above all a pragmatist, comfortable with compromise, solicitous of experts, disinclined to sacrifice the good in pursuit of the ideal."[3]

Obama's management style was collaborative. He participated in endless debates within the White House about policy that did not always result in decisions. Critics noted that Obama did not always lead, and they were right, especially in his first two years in office. Ron Suskind called Obama a "brilliant amateur."[4] Professor David Garrow wrote rather scathingly of Obama that "the vessel was hollow at its core," as if he were a man who had sold his soul to win the presidency. One senses in Garrow's biography a feeling of being left at the altar, that Obama could never meet the heightened expectations the public had of him.[5]

One thing missing from Obama's personality was what journalist Jonathan Alter called the "schmooze gene."[6] Obama enjoyed governing, but he wasn't a particularly gifted politician. Chuck Todd, a White House correspondent during both the Bush and Obama eras, noted about Obama, "At times both passive and arrogant, this is a president who is brilliant at communicating with voters and miserable at communication with the folks they voted for. It's no secret he despises the glad-handing, backslapping necessities of his chosen profession." He often delegated political affairs to Joe Biden, his vice president, and seldom got involved in the sausage-making of drafting laws. This would be problematic with a chaotic Congress that needed direction and leadership from the president.[7]

As president, Obama spent little time on racial issues. He played up his personal and family story, but downplayed being black and spent little political capital on black issues. Obama steered clear of involving himself in black-specific issues at the risk of being seen as pandering to that community. As an African American, Obama was a symbolically potent president, but ultimately did little to specifically address black civil rights, prison reform, and the war on drugs, or economic issues like high black unemployment and housing foreclosures. Obama's view was that he couldn't just be president for one group of people—he had to be president for everyone.

President Obama told New Yorker editor David Remnick, "And so I think that nobody should have ever been under the illusion—certainly I wasn't, and I was very explicit about this when I campaigned—that by virtue of my election, suddenly race problems would be solved or conversely that the American people would want to spend all their time talking about race."[8]

"Symbolically, the election of Obama as the first black president represents the apex of black politics," wrote Professor Fredrick Harris in The Price of the Ticket. "Substantively, however, Obama's ascendancy illustrates the continued decline of black politics' inability to set a political agenda in national politics." The black community, some of whom had initially questioned Obama's blackness, rallied around the president. "Black voters put aside policy demands for the prize of electing one of their own to the White House," Harris concluded.[9]

Some naively believed that the U.S. was reaching a post-racial era where racism was banished for good. "The emerging official story of American progress goes something like this: Obama's ascendancy proves, once and for all, that America has overcome its racism," Professor Harris stated. He was deeply skeptical of such claims, and he was right to be. Indeed, how was one ever to pretend that race simply didn't exist? Some hoped for a color-blind society, but a more realistic view was to realize that race would always be there—and that the U.S. was a multiracial society.[10]

"When Barack was first elected, various commentators had naively declared that our country was entering a 'post-racial' era, in which skin color would no longer matter," noted First Lady Michelle Obama, even as young black men continued to be killed by police. "Here was proof of how wrong they'd been. As Americans obsessed over the threat of terrorism, many were overlooking the racism and tribalism that were tearing our nation apart."[11]

In July 2009, Harvard Professor Henry Louis Gates Jr. found himself locked out of his own house in Cambridge, Massachusetts, as he returned from a trip to China. As he tried to force the front door open, a neighbor called the police. A Cambridge police officer arrested Gates, one of the most prominent African American academics in the country, despite his protests that this was his own house. Obama stated that the Cambridge police "acted stupidly," which drew protest from police everywhere. The president regretted the comment and invited Gates and the police officer to a "beer summit" at the White House. What was meant as a teachable moment seemed a little pathetic.

Most Americans had no clue how deadly it was to be black in America. White families never had to give their sons "the talk" about how not to go out in public wearing a hoodie or risk being arrested; how never to talk back to police officers; and above all, to keep your hands on the steering wheel if a police officer pulled you over so you don't get shot. The Black Lives Matter movement formed in 2013 to protest the continuing police violence against black people.

Obamanomics

As Obama came into office, the financial markets were still in free fall. He inherited the economic crisis from President Bush. One of Obama's first tasks was to restore public confidence in the economy.

The economic news was frightful as the country plunged into a deep recession. Obama had to catch a falling knife. He selected New York Federal Reserve president Tim Geithner as his treasury secretary. Having stood at the epicenter of the banking rescue in 2008, Geithner's appointment signaled Obama's commitment to the ongoing efforts. Geithner was a career public servant who had never worked in the banking industry or on Wall Street.

The president gathered a brain trust of economists to steer the economy, including Tim Geithner, Larry Summers as national economic adviser, Peter Orszag as budget director, and Christina Romer as chair of the Council of Economic Advisors. Summers was a brilliant but arrogant man, having served earlier as head of Treasury, and wanted his old job back. In the interim, he had served as president of Harvard University, where he resigned after a no-confidence vote from the faculty. Obama's economic team soon proved dysfunctional as they frequently clashed with the argumentative and contrarian Summers, and only Geithner would stay in the cabinet longer than two years. These four plus their extensive teams were to lead the president's efforts to rescue the economy.[12]

The week before entering the Oval Office, Obama requested the other half of the TARP funds, $350 billion, promising to better spend and monitor the money. The first half had not bought up troubled assets, but had largely shored up the balance sheets of banks, some of which did not need the capital but took it anyway because it was a cheap loan. Congress quickly voted to allow the new president to use the money.

December's retail numbers were terrible as consumers reduced their spending at a time of year when many businesses count on Christmas sales. Housing starts fell to an all-time low. It was clear that this was the most serious economic recession since the Great Depression of the 1930s.

Newly sworn-in Treasury Secretary Tim Geithner immediately pointed out that five major financial institutions were still in trouble: AIG, Bank of America, and Citigroup, along with Fannie Mae and Freddie Mac. On top of that, the Detroit automakers were in serious trouble. Geithner noted that "Citi and Bank of America were the biggest of the bombs, Exhibit A and B for the outrage over 'too big to fail' banks; my aides called them the Financial Death Stars." Geithner noted there was need for another TARP-like solution.[13]

In January 2009, the financial giant Citigroup reported an $8.29 billion loss for the fourth quarter and decided to split itself up. It would spin off its Smith Barney brokerage into a joint venture with Morgan Stanley, and divide the rest into two separate companies: Citicorp and Citi Holdings. The era of the one-stop financial supermarket had come to an end. The stock market did not like the news and shares tanked.

Meanwhile, Bank of America reported its first quarter after absorbing Merrill Lynch. It discovered that Merrill was far more toxic than it had anticipated: BofA had a $15.3 billion loss for the fourth quarter of 2008. The federal government stepped in, offering a rescue package similar to the Citigroup bailout from November: $20 billion in new capital was injected into the company, and $118 billion worth of troubled assets were guaranteed.[14]

Both Fannie Mae and Freddie Mac asked for more federal money to cover their widening mortgage-related losses. Then the unthinkable happened: technology giant Microsoft cut 5,000 jobs, its first major layoffs ever. On January 26, just six days after Obama's inauguration, large corporations announced a bloodbath of 55,000 job cuts in one day, including 20,000 at Caterpillar, 8,000 at Pfizer, 8,000 at Sprint Nextel, and 7,000 at Home Depot.[15] The list of corporate layoffs continued to mount. The unemployment rate for January spiked to 7.6 percent as a total of 598,000 jobs were lost just in that one month.[16]

The Federal Reserve had already used its last interest rate tool—they were effectively set at zero percent—and now promised to buy mortgage-backed securities to help corporations get these bad debts off their books. The Obama administration was quickly assembling a financial relief package for Congress to approve.

Two weeks into office, Obama suffered his first misstep. Three political nominations had all run afoul of tax rules. Former senator Tom Daschle was appointed to lead Health & Human Services and be the administration's point man on health care reform; he belatedly disclosed that he had failed to pay $146,000 in taxes for the personal use of a limousine and other services. He paid the taxes, then withdrew his name from nomination. Nancy Killefer, Obama's chief performance officer, withdrew after revealing she had not paid unemployment taxes for her nanny. Treasury Secretary Tim Geithner belatedly paid his self-employment taxes for four years at the International Monetary Fund, but the Senate confirmed him anyway.

Public figures are held to a zero-defect ethical standard. Olympic swimmer Michael Phelps was heavily criticized after a photograph taken on a mobile phone showed him smoking marijuana, even though millions of Americans themselves did exactly the same thing. He issued a public apology, though many of his sponsors rescinded their financial support for the athlete. Phelps's mistake wasn't that he smoked pot, but rather that he allowed himself to be photographed doing it.

After Wall Street firms announced $38 billion in bonuses in 2008—a significant sum, though also a significant decline from the year before—the public responded with anger that companies receiving so much in taxpayer dollars were still rewarding the wealthy with bonuses that they certainly did not deserve. The Obama administration proposed a $500,000 pay cap on senior executives of companies that received federal assistance.[17]

On February 10, Treasury Secretary Geithner announced the administration's bailout package. This was the successor to TARP, which was renamed the Financial Stability Plan. It consisted of $1.5 trillion of both public and private funds. It would use the remaining $350 million from TARP, as well as moneys from various federal institutions, such as the Federal Reserve and the FDIC. The stock market did not like the package and promptly tanked 5 percent. Steven Pearlstein, financial columnist of the *Washington Post*, wrote a scathing editorial on Wall Street's response.

> By now, I hope you've learned enough not to be taken in by the self-serving floor patter. These guys won't be happy until the government agrees to relieve them of every last one of their lousy loans and investments at inflated prices, recapitalize every major bank and brokerage and insurance company on sweetheart terms and restore them to the glory days, so they can once again earn inflated profits and obscene pay packages by screwing over their customers and their shareholders.[18]

Meanwhile, Congress pared down the president's economic stimulus request to $787 billion. This huge package of government spending, consisting of infrastructure, state aid, and tax cuts, was nearly the cost of the Iraq

War. Obama signed the American Recovery and Reinvestment Act into law on February 17, less than a month after he had been sworn in. At more than 5 percent of GDP, it was far larger than Roosevelt's New Deal (2 percent of GDP), and yet there was not much focus on creating jobs, unlike the New Deal. Obama's financial advisers, many of them veterans of the Clinton administration, an era when fiscal deficits were considered evil, were more concerned with fiscal solvency and stability than with anything radical like a huge stimulus program. [19]

FDR's famed New Deal was a series of small make-work programs. Obama's Recovery Act included a huge infusion of research money and changed the country's energy policy toward a greener future. Renewables such as solar and wind power sprung to life, setting the stage for major CO_2 reductions in following decades. The Recovery Act saved an estimated three million jobs. This was a fraction of all the jobs lost from the Great Recession. Meanwhile unemployment continued to worsen. [20]

Obama championed "shovel-ready" construction projects that the federal government would fund. The problem was, the shovel-ready projects weren't really ready—construction takes a long time to prepare for and finally build. Shovel-ready turned into an embarrassment.

The stimulus package reflected Keynesian spending, named after John Maynard Keynes, the British economist who recommended that governments deficit-spend during the Great Depression to pick up the slack from the private sector until consumer confidence returned. The GOP, in contrast, preferred tax cuts, which largely went to the wealthy, in the hope that their spending would trickle down to the masses. That rarely worked out (Exhibit A was the Bush tax cuts); the wealthy often invested or saved the difference, rather than spending it. Yes, investment is important, but in an economic crisis what is needed is open wallets.

When President Bush left the White House, the GOP was bankrupt. Its working-class base was in rebellion, and a power vacuum existed that would be filled. Obama essentially continued the economic rescue that the Bush administration had started (was there any other choice?), including TARP, a program that was toxic to the populist right wing.

Republicans in Congress had initially been supportive, particularly around infrastructure spending in the stimulus bill, but when the president met with them and brazenly told them, "Elections have consequences. And I won," he alienated potential supporters. Not a single Republican voted for the recovery act, the first of many obstructionist stances the GOP would take against Obama.

From nearly the moment Obama was sworn in, Republicans stonewalled against supporting the new president, even during the economic emergency. They painted Obama as a big-spending liberal with the stimulus bill. The Bush administration got far more help from Democrats in Congress, but the Republicans by 2009 had become the party of "just say no." Whatever Obama proposed, they would reject. Many Republicans railed against Obama as a radical and a socialist, when he was in fact a centrist. He faced a deeply hostile GOP that opposed his agenda at nearly every turn. Obama's "honeymoon was over before it had started," quipped *Time* reporter Michael Grunwald.[21]

There was no other fiscal stimulus beyond the American Recovery and Reinvestment Act. There was simply too much political opposition. The $787 billion was what was politically feasible, though the government had nearly limitless means for fiscal stimulus.

Americans often confused the Recovery Act with TARP, both of whose price tags ran in the $700-billion range. They were two separate laws, passed by two different presidential administrations. Both angered the populists of the Republican Party and set the stage for the Republican resurgence in the 2010 midterm election. Neither proved a solution to the problem of rampant unemployment.

The federal government had bailed out the banks, so Congress took a politically popular step that ultimately had little impact: for the first time ever, the U.S. government would determine executive compensation, specifically for those seven firms that the government had rescued (AIG, Bank of America, Citigroup, Chrysler, Chrysler Financial, General Motors and GMAC). A special master was appointed, Kenneth Feinberg, who had overseen the September 11th Victim Compensation Fund. Feinberg wrote in *Who Gets What* that his goal:

> was to determine payments for senior corporate officials that would maximize the likelihood that the designated companies would repay TARP loans as quickly as possible. The taxpayers had to be made whole. This was the top priority—not any effort to "punish" corporate officials by cutting their pay to rock bottom or any attempt to placate congressional critics saddling up to pit Main Street against Wall Street.

This limited compensation for 175 individuals, ensuring that they did not get exorbitant bonuses or cash, while giving them an incentive to pay back taxpayer dollars as soon as possible.[22]

Meanwhile, the economic news kept getting worse: four weeks after Obama's inauguration, markets realized that the global economy was sliding deeper into recession, and the Dow Jones tanked nearly 4 percent to 7552.60. GDP fell by an annual rate of 6.2 percent in the fourth quarter of 2008. That news was sobering, and the first quarter of 2009 was expected to be equally dire. The Federal Reserve released a sharply downgraded economic forecast that predicted a much longer recession. Unemployment would remain high through 2011, and economic growth would be minimal. The market continued its free fall, ending that week at 7365.67, a six-year low. The Dow had fallen by half after hitting its all-time peak in October 2007, just sixteen months before. The next Monday, February 24, the market fell another 3.4 percent to 7114.78—a twelve-year low.[23]

There was no bottom in sight. Investors feared another collapse of major financial institutions, and despite earlier federal interventions, Citigroup, Bank of America, and other banks were pummeled until they were but penny stocks. The rumor of nationalization was in the air. Indeed, the Obama administration signaled its willingness to allow Citigroup to convert government-owned preferred shares into common stock. This provided an immediate boost in capital for the struggling bank, though it shifted the risk to the taxpayers and government. It was now the federal government's third intervention to prop up the company since October 2008.

Seeking to address the root cause of the economic crisis—the housing market—Obama announced a $75 billion plan to help homeowners in danger of foreclosure to refinance their houses. This did virtually nothing. The government also doubled the guarantees it provided to Fannie Mae and Freddie Mac to $400 billion. This latter measure finally marked the turnaround in the housing market, which finally stabilized.

Obama addressed a joint session of Congress on February 24 in a speech that was very much like a State of the Union address. He laid out an ambitious domestic agenda: how the United States would recover from the Great Recession, and how the country would make key investments in education, energy, and health care—all areas that he believed would contribute to future growth in the economy. This was an activist government program that hearkened to the days of FDR's New Deal and LBJ's Great Society. Only Obama did not

have a name for it. It sought to undo three decades of laissez-faire government ushered in by Ronald Reagan. People began calling it *Obamanomics*.

The federal government projected a stunning fiscal deficit of $1.75 tril-
lion, or 12.3 percent of GDP, during Obama's first year in office. He proposed
paying this down by allowing the Bush tax cuts to expire in 2011—largely
impacting the wealthy—and by creating a cap-and-trade system for carbon
emissions. This would redistribute part of the nation's wealth from the rich,
whose incomes had grown sizably, to the middle and working class, whose
wages had stagnated. Obama also signaled that he might ask for another
$750 billion for the Financial Stability Plan to shore up the nation's teetering
banking system. The Congressional Budget Office assessed Obama's budgets
and projected enormous deficits at $9.3 trillion over the next ten years. [24]

On March 2, American International Group reported the worst quarterly
loss in history for the fourth quarter of 2008: $61.7 billion. The federal gov-
ernment immediately pumped in another $30 billion to stabilize the company
and changed the terms on earlier loans to allow lower interest payments. This
was the fourth time the feds had intervened to save AIG, which was deemed
too crucial for the global economy to fail. The market perceived that this
would not be the last intervention either, and stocks continued to tank. The
Dow Jones fell 4.2 percent that day to 6763.29.

February's unemployment numbers continued upward: 651,000 jobs were
lost, and the unemployment rate rose to 8.1 percent. This was the highest level
since 1983. The economy was in a tailspin with no bottom in sight. Construction, finance, manufacturing, and retail were hit particularly hard, and men
were more likely to be laid off than women, as men tended to dominate in
these fields. Hispanic men, who were heavily concentrated in construction,
bore the brunt of job losses from the collapse of the housing boom. [25]

Small glimpses of hope began to appear. Citigroup reported in an internal
memo that it was profitable in January and February 2009. The trade deficit
shrank noticeably. The retail market had stabilized after a terrible Christmas.
The Dow reached its lowest point of the Great Recession on March 9, 2009,
when it declined to 6,547.05. This was ironic: the NASDAQ hit its all-time
high nine years earlier on March 10, 2000. No one could know it at the
time, but the stock market was about to commence the longest bull market
in its history.

Just two weeks after its latest bailout, AIG revealed it would pay out
$165 million in bonuses to the business unit that had created the company's

financial difficulties, including to a number of people who were no longer at the company. AIG was contractually obligated to pay these bonuses, yet the public backlash was fierce. Nearly everyone condemned the bonuses, given that the taxpayers had already invested $180 billion to rescue the company, and now they were giving treats to executives who had been part of the problem. The House of Representatives quickly passed a punitive 90 percent tax rate on bonuses for companies that had accepted taxpayer dollars, but both the Senate and the president thought better of this knee-jerk reaction. AIG's executives pleaded with its employees to return the bonuses. Some but not all of them complied. [26]

The Federal Reserve noted how much wealth Americans had lost: since the start of the Great Recession, four years of gains in net worth had been wiped out. The recession was a wealth destroyer. It hit hard those who had diligently saved for retirement and their kids' college education. For retirees, it was especially cruel, as they did not have the time to earn the money back. [27]

One of the key problems that acerbated the Great Depression in the 1930s was that the money supply shrank significantly, removing a key source of capital that the private sector depended on. In the Great Recession, the Federal Reserve had already taken interest rates down to nearly zero percent, and in March it pumped $1.2 trillion into the markets—essentially printing money to loan at low interest rates. If banks wouldn't loan to one another or to businesses, the Fed stood by to keep the cash flowing. The federal government had become the lender not only of last resort, but the lender of first resort.

Home prices had fallen so far that they were now affordable again to the middle class, and home sales began to tick upward. But the old days of zero-down loans were gone: banks had tightened their lending standards to where they should have been all along. Home buyers now had to cough up down payments and provide proof of income. On the upside, home loan interest rates were at an historic low, and there were plentiful houses for people to buy.

On March 23, six weeks after presenting his initial (but blank) proposal to deal with toxic assets, Treasury Secretary Tim Geithner stepped in front of the cameras again, and this time spelled out the details. The government would team up with private investors to buy up toxic assets from firms' balance sheets. The government guaranteed losses beyond 15 percent, and if the partnerships made money, the firms and the government would split the profits. In addition, Treasury would perform stress tests on the country's nineteen largest banks to determine if they needed additional capital to weather the economic storm. The market was enthusiastic and soared 7 percent that day.

Despite the hints of economic improvement, the unemployment rate continued to rise. The U.S. economy shed 663,000 jobs in March, and the unemployment rate hit 8.5 percent. Even though the stock market had started to rise as the recession bottomed out, layoffs were a lagging indicator. In fact, unemployment would continue to worsen for the next seven months.[28]

First quarter GDP showed an economic decline at an annual rate of 6.1 percent. However, there were signs that the market was bottoming out: business inventories were empty, meaning they would have to start ordering more goods, and consumer confidence started to rise. The stock market trended upward as a leading indicator. The Federal Reserve estimated that Americans had lost $1.33 trillion in net worth in the first quarter of 2009, largely from falling house prices and stock portfolios.[29]

All of this happened under the shadow of a global outbreak of swine flu that killed dozens and sickened hundreds in Mexico, then quickly traveled around the world. The World Health Organization declared a pandemic, but just like that, the danger level dropped as researchers realized this virus was no more dangerous than the regular flu. Over the course of the year, the federal government worked with scientists to produce enough vaccine for every American.

Just four months into the Obama presidency, Justice David Souter announced he was retiring from the Supreme Court and returning to his home state of New Hampshire. Souter was appointed by George H. W. Bush, a Republican, but had always voted with the liberal wing of the court, surprising many conservatives. Obama appointed Sonia Sotomayor, the court's first Latina, to replace him on May 26. The balance on the court remained the same with five conservatives and four liberals.

On May 6, the Treasury Department published the results of its stress tests on nineteen large banks. It determined that most of the banks were well capitalized. Bank of America needed another $33.4 billion in capital, but Treasury only required the bank to raise its reserves. Most of the banks' needs were more modest. Wells Fargo required $15 billion, Citigroup required $5 billion, but had to increase its common equity by $50 billion, while some such as JPMorgan Chase did not need any new capital. Those that were found to be fully capitalized could repay the TARP money to the government. On June 9, Treasury announced that ten large banks could repay their TARP loans worth more than $68 billion. These banks were deemed financially healthy, and their boards were eager to return the money that had strings attached, such as strict limits on executive compensation. [30]

The April unemployment rate rose to 8.9 percent as the economy shed another 539,000 jobs—but the good news was that layoffs seemed to be easing, and economists predicted an upturn later in the year. They said the same thing a month later when the May unemployment rate rose to 9.4 percent when the economy lost 345,000 jobs. This was the highest rate since 1983. Steadily decreasing layoffs was "good news," but it was also obvious that the economy was not creating new jobs yet. So much for good news: June unemployment rose to 9.5 percent as 467,000 workers lost their jobs that month. July's unemployment rate dipped to 9.4 percent as the economy lost fewer jobs: only 247,000 that month. The number of layoffs were declining, even though the economy still was not creating jobs. Unemployment would continue to get worse.

The largest banking institutions on Wall Street returned to profitability in the second quarter of 2009. Goldman Sachs made a huge profit by betting on a stock market rebound and in selling shares for companies that needed more capital. JPMorgan Chase likewise did quite well. Goldman quickly repaid its TARP money at a large profit to the government, and indicated it would pay out sizable bonuses to its employees (many criticized the bank as returning to Wall Street's business as usual ways). Two other banks, Citigroup and Bank of America, were also profitable, but only because they had sold off significant assets. They still had many toxic loans on their books to clean up.

Trouble in Detroit

When gas prices rose above $4 a gallon in July 2008 and the financial markets roiled with the Lehman Brothers collapse two months later, Americans simply stopped buying cars. The Big Three automakers in Detroit were in trouble, a mess that was years in the making.

Detroit began massive layoffs as the carmakers tried to cut costs to stay afloat. The automobile industry came to Washington, hat in hand, in November 2008 to ask for $25 billion in federal loans. President Bush defied his own advisers by supporting a rescue package for Detroit. He was also cognizant that he was about to leave the Oval Office and didn't want to leave a steaming mess for his successor, Barack Obama.

Chrysler, Ford, and General Motors "had made Detroit the Silicon Valley of the mid–20th century, a place of economic opportunity, where hillbillies from Appalachia and sharecroppers from the South could break out of poverty and grab a piece of America's bounty," wrote Paul Ingrassia in *Crash Course*. Detroit employed hundreds of thousands of workers, and its supply chain was enormous and global. Idle workers would be listed on the Jobs Bank, drawing full salaries for doing nothing. They earned big pensions and free medical care for life. You could be an unskilled worker with little education and still reach the middle class. That's what Detroit meant to America.[31]

And all that came crashing down. Over the course of the first decade, the Big Three carmakers laid off 330,000 workers as they made dramatic cutbacks simply to survive as they came to the brink of disaster.[32]

After the 1970s oil crises, Detroit yielded the small, fuel-efficient car market to the Germans and Japanese and focused on building larger, more profitable cars and trucks. They sowed the seeds of their near-destruction. (Chrysler had a government-backed bailout in 1979, and history would repeat itself three decades later.) As small cars became popular, the U.S. slapped quotas to halt the imported onslaught. The Japanese responded by opening car factories in the U.S. that were competitive and nonunionized.

General Motors and other carmakers concentrated on making SUVs because these were the most profitable cars for them, not just to please their shareholders, but because of their staggering health care and pensions costs, especially for retirees. Between 1991 and 2006, GM paid out $55 billion in retiree pension benefits (not counting health care), while only paying $13 billion in dividends to stockholders. Wall Street historian Roger Lowenstein wrote, "It was a pension firm on wheels, so went the joke—an HMO [health maintenance organization] with a showroom." Foreign companies were not saddled with those costs, as the state picked up the tab for health care and retirement.[33]

In 2003, GM had 460,000 retirees and spouses to support—more than three times the number of its employees. This would get worse, rising to five times the number of employees by 2007. The cost of supporting so many retirees was a heavy anchor that would drag down GM. GM's CEO Rick Wagoner called for Congress to reform health care. The cost was crippling to the automobile industry.[34]

The SUV party came to an end in 2005 after Hurricane Katrina sent gas prices above $3 a gallon. SUVs were now too expensive to operate and consumers stopped buying them. Detroit lost its pathway to profitability. The stock prices of the Big Three tanked. It was especially bad for GM: in 1999 it had spun off Delphi, its parts manufacturer, but saddled the company with identically high labor and pension costs. Delphi filed for Chapter 11 bankruptcy in October 2005. GM was one of its biggest creditors. That year, GM took a $10.6 billion loss. The company sold off GMAC, its profitable financing arm, to raise money.[35]

Desperate, GM and the United Auto Workers union came to a new accord in 2007: GM would transfer $30 billion to a UAW-operated trust fund for retiree health care, and agree to a two-tier wage system, paying new hires much less. GM finally got this huge liability off its books. Chrysler and Ford soon came to similar agreements with the UAW.[36]

German luxury car manufacturer Daimler-Benz acquired Chrysler in 1998 for $36 billion, but the relationship was disastrous. The two corporate cultures simply didn't blend. The Germans eventually asserted control of the combined company and discovered that the cost synergies didn't exist. By 2007, Daimler had had enough of Chrysler. It offloaded Chrysler to private equity firm Cerberus Capital Management for $7.4 billion, a fifth of the price it had spent to buy the company. Daimler essentially paid Cerberus to take the company, freeing Daimler from pension and retiree health care obligations.

The third Detroit carmaker, Ford, was in better shape than the other two. Ford recognized earlier that the automobile market was fundamentally changing, and so it took a different path than Chrysler or GM. A new CEO, Alan Mulally, came aboard in 2006. He immediately mortgaged every bit of the company for $23.6 billion to finance a turnaround. This bought the company time while it retooled, and it never had to take federal bailout money.

Chrysler and General Motors entered into negotiations to merge. Survival mergers usually involved at least one healthy partner that could nurse the other back to health. But when they were both sick? Perhaps allowing them to file for Chapter 11 to reorganize would be better. The two companies asked for billions from the federal government in assistance. After all, the finance industry was being bailed out, so why not Detroit? The Treasury Department rejected the request, deciding not to get involved in bailing out industrial companies.

The car companies were hemorrhaging cash, so they came back to Washington in fall 2008 to ask for $25 billion in emergency loans. Congress balked, requiring the companies to come up with a business plan for how they would use the money to restructure the industry. These companies had enormous legacy costs: retiree benefits, health care, guaranteed hours for workers, and far too many dealerships. But with the implosion of the credit markets, who else could possibly save Detroit? Certainly not the banks. The federal government was the lender of last resort.

The CEOs of the Big Three returned to Congress after Thanksgiving 2008 to plead their case. Congress was skeptical, but after the Labor Department published the 533,000-job loss figure for November, Democrats quickly proposed a short-term, $14 billion loan that would bridge GM and Chrysler to March, when the new Obama administration could then package a more permanent solution. The Bush White House threw its support behind the loan and the idea to appoint a "car czar" to oversee the industry's restructuring, but Senate Republicans said no when they voted on December 11.

With George W. Bush's term in office winding down, he realized the country could not afford to let Detroit collapse. The White House tapped into TARP to provide the Detroit automakers with a survival loan. GM and Chrysler received a $17.4 billion loan providing them a bridge. (Ford was not included, as it had enough cash to survive.) It came with strict conditions: the government would receive warrants to purchase up to 20 percent of the companies, and the United Auto Workers had to accept wages equal to pay of nonunion auto workers. The Bush administration required the companies to provide proof of restructuring by March 31, 2009, or they would be forced into Chapter 11 to reorganize.[37]

As Barack Obama came into the Oval Office in January 2009, his first crisis stared him in the face: what to do about Detroit? He inherited the problem, and he largely continued the Bush administration's rescue. Continuity was vital for restoring faith in the market. If one of the Big Three auto makers went under, the effects would have rippled disastrously throughout the economy.

As the March deadline approached, Detroit finalized its restructuring plan: Chrysler and GM between them proposed cutting six brands and asked for $21.6 billion more from the federal government just to survive. Workers and retirees were asked to make dramatic cuts. This would especially impact the estimated 800,000 retirees who counted on healthcare from Detroit.[38]

Detroit's news turned even grimmer when GM's own auditor revealed that the company was probably untenable. Despite the company's efforts toward trimming costs, GM's future was in doubt. There was the genuine fear that GM would be another Lehman Brothers, only for the manufacturing sector. On March 5, the Dow Jones fell another 4.1 percent to 6594.44. It had nearly reached the bottom.

The Obama administration rejected Detroit's restructuring plans as insufficient. It took a hard line against the automakers, questioned their survivability and imposed strict conditions if the companies wanted additional taxpayer funding. It requested and received the ouster of GM CEO Rick Wagoner on March 29, and gave the company sixty days to redraw its business plans. Chrysler had thirty days to finalize its proposed alliance with Italian carmaker Fiat. This was done, in part, to satisfy a public that was increasingly angry at the scope and scale of corporate bailouts.

On his first day on the job, GM's new CEO, Fritz Henderson, indicated that it was more than likely the company would file for Chapter 11 in order to quickly reorganize. The federal government set up a program to guarantee car warranties, lest people stop buying cars for fear their warranties would no longer be valid.

In its fourth business plan since the start of the year, GM proposed radical cuts to win new government aid: it would kill an additional brand, Pontiac, cut another 21,000 jobs, and swap much of its debt for equity. As the government was now a major bondholder, it would in effect partly nationalize the company.[39]

These steps were still too incremental to actually save the automakers. The Obama administration concluded that there was only way that could radically restructure the ailing car companies: bankruptcy court. The federal government worked out agreements with the unions to guarantee some benefits, though retirees were hit hard with benefit cuts. Decades of UAW bargaining would be undone by the Obama administration and the bankruptcy courts.

The federal government and Chrysler negotiated with the company's bondholders, but failed to come to an agreement by the April 30 deadline. At noon, President Obama held a press conference declaring that Chrysler was in Chapter 11 to reorganize. Fiat had offered to assume an ownership stake and the burden of leading the company, and it bid exactly zero dollars to do so. The merger with Fiat would move forward and the government would provide another $10 billion in assistance.

The Chrysler bankruptcy progressed through the bankruptcy court with remarkable speed. Chrysler closed almost eight hundred dealerships, a quarter of its total, using the bankruptcy court to dissolve them. Many states had strong laws protecting the dealers, but bankruptcy law trumped those. The first week of June 2009, the bankruptcy court agreed to Fiat's acquisition of Chrysler, allowing Chrysler to exit bankruptcy just one month after filing for Chapter 11. The Supreme Court granted a stay in the Chrysler bankruptcy process at the behest of some creditors, then declined to review the case. On June 10, Fiat took possession of most of Chrysler's assets, and the company exited bankruptcy after a quick forty-two days.

Seeing how fast Chrysler had progressed in its bankruptcy proceedings, the Obama administration prepared to do the same for GM. GM was a much larger company than Chrysler. The government shored up final concessions from the UAW and sweetened the pot for bondholders before directing the company into an orderly Chapter 11. The U.S. government invested another $30 billion, totaling $50 billion in taxpayer financing for GM. In return, the government now owned 60 percent of the company, while the Canadian government owned 12 percent. The UAW's health trust received 17.5 percent ownership, while the bondholders got 10 percent. The company was effectively nationalized, albeit temporarily. Some referred to GM as "Government Motors." GM filed for Chapter 11 on June 1 and declared it would close fourteen plants, jettison four of its eight brands, and close 1,100 dealers nationwide. By the time it emerged from bankruptcy, this onetime icon of American industry and manufacturing was significantly diminished.[40]

GM's speed through bankruptcy court matched Chrysler's. There was no appeal to the Supreme Court. A judge approved the deal: GM would spin off its most valuable assets into a new GM that was government-backed and had strong union ownership. The losers were the many dealers who were closed, as well as many workers from the discontinued brands. GM emerged from bankruptcy on July 10, five weeks after filing for Chapter 11. Despite the $67 billion that the federal government had invested in Chrysler and GM, it was unlikely that this money would ever be paid back. Both companies went to the brink, and both survived, but only because of massive federal intervention.

Ford was the only one of the Big Three automakers that did not file for bankruptcy, nor did it take bailout funds. However, it took a $5.9 billion federal loan, part of a $25 billion federal program to help automakers retool their factories to make more fuel-efficient cars. The company posted a

$1 billion profit for the third quarter of 2009. The company was making cars and people were buying them. Ford lacked the stigma of bankruptcy, and it had heavily streamlined its operations in recent years. It had also slashed its workforce in half since 2005. This was the first time the car manufacturer had reported profitability in four years.

Four months into office, Obama announced a major agreement, tightening vehicle emissions and raising car mileage standards by 2016. California had led a coalition of states that demanded carmakers raise fuel efficiency. Obama got the states and car manufacturers to agree on a single federal standard, which was what Detroit wanted. Detroit had spent years fighting efficiency, but now with the Big Three in trouble, they embraced it.

The automobile industry's near implosion had a sharp impact on Michigan. The state had lost 840,000 jobs during the decade as manufacturing was hit hard, and unemployment stood at 14.7 percent at the end of 2009—the highest in the nation. The city of Detroit lost 25 percent of its population over the decade, as the 2010 Census showed. No other city had suffered such a devastating loss, not even New Orleans, which was swamped by Hurricane Katrina. [41]

What happened to the Detroit carmakers was emblematic of the broader problems facing American labor. Unskilled labor was being squeezed out by automation and outsourcing. Those workers who survived had education and skills to survive in a technology-driven work environment, and often they would be paid less than before. The Great Recession sped up the process of deindustrialization that had been underway for years.

Obamacare

After dealing with the stimulus package and rescuing Detroit, President Obama turned to other legislative priorities. The White House could choose from financial reform (the most obvious in the wake of the economic crisis), health care reform, or addressing climate change through a cap-and-trade program, whose failure we discussed earlier. Obama chose health care, a key campaign promise he had made to Senator Ted Kennedy to win his endorsement.

Health care reform was long overdue. President Harry Truman has been called the father of "Medicare for all," and he attempted but failed to create universal health care after World War II. Instead, most Americans received health insurance through their employers, and as premiums rose, companies cut back on salary increases and financed health care instead. This contributed to a long period of stagnant wages throughout the first decade. It also contributed to job lock as people stayed at their jobs, when they could have been out forming new businesses, out of fear of losing health care.

In 2001, insuring a family of four cost only $8,414. By 2012, the average health care spending for that same family was $20,728.[42] In 2010, the U.S. spent $2.7 trillion on health care, or 17 percent of GDP. Health care costs were rising at twice the rate of inflation. Americans were living longer, thanks to modern medicine. Pharmaceuticals and expensive, experimental medical treatments could keep people alive longer, but that also came with a heavy cost. Americans were spending twice that of other industrialized nations on health care, but without better results. Other nations, however, had heavy government regulation of health care, but the U.S. was leery of taking this approach. Only the U.S. left it open to the market to determine pricing, and what a distorted market it was.[43]

Health care in the U.S. was a patchwork. Many people didn't have it or were inadequately covered. Many couldn't afford health insurance, even as the public was shifting toward viewing health care as a basic right. Health care was certainly a painful issue for many Americans and it needed reforming, but it was far down the list compared to strengthening the economy, which was job number one. The problem in 2009 was that unemployment was still getting worse, even as Wall Street was rebounding from its lows.

Obama hoped to have health care reform signed by the fall of 2009, but it was not to be. It was a long slog trying to woo Republicans in Congress to support the legislation, which finally passed the Senate on Christmas Eve with no Republican votes. The House likewise passed its own bill with no Republican support, and these two bills needed to be reconciled. The issue was punted to 2010.

Further complicating the matter was the fact that Senator Ted Kennedy died on August 25, opening his Senate seat. The Democratic giant was diagnosed with a brain tumor, and so he was largely absent from the Senate in 2009 during his treatment, and right when he was most needed. His death meant a special election would be held for his seat.

And then the unexpected happened: Democrats lost Kennedy's seat. Their candidate, Martha Coakley, ran a lackluster campaign in the country's most liberal state and lost to a Republican, Scott Brown. This threw the entire equation around health care reform into question, as Democrats had lost their sixty-seat supermajority by one. Yet Obama pushed health care reform through Congress through legislative maneuvering to avoid the Senate's arcane rules. Democrats in the House first passed the earlier Senate-approved version of reform, then immediately voted and passed a reconciliation bill that had been previously negotiated with senators.

Obama took a centrist approach, modeling his health care reform on the conservative Heritage Foundation's proposal and Massachusetts's experience with Romneycare, named after Republican governor Mitt Romney, who created the statewide system in 2004. Rather than a federal takeover of health care, states instead would set up exchanges where people could compare rates and buy health insurance. Those who fell under an income threshold of four times the federal poverty rate would get a subsidized rate. The working poor would be covered through an expansion of Medicaid; the federal government paid for 90 percent of the cost, while states would pick up 10 percent. This was, essentially, the free-market approach, modeled on Republican ideas. And yet Republicans ran away from it. Not a single Republican in Congress voted in favor of the Affordable Care Act. In fact, the ACA became a toxic issue to the political right.

Many liberals wanted a public option, an alternative alongside private insurance, which would allow people to buy into a federal health care program. After an intense public debate, Obama yielded to the political reality and gave up the public option. (Joe Lieberman was the one Democratic holdout in the Senate; it would have passed had he voted aye.) Liberals were incensed, while conservatives remained deeply distrustful of any tampering with the free market or giving the federal government more power.

The Affordable Care Act fundamentally changed health care in the country, even for those who already had it through their employer. Children up to twenty-six years of age could remain on their parents' insurance plan. There was now a mandate to buy health insurance, along with a penalty for failing to be insured. The law instituted a tax on expensive "Cadillac" plans, and also taxed wealthier people to pay for the state subsidies. Most importantly, it prevented insurers from blocking coverage to people with preexisting conditions. Although the idea of a public option was popular, it was nixed in the final bill for political expediency. It was the great might-have-been of health care reform.

Ultimately the Affordable Care Act wasn't about making health care more affordable, but rather about extending coverage to more people. Democrats in Congress passed the ACA which Obama signed into law on March 23, 2010. It was the signature achievement of the Obama administration. Despite the victory—the first major health care overhaul since Medicaid and Medicare were created in the 1960s—many Americans were angry over reform, viewing it as socialized medicine and worried about the fiscal cost. In fact, it reduced the federal deficit through cost controls.

The ACA hung like an albatross around the Obama administration's neck. Obama promised that people could keep their existing health care plans, which often proved untrue, and would become a sizable talking point for Republicans in the 2010 election. Conservatives started derisively calling it "Obamacare," a name that everyone quickly embraced, including the president. The rollout of the government exchange in 2013, healthcare.gov, was botched, and gave the Obama administration a black eye.

It was probably a mistake for Obama to push health care reform so early, rather than focusing on creating jobs. Franklin Roosevelt waited until 1935—his third year in office—before proposing Social Security. If Obama had focused on creating jobs instead, he might have avoided the "shellacking" in the 2010 midterm election.

Obama at War

In addition to the financial crisis, Obama inherited Bush's three wars: Afghanistan, Iraq, and the War on Terror. There were still 38,000 American soldiers in Afghanistan and 161,000 in Iraq when he entered the White House. [44]

Obama had campaigned on rolling back much of George W. Bush's foreign policy and War on Terror initiatives, but as president Obama didn't entirely succeed. He revoked the "Torture Memos" that had allowed enhanced interrogation techniques and banned the CIA's secret prisons. In other areas, such as surveillance and Predator drone strikes, he continued or expanded the Bush policies. Nor did he completely sever the wars in Afghanistan and Iraq.

Because of the military's successful surge in 2007–2008, Iraq seemed to be stabilized. Obama pulled out the last combat brigade from Iraq in August 2010, leaving behind 50,000 support troops to help steady the country. The remainder would be withdrawn within sixteen months in accordance with the agreement George Bush had made with the Iraqi government. The Iraqis were now on their own for protecting their country. However, when the Islamic State overran northern Iraq in 2014, American forces returned to bolster the government.

In June 2009, Obama flew to the Middle East and gave a stirring address in Cairo, Egypt, directed at closing the rift between the U.S. and the Muslim world, which had come to distrust the U.S. over the invasion and occupation of Iraq. In a well-received speech, he declared, "I've come here to Cairo to seek a new beginning between the United States and Muslims around the world, one based on mutual interest and mutual respect, and one based upon the truth that America and Islam are not exclusive and need not be in competition."[45]

In fact, in early 2011 revolutions broke out around the Middle East in what became known as the Arab Spring. Nonviolent protesters overthrew Egypt and Tunisia's long-standing presidents. Things were not quite so peaceful in Libya and Yemen, which endured heavy fighting—and in the case of Libya, NATO intervened to prevent Muammar Gaddafi from massacring his own people. Gaddafi was eventually overthrown and killed. The most violent outbreak resulted in a years-long civil war in Syria that killed hundreds of thousands and created several million refugees, many of whom fled to Europe.

Obama carried forward Bush's earnestness for protecting the U.S., including many of the electronic surveillance measures. He stepped up Predator drone attacks to assassinate al-Qaeda leaders in Pakistan, Yemen, and elsewhere. The new president no longer called it the War on Terror, but the war continued nonetheless.

Former CIA director George Tenet had presciently written how U.S. intelligence had focused on screening Arab males, which would lead al-Qaeda to broaden its base of recruits to non-Arabs. "I am convinced the next major attack against the United States may well be conducted by people with Asian or African faces, not the ones that many Americans are alert to." On Christmas Day 2009, a Nigerian named Umar Farouk Abdulmutallab tried to blow up a Delta Airlines plane as it landed in Detroit after flying over from Amsterdam. As he had plastic explosives sewn into his underwear, he became known as the Underwear Bomber, and he tried to ignite it with a syringe. Alert crew and passengers jumped on him just as the fire began and managed to extinguish it. Al-Qaeda claimed responsibility for the incident, and Abdulmutallab had claimed he had received the explosives and training from al-Qaeda in Yemen, which was shaping up to be a new base for the terrorist organization. [46]

On May 1, 2010, a near disaster in New York's Times Square was averted by two alert vendors. A naturalized American citizen from Pakistan, Faisal Shahzad, had parked an explosives-filled SUV on a busy street, set the timer to detonate, then fled the scene. The car began to emit smoke, and that's when the street vendors called the police, who evacuated the area. The FBI sprang into action and arrested Shahzad just fifty-two hours later. He was believed to be a terrorist working for the Pakistani Taliban. Shahzad pleaded guilty and was given a life sentence in prison.

The Pakistanis both helped the U.S. in the War on Terror but also supported the Taliban, their goal being to keep Afghanistan destabilized so it couldn't ally with Pakistan's archrival, India. Obama had to decide what to do about Afghanistan.

By the end of the decade, the American public had largely lost interest in the war in Afghanistan or its outcome. Let's declare victory, people said, and bring our soldiers home. But to do so would allow the Taliban to reclaim the country and possibly give al-Qaeda its sanctuary again. The hard truth was that Afghanistan was an unwinnable war, and everyone knew it.

General David Petraeus, the architect of the surge in Iraq, was promoted to head Central Command in Tampa in October 2008, which had responsibility for military operations in the Middle East. Obama would come to rely on him as a key general and later CIA director.

Because of the heavy violence in Iraq, the American military had spent most of its efforts in the decade to stabilize the country. The U.S. had taken its eye off the ball in Afghanistan. Joe Biden pronounced, "This has been on autopilot." General Stanley McChrystal, the new commander there, won approval to raise the force in the country to 68,000 soldiers in early 2009, but soon came back with another request for 40,000 more troops to stabilize a country long ignored and whose government was noticeably corrupt and ineffective. This exasperated Obama. [47]

A counterinsurgency strategy would take years to implement in Afghanistan. There was strong opposition to the plan: the American public was divided on the question of Afghanistan, as troops had been there for eight years already and the situation still was not under control. The public was tired of these expensive wars. Opposition to escalation in Afghanistan was the result, in part, because of the long, drawn-out war in Iraq.

After three months of deliberation, Obama finally made his decision about Afghanistan after Thanksgiving 2009. In a nationally televised address from West Point on December 1, he declared that he would send an additional 30,000 troops to the country. This would raise the American commitment to more than 100,000 soldiers. It was designed to shore up the corrupt government and train Afghan security forces so they could defend their own country. Obama was wary of an open-ended commitment, and thus put a timeline in place, saying that the surge would draw down after eighteen months in July 2011. In this he replicated President Bush's successful surge in Iraq.[48]

Unfortunately for General McChrystal, he couldn't keep his mouth shut. *Rolling Stone* magazine published a candid and unsavory profile of the general in June 2010. McChrystal resigned and Petraeus took over military operations in Afghanistan. And the war continued on. As of 2020, the United States still had a military presence in the country. It had become our longest war.[49]

Obama inherited 242 detainees at the controversial Guantanamo Bay detention center in Cuba, and signed an executive order closing the prison within one year. This was one of his campaign promises that he could never fulfill.

In November 2009, the Obama administration determined that Khalid Sheik Mohammed, the mastermind behind 9/11, would be transferred out of Guantanamo Bay to New York City, where he and four other al-Qaeda ringleaders would stand trial in federal district court. New York howled in protest, noting how much the security for such a trial would cost. Obama relented and picked a rural location. Congress objected and passed a law forbidding Guantanamo detainees to be transferred to the U.S. for prosecution. Obama also found it difficult to repatriate some detainees to their home countries—these countries often didn't want these people. Some of these men, despite our love for the rule of law, were simply too dangerous to release, with or without a trial. Indefinite detention would continue with some combatants never being charged with a crime.

In April 2011, having run out of political options and stymied on every front, Obama reversed course on civilian trials, ordering the five key 9/11 suspects, including Khalid Sheik Mohammed, to be tried by military tribunal. The process bogged down, however, and as of 2020 the five detainees had still not been tried. The prison at Guantanamo remained open, despite Obama's pledge to close it.[50]

Just a week after Obama relented on closing Guantanamo, the president announced that Osama bin Laden was dead. Nearly a decade after 9/11, bin Laden was discovered living in a mansion in the northern Pakistani city of Abbottabad. A Navy SEAL team was dispatched by helicopter from Afghanistan to raid the compound on the night of May 2. They killed the terrorist leader, retrieved an enormous amount of documentation about al-Qaeda, then buried bin Laden's body at sea. There was no way that bin Laden could be taken prisoner; how would you ever put a man like that on trial? "We got him," Obama announced on television.

Another war that the United States had fought since the 1970s was the war on drugs. It had dragged on for decades with no end—or victory—in sight. The U.S. had high demand for drugs, despite extensive efforts to eradicate drug importation, and yet, doing too little for prevention or treatment. It treated addiction as a crime, rather than as an illness. South of the border, Mexican drug cartels battled for control of who got to feed America's staggering drug addiction. The violence was appalling: nearly 5,400 people were killed in Mexico in 2008 alone from battling cartels. The violence ebbed as the Sinaloa cartel defeated its main rival, the Juárez cartel.[51]

Meanwhile, Americans were reconsidering their opposition to marijuana, a drug demonized since Richard Nixon's day for its popularity among Haight-Ashbury hippies who opposed the Vietnam War. It had been declared a Schedule 1 drug, placing it in the same category of controlled substances as cocaine, heroin, and methamphetamines.

During the first decade, many Americans came out as pot smokers. By 2009, thirteen states and Washington, D.C., had made marijuana legal for medicinal purposes. (There is a historic echo to Prohibition of the 1920s, which made medicinal whiskey legal.) Pot was especially helpful for people with AIDS or cancer, as it stimulated appetite and reduced nausea. California became the poster child for medical marijuana: cannabis clinics and dispensaries sprouted, and it was easy to get a doctor's prescription. The Golden State was in a severe fiscal crisis because of the housing bubble collapse and considered legalizing marijuana for recreational use, and thus could tax and regulate it. The city of Stockton, which had a high number of housing foreclosures, witnessed many of its homes turned into marijuana grow houses.

Increasing majorities of Americans now believed that marijuana should be legalized. The Obama administration recognized that the marijuana fight was not one it could win and punted the issue to the states. Attorney General Eric Holder tepidly reminded Americans that it was still a federal crime to possess marijuana, but even local law enforcement had tired of arresting people for smoking weed. The zero-tolerance policies of the 1980s and 1990s had yielded prisons full of people, largely for low-level drug offenses, and the public was realizing just how expensive incarceration is.

A ballot initiative in California in 2010 narrowly rejected marijuana legalization. Colorado and Washington State became the first two states to legalize pot in 2012, and after that the floodgates opened as ever more states legalized medicinal marijuana. California voters revisited the issue in 2016, approving marijuana legalization for recreational use. It was probably just a question of time before marijuana became legal nationally, but that would take an act of Congress and a president who supported legalization.

The Deepwater Horizon

On April 20, 2010, a deepwater exploratory oil rig, the *Deepwater Horizon*, was completing the mile-deep Macondo well in the Gulf of Mexico when something went terribly wrong. Pressurized oil and gas shot up the well after the crew thought they had cemented it shut. The blowout preventer, a five-story shutoff valve capping the well, failed to seal the well. A massive bubble of oil and gas rose a mile to the surface, engulfing the *Deepwater Horizon* in an explosion that killed eleven crewmen. Thus began the worst accidental marine oil spill, one that far exceeded the *Exxon Valdez's* eleven-million-gallon spill in 1989. This came just fifteen days after twenty-nine miners were killed in a coal dust explosion at the Upper Big Branch coal mine in West Virginia after an explosive gas buildup.

The oil turned the waters of the Gulf of Mexico black. Oil soon threatened to taint the beaches and marshlands of Alabama, Florida, Louisiana, and Mississippi. The federal government put a deepwater drill moratorium in place and halted fishing in large portions of the gulf, while the Coast Guard, British Petroleum (BP), and the gulf states erected hundreds of miles of booms to contain the oil from contaminating beaches and wetlands. Joel Achenbach, author of *A Hole at the Bottom of the Sea*, called it "a kind of environmental 9/11." Technology allowed humans to drill in the heavily pressured waters of the deep, and technology failed.[52]

BP owned the Macondo well, and it immediately took responsibility for the failure. But it also cast blame on the *Deepwater Horizon*'s owner, Transocean, and other contractors such as Halliburton, which made the cement for the well. At the Obama administration's demand, BP put $20 billion into an escrow account to pay for the damages, cleanup, and potential losses to the states and industries like tourism and fishing. This was just a starting point: BP would fund the entire cleanup, including what the government spent on operations. The president appointed Coast Guard Commandant Admiral Thad Allen as the federal point man on the response. For three months, the *Deepwater Horizon* disaster was all-consuming for the White House.

On July 15, nearly three months after the Macondo well started spewing oil, BP engineers finally put a tight-fitting cap over the well, effectively sealing it. The leak had stopped. It was not until early August that engineers could pump heavy drilling mud and cement down the well, known as a static kill, while another rig drilled a relief well that sealed Macondo from the bottom in a double kill on September 18.

BP initially downplayed the size of the oil spill. After the well was finally sealed, the federal government reported that the Macondo well had spilled 4.9 million barrels of oil (205.8 million gallons). The well had initially released 62,000 barrels a day, though that gradually reduced to 53,000 barrels as the pressure weakened.[53]

Why do some disasters stick to presidents, while others don't? George W. Bush was blamed for the lackadaisical federal response to Hurricane Katrina, yet the Macondo well disaster failed to stick to Obama. This was in part because it was the private sector's fault for allowing the well to blow—and it was the private sector that had the technology to kill the well. Still, the public wanted the president to hold BP accountable for the spill, and wondered why he wasn't spitting mad at the company. "The president still had that 'No Drama Obama' thing going, that ability to ratchet crises down to the level of mere *challenges*," wrote Joel Achenbach. "His equanimity was one of his great qualities, but suddenly he seemed like the guy who orders a fine Vouvray at a biker bar."[54]

The Jobless Recovery

The national unemployment rate climbed to 9.8 percent in September 2009, the highest rate in twenty-six years. The economy was still shedding jobs; it seemed to be a jobless recovery, and economists forecast it would stay this way well into 2010. The Federal Reserve meanwhile declared that the recession was over, as the economy was growing again, but with so little growth or job creation that they continued to hold interest rates near zero percent.[55]

The 2009 fiscal year ended in September with a massive and record fiscal deficit of $1.4 trillion. This was actually lower than forecast, as Wall Street did not need as much bailout money as anticipated, though the deficit was 10 percent of the overall economy. This put a brake on Obama's spending plans.[56]

The unemployment rate for the Great Recession peaked at 10.2 percent in October 2009. Some called it the Great Mancession, as working-class men were hit particularly hard. Non-college-educated men were overly represented in construction and manufacturing, and when the economy turned south, they suffered the most layoffs. Hardest hit were the nation's minorities, African Americans and Hispanics, who were poorer and lacked the high-paying jobs and savings that would allow them to weather the storm. Women tended to work in service industries, which weren't hit as hard. Thus during the worst of the layoffs, women became the majority of the American workforce for the first time ever.

At the same time, the government reported that GDP grew 3.5 percent on an annual basis in the third quarter, but that was partly because of massive federal stimulus spending. Many were worried about the enormous sums that the government borrowed to finance the stimulus. Although unemployment was high, there was the fear that high borrowing would lead to high interest rates if foreign investors decided that the U.S. was too much of a risk. The Federal Reserve also warned of a jobless recovery, forecasting that unemployment might stay high for five or six years. However, in November the unemployment rate fell slightly to 10 percent.[57]

After less than nine months in office, Obama was awarded the Nobel Peace Prize. Many scratched their heads, wondering what the president had done in his short time in office to deserve such a prestigious humanitarian award. It was as if the European prize committee was so enamored of Obama's rock star status—and that above all he wasn't George W. Bush—that qualified him for the prize. He admitted candidly, "It was not helpful to us politically."[58]

Over the course of 2009, most of the large banks that were forced to take federal guarantees during the previous year paid the TARP loans back. The Treasury estimated that, of the $370 billion it had lent, it would recover all but $42 billion, largely from AIG, Chrysler, and GM. In December, Bank of America declared that it would repay its $45 billion loan. That left Citigroup as the only large bank not to pay back its TARP loan, but it soon came to an agreement with the feds on repayment. The federal government declared that it would spend $200 billion less on rescue efforts than anticipated, and the loans were coming back with interest.[59] The Congressional Oversight Panel, which was created to oversee the rescue program, summarized that TARP had largely done its job to stabilize the financial markets, even while acknowledging that it had done little to stem high home foreclosures.[60] The Federal Reserve ended up making $45 billion in profit in 2009, and returned this money to the Treasury.[61]

With the repayment of TARP money, large financial institutions had freed themselves from stringent crisis-era federal oversight. Despite the fear that Wall Street firms were too big to fail, the banking sector was even more concentrated now than it was before the crisis. There was now the implicit assumption that the feds would rescue the banks whenever the financial markets got into trouble. Banking reform was stalled in Congress and had done little to provide new oversight. At the same time, Wall Street paid out nearly $21 billion in bonuses in 2009, a 17 percent increase from the year before, though still far below the peak of $33 billion in 2007.[62] Meanwhile, banks pulled back lending significantly, reducing their lending 7.5 percent or $587 billion in 2009, even though interest rates were at a record low. The lack of credit continued to stymie the economic recovery. This made it more difficult for businesses to operate, leaving the government to be the lender of last (or sometimes only) resort.[63]

TARP was widely reviled as a government bailout, and government largesse helped spawn the reactionary Tea Party, which we will discuss in the next chapter. It arose as a political force in 2009, but the strong populist anger against the bailouts during Bush's waning days served as a warning of what was to come. Critics carped that the bailout benefited big business more than anyone, which was true. Chrystia Freeland wrote in *Plutocrats*: "the super-elite got a rescue that was denied everyone else." The flip side of that argument was that the entire economy was rescued.[64]

The fact is: TARP worked. The $700 billion emergency fund had in fact stabilized the banking system and thus the broader economy. Without it, unemployment would have gone much higher. By extending credit to the banking system right when it needed it, the federal government had prevented another Great Depression. The banks had returned the money at a profit to the taxpayers. However, not all of the money had been paid back—Fannie Mae and Freddie Mac were still ingesting funds, and it was questionable whether the automakers and AIG would ever be able to completely repay their TARP loans. The Congressional Budget Office calculated that the taxpayers would only lose $25 billion out of the $700 billion that the U.S. government authorized during the economic crisis.[65]

As TARP expired in October 2010, much of the American population was angry at the program for its costly bailout of Wall Street. Geithner noted that TARP "was perhaps the most maligned yet most effective program in recent memory." He explained its unpopularity. "The TARP was doomed to be unpopular from inception, because Americans were rightfully angry that the same firms that helped create the economic crisis got taxpayer support to keep their doors open." He finally noted in TARP's defense that it had not cost the taxpayers nearly as much as people had feared. "In the end, 90 percent of that once-feared $700 billion TARP price tag either will not have been spent or will be returned to the taxpayers."[66]

The International Monetary Fund calculated in 2013 that the U.S. had invested around $2 trillion on its various economic rescue packages—and that it had earned $166 billion in return. Half of that ($88 billion) came from the Fannie Mae and Freddie Mac conservatorships. Even the $180 billion injected into AIG earned $23 billion in interest, all profit to the taxpayers. The federal government sold off its last shares in the company in 2012.[67]

The American automobile industry, which had seemed near the brink of collapse, had shrunk from 1.32 million workers down to 626,000 by 2009. A year after the massive federal intervention, the car industry had grown by 55,000 jobs as Detroit started making more fuel-efficient, smaller cars that Americans now wanted. Just a year after filing for bankruptcy to reorganize, GM filed for its initial public offering in August 2010.[68]

The stock market ended down for the decade, a rare occurrence. For many investors, these were lost years: the Dow Jones was down 8.25 percent compared to its close in 1999, while the S&P 500 was down 23 percent, and the NASDAQ closed 44 percent lower than a decade before.[69] The recession may have officially been over, but the economy was anemic and consumers still weren't in a mood to spend—they preferred to pay off debt and put more into savings. There did not seem to be much of an economic recovery, especially with unemployment above 10 percent, and so many people looking over their shoulders, wondering if it would be their turn soon. Mortgage rates may have been at historic lows—you could get a thirty-year mortgage for under 5 percent—but that was only because the Federal Reserve was buying mortgage-backed securities, artificially driving rates low. That program ended in March 2010, but surprisingly, rates continued to fall on the weakness of the economy and deflation.

The first decade ended with unemployment stuck at 10 percent. The economy lost 85,000 jobs in December 2009, and hundreds of thousands of the unemployed had simply stopped job hunting in despair.[70] On the upside, the housing market seemed to have stabilized, and prices in some places were beginning to creep upward again. The Standard & Poor's/Case-Shiller Home Price Index showed that nationwide, home prices ended the decade 30 percent below their peak in April 2006.[71]

Over the course of the next year, the job numbers improved somewhat, but not nearly enough. Unemployment stubbornly stood at 9.6 percent in October 2010, just slightly down from 10.2 percent a year earlier. The stock market was recovering, but this mattered little to the worker who couldn't find a job. The jobless recovery was disastrous for Obama as he faced the midterm election, and he did a poor job explaining how his administration was improving the economy, despite his rhetorical skills as a public speaker.

Without a doubt, the massive federal intervention started under Bush and completed under Obama rescued the economy. Yet Obama failed to build policies that would create jobs. He had the onetime stimulus bill in 2009, but that was it. There was no jobs bill. Democrats controlled Congress, but he offered too little leadership. The White House proposed no ideas to help the unemployed. "There was no narrative, no story to tell, because there was no guiding vision," wrote reporter Ron Suskind.[72]

The country forecast deficits as far as the eye could see: shortfalls of more than $1 trillion or more each year through 2011, and then declining to about $700 billion a year through 2019. Already the country owed $7.9 trillion to investors, which was just over half of GDP, but this was forecast to more than double to $17.5 trillion by 2019. Deficits—and interest rates—would rise unless spending could be brought under control, new sources of revenue tapped into, and economic growth rejuvenated. With a tenth of the work-force unemployed, and everyone else fearing for their jobs, the economy was anemic. [73]

Banking reform finally passed Congress in July 2010, almost two years after Lehman Brothers collapsed. It was a victory for the Obama administration. The Dodd-Frank Act intended to keep a financial meltdown like 2008 from reoccurring. The new law gave Treasury and the Federal Reserve greater powers to deal with the next crisis, including annual stress tests. "We had passed the most important financial reforms since the Great Depression," claimed Congressman Barney Frank, who had chaired the House Financial Services Committee. [74]

Banking lobbyists delayed implementation of Dodd-Frank as long as they could, then attempted to sabotage the new Consumer Financial Protection Bureau created by the law. Obama's choice to lead the bureau, Harvard professor Elizabeth Warren, faced major opposition by the bankers and had to withdraw. She soon found herself in the U.S. Senate in Ted Kennedy's old seat, where she continued to snipe at Wall Street. One might ask the bankers: How'd that work out for you?

Human nature being what it is, bankers will chase after the next hot investment to make more money, and no doubt there will be future bubbles that will burst and cause financial harm. Kenneth Feinberg, special master for a wide array of victims' compensation funds, wrote: "In past times of public anger over financial industry excesses, Wall Street has played a waiting game, lying low until the political storm subsides. History is on Wall Street's side." [75]

Obama had achieved much in his first two years in office: he engineered rescues for Wall Street and Detroit, reformed health care, and passed a financial reform bill. But the voters were deeply dissatisfied with the direction the country was moving. The economy weighed on everyone's minds. When would the job market get better? Would we be able to make next month's mortgage payment? What will this deficit spending do to the economy, and are we not saddling our kids with a tremendous amount of debt? Would Obamacare lead to a government takeover of health care?

Obama experienced one particular failure during his first two years in office: Congress had not come to a workable compromise on carbon emissions. Cap-and-trade was effectively dead. Despite the massive *Deepwater Horizon* oil spill in the Gulf of Mexico, there was no action on a climate bill.

Rather, the key issue for the 2010 midterm elections was the glacial economic recovery. Unemployment was stalled at 9.6 percent. Given the fragile state of the economy, no one wanted to raise energy costs.

Franklin Roosevelt provided the benchmark for any president leading the country during an extreme financial crisis. Roosevelt was elected in 1932 in the darkest part of the Great Depression, when the Republicans had been thoroughly discredited after a decade of rule and the Democrats took over the political direction of the country. In Obama's case, the economy was still falling, and the economy was hemorrhaging more jobs than the Obama team had forecast.

Unlike Roosevelt, Obama did not translate the successes of his administration into public enthusiasm, nor did he relate to how it impacted the regular citizen. The raw enthusiasm for Obama in 2008 quickly diminished. *New York Times* columnist Thomas Friedman wrote, "Barack Obama is a great orator, but he is the worst president I have ever seen when it comes to explaining his achievements, putting them in context, connecting with people on a gut level through repetition and thereby defining how the public views an issue." He used his bully pulpit too little, and critics long argued that he did not lead. [76]

Both Roosevelt and Obama benefited from having their party, the Democrats, control both houses of Congress. It is here where the comparison to FDR ends: Roosevelt's party had control over Congress for his entire presidency. Obama was about to lose control of the House of Representatives to a right-wing insurgency, a new breed of political opponents who would make his remaining six years as president a challenge to govern. They called themselves the Tea Party.

16

The Tea Party Strikes Back

Even before President Obama was sworn into office in January 2009, there was a populist outpouring against the banking bailouts. These were mostly libertarian, small-government conservatives who believed the banks shouldn't be rescued. To them, TARP was a four-letter word. They were angry at the Bush administration, and they transferred that anger to Obama. As Obama proposed big-government solutions to rescue the economy in the Great Recession, the populists coalesced into a protest movement shortly after the new president was sworn in.

The U.S. public debt had gone from surplus to massive deficit in a few short years, largely because of Bush's tax cuts, the nation's wars, and the response to the financial crisis. This had political consequences: a vocal minority of conservative Republicans decried the heavy borrowing and financial bailouts. They named the movement after the Boston Tea Party, and protests witnessed men and women dressed in Revolutionary War–era costumes and carrying Don't Tread on Me flags and signs.

The Tea Party was a grassroots, populist movement with no central leadership or national organization, but one that harnessed voter anger. It was a complaint movement like the Know Nothings of the 1850s. The *Washington Post* called it "a movement without a compass." Tea Party activists ranked the economy as their primary concern, along with distrusting government and opposing Obama's policies, all while expressing deep dissatisfaction with the Republican Party. Like much of the Republican demographic, the Tea Party was middle-aged or older and white.[1]

But the Tea Party was not just an economic protest movement; it was a reaction to the nation's changing culture and demographics. Non-college-educated whites had lost much of their economic power during the Great Recession, and their anger simmered and boiled over. They were resentful of the elites who had failed them, and resentful of their declining cultural, economic, and racial majority status. The working class became populist right wingers, though no one was really sure what to do with all this brimming anger.

The Tea Party did not want compassion, compromise, or moderation; it wanted red meat and heads on a platter. The populist movement hated big government spending and happily demanded that government be dismantled, but paradoxically insisted that they receive their Medicare and Social Security benefits, even though those two areas were major contributors to the federal deficit. The irony was the Tea Party was largely made up of people who would be affected by cuts to the safety net. Former congressional analyst Mike Lofgren called the Tea Party "people covered by Medicare who hate socialized medicine."[2]

The Republican Party was once known for its fiscal prudence; now it had become ideologically rigid and beholden to one principle: keeping taxes low, something that overwhelmingly benefited the wealthy. "The version of the Republican Party that greeted the second decade of the 21st century was one that apparently was in the process of shucking off most of its own history and heritage," observed historian Geoffrey Kabaservice. "Its leaders showed little interest in appealing to moderates, repudiating extremism, reaching out to new constituencies, or upholding the party's legacy of civil rights and civil liberties."[3]

During the Bush years, the Republican-led Congress greatly increased government spending, especially on the Pentagon and the Medicare prescription drug benefit, but without finding ways to pay for these except through more debt. But as a minority party, the GOP suddenly became terribly concerned about out-of-control spending and demanded immediate cuts.

Moderate Republicanism had become an endangered species, stung by the accusation of being a RINO (Republican in name only). Every Republican political candidate now campaigned on their conservative bona fides, not on how they worked with colleagues across the aisle. The conservative base did not want collaborators; they wanted representatives to take an unyielding stance on issues. This made for bad politics and gridlock, which was what happened during the second half of Barack Obama's first term.

Establishment Republicans were reluctant to engage with the Tea Party, and the GOP effectively split into an ungovernable party. But billionaire free-market advocates who wanted to lower taxes and stymie government regulations jumped on the bandwagon, sensing an opportunity to coopt this scorched-earth populism, while right-wing Fox News fanned the flames. They had assistance from the U.S. Supreme Court.[4]

The most controversial and bitterly fought-over Supreme Court decision of the decade came on January 21, 2010. The court split 5–4 in *Citizens United v. Federal Election Commission* in deciding that the federal government could not ban or limit corporate political spending and campaign donations on free speech grounds. It overturned a 2002 campaign finance reform law known as McCain-Feingold. Shadow money poured into the Tea Party as a number of plutocrats attempted to harness the populist anger for their benefit.[5]

One thing was certain: the Tea Party *despised* Barack Obama, and despite their heated denials, this was largely based on race. They simply didn't like that the country was becoming ever browner, which was a challenge to the dominant status of white people. Obama represented the country's demographic destiny. In their landmark study of the Tea Party, Theda Skocpol and Vanessa Williamson wrote:

> The son of an African father and a white American mother, Obama is perceived by many Tea Partiers as a foreigner, an invader pretending to be an American, a fifth columnist. Obama's past as a community organizer is taken as evidence that he works on behalf of the undeserving poor and wishes to mobilize government resources on their behalf. His academic achievements and social ties put him in league with the country's intellectual elite, whose disdain feels very real to many Americans, and whose cosmopolitan leanings seem unpatriotic. For so many reasons, therefore, Obama's social ambiguities as well as his political stands make him easy to portray as a threat—especially in the eyes of very conservative Americans.[6]

The Tea Party spawned a left-wing counterweight called Occupy Wall Street. It began, literally, with protests on Wall Street and spread to cities around the country as youthful (and often unemployed) leftists staged protests. "We are the 99%" was the movement's claim as they protested against the 1 percent, the wealthiest of the wealthy, who were capturing ever more of the nation's wealth. The movement "occupied" Zuccotti Park in Manhattan and McPherson Square in Washington, D.C., along with public spaces in other cities, for months before they finally cleared out. The Occupy movement certainly helped reframe the debate over economic inequality, but ultimately its message was too diffuse, and lacking any central leadership it had no goals. As a result, the protest movement faded quickly. There were no Occupy candidates who entered the halls of Congress, unlike the Tea Party.

In a warning that foreshadowed what was to come, the Tea Party flexed its political muscles and helped an unknown Massachusetts Republican state senator, Scott Brown, take liberal Ted Kennedy's seat in the U.S. Senate in a special election in January 2010. Kennedy, the youngest brother of JFK and Bobby, had died the summer before after holding the seat for nearly a half century. Brown's election made him the forty-first Republican senator, breaking the Democratic supermajority. As we've seen, the Democrats then had to jump through legislative hoops to pass the Affordable Care Act in March.

The Tea Party dubbed health care reform "Obamacare" and denounced Obama as a socialist, although there was nothing socialist about Obama's agenda. (As a reminder to the reader, socialism is where the state owns the means of production. With Obamacare, people bought private insurance. This was not socialism.). The name Obamacare came into mainstream usage.

Former vice presidential candidate Sarah Palin latched onto the populist Tea Party. Folksy and always entertaining, she had a way of galvanizing the political right. She made for excellent political theater. Palin was famous for quipping facetiously about President Obama, "How's that hopey-changey stuff working out for you?" She declared that Medicare-financed patient-physician end-of-life counseling were "death panels." This was irresponsible and outright false; on the other hand, she tapped into widespread fear, especially among the already retired, that their Medicare would somehow be taken away, or that undeserving people would take their well-deserved benefits.

President Bill Clinton and his wife Hillary had pushed for health care reform in the early 1990s. Their efforts never passed Congress, but so galvanized conservatives that the 1994 midterm witnessed the Republican Revolution, which saw Newt Gingrich rise to lead the House of Representatives. History seemed to repeat itself in 2010 after Obamacare passed and angry

Republicans stormed the precincts in protest. They saw it as a big government program and demanded its repeal.

An angry electorate went to the polls in the midterm election. Some 80 million people voted, compared to 130 million two years earlier. Essentially, fifty million people didn't show up at the polls in 2010, but those who did were angry whites who voiced their disaffection with Obama. The under-thirty young adults (Millennials), who were so instrumental in getting Obama elected, largely stayed at home on election day, too unenthusiastic to cast a ballot. In many ways, the election was about the late middle-aged white voter striking back.[7]

The Tea Party wrenched the Republican Party to the right, replacing conservative "blue dog" Democrats with Tea Party–friendly Republicans. The GOP seized control of the House of Representatives and significantly closed the gap in the Senate, though the Democrats still controlled that chamber, as well as the presidency. The right wing mobilized its base, while the Democrats stayed home and got their "shellacking," as President Obama phrased it. Democrats lost the House after only four years.[8]

The Tea Party's victory in the midterm elections divided the government and weakened Obama's presidency, as Republicans were now a force to obstruct legislative progress. This was a group of reactionaries who did not want compromise—they were like Luddites who would sooner see the entire machine collapse rather than cooperate. They argued, in fact, that they were elected *not* to compromise.

Republicans captured dozens of statehouses as well, which meant they were in power for the Congressional and state redistricting that takes place every ten years after the U.S. Census. Through gerrymandering, Republicans redrew state districts that benefited their party. In states like Pennsylvania, North Carolina, and Wisconsin that were evenly split politically, Republicans built supermajorities through gerrymandering, designed to cement their wins and effectively hobble Democrats.

Congress reached gridlock as it stopped doing the work of the people, and instead was hell-bent on stymieing anything President Obama proposed. The GOP had lost its collective mind and its willingness to reach deals. It would sooner see the country default than negotiate with the president. Some regarded the president as illegitimate, refusing to see the validity of his views or that of the Democratic Party. Tea Party governance meant making demands, not concessions or reaching compromise.

Two highly regarded independent researchers, Thomas Mann and Norman Ornstein, placed the blame squarely on the Republican Party. They wrote in *It's Even Worse Than It Looks*: "As bad as the atmospherics were, the new and enhanced politics of hostage taking, of putting political expedience above the national interest and tribal hubris above cooperative problem solving, suggested something more dangerous, especially at a time of profound economic peril." Republicans took the government hostage to demand a radical down-sizing in federal spending—their ultimate goal being to dismantle much of the Great Society social programs of the 1960s, and even some of the New Deal programs of the 1930s. Led by anti-tax crusader Grover Norquist, they wanted a return to lean government that did little, that asked little of its citizens, and took little from them. They wanted to turn the clock back to 1900, before the Progressive Era instilled permanent federal involvement in improving society and greatly increased its power and size. [9]

Mike Lofgren worked as a Republican budget analyst in Congress for twenty-eight years. After retiring, he wrote a score-settling manifesto about how the GOP had become part of the fringe:

> In particular, my own party, the Republican Party, began to scare me. After the 2008 election, Republican politicians became more and more intransigently dogmatic. They doubled down on advancing policies that transparently favored the top 1 percent of earners in this country while obstructing measures such as the extension of unemployment insurance. They seemed to want to comfort the comfortable and afflict the afflicted in the middle of the worst economic meltdown in eighty years. [10]

Tea Party recalcitrance made the GOP dysfunctional. Speaker of the House John Boehner, a pragmatic man known to cut deals, had probably the most difficult job in the world governing a caucus that was at war with itself. The Democrats "do not match the current crop of zanies who infest the Republican Party," Lofgren concluded. "The GOP has gone off the rails." [11]

Sensing an opportunity to tap into this populist anger, brash New York real estate developer Donald Trump considered running for president as a Republican in 2012. He had long harbored dreams of the presidency. A keynote of his unannounced campaign was questioning President Obama's birthplace. Trump became a birther. Though he did not invent the fable of

Obama's overseas birth, he became its leading proponent. "The whole thing was crazy and mean-spirited, of course, its underlying bigotry and xenophobia hardly concealed," wrote First Lady Michelle Obama. "Donald Trump, with his loud and reckless innuendos, was putting my family's safety at risk. And for this, I'd never forgive him."[12]

In response to Trump, Obama released his birth certificate in April 2011, which confirmed that he was born in Hawaii and was an American citizen. Trump soon bragged, "I'm very proud of myself, because I've accomplished something that no one else has been able to accomplish." He added in self-congratulatory Trumpian style: "I really did a great job." Obama largely ignored the birthers, but used the episode to take a swipe at Trump: "We're not going to be able to solve our problems if we get distracted by sideshows and carnival barkers," implying that Donald Trump was a clown. One has to ask: what other president would have been questioned in such a way, had it not been for his race?[13]

At the White House Correspondents' Dinner in April 2011, Obama teased Trump from the stage about being a birther. Trump grimaced at the jokes at his expense, but many would subsequently wonder if this was the moment when Trump decided to demolish everything Obama accomplished once he too reached the White House. One day he would harness the right wing's populist anger to ascend to the presidency and bring a wrecking ball. In the meantime, Trump continued to beat the racist birther drum for the next five years.

That same night, Obama returned to the White House to watch SEAL Team 6 raid Osama bin Laden's compound and kill the most wanted man in the world.

After the Shellacking

After the midterm shellacking, Obama found his footing. He regained his confidence and became a more self-assured, involved leader. He grew into the presidency. In December 2010, Obama reached out to Congress during the lame-duck session and cut deals directly with the GOP with the help of Joe Biden. Republican leaders understood that Tea Party representatives entering Congress in January would make deal-making far more difficult. The last month of Congress proved astonishingly productive.

As the clock ticked down on 2010, President Obama still had significant agenda items to address, but the Republicans refused to go along until the Bush-era tax cuts were addressed. Obama quickly reached a compromise: the tax cuts were extended for two years, unemployment benefits were extended through 2011, and payroll taxes (these funded Medicare and Social Security) for workers were cut by 2 percent for one year. This would provide workers more cash in their wallets for the coming year, though it would all be financed through deficit spending. The cost of the entire package was $858 billion.

The tax agreement enabled Obama's broader agenda to move forward, and it signaled that he was willing to compromise with Republicans in the coming years of divided government. In a lightning-fast final session of Congress, Democrats achieved a remarkable amount of policy changes. "Don't ask, don't tell" was repealed, and the Senate approved a nuclear arms treaty, New START, with Russia. Congress then adjourned, making the 111th Congress one of the most productive for the sheer volume of legislation it had passed. The only major issues unresolved were a budget, climate change legislation, and immigration reform. Otherwise this Congress had accomplished a great deal, including health care and Wall Street reform.

Just a day after the 2010 midterm election, the Federal Reserve agreed to purchase $600 billion in Treasury bonds. The governors called this quantitative easing, a strategy that they had used before, purchasing $2.3 trillion in bonds on the open market after the 2008 meltdown. With these new bond purchases, the Fed would have nearly $3 trillion under its belt. The governors had hoped to sell these bonds, rather than continue purchasing them, but the slow economy had forced their hand. Interest rates were still at zero, inflation was almost nonexistent, so the Fed had few tools left in its shed to stimulate the economy. Still, the stock market loved quantitative easing, and its end-year rally finally wiped out the losses after the Lehman Brothers collapse two years earlier.[14] By the time the Fed ended quantitative easing in October 2014, it had $4.5 trillion in the bank.[15]

The stock market ended the year up 11 percent, closing at 11,577.51. That was still below its all-time peak. Unemployment ended the decade at 9.8 percent, stubbornly high and showing little trend toward heading down. More than 15 million Americans were jobless. The economy simply wasn't creating enough new jobs; it was growing, but corporations were still in cost-cutting and productivity-raising mode and leery of large-scale hiring.

Consequences of the Great Recession

In September 2010, the National Bureau of Economic Research declared that the Great Recession had officially ended in June 2009 after eighteen months. This made it the longest recession since World War II. However, growth was so slow that it was almost unnoticeable, and by the end of that year, unemployment was stubbornly lodged at 9.6 percent. The high unemployment rate was ammunition for critics to claim that Obamanomics was ineffective at improving the economy and drove Republican voters to the polls.[16]

Federal debt as a percentage of the nation's GDP hit 94.3 percent in 2010. State and local debt had also inched up. The U.S. was awash in a sea of red ink. Liberal economists argued all this borrowing was necessary to sustain a fragile economy. Conservatives and Tea Party activists wanted the debt cut pronto, though if the government suddenly stopped spending it would hobble the recovery.[17]

The Great Recession wreaked havoc on city, county, and state budgets as people were laid off and stopped paying taxes. The stock market decline punched a massive hole in state budgets. States were partly able to make up the loss of income through short-term federal stimulus funds, but once those dried up the states were on their own and forced to cut even more. The Census Bureau reported that overall state revenues dropped by almost 31 percent between 2008 and 2009. Since no one wanted to raise taxes during a recession, the states closed the gap though significant safety-net cuts while requiring state workers and teachers to contribute more to health care, pensions, and forgo pay raises.[18]

No state was devastated more than California, where decades of voter initiatives had put sizable parts of the budget into lock boxes. Unemployment in the state soared above 12 percent. Governor Arnold Schwarzenegger and the state legislature deeply cut the state budget and adopted austerity measures that gutted state services. Years of profligate spending had caught up.

The Great Recession triggered a massive restructuring of the American economy. This was a significant setback for many Americans. So many people had been laid off—older workers were particularly vulnerable, as they tended to earn more money and were more expensive to insure. Unskilled workers were quickly thrown overboard. As the economy slowly improved, companies were fixated not on hiring employees, but on raising productivity to obviate the need for more workers—even as their return to profitability left them sitting on a mountain of cash. Younger workers fresh from college, though they were cheaper to hire, were deemed unnecessary as entry-level positions seemed to vanish, and a company's existing workforce was tasked with ever more responsibilities but seldom with a raise in pay. The refrain "Be thankful you have a job" became common.

Many union-based, working-class jobs that were formerly gateways to the middle class simply vanished. The working class slid backward economically as people were laid off and the only jobs available paid less, such as working at restaurants and retail. Businesses focused on automation, cost-cutting, and efficiency. Gallows humor of the time held that there would be only two workers in the manufacturing plant of the future: an employee and a dog. The employee would feed the dog and oversee the equipment, and the dog would make sure the employee did not steal anything.

The Millennial generation was just entering the workforce and was traumatized by the recession. This was a generation raised in the cauldron of competition and helicopter-parent surveillance, their every youthful activity and playdate geared toward getting them into college. "Their lives center around production, competition, surveillance, and achievement in ways that were totally exceptional only a few decades ago," observed Malcolm Harris in *Kids These Days*, his investigation of Millennial life in the 21st century. They graduated from college into what felt like permanent financial insecurity with high student loan debts, few career opportunities, and stagnant wages. It was an anxiety-inducing age. Millennials were a low-trust generation and adapted to the times by continually focusing on building their personal brand through networking and social media, knowing that work was always tenuous. [19]

Earlier generations could count on leaving the world a better place for their children, but the Great Recession threw that into doubt. College costs continued to rise exorbitantly, far beyond the rate of inflation, and even with an education, there was so seldom a job at the end of the rainbow that graduates moved back in with their parents. Meanwhile savings stagnated as the stock market failed to deliver its traditional ten percent a year gain. With two enormous stock market declines that bookended the decade, many people were no better off at the end than they were at the beginning. Even people who had responsibly saved had little to show for it. People quipped that their 401(k)s had become 201(k)s. Interest rates were so low that you may as well have stuffed your savings in a mattress, rather than put it in a bank account that earned almost nothing. Retirees on fixed incomes were squeezed as their dividends and interest plummeted. Many people openly wondered, Is this the end of the American dream? Was America becoming downwardly mobile?

"In the 1970s, the top 1 percent of earners captured about 10 percent of the national income," wrote Chrystia Freeland in *Plutocrats*. "Thirty-five years later, their share had risen to nearly a third of the national income, as high as it had been during the Gilded Age, the previous historical peak." The plutocrats were capturing ever more of the economy while the middle and working class could barely pay their bills. [20]

"Today, the gravest challenge and the most corrosive fault line in our society is the gross inequality of income and wealth in America," observed Hedrick Smith in *Who Stole the American Dream?* This was a struggle that had persisted since the late 19th century, when wealth became concentrated in just a lucky few, while the rest of society struggled. Reforming presidents such as Theodore Roosevelt, Woodrow Wilson, Franklin Delano Roosevelt, and Lyndon Johnson had all taken on the issue of economic inequality, but Republican presidents from Ronald Reagan on reduced taxes on the super-rich, allowing them to concentrate their wealth even more. "In our New Economy, America's super-rich have accumulated trillions in new wealth, far beyond anything in other nations, while the American middle class stagnated," Smith wrote. "What separates the Two Americas is far more than a wealth gap. It is a wealth chasm." [21]

To get ahead in the modern, increasingly digital-based economy, you needed an education and skills. "We're facing a fundamental skills mismatch, and the U.S. labor market is increasingly divided into a group that can keep up with technical work and a group that can't," noted economist Tyler Cowen. Without an education, the pathways to the middle class became narrower, as companies found ways to replace low-skill, low-wage jobs through automation. There were fewer opportunities for well-paying jobs protected by a union, and unions continued to decline. Inequality widened further as the educated commanded good salaries, while the working class fell behind. This was a key reason for populist anger on the left and the right—they felt America was slipping away from them. [22]

After the banking failures of the Great Recession, only one person ever went to jail: an investment banker at Credit Suisse. Two hedge fund managers from Bear Stearns were charged, but they were acquitted in trial and released. The Obama Justice Department decided not to prosecute further cases, out of fear that it would cause panic in the financial markets. This was a leadership failure. The SEC fined Bank of America, Citigroup, Goldman Sachs, JPMorgan Chase, and others billions for malfeasance, which should have led to prosecutions, convictions, and jail time for greedy executives and to serve as a deterrence. The Bush DOJ had tried and convicted executives at Enron, Qwest, Tyco, and WorldCom. Ultimately there was too little accountability for the corporate malfeasance that led to the Great Recession.[23]

In 2012, the Federal Reserve noted just how devastating the Great Recession had been to the nation's wealth. American's median net wealth had shrunk 39 percent from $126,400 in 2007 to $77,300 in 2010. This was about where Americans were in 1992, meaning that two decades of wealth creation had vanished. The biggest factor was shrunken home values, where middle-class America concentrated its wealth.[24]

By the end of the decade, 9/11 seemed like a distant memory—not forgotten, but somehow blurred by all the events it had triggered: Afghanistan, Guantanamo Bay, the Iraq War, increased airport security, enhanced surveillance, the Patriot Act, secret CIA prisons, waterboarding, Abu Ghraib prison photos, Predator drone strikes, and elections about who could best keep us safe. By the end of the decade, the U.S. was still the only superpower, but its moral authority was diminished.

The first decade started in prosperity, and ended in financial crisis. The twin bursting of the dot-com and housing bubbles, followed by the Great Recession, significantly harmed the nation's wealth and reset the economy. These ten years ended with no net job creation while wages declined in real terms, in part because of rising health care costs. Bush's tax cuts and the Medicare drug program knocked a hole in the federal budget, the wars in Afghanistan, Iraq, and on Terror were frightfully expensive, and the economic stimulus was one giant IOU. Economically speaking, many Americans were worse off in 2009 than in 1999, though the U.S. was still by far the wealthiest country in the world. The first decade proved to be a lost decade.[25]

17

History Is Not Over

B ut that's not the end of the story. Far from it. People thought history ended with the Cold War, but it continued—and it will continue until the end of time.

If the first decade of the 21st century was a lost decade, the following decade was defined by populism, not just in the United States but worldwide. The Great Recession fueled populist resentment on both the left and the right, though it was initially far more visible on the right with the Tea Party.

Populism by definition is anti-establishment, as it reflects a loss of faith in institutions. It often takes on the mantle of victimhood and a feeling of being betrayed. Populism drives tribal identity and blasts opponents as not being *real* Americans. In his insightful book *What is Populism?*, Jan-Werner Müller wrote, "This is the core claim of populism: only some of the people are really the people." The right-wing populists staked a claim that only non-college-educated whites were the real Americans. Everyone else was an elitist or a phony.[1]

The rescue of the banks and the stimulus in 2008–2009 fueled this populist backlash. Why were the banks bailed out while the little guy who lost his house wasn't? This was in part what drove the Tea Party and its counterweight Occupy Wall Street, and later the post-truth era, when trust in business and governmental institutions plummeted, conspiracy theories ran rampant, and anti-establishment forces ran amok. The financial meltdown of 2008 poisoned American politics. As Neil Irwin of the *New York Times* wrote on the tenth anniversary of the crisis, "It turns out, when you throw trillions of dollars at rescuing a system that most people don't like very much in the first place, the result isn't relief. It's anger."[2]

Many thought the American dream was dead, and therefore it was time to bulldoze it and start over. The left disliked Wall Street, the right distrusted government, but neither could propose a viable alternative. And neither could quite recognize that both are necessary for a viable democratic society to function.

❖

Barack Obama had been elected to the presidency in 2008 with a great deal of optimism; however, the excitement for the country's first black president dissipated with the gruelingly slow economic recovery. He ran for reelection four years later. The idealist of 2008 had transformed into the partisan fighter of 2012. Obama's slogan in 2008 was Change; in 2012 it was Forward. The big question on everyone's mind was, Are you better off now than you were four years ago? It certainly didn't feel like it, but then again, given how close the economy came to another Great Depression, it certainly could have been worse. Vice President Joe Biden summarized the Obama administration's case as: "Osama bin Laden is dead, and General Motors is alive."

Obama faced off against Mitt Romney, a former Massachusetts governor and establishment conservative who had created the state's Romneycare health system, the model for Obamacare. The GOP faced the same challenge that it had four years before: it was largely a party of older white voters, a demographic that was shrinking as a proportion of the electorate. The GOP also had a women problem: its strident stance against abortion, including several candidates who made jaw-dropping remarks about pregnancies that resulted from rape, was seen as a threat to many women and cut against the grain of where most Americans were on this issue.

The Supreme Court's 2010 decision in *Citizens United* opened the floodgates to corporate and union political spending. The decision helped drive up the cost of campaigning, as corporate money could easily turn an election into an arms race. Congressmen and senators were in nonstop campaign mode, having to fundraise every weekend in their home districts. And it made them especially susceptible to special interests, since corporations had far deeper pockets than Joe Citizen. As they say, money talks.

During the election campaign, Romney gaffed, "Corporations are people," and that fairly well summarized the Supreme Court's decision in *Citizens United*. Money poured into both political parties—much of it anonymously. A number of wealthy conservatives donated more than $1 billion to political action committees, and this in turn fueled a relentless media campaign. You couldn't watch television or listen to the radio without being bombarded by ads. People complained about the invasiveness of it all. Yet in the end, all this spending spent bought very little. Obama was reelected, and the Democrats retained control of the Senate and narrowed the Republican lead in the House. The 2012 election brought a record twenty women to the U.S. Senate—sixteen of them Democrats. [3]

The 2012 election sealed the status quo of divided government. The election meant that the Dodd-Frank finance reform law would stand, as would Obamacare. Ever since the Affordable Care Act became law in 2010, the Republican Party had pledged to repeal and replace it. This was a campaign slogan, not a policy position. It was an empty promise, as the GOP had no ideas about what to replace Obamacare with. But the ACA was unpopular with the Republican base because Obama had passed it—no matter that the law actually helped many of them—and therefore it had to go.

The Supreme Court upheld most of the Affordable Care Act in June 2012. Republicans would spend the next decade trying to legislatively destroy or bureaucratically undermine Obamacare. However, as time progressed and people realized that the "death panels" that Sarah Palin had said would result from Obamacare were just hyperbole, public opinion swayed ever more toward supporting the law. Some parts of it became downright popular, such as blocking insurers from banning coverage based on preexisting conditions, and keeping your children on your insurance coverage until they were twenty-six.

Because of the Great Recession, the loss of good jobs, and the sluggish economic recovery, many Americans lost faith in their institutions. Americans were famous as joiners for most of our history, but were becoming more hesitant to join civic organizations as trust in society weakened. Tribalism threatened the civility of the country and made people intolerant, even hostile, to opposing viewpoints. Americans were becoming increasingly secular, with rising numbers of people declaring no religious affiliation. The U.S. had a long way to go to reach Europe's agnosticism, but it was rapidly catching up. Church attendance had fallen far from its post–World War II peak. Americans had fewer ways to connect with different people as they retreated to the safety of their bubbles. As religion waned and small-town America folded, many turned to political affiliation as their sole identity.[4]

Without a commitment to our institutions, Americans devolved into individuals who only saw how they differed, not what they had in common. Yuval Levin wrote in *The Fractured Republic*, "Increasingly, society consists of individuals and a national state, while the mediating institutions—family, community, church, unions, and others—fade and falter." While every American loves liberty, "The age of individualism produced its opposite: a deep and anxious loneliness."[5]

Americans were self-segregating themselves into like-minded communities: college-educated with college-educated, conservative with conservative, liberal with liberal, and working class with working class. This was happening geographically, as people relocated to be with their own kind, which served only to reinforce their thinking and their prejudices. This led to political tribalism and blind partisanship. The country evolved into two separate political camps with little overlap.

Economists Linda Bilmes and Joseph Stiglitz wrote presciently in 2011 about the agonizingly slow economic recovery after the Great Recession, drawing comparison to the tumultuous economic reset during the 1930s:

> The trauma we're experiencing right now resembles the trauma we experienced 80 years ago, during the Great Depression, and it has been brought on by an analogous set of circumstances. Then, as now, we faced a breakdown of the banking system. But then, as now, the breakdown of the banking system was in part a consequence of deeper problems. Even if we correctly respond to the trauma—the failures of the financial sector—it will take a decade or more to achieve full recovery. Under the best of conditions, we will endure a Long Slump.[6]

The Long Slump might be a good name for the 2010s, the years following the first decade. It was a time of continuing but slow economic recovery with significant headwinds, especially from large numbers of retiring Baby Boomers and others who had permanently left the workforce. Wage growth stagnated, even as employment improved.

Bilmes and Stiglitz argued that the demand for fiscal austerity slowed the economic recovery. The economy needed massive stimulus through government spending, but Tea Party–influenced budget hawks shot this down, though austerity ultimately hurt workers the most. The rich did fine as the stock market rebounded, but the middle and working class shrank, widening the inequality gap between the very rich and the rest of us.

The American working class had been experiencing a long, slow, and painful decline. The Great Recession accelerated that, leaving a whole class of people insecure and uprooted. The U.S. was becoming a postindustrial economy as it shifted toward services, and this left a generation of resentment among the unskilled who could not find gainful employment. Many turned to disability and opioids to bury their despair.

The day was over that someone could graduate high school and start the next day in the factory or on the shop floor for high wages. No amount of wishful thinking would bring back coal mines or steel mills that employ tens of thousands of people. Low-skill jobs were largely replaced by automation, and it was the high-skill or college-educated worker who had a future in the new economy.

"Alienation is the disease of working-class America," wrote Timothy Carney in *Alienated America*. Metropolitan areas captured ever more of the nation's opportunities and wealth, while many rural areas hollowed out. Carney observed, "When a factory leaves, it takes many things with it, but it often leaves people behind." Communities faced breakdown and collapse.[7]

Like all political parties, the Republican Party was a coalition of interests. The pro-business, Chamber of Commerce wing had long dominated the GOP. It focused on rewarding its wealthy donors with deregulation, tax cuts, trade deals, and trickle-down economics. The party's base—the non-college-educated whites who were increasingly left out of the economy—had legitimate grievances that the political system had counted on their votes while acting against their interests. Their concerns were dismissed. And this stoked a great rebellion within the GOP. Thomas Friedman wrote presciently in *The World is Flat* (2005) about how just such a revolt could lead to a political realignment:

> Given these conflicting emotions and pressures, there is potential here for American politics to get completely reshuffled—with workers and corporate interests realigning themselves into different parties. Think about it: Social conservatives from the right wing

of the Republican Party, who do not like globalization or closer integration with the world because it brings too many foreigners and foreign cultural mores into America, might align themselves with unions from the left wing of the Democratic Party, who don't like globalization for the way it facilitates the outsourcing and offshoring of jobs. They might be called the Wall Party. [8]

Eleven years after Friedman wrote these prophetic words, his prediction came true: the Wall Party took over the GOP with help from unionized Democrats in the Rust Belt in the presidential election of 2016. The uprooted whites revolted against the establishment and voted for New York real estate developer Donald Trump. There were many causes that led to this, including cultural, economic, and racial anxiety. They saw Trump as their savior who would Make America Great Again, who would build a "big, beautiful wall" to keep Hispanic immigrants from crossing our southern border.

The Tea Party had faded as a protest movement, but its populist outrage was still simmering. It morphed into anger against the Republican establishment for not fulfilling its unrealistic campaign promises, like repealing Obamacare. Trump harnessed this anger by speaking their language of disaffection, grievance, and victimhood. Trump was a symptom, not a cause of populist discontent. The populists who had opposed the TARP bailouts and supported Sarah Palin in 2008 rallied around Trump eight years later. There was a direct ideological line connecting these.

Jeb Bush, brother of the former president, was the establishment Republican choice in 2016, but the base wanted nothing to do with him and his presidential campaign went nowhere. In the primaries, Trump mopped the floor with his sixteen Republican rivals and captured the nomination. It was the most stunning political upset in modern American history.

The GOP capitulated to Donald Trump. Conservatives abandoned their principles of civility, free trade, and small government and climbed in bed with a noxious demagogue who completely lacked experience in the world of politics or statesmanship, but believed that only he could fix America.

Republicans had long run on American exceptionalism. Ronald Reagan–era conservatism painted America as a shining city on a hill that took on the Soviet Union and won. It was pro-business and pro-immigrant. It promoted democracy abroad. But Trump repudiated this optimism, running instead on a nativist, nationalist platform of American carnage.

Trump was questionable as anyone's role model. He was a serial phi-landerer who had been married three times and bragged about sexually assaulting women and not paying taxes, though he refused to release his tax returns. As the emperor of a private real-estate empire, Trump's instincts were autocratic. He was a bully and thin-skinned, which masked deep-seated insecurities.

A serial attention-seeker and narcissist, Trump had learned early in his career how to manipulate the media to draw attention to himself. He wasn't frightened of saying controversial things or repeating unfounded rumors or trafficking in quack conspiracy theories, as long as it brought him attention. He didn't give a fig about the truth. He was a patently dishonest person with absolutely no moral compass.

Trump appealed to peoples' worst instincts by treating every public debate as if it were a knife fight. He stoked anti-immigrant and anti-Muslim fervor. His nativism struck a chord with white supporters who feared the nation becoming brown. His five-year role as the nation's birther-in-chief, ques-tioning President Obama's birth as an American, was tinged with racism. "Our presence in the White House had been celebrated by millions of Ameri-cans, but it also contributed to a reactionary sense of fear and resentment among others," wrote former First Lady Michelle Obama. "The hatred was old and deep and as dangerous as ever."[9]

Trump and his followers often sported red ballcaps with the words MAKE AMERICA GREAT AGAIN printed on them. They bore a subliminal mes-sage: make America *white* again. They represented the fear that the country was changing too rapidly, the fear that white Protestants would no longer be a majority—and thus no longer in charge. And yet this was like Don Quixote tilting at windmills: the demographics of the country were changing. America was becoming ever browner. No amount of populist anger would change that—not even a wall.

An oft-noted comment was that conservatives took Trump seriously but not literally, while liberals took him literally but not seriously. They should have taken him both literally and seriously. Most voters agreed he lacked the temperament to be president. Trump won virtually no newspaper endorse-ments, largely because of his personality and his lack of principles.

On election day, November 8, 2016, Trump's Democratic opponent Hillary Clinton won the popular vote by more than 2.8 million votes, but Trump took the electoral college. Many working class, unionized white voters who traditionally voted Democratic voted for The Donald instead. Conservative radio talk show host Charles Sykes quipped, "After Trump's defeat of Hillary Clinton, the Democrats need to perform an autopsy; Republicans need an exorcism."[10]

As president, rather than attempt to unify the country or provide an optimistic vision for the country, Trump demagogued against immigrants and waged war against opponents with his many petty resentments, often through Twitter. He drove a red-hot poker into America's cultural fissures and fanned the flames, widening an already divided country into hostile camps. He was a fabulist who constantly delivered self-serving and easily fact-checked lies. He denounced any news that was critical toward him as "fake news," and even called the media "the true Enemy of the People" in Stalinist terms. Trump governed through grievance and self-aggrandizement. He undermined American institutions, frayed relationships with America's allies, coddled dictators, and emboldened white nationalists. His message of "America First" really meant America Alone. America's global reputation suffered and moral influence diminished.

President Trump harnessed the right's populist furor while jettisoning the Tea Party's ideas, notably around fiscal discipline, reducing the deficit, and smaller government. Trump gave Corporate America a huge tax cut and juiced budget deficits to well above $1 trillion annually, but Republicans had once again fallen silent on deficits, only caring about them when Democrats were in power. Trump served the interests of big business, rather than the political base that elected him, but they still loved him.

Trump was neither a conservative nor a liberal, but a nationalist with authoritarian instincts, and he spoke the language that the Republican Party's white working-class base wanted to hear: that brown immigrants were a threat to their status, that America's allies were screwing the country, that trade deals that had enriched the U.S. were a raw deal, and that the politically correct elite looked down on them. Evangelicals knew the man was shady, but supported him because they wanted *Roe v. Wade* overturned. Trump hijacked the GOP and turned it into the Party of Trump. Establishment Republicans were sent into political exile or silenced out of fear of his Twitter handle and his vehement red MAGA hat–wearing followers. "Rarely has a president so thoroughly altered the identity of his party," wrote Tim Alberta in *American Carnage*. "Never has a president so ruthlessly exploited the insecurity of his people."[11]

Outrage became the nation's default setting. Everyone was angry and outraged all the time, triggered by a simple mention of Trump. The anger of Trump's followers was matched in fervor by the populist left with the illiberal call-out and cancel culture, the circular firing squad of zero tolerance, the privilege checkers, and the newly woke social justice warriors who bullied dissenters on social media. The nation had a serious empathy gap, splitting into hostile camps shouting at each other, with neither side listening to the concerns of the other. It was pure tribalism. The 24/7 news cycle blew up incidents before they were properly analyzed, investigated, and reported on. The news could be weaponized as an instrument of propaganda. And this suited Trump, who was the nation's first reality TV president.

The right wing eschewed the mainstream media (the "lamestream media," as Sarah Palin called it) and developed its own propaganda machine and echo chamber. This went far beyond conservative Fox News and the editorial page of the *Wall Street Journal*. News outlets like Breitbart and InfoWars were conspiratorial and fringy. They lived in a parallel universe with their own set of realities, demonstrating a propensity to believe the sensational and dismiss documented facts. They cast doubt on the very notion of objective truth.

Earlier conspiracy theories had posited that UFOs had landed at Roswell or that the moon landings were staged. Modern conspiracy theories ran amok in this post-truth era: that the Sandy Hook school massacre was fake; that Barack Obama was a Kenyan-born Muslim; that vaccines cause autism in children; that global warming was a manufactured hoax to increase government power; that Muslim immigrants wanted to force Sharia law upon the country; that 9/11 was an inside job; that an underground conspiracy known as the deep state operated as a shadow government; or that Hillary Clinton was running a child sex trafficking ring out of the basement of a D.C. pizza parlor. But the facts are knowable, and the truth can be attained. Truth is not relative.

The Donald Trump era was simply exhausting. After a decade of disruption, Trump proved to be the ultimate disrupter.

The United States has often elected a president who is the polar opposite of the previous one. The academic and righteous Woodrow Wilson was succeeded by the corrupt Warren Harding. The libertine Bill Clinton gave way to the moralist George W. Bush. And the bookish Barack Obama gave way to the populist demagogue Donald Trump. After Trump, the nation will need a president who is capable of healing the nation's raw emotions and self-inflicted wounds. They will need to be a person of profound empathy.

Can America regain its moral compass and its soul, and once again be the beacon of liberty to the world? Can Americans empathize with each other and end this senseless tribalism? Can we understand the travails of our workers and how much the Great Recession took from them, and help people build skills so they can thrive in the digital economy? Can we build a sustainable economy that addresses inequality while providing upward mobility to its citizens once again? Can we welcome the immigrant as our neighbor again, recognizing that all of us once came from somewhere else?

The coming years will have their own challenges. We must have faith in the American democracy that we will eventually get it right. History is not over.

Acknowledgments

This has been a dream book that was long in the making. I was inspired to write *A Decade of Disruption* after reading Frederick Lewis Allen's *Only Yesterday: An Informal History of the 1920's*. I simply started taking notes in 2007 as the bursting housing bubble led to the Great Recession and economic Armageddon. It felt like we were living in 1929 on the cusp of the Great Depression, and looking back I'm amazed at how close we came to falling off the financial cliff. One economic meltdown was enough for a lifetime. Let's not do that again, okay?

Once again, I'm indebted to my literary agent and dear friend Tom Miller of Liza Dawson Associates. He has spent his career editing, writing, and nurturing authors. Tom is a rare breed indeed.

Once again, I've had the privilege of working with the Pegasus Books team to bring a book from conception to publication. We had such a fantastic experience working together on my last book, *The Great War in America*, and I was thrilled beyond words that they were interested in *A Decade of Disruption*. Founder and publisher Claiborne Hancock is everything you hope for in a publisher—enthusiastic about books and ideas and kind to everyone he meets. Associate publisher and publicist Jessica Case has opened more doors than I can count. She is a champion for writers, as is publicist Lauren Rosenthal. My thanks to Drew Wheeler and Maria Fernandez for their work editing and preparing the manuscript.

My friend Brian Robinson, a wealth adviser at Ameriprise Financial, has long expressed enthusiasm for this project, and added in more than a few insights, especially around the ideas of retirement and life's next chapter.

The staff at Arlington Public Library has once again pulled out the stops. I've lost count how many books I ordered through interlibrary loan in researching *A Decade of Disruption*, and I visited the information desk so many times that it became a standing joke between me and the staff. Thanks for your aplomb and timely help.

I want to send my heartfelt gratitude to the staff of Politics and Prose Bookstore in Washington, D.C., truly one of the country's great bookstores, which has become a second home to me as they've invited me to give author talks, lead tours, and teach classes. Extra special thanks to Kate Shawcross, Bob Attardi, Allison Witten, and Jack Bennett.

It was crushing to see so many bookstores close because of the Great Recession. I had my very first book signing ever on August 27, 2009, at Now Voyager in Provincetown (this was two days after Senator Ted Kennedy died). That bookstore closed like so many others. I'm thrilled to see consumers embrace books again and see new bookstores open as vital community gathering points for readers. Long live local independent bookstores!

Wherever you live, there is probably an annual book festival nearby that is organized by a small army of book-loving volunteers. My hat goes off to all of you who dedicate your time to make these possible. Special thanks to Jud Ashman, the mayor and brainchild behind the Gaithersburg Book Festival, Karen Lyon of the Literary Hill BookFest, and Judy Gutierrez of the University Club book fair.

Lastly, a shout-out to the journalists who write the first draft of history, without which this book would not be possible. The truth can be determined, and journalists are dedicated to getting the story right. As the *Washington Post* displays on its masthead, Democracy dies in darkness.

Garrett Peck
Arlington, Virginia

Bibliography

BOOKS

The 9/11 Commission Report: Final Report of the National Commission on Terrorist Attacks Upon the United States. New York: Norton, 2004.

Abramoff, Jack. *Capitol Punishment: The Hard Truth About Washington Corruption from America's Most Notorious Lobbyist.* Washington, D.C.: WND Books, 2011.

Achenbach, Joel. *A Hole at the Bottom of the Sea: The Race to Kill the BP Oil Gusher.* New York: Simon & Schuster, 2011.

Alberta, Tim. *American Carnage: On the Front Lines of the Republican Civil War and the Rise of President Trump.* New York: HarperCollins, 2019.

Alter, Jonathan. *The Center Holds: Obama and His Enemies.* New York: Simon & Schuster, 2013.

———. *The Promise: President Obama, Year One.* New York: Simon & Schuster, 2010.

Anderson, Chris. *The Long Tail: Why the Future of Business is Selling Less of More.* New York: Hyperion, 2006.

Auletta, Ken. *Googled: The End of the World as We Know It.* New York: Penguin Press, 2009.

Bacevich, Andrew J. *The Limits of Power: The End of American Exceptionalism.* New York: Metropolitan Books, 2008.

Balz, Dan and Haynes Johnson. *The Battle for America 2008: The Story of an Extraordinary Election.* New York: Viking, 2009.

Bernanke, Ben S. *The Courage to Act: A Memoir of a Crisis and Its Aftermath.* New York: Norton, 2015.

Blinder, Alan S. *After the Music Stopped: The Financial Crisis, the Response, and the Work Ahead.* New York: Penguin, 2013.

Brandt, Richard L. *One Click: Jeff Bezos and the Rise of Amazon.com.* New York: Penguin, 2011.

Brinkley, Douglas. *The Great Deluge: Hurricane Katrina, New Orleans, and the Mississippi Gulf Coast.* New York: William Morrow, 2006.

Bush, George W. *Decision Points.* New York: Crown, 2010.

Carney, Timothy. *Alienated America: Why Some Places Thrive While Others Collapse.* New York: HarperCollins, 2019.

Chandrasekaran, Rajiv. *Imperial Life in the Emerald City: Inside Iraq's Green Zone.* New York: Alfred A. Knopf, 2006.

Cheney, Dick. *In My Time: A Personal and Political Memoir.* New York: Threshold Editions, 2011.

Clarke, Richard A. *Against All Enemies: Inside America's War on Terror.* New York: Free Press, 2004.

Comey, James. *A Higher Loyalty: Truth, Lies, and Leadership*. New York: Flatiron Books, 2018.

Continetti, Matthew. *The K Street Gang: The Rise and Fall of the Republican Machine*. New York: Doubleday, 2006.

Cooper, Cynthia. *Extraordinary Circumstances: The Journey of a Corporate Whistleblower*. New York: John Wiley & Sons, 2008.

Cowen, Tyler. *The Great Stagnation: How America Ate All the Low-Hanging Fruit of Modern History, Got Sick, and Will (Eventually) Feel Better*. New York: Dutton, 2011.

Díaz, Junot. *The Brief Wondrous Life of Oscar Wao*. New York: Riverhead Books, 2007.

Draper, Robert. *Dead Certain: The Presidency of George W. Bush*. New York: Free Press, 2007.

Duelfer, Charles. *Hide and Seek: The Search for Truth in Iraq*. New York: PublicAffairs, 2009.

Eichenwald, Kurt. *Conspiracy of Fools: A True Story*. New York: Broadway, 2005.

Farrell, Chris. *Unretirement: How Baby Boomers Are Changing the Way We Think About Work, Community and the Good Life*. New York: Bloomsbury Press, 2014.

Feinberg, Kenneth R. *Who Gets What: Fair Compensation after Tragedy and Financial Upheaval*. New York: PublicAffairs, 2012.

Financial Crisis Inquiry Commission, *The Financial Crisis Inquiry Report: Final Report of the National Commission on the Causes of the Financial and Economic Crisis in the United States*. New York: PublicAffairs, 2011.

Florida, Richard. *The Rise of the Creative Class, Revisited*. New York: Basic Books, 2012.

Frank, Barney. *Frank: A Life in Politics from the Great Society to Same-Sex Marriage*. New York: Farrar, Straus and Giroux, 2015.

Frank, Nathaniel. *Awakening: How Gays and Lesbians Brought Marriage Equality to America*. Cambridge, Mass.: Belknap Press, 2017.

Freeland, Chrystia. *Plutocrats: The Rise of the New Global Super-Rich and Fall of Everyone Else*. New York: Penguin Press, 2012.

Friedman, Thomas L. *Hot, Flat, and Crowded: Why We Need a Green Revolution—And How It Can Renew America*. New York: Farrar, Straus and Giroux, 2008.

———. *The World is Flat: A Brief History of the Twenty-first Century*. New York: Farrar, Straus and Giroux, 2005.

Garrow, David J. *Rising Star: The Making of Barack Obama*. New York: HarperCollins, 2017.

Geithner, Timothy S. *Stress Test: Reflections on Financial Crises*. New York: Crown, 2014.

Gellman, Barton. *Angler: The Cheney Vice Presidency*. New York: Penguin, 2008.

Greenspan, Alan. *The Age of Turbulence: Adventures in a New World*. New York: Penguin, 2007.

Grunwald, Michael. *The New Deal: The Hidden Story of Change in the Obama Era*. London: Simon & Schuster, 2012.

Haass, Richard N. *War of Necessity, War of Choice*. New York: Simon & Schuster, 2009.

Harrington, Samuel, MD. *At Peace: Choosing A Good Death After a Long Life*. New York: Grand Central Life & Style, 2018.

Harris, Fredrick C. *The Price of the Ticket: Barack Obama and the Rise and Decline of Black Politics*. New York: Oxford University Press, 2012.

Harris, Malcolm. *Kids These Days: Human Capital and the Making of Millennials*. New York: Little, Brown, 2017.

Hart-Brinson, Peter. *The Gay Marriage Generation: How the LGBTQ Movement Transformed American Culture*. New York: New York University Press, 2018.

Hirshman, Linda. *Victory: The Triumphant Gay Revolution*. New York: HarperCollins, 2012.

Horne, Jed. *Breach of Faith: Hurricane Katrina and the Near Death of a Great American City*. New York: Random House, 2006.

Ifill, Gwen. *The Breakthrough: Politics and Race in the Age of Obama*. New York: Doubleday, 2009.

Ingrassia, Paul. *Crash Course: The American Automobile Industry's Road from Glory to Disaster*. New York: Random House, 2010.

Isaacson, Walter. *Steve Jobs*. New York: Simon & Schuster, 2011.

Jackson, Maggie. *Distracted: The Erosion of Attention and the Coming Dark Age*. Amherst, N.Y: Prometheus Books, 2008.

Jacoby, Susan. *Never Say Die: The Myth and Marketing of the New Old Age*. New York: Pantheon, 2011.

Jeter, Lynne W. *Disconnected: Deceit and Betrayal at WorldCom*. New York: John Wiley & Sons, 2003.

Johnson, Steven. *Everything Bad Is Good for You*. New York: Riverhead, 2005.

Kabaservice, Geoffrey. *Rule and Ruin: The Downfall of Moderation and the Destruction of the Republican Party, from Eisenhower to the Tea Party*. New York: Oxford University Press, 2012.

Kantor, Jodi. *The Obamas*. New York: Little, Brown, 2012.

Keating, Gina. *Netflixed: The Epic Battle for America's Eyeballs*. New York: Penguin, 2012.

Kirkpatrick, David. *The Facebook Effect: The Inside Story of the Company That Is Connecting the World*. New York: Simon & Schuster, 2010.

Kornacki, Steve. *The Red and the Blue: The 1990s and the Birth of Political Tribalism*. New York: HarperCollins, 2018.

Levin, Yuval. *The Fractured Republic: Renewing America's Social Contract in the Age of Individualism*. New York: Basic Books, 2016.

Lewis, Michael. *The Big Short: Inside the Doomsday Machine*. New York: Norton, 2010.

Lewis, Sinclair. *Babbitt*. New York: Bantam Dell, 1998.

Lofgren, Mike. *The Party Is Over: How Republicans Went Crazy, Democrats Became Useless, and the Middle Class Got Shafted*. New York: Viking, 2012.

Lord, Alexandra M. *Condom Nation: The U.S. Government's Sex Education Campaign from World War I to the Internet*. Baltimore: Johns Hopkins University Press, 2010.

Losse, Katherine. *The Boy Kings: A Journey into the Heart of the Social Network*. New York: Free Press, 2012.

Lowenstein, Roger. *The End of Wall Street*. New York: Penguin, 2010.

———. *Origins of the Crash: The Great Bubble and Its Undoing*. New York: Penguin, 2004.

———. *While America Aged: How Pension Debts Ruined General Motors, Stopped the NYC Subways, Bankrupted San Diego, and Loom as the Next Financial Crisis*. New York: Penguin Press, 2008.

Magnus, George. *The Age of Aging: How Demographics are Changing the Global Economy and Our World*. Hoboken, N.J.: John Wiley & Sons, 2009.

Mahler, Jonathan. *The Challenge:* Hamdan v. Rumsfeld *and the Fight over Presidential Power*. New York: Farrar, Straus and Giroux, 2008.

Mann, James. *George W. Bush*. New York: Times Books, 2015.

Mann, Michael E. *The Hockey Stick and the Climate Wars: Dispatches from the Front Lines*. New York: Columbia University Press, 2012.

Mann, Thomas E. and Norman J. Ornstein. *It's Even Worse Than It Looks: How the American Constitutional System Collided with the New Politics of Extremism*. New York: Basic Books, 2012.

Maraniss, David. *Barack Obama: The Story*. New York: Simon & Schuster, 2012.

Mazarr, Michael J. *Leap of Faith: Hubris, Negligence, and America's Greatest Foreign Policy Tragedy*. New York: PublicAffairs, 2019.

McLean, Bethany and Peter Elkind. *The Smartest Guys in the Room: The Amazing Rise and Scandalous Fall of Enron*. New York: Portfolio, 2003.

McLean, Bethany and Joe Nocera. *All the Devils Are Here: The Hidden History of the Financial Crisis*. New York: Penguin, 2010.

McClellan, Scott. *What Happened: Inside the Bush White House and Washington's Culture of Deception*. New York: PublicAffairs, 2008.

McQuaid, John and Mark Schleifstein. *Path of Destruction: The Devastation of New Orleans and the Coming Age of Superstorms*. New York: Little, Brown, 2006.

Mezrich, Ben. *The Accidental Billionaires: The Founding of Facebook*. New York: Doubleday, 2009.

Müller, Jan-Werner. *What is Populism?* Philadelphia: University of Pennsylvania Press, 2016.

Murray, Charles. *Coming Apart: The State of White America, 1960–2010*. New York: Crown Forum, 2012.

Neumann, Ann. *The Good Death: An Exploration of Dying in America*. Boston: Beacon Press, 2016.

Obama, Michelle. *Becoming*. New York: Crown, 2018.

Oreskes, Naomi and Erik M. Conway. *Merchants of Doubt*. New York: Bloomsbury, 2011.

Paulson, Henry M., Jr. *On the Brink: Inside the Race to Stop the Collapse of the Global Financial System*. New York: Business Plus, 2010.

Plouffe, David. *The Audacity to Win: The Inside Story and Lessons of Barack Obama's Historic Victory*. New York: Viking, 2009.

Pooley, Eric. *The Climate War: True Believers, Power Brokers, and the Fight to Save the Earth*. New York: Hyperion, 2010.

Powell, Colin. *It Worked for Me: In Life and Leadership*. New York: HarperCollins, 2012.

Remnick, David. *The Bridge: The Life and Rise of Barack Obama*. New York: Alfred A. Knopf, 2010.

Rice, Condoleezza. *No Higher Honor: A Memoir of My Years in Washington*. New York: Crown, 2011.

Ricks, Thomas E. *Fiasco: The American Military Adventure in Iraq*. New York: Penguin, 2006.

———. *The Gamble: General David Petraeus and the American Military Adventure in Iraq, 2006–2008*. New York: Penguin, 2009.

Ridge, Tom. *The Test of Our Times: America Under Siege . . . and How We Can Be Safe Again*. New York: Thomas Dunne, 2009.

Rove, Karl. *Courage and Consequence: My Life as a Conservative in the Fight*. New York: Threshold, 2010.

Rumsfeld, Donald. *Known and Unknown: A Memoir*. New York: Sentinel, 2011.

Saylor, Michael. *The Mobile Wave: How Mobile Intelligence Will Change Everything*. New York: Vanguard Press, 2012.

Shiller, Robert J. *The Subprime Solution: How Today's Global Financial Crisis Happened, and What to Do About It*. Princeton, N.J.: Princeton University Press, 2008.

Skeel, David. *Icarus in the Boardroom: The Fundamental Flaws in Corporate America and Where They Came From*. New York: Oxford University Press, 2005.

Skocpol, Theda and Vanessa Williamson. *The Tea Party and the Remaking of Republican Conservatism*. New York: Oxford University Press, 2012.

Smith, Hedrick. *Who Stole the American Dream?* New York: Random House, 2012.

Smith, Jean Edward. *Bush*. New York: Simon & Schuster, 2016.

Smith, Rebecca and John R. Emshwiller. *24 Days: How Two Wall Street Journal Reporters Uncovered the Lies That Destroyed Faith in Corporate America*. New York: HarperCollins, 2003.

Sorkin, Andrew Ross. *Too Big to Fail: The Inside Story of How Wall Street and Washington Fought to Save the Financial System from Crisis—and Themselves*. New York: Penguin, 2009.

Spector, Robert. *Amazon.com: Get Big Fast*. New York: HarperCollins, 2000.

Stone, Peter H. *Heist: Superlobbyist Jack Abramoff, His Republican Allies, and the Buying of Washington*. New York: Farrar, Straus and Giroux, 2006.

Suarez, Ray. *The Holy Vote: The Politics of Faith in America*. New York: HarperCollins, 2006.

Suskind, Ron. *Confidence Men: Wall Street, Washington, and the Education of a President*. New York: HarperCollins, 2011.

Sykes, Charles J. *How the Right Lost Its Mind*. New York: St. Martin's Press, 2017.

Tenet, George. *At the Center of the Storm: My Years at the CIA*. New York: HarperCollins, 2007.

Thomas, Helen and Craig Crawford. *Listen Up, Mr. President: Everything You Always Wanted Your President to Know and Do*. New York: Scribner, 2009.

Todd, Chuck. *The Stranger: Barack Obama in the White House*. New York: Little, Brown, 2014.

Tooze, Adam. *Crashed: How a Decade of Financial Crises Changed the World*. New York: Viking, 2018.

Van Heerden, Ivor and Mike Bryan. *The Storm: What Went Wrong and Why During Hurricane Katrina—The Inside Story from One Louisiana Scientist*. New York: Viking, 2006.

Vanderbilt, Tom. *Traffic*. New York: Alfred A. Knopf, 2008.

Wolffe, Richard. *Revival: The Struggle for Survival Inside the Obama White House*. New York: Crown, 2010.

Woodward, Bob. *Obama's Wars*. New York: Simon & Schuster, 2010.

———. *Plan of Attack*. New York: Simon & Schuster, 2004.

Yergin, Daniel. *The Quest: Energy, Security, and the Remaking of the Modern World*. New York: Penguin, 2011.

Zakaria, Fareed. *The Post-American World Release 2.0*. New York: W.W. Norton, 2011.

Zogby, John. *The Way We'll Be: The Zogby Report on the Transformation of the American Dream*. New York: Random House, 2008.

NEWSPAPERS AND PERIODICALS

"A $1.33 Trillion Drop in Net Worth in First Quarter," *New York Times*, June 12, 2009.

Abramowitz, Michael. "Administration Strategy for Detention Now in Disarray," *Washington Post*, June 13, 2008.

Achenbach, Joel. "In Debate Over Nation's Growing Debt, a Surplus of Worry," *Washington Post*, December 8, 2009.

Achenbach, Joel and David A. Fahrenthold, "Gulf Disaster is Biggest Accidental Spill in History, Analysis Says," *Washington Post*, August 3, 2010.

Adams, Scott. "Dilbert," *Washington Post*, February 10, 2011.

Allen, Mike. "Confident Bush Vows to Move Aggressively; Second-Term Agenda Includes Social Security, Tax Code," *Washington Post*, November 5, 2004.

Allen, Mike and Dana Priest. "Report Discounts Iraqi Arms Threat; U.S. Inspector Says Hussein Lacked Means," *Washington Post*, October 6, 2004.

Andrews, Edmund L. and Vikas Bajaj, "U.S. Plans $500,000 Cap on Executive Pay on Bailouts," *New York Times*, February 3, 2009.

Andrews, Edmund L. and Peter Baker. "A.I.G. Planning Huge Bonuses after $170 Billion Bailout," *New York Times*, March 14, 2009.

Appelbaum, Binyamin. "Family Net Worth Drops to Level of Early '90s, Fed Says," *New York Times*, June 11, 2012.

———. "Stress Test Finds Strength in Banks," *Washington Post*, May 7, 2009.

———. "Troubled Banking Industry Pulls Back," *Washington Post*, February 24, 2010.

Appelbaum, Binyamin and Neil Irwin, "Bank of America Gets New Round of U.S. Aid," *Washington Post*, January 16, 2009.

Arango, Tim. "How the AOL-Time Warner Merger Went So Wrong," *New York Times*, January 11, 2010.

"Barack Obama's Inaugural Address," *New York Times*, January 20, 2009.

Bagli, Charles V. "Due Diligence on the Donald," *New York Times*, January 25, 2004.

Bagli, Charles V. and Christine Haughney. "Fallout is Wide in Failed Deal for Stuyvesant Town," *New York Times*, January 25, 2010.

Bajaj, Vikas. "Heart-Stopping Fall, Breathtaking Rally," *New York Times*, December 31, 2009.

———. "Markets Limp Into 2009 After a Bruising Year," *New York Times*, December 31, 2008.

"Barack Obama's Speech on Race," *New York Times*, March 18, 2008.

Barnes, Robert. "Court Hears Global Warming Case," *Washington Post*, November 30, 2006.

———. "A Deeply Divided Supreme Court on Friday Delivered a Historic Victory," *Washington Post*, June 27, 2015.

———. "Justices Say Detainees Can Seek Release," *Washington Post*, June 13, 2008.

———. "Ruling Threatens Enron Conviction," *Washington Post*, June 25, 2010.

———. "Victories for Gay Marriage," *Washington Post*, June 27, 2013.

Barnes, Robert and Juliet Eilperin. "High Court Faults EPA Inaction on Emissions," *Washington Post*, April 3, 2007.

Barrionuevo, Alexei. "Enron's Skilling is Sentenced to 24 Years," *New York Times*, October 24, 2006.

———. "Two Enron Chiefs Are Convicted in Fraud and Conspiracy Trial," *New York Times*, May 25, 2006.

Barstow, David, Susanne Craig, and Russ Buettner. "Trump Engaged in Suspect Tax Schemes as He Reaped Riches from His Father," *New York Times*, October 2, 2018.

Behr, Peter. "Hidden Numbers Crushed Enron; 'Partnerships' Shielded $600 Million Debt," *Washington Post*, January 12, 2002.

Bernstein, Lenny. "World's Fish on Move to Cooler Waters, Study Finds," *Washington Post*, May 16, 2013.

Brinkley, Joel. "Supreme Court Strikes Down Texas Law Banning Sodomy," *New York Times*, June 26, 2003.

Broder, John M. "Past Decade Warmest Ever, NASA Data Shows," *New York Times*, January 21, 2010.

Brooks, David. "When Trolls and Crybabies Rule the Earth," *New York Times*, May 30, 2019.

Brown, David. "Life Expectancy Hits Record High in United States," *Washington Post*, June 12, 2008.

"The Browning of America," *Washington Post*, May 18, 2012.

Brubaker, Bill. "GWU Raises Tuition to Over $50,000 a Year," *Washington Post*, February 9, 2007.

Bumiller, Elisabeth. "Amid Talk of War Spending, Bush Urges Fiscal Restraint," *New York Times*, September 17, 2002.

Bumiller, Elisabeth and James Dao. "Cheney Says Peril of a Nuclear Iraq Justifies Attack," *New York Times*, August 27, 2002.

Burns, Alexander. "Choice Words from Donald Trump, Presidential Candidate," *New York Times*, June 16, 2015.

"Bush's Approval Rating," *Washington Post*, January 13, 2009.

Calmes, Jackie. "TARP Bailout to Cost Less Than Once Anticipated," *New York Times*, October 1, 2010.

———. "U.S. Forecasts Smaller Loss from Bailout of Banks," *New York Times*, December 7, 2009.

———. "Year-End Audit Finds TARP Program Effective," *New York Times*, December 9, 2009.

Cha, Ariana Eunjung. "China's Cars, Accelerating a Global Demand for Fuel," *Washington Post*, July 28, 2008.

Chan, Sewell and Jackie Spinner. "Allegations of Abuse Lead to Shakeup at Iraqi Prison," *Washington Post*, April 30, 2004.

Cho, David. "A Conversion in 'This Storm,'" *Washington Post*, November 18, 2008.

Clement, Scott and Sandhya Somashekhar. "Opposition to Gay Marriage Hits a Low," *Washington Post*, May 23, 2012.

Copeland, Michael V. "Reed Hastings: Leader of the Pack," *Fortune*, November 18, 2010.

Cushman, John H., Jr. "Appeals Court Overturns Terrorism Conviction of Bin Laden's Driver," *New York Times*, October 16, 2012.

Dabrowski, Wojtek. "Buffett: Bank Woes are 'Poetic Justice,'" *Reuters*, February 6, 2008.

Davey, Monica. "Iowa Court Voids Gay Marriage Ban," *New York Times*, April 4, 2009.

Dennis, Brady. "TARP at 2: Officials Assess Bailouts," *Washington Post*, October 1, 2010.

DeYoung, Karen. "Powell Reverses View on Gays in Military," *Washington Post*, February 4, 2010.

"Dow's 778-Point Tailspin is Bigger Loss Than First Trading Day After 2001 Attacks," *Washington Post*, September 30, 2008.

Drew, Jill. "The Crash: What Went Wrong," *Washington Post*, December 16, 2008.

Eder, Steve. "Donald Trump Agrees to Pay $25 Million in Trump University Settlement," *New York Times*, November 18, 2016.

Edwards, Mickey. "Dick Cheney's Error," *Washington Post*, March 22, 2008.

Eggen, Dan and T. W. Farnam. "Spending a Lot, With Little Effect," *Washington Post*, November 8, 2012.

Eggen, Dan and Michael A. Fletcher. "Embattled Gonzales Resigns," *Washington Post*, August 28, 2007.

Eichenwald, Kurt. "Ex-Chief Financial Officer of Enron and Wife Plead Guilty," *New York Times*, January 15, 2004.

Eilperin, Juliet. "Long Droughts, Rising Seas Predicted Despite Future CO2 Curbs," *Washington Post*, January 27, 2009.

———. "Nation Set Record for Heat Last Year," *Washington Post*, January 9, 2013.

Eisinger, Jesse. "Why Only One Top Banker Went to Jail for the Financial Crisis," *New York Times*, April 30, 2014.

Elmer-DeWitt, Philip. "Fortune Magazine Names Apple's Steve Jobs CEO of the Decade," *Fortune*, November 5, 2009.

Farhi, Paul. "A Caller Had a Lewd Tape on Donald Trump," *Washington Post*, October 8, 2016.

Fears, Darryl. "Hispanics in the U.S.," *Washington Post*, October 3, 2006.

Feuer, Alan. "Four Charged with Running Online Prostitution Ring," *New York Times*, March 7, 2008.

Finn, Peter. "Sept. 11 Suspects Will Be Tried by a Military Panel," *Washington Post*, April 5, 2011.

Finn, Peter and Anne E. Kornblut. "How the White House Lost on Guantanamo," *Washington Post*, April 24, 2011.

Fletcher, Michael A. "Detailing How the Recession Imploded States' Finances," *Washington Post*, January 6, 2011.

Friedman, Thomas L. "China Deserves Donald Trump," *New York Times*, May 21, 2019.

———. "Obama Should Seize the High Ground," *New York Times*, May 26, 2012.

Gardner, Amy. "A Movement Without a Compass," *Washington Post*, October 24, 2010.

Geithner, Timothy F. "5 Myths About TARP," *Washington Post*, October 10, 2010.

Glaberson, William. "Bin Laden Driver Sentenced to a Short Term," *New York Times*, August 7, 2008.

———. "Detainee Convicted on Terrorism Charges," *New York Times*, November 3, 2008.

———. "Judge Declares Five Detainees Held Illegally," *New York Times*, November 20, 2008.

Goldfarb, Zachary A. and Alec Klein. "The Bubble, Part II: Bust," *Washington Post*, June 16, 2008.

Goodman, Peter S. and Jack Healy. "663,000 Jobs Lost in March; Total Tops 5 Million," *New York Times*, April 3, 2009.

Goodstein, Laurie. "After the Attacks: Finding Fault; Falwell's Finger-Pointing Inappropriate, Bush Says," *New York Times*, September 14, 2001.

Gordon, Michael R. and Judith Miller. "U.S. Says Hussein Intensifies Quest for A-Bomb Parts," *New York Times*, September 8, 2002.

Graham, Bradley. "Rumsfeld Tells of Regrets," *Washington Post*, February 3, 2011.

Greenberg, Jonathan. "Saving Face: How Donald Trump Silenced the People Who Could Expose His Business Failures," *Washington Post*, June 14, 2019.

———. "Trump Lied to Me About His Wealth to Get onto the Forbes 400. Here Are the Tapes," *Washington Post*, April 20, 2018.

Greenhouse, Linda. "The Gay Rights Ruling," *New York Times*, May 21, 1996.

———. "Justices, 5–3, Broadly Reject Bush Plan to Try Detainees," *New York Times*, June 30, 2006.

Harden, Blaine. "America's Population Set to Top 300 Million," *Washington Post*, October 12, 2006.

Hastings, Michael. "The Runaway General: The Profile That Brought Down McChrystal," *Rolling Stone*, June 22, 2010.

Haynes, V. Dion. "Downturn Pummels Consumer Confidence," *Washington Post*, October 29, 2008.

Healy, Jack. "Home Prices Fell at Record Pace in October," *New York Times*, December 30, 2008.

Hedgpeth, Dana and Jennifer Agiesta. "A Hard Downshift in Detroit," *Washington Post*, January 3, 2010.

Helderman, Rosalind S. "Trump Agrees to $25 Million Settlement in Trump University Fraud Cases," *Washington Post*, November 18, 2016.

Hsu, Spencer S. "Immigration Arrests Down 8% for Year," *Washington Post*, October 31, 2006.

"Iraq and the Economy," *Washington Post*, September 20, 2002.

Irwin, Neil. "Aughts Were a Lost Decade for U.S. Economy, Workers," *Washington Post*, January 2, 2010.

———. "Central Bank Chief Forecasts a Sluggish Recovery," *Washington Post*, December 8, 2009.

———. "Economic Signs Point to Longer, Deeper Recession," *Washington Post*, December 2, 2008.

———. "Fed Cuts Key Rate to Record Low," *Washington Post*, December 17, 2008.

———. "Fed to Inject $600 Billion Into Economy," *Washington Post*, November 4, 2010.

———. "In Crisis, Fed Made a Record Profit," *Washington Post*, January 12, 2010.

———. "The Policymakers Saved the Financial System. And America Never Forgave Them," *New York Times*, September 12, 2018.

Irwin, Neil and David Cho. "U.S. Offers Citigroup Sweeping Safety Net," *Washington Post*, November 24, 2008.

Irwin, Neil and Dan Eggen. "Economy Made Few Gains in Bush Years," *Washington Post*, January 12, 2009.

Irwin, Neil and Zachary A. Goldfarb. "U.S. Seizes Control of Mortgage Giants," *Washington Post*, September 8, 2008.

Irwin, Neil, Annie Gowen and Ben Pershing. "Job Losses a Blow to Still Fragile Economy," *Washington Post*, January 9, 2010.

Irwin, Neil and Nia-Malika Henderson. "Recession is Officially Over, But Anxiety Lingers," *Washington Post*, September 21, 2010.

Irwin, Neil and Steven Mufson. "Economic Indicators Continue Nose Dive," *Washington Post*, December 6, 2008.

Irwin, Neil and Amit R. Paley. "Greenspan Says He Was Wrong on Regulation," *Washington Post*, October 24, 2008.

Irwin, Neil and Annys Shin. "598,000 Jobs Shed in Brutal January," *Washington Post*, February 7, 2009.

———. "Fed Leaders Issue Bleak Forecast," *Washington Post*, February 19, 2009.

Jehl, Douglas. "U.S. Report Finds Iraq Was Minimal Weapons Threat in '03," *New York Times*, October 6, 2004.

Johnson, Carrie. "Internal Justice Dept. Report Cites Illegal Hiring Practices," *Washington Post*, July 29, 2008.

Johnson, Carrie, Del Quentin Wilber, and Dan Eggen. "Government Asserts Ivins Acted Alone," *Washington Post*, August 7, 2008.

Klein, Alec and Zachary A. Goldfarb. "The Bubble, Part I: Boom," *Washington Post*, June 15, 2008.

Knowlton, Brian. "Battle Ends Quietly as Kerry Concedes: Bush Wins 2nd Term by a Solid Margin," *New York Times*, November 4, 2004.

Krauthammer, Charles. "Phony Theory, False Conflict," *Washington Post*, November 18, 2005.

Lacey, Marc. "Hispanics Are Surging in Arizona," *New York Times*, March 10, 2010.

———. "Killings in Drug War in Mexico Double in '08," *New York Times*, December 8, 2008.

Leonhardt, David. "The Big Fix," *New York Times*, January 27, 2009.

———. "Job Losses Show Breadth of Recession," *New York Times*, March 3, 2009.

Liptak, Adam. "Justices, 5–4, Reject Corporate Spending Limit," *New York Times*, January 21, 2010.

———. "Supreme Court Ruling Makes Same-Sex Marriage a Right Nationwide," *New York Times*, June 26, 2015.

Lohr, Steve. "Smartphone Rises Fast from Gadget to Necessity," *New York Times*, June 10, 2009.

Londoño, Ernesto. "Iraq and Afghan Wars Will Cost Up to $6 Trillion, Study Says," *Washington Post*, March 29, 2013.

Lowenstein, Roger. "A Legacy of the Financial Crisis? The Makings of the Next One," *Washington Post*, September 7, 2018.

Lyall, Sarah. "Heat, Flood or Icy Cold, Extreme Weather Rages Worldwide," *New York Times*, January 10, 2013.

MacGillis, Alec and Jon Cohen. "Democrats Add Suburbs to Their Growing Coalition," *Washington Post*, November 6, 2008.

Mayes, Brittany Renee, Aaron Williams, and Laris Karklis. "The History of U.S. Border Apprehensions," *Washington Post*, January 9, 2019.

McCarthy, Justin. "Two in Three Americans Support Same-Sex Marriage," *Gallup*, May 23, 2018.

McGeehan, Patrick. "$100 Million Fine for Merrill Lynch," *New York Times*, May 22, 2002.

McNamee, Roger. "A Brief History of How Your Privacy Was Stolen," *New York Times*, June 3, 2019.

Merle, Renae. "Recession Weighs on Home Prices, Consumers," *Washington Post*, December 31, 2008.

———. "Stocks Tank as Recession Declared," *Washington Post*, December 2, 2008.

———. "Wall Street's Final '08 Toll: $6.9 Trillion Wiped Out," *Washington Post*, January 1, 2009.

Meyerson, Harold. "A Useful Nudge in California," *Washington Post*, May 21, 2008.

Miroff, Nick and William Booth. "Border Arrests Fall Sharply, U.S. Says," *Washington Post*, December 4, 2011.

Mitchell, Alison and Carl Hulse. "Congress Authorizes Bush to Use Force Against Iraq, Creating a Broad Mandate," *New York Times*, October 11, 2002.

Montgomery, Lori. "Deficit Projected to Swell Beyond Earlier Estimates," *Washington Post*, March 21, 2009.

———. "Obama Predicts Years of Deficits Over $1 Trillion," *Washington Post*, January 7, 2009.

———. "U.S. to Pay $25 Billion for TARP, CBO Says," *Washington Post*, November 30, 2010.

Montgomery, Lori and Neil Irwin. "Record-High Deficit May Dash Big Plans," *Washington Post*, October 17, 2009.

Morello, Carol. "9 Million Americans Said to Be Gay or Bisexual," *Washington Post*, April 8, 2011.

Morello, Carol and Dan Balz. "Calif. Latino Population Burgeons," *Washington Post*, March 9, 2011.

Morello, Carol and Ted Mellnik. "Minority Babies Majority in U.S.," *Washington Post*, May 17, 2012.

Morgenson, Gretchen. "Bullish Analyst of Tech Stocks Quits Salomon," *New York Times*, August 16, 2002.

———. "Seeing a Fund as Too Big to Fail, New York Fed Assists Its Bailout," *New York Times*, September 24, 1998.

Mouawad, Jad. "Wind Power Grows 39% for the Year," *New York Times*, January 26, 2010.

Mufson, Steven. "Calif. Field Goes from Rush to Reflection of Global Limits," *Washington Post*, July 29, 2008.

———. "Debt Across U.S. Hits Post-WWII Levels," *Washington Post*, February 23, 2011.

———. "Flight to U.S. Treasury Bonds is Bad News for the Economy," *Washington Post*, December 2, 2008.

———. "GM's New Road Map: Partial Nationalization," *Washington Post*, April 28, 2009.

———. "Power-Sector Emissions of China to Top U.S.," *Washington Post*, August 27, 2008.

———. "This Time, It's Different," *Washington Post*, July 27, 2008.

Mufson, Steven and Blaine Harden. "Around the World, the Signs of Slowdown Spiral Outward," *Washington Post*, October 25, 2008.

Mufson, Steven, David Cho, and Cecilia Kang. "Aid in Hand, Clock Ticks for Detroit," *Washington Post*, December 20, 2008.

Mui, Ylan Q. "Families See Their Wealth Sapped," *Washington Post*, June 12, 2012.

Murray, Shailagh and Paul Kane. "Congress Passes Stimulus Package," *Washington Post*, February 14, 2009.

Nagl, John. "What America Learned in Iraq," *New York Times*, March 20, 2013.

Nagourney, Adam. "Reform Bid Said to Be a No-Go for Trump," *New York Times*, February 14, 2000.

Nakamura, David. "Obama on Same-Sex Marriage Ruling," *Washington Post*, June 26, 2015.

Newport, Frank. "In U.S., Estimate of LGBT Population Rises to 4.5%," *Gallup*, May 22, 2018.

Noguchi, Yuki and Renae Merle. "WorldCom Says Its Books Are Off $3.8 Billion; U.S. Criminal Probe Reported," *Washington Post*, June 26, 2002.

Novak, Robert. "Mission to Niger," *Washington Post*, July 14, 2003.

O'Brien, Timothy L. "Blix Tells Security Council That Iraq's Cooperation is Limited," *New York Times*, January 27, 2003.

O'Connell, Jonathan, David Fahrenthold, and Jack Gillum. "As the 'King of Debt,' Trump Borrowed to Build His Empire. Then He Began Spending Hundreds of Millions in Cash," *Washington Post*, May 5, 2018.

O'Keefe, Ed and Craig Whitlock. "'Don't Ask' Opponents Get a Boost,'" *Washington Post*, December 1, 2010.

O'Keefe, Ed and Jennifer Agiesta. "75% Back Letting Gays Serve Openly," *Washington Post*, February 12, 2010.

Pearlstein, Steven. "Big Lessons in Finance from a Little Bank You've Never Heard Of," *Washington Post*, February 11, 2009.

———. "In Crisis, Paulson's Stunning Use of Federal Power," *Washington Post*, September 8, 2008.

Perlroth, Nicole. "The BlackBerry as Black Sheep," *New York Times*, October 16, 2012.

Perry v. Schwarzenegger, No. C 09-2292 VRW, United States District Court for the Northern District of California, August 4, 2010.

Pincus, Walter. "CIA Did Not Share Doubt on Iraq Data; Bush Used Report of Uranium Bid," *Washington Post*, June 12, 2003.

Plumer, Brad. "U.S. Oil Imports are Falling to Their Lowest Level Since 1987," *Washington Post*, January 9, 2013.

Powell, Michael. "Judge Rules Against 'Intelligent Design,'" *Washington Post*, December 21, 2005.

"President Bush's Remarks," *Washington Post*, September 12, 2001.

"President-Elect Obama," *Washington Post*, November 5, 2008.

Priest, Dana. "CIA Holds Terror Suspects in Secret Prisons," *Washington Post*, November 2, 2005.

Priest, Dana and R. Jeffrey Smith. "Memo Offered Justification for Use of Torture," *Washington Post*, June 8, 2004.

"Queen Teases Bush over Verbal Gaffe," *The Guardian*, May 9, 2007.

Reinhardt, Uwe E. "The Fork in the Road for Health Care," *New York Times*, May 25, 2012.

"Remarks by the President and Vice President at Signing of the Don't Ask, Don't Tell Repeal Act of 2010" (official White House transcript), December 22, 2010.

Revkin, Andrew C. "Climategate Fever Breaks," *New York Times*, July 7, 2010.

Revkin, Andrew C. and Seth Mydans, "Climate Panel Reaches Consensus on the Need to Reduce Harmful Emissions," *New York Times*, May 4, 2007.

Richburg, Keith B. "'Old Europe' Reacts to Rumsfeld's Label," *Washington Post*, January 24, 2003.

Risen, James. "The Struggle for Iraq: Treatment of Prisoners," *New York Times*, April 29, 2004.

Risen, James and Eric Lichtblau. "Bush Lets U.S. Spy on Callers Without Courts," *New York Times*, December 16, 2005.

Roberts, Sam. "Minorities in U.S. Set to Become Majority by 2042," *New York Times*, August 14, 2008.

Romero, Simon and Alex Berenson. "WorldCom Says It Hid Expenses, Inflating Cash Flow $3.8 Billion," *New York Times*, June 26, 2002.

Roose, Kevin. "A Farewell for iTunes," *New York Times*, June 3, 2019.

Rosenwald, Michael S. "AOL Tries to Navigate the Web It Helped You Find," *Washington Post*, December 9, 2009.

Sanger, David E. "Bush Aides Say Tough Tone Put Foes on Notice," *New York Times*, January 31, 2002.

Schmidt, Susan. "A Jackpot from Indian Gaming Tribes," *Washington Post*, February 22, 2004.

Schmidt, Susan and James V. Grimaldi. "Abramoff Pleads Guilty to 3 Counts; Lobbyist to Testify About Lawmakers in Corruption Probe," *Washington Post*, January 4, 2006.

Schneider, Richard, Jr. "Pride Issue: Stonewall Special," *The Gay & Lesbian Review Worldwide*, May–June 2019.

Seelye, Katharine Q. "A National Challenged: Captives; Detainees are Not P.O.W.'s, Cheney and Rumsfeld Declare," *New York Times*, January 28, 2002.

Serwer, Amy. "The '00s: Goodbye (at Last) to the Decade from Hell," *Time*, November 24, 2009.

Shales, Tom. "Aboard the Abraham Lincoln, A White House Spectacular," *Washington Post*, May 2, 2003.

Shear, Michael D. "With Document, Obama Seeks to End 'Birther' Issue," *New York Times*, April 27, 2011.

Shear, Michael D. and Peter Whoriskey. "Obama Takes Auto Bailout Victory Lap," *Washington Post*, July 31, 2010.

Shiller, Robert J. "The Housing Boom is Already Gigantic. How Long Can It Last?" *New York Times*, December 7, 2018.

Shin, Annys. "Stocks Soar, But Dismal Signs Remain," *Washington Post*, March 13, 2009.

Shin, Annys and Neil Irwin. "Layoffs Cut Deeper into Economy," *Washington Post*, January 27, 2009.

Sidarth, S. R. "I Am Macaca," *Washington Post*, November 12, 2006.

Smith, Craig S. "Threats and Responses: The Allies," *New York Times*, January 24, 2003.

Somashekhar, Sandhya. "Troops Express Views on Gay Ban," *Washington Post*, December 1, 2010.

Sorkin, Aaron Ross. "From Trump to Trade, The Financial Still Resonates 10 Years Later," *New York Times*, September 10, 2018.

St. George, Donna. "Internet, Cellphones May Strengthen Family Unit, Study Finds," *Washington Post*, October 20, 2008.

Stein, Ben. "In Class Warfare, Guess Which Class is Winning," *New York Times*, November 23, 2006.

Stein, Rob. "Premarital Abstinence Pledges Ineffective, Study Finds," *Washington Post*, December 29, 2008.

Steinhauer, Jennifer. "Senate Races Expose Extent of Republicans' Gender Gap," *New York Times*, November 7, 2012.

Stern, Christopher and Carrie Johnson. "WorldCom Files Record Bankruptcy Case," *Washington Post*, July 22, 2002.

Stiglitz, Joseph E. and Linda J. Bilmes. "The Book of Jobs," *Vanity Fair*, December 6, 2011.

Stolberg, Sheryl Gay. "Tremors Across Washington as Lobbyist Turns Star Witness," *New York Times*, January 4, 2006.

Stolberg, Sheryl Gay and Helene Cooper. "Obama Adds Troops, but Maps Exit Plan," *New York Times*, December 1, 2009.

Story, Louise and Jo Becker. "Bank Chief Tells of U.S. Pressure to Buy Merrill Lynch," *New York Times*, June 12, 2009.

Stout, David. "Bush Backs Ban in Constitution on Gay Marriage," *New York Times*, February 24, 2004.

———. "Bush Expresses 'Deep Disgust' Over Abuse of Iraqi Prisoners," *New York Times*, April 30, 2004.

Streitfeld, David and Jack Healy. "Phoenix Leads the Way Down in Home Prices," *New York Times*, April 29, 2009.

Tavernise, Sabrina. "Numbers of Children of Whites Falling Fast," *New York Times*, April 6, 2011.

"Text of Bush's Speech at West Point," *New York Times*, June 1, 2002.

Thompson, Krissah and Felicia Sonmez. "To N.Y. Muslims, Islamic Center Near Ground Zero Would Be More Than a Mosque," *Washington Post*, August 19, 2010.

Thorstad, David. "Can the LGBT+ Coalition Survive?" *The Gay & Lesbian Review Worldwide*, March–April 2019.

"Transcript of President Bush's Address to Nation on U.S. Policy in Iraq," *New York Times*, January 11, 2007.

Trejos, Nancy. "Retirement Savings Lose $2 Trillion in 15 Months," *Washington Post*, October 8, 2008.

Trump, Donald J. "What I Saw at the Revolution," *New York Times*, February 19, 2000.

Tse, Tomoeh Murakami. "Financial Firms Pay Out 17% More in Bonuses," *Washington Post*, February 24, 2010.

Tsukayama, Hayley. "Facebook Nearly Flat After Glitches and Chaotic Trading," *Washington Post*, May 19, 2012.

Uchitelle, Louis. "Unemployment Hits 7.2%, a 15-Year High," *New York Times*, January 9, 2009.

"U.S. Home Price Index Rose Slightly in November," *New York Times*, January 26, 2010.

"U.S. Stocks Gain on Speculation That Fed Will Cut Rates Again," *New York Times*, January 28, 2008.

Vedantam, Shankar. "U.S. Deportations Reach Record High," *Washington Post*, October 7, 2010.

Vick, Karl and Ashley Surdin. "Most of California's Black Voters Backed Gay Marriage Ban," *Washington Post*, November 7, 2008.

Wallsten, Peter. "Party Coalition at a Crossroads," *Washington Post*, November 8, 2012.

Wallsten, Peter and Scott Wilson. "Historic Step by Obama on Gay Marriage," *Washington Post*, May 10, 2012.

Walsh, Edward. "Bush Encourages N.Y. Rescuers," *Washington Post*, September 15, 2001.

Weiss, Eric M. "Around D.C., a Cheaper House May Cost You," *Washington Post*, October 12, 2006.

Whitlock, Craig and Greg Jaffe. "Pentagon Now Backs Gays Serving Openly in Military," *Washington Post*, February 3, 2010.

Whoriskey, Peter. "The 'Lake Wobegon Effect' Lifts CEOs' Pay," *Washington Post*, October 4, 2011.

———. "U.S. Gets Majority Stake in New GM," *Washington Post*, June 1, 2009.

———. "Weak Data Signal Grim Prospects for Workers," *Washington Post*, October 3, 2009.

Whoriskey, Peter and Kendra Marr. "In Auto Talks, No Cure-All for Health Care Costs," *Washington Post*, February 27, 2009.

Wilentz, Sean. "George W. Bush: The Worst President in History?" *Rolling Stone*, May 4, 2006.

Williams, Krissah. "Immigrants Sending $45 Billion Home," *Washington Post*, October 19, 2006.

Wilson, Joseph C. "What I Didn't Find in Africa," *New York Times*, July 6, 2003.

Wilson, Scott. "Obama Calls for Fresh Start with Muslims," *Washington Post*, June 5, 2009.

Woodward, Bob. "Detainee Tortured, Says U.S. Official," *Washington Post*, January 14, 2009.

———. "Why Did Violence Plummet? It Wasn't Just the Surge," *Washington Post*, September 8, 2008.

Zak, Dan. "'Google:' After Searching High and Low, Group Picks 'Word of the Decade,'" *Washington Post*, January 9, 2010.

Zeleny, Jeff. "Opponents Call Obama Remarks 'Out of Touch,'" *New York Times*, April 12, 2008.

Zernike, Kate. "Amid Small Wins, Advocates Lose Marquee Battles," *New York Times*, December 3, 2009.

Zezima, Katie. "Boston Archdiocese to Sell Land to Raise $100 Million," *New York Times*, April 21, 2004.

ONLINE RESOURCES

Frank, Robert. "Jeff Bezos Is Now the Richest Man in Modern History," CNBC, July 16, 2018. cnbc.com.

"Morbidity and Mortality Weekly Report (MMWR)," Centers for Disease Control and Prevention. cdc.gov.

"Novak: 'No Great Crime' with Leak," CNN, October 1, 2003. cnn.com.

Simon, Scott. "Unrighteous Reverends," National Public Radio, September 22, 2001. npr.com.

"CIA's 'Facebook' Program Dramatically Cuts Agency's Costs," *The Onion*, March 21, 2011. theonion.com.

"Top Bush Officials Push Case Against Saddam," CNN, September 8, 2002. cnn.com.

Notes

INTRODUCTION

1 Amy Serwer, "The '00s: Goodbye (at Last) to the Decade from Hell," *Time*, November 24, 2009.

1: FROM DOT-COM TO DOT-BOMB

1 Alan Greenspan, *The Age of Turbulence* (New York: Penguin, 2007), 182–83.

2 Ibid., 185, 186, 207.

3 Ibid., 197.

4 Peter Whoriskey, "The 'Lake Wobegon Effect' Lifts CEOs' Pay," *Washington Post*, October 4, 2011.

5 Roger Lowenstein, *Origins of the Crash: The Great Bubble and Its Undoing* (New York: Penguin, 2004), 3.

6 Chrystia Freeland, *Plutocrats: The Rise of the New Global Super-Rich and Fall of Everyone Else* (New York: Penguin Press, 2012), 92.

7 Greenspan, *The Age of Turbulence*, 206–7.

8 Lowenstein, *Origins of the Crash*, 211; Financial Crisis Inquiry Commission, *The Financial Crisis Inquiry Report* (New York: PublicAffairs, 2011), 391.

2: DUBYA

1 Steve Kornacki, *The Red and the Blue: The 1990s and the Birth of Political Tribalism* (New York: HarperCollins, 2018), 377, 417.

2 George W. Bush, *Decision Points* (New York: Crown, 2010), 74.

3 Kornacki, *The Red and the Blue*, 5, 419.

4 John Zogby, *The Way We'll Be: The Zogby Report on the Transformation of the American Dream* (New York: Random House, 2008), 8–9.

5 Karl Rove, *Courage and Consequence: My Life as a Conservative in the Fight* (New York: Threshold, 2010), 200.

6 Bush, *Decision Points*, 300.

7 Kornacki, *The Red and the Blue*, 412.

8 David Barstow, Susanne Craig, Russ Buettner, "Trump Engaged in Suspect Tax Schemes as He Reaped Riches from His Father," *New York Times*, October 2, 2018.

9 Jonathan Greenberg, "Trump Lied to Me About His Wealth to Get onto the Forbes 400. Here Are the Tapes," *Washington Post*, April 20, 2018; Jonathan Greenberg, "Saving Face: How Donald Trump Silenced the People Who Could Expose His Business Failures," *Washington Post*, June 14, 2019.

10   Adam Nagourney, "Reform Bid Said to Be a No-Go for Trump," *New York Times*, February 14, 2000; Donald J. Trump, "What I Saw at the Revolution," *New York Times*, February 19, 2000.

11   Scott McClellan, *What Happened: Inside the Bush White House and Washington's Culture of Deception* (New York: PublicAffairs, 2008), 79.

12   Donald Rumsfeld, *Known and Unknown: A Memoir* (New York: Sentinel, 2011), 319.

13   James Comey, *A Higher Loyalty: Truth, Lies, and Leadership* (New York: Flatiron Books, 2018), 123–4.

14   "Queen Teases Bush over Verbal Gaffe," *The Guardian*, May 9, 2007.

15   James Mann, *George W. Bush* (New York: Times Books, 2015), 1–2.

16   Jean Edward Smith, *Bush* (New York: Simon & Schuster, 2016), 128.

17   Barton Gellman, *Angler: The Cheney Vice Presidency* (New York: Penguin, 2008), 58.

18   Dick Cheney, *In My Time: A Personal and Political Memoir* (New York: Threshold Editions, 2011), 305.

19   Ibid., 305

20   Ibid., 413.

21   Bush, *Decision Points*, 87.

22   Gellman, *Angler* (New York: Penguin, 2008), 87.

23   Rumsfeld, *Known and Unknown*, 320.

24   Gellman, *Angler*, 128.

25   Bradley Graham, "Rumsfeld Tells of Regrets," *Washington Post*, February 3, 2011.

26   Richard N. Haass, *War of Necessity, War of Choice* (New York: Simon & Schuster, 2009), 195.

27   Rumsfeld, *Known and Unknown*, xiii.

28   Greenspan, *The Age of Turbulence*, 224.

29   Ben Stein, "In Class Warfare, Guess Which Class is Winning," *New York Times*, November 23, 2006.

30   Hedrick Smith, *Who Stole the American Dream?* (New York: Random House, 2012), 137.

31   Greenspan, *The Age of Turbulence*, 235.

32   Dan Eggen and Michael A. Fletcher, "Embattled Gonzales Resigns," *Washington Post*, August 28, 2007.

33   Carrie Johnson, "Internal Justice Dept. Report Cites Illegal Hiring Practices," *Washington Post*, July 29, 2008.

34   "Morbidity and Mortality Weekly Report (MMWR)," Centers for Disease Control and Prevention, www.cdc.gov

35   Rob Stein, "Premarital Abstinence Pledges Ineffective, Study Finds," *Washington Post*, December 29, 2008; Alexandra M. Lord, *Condom Nation: The U.S. Government's Sex Education Campaign from World War I to the Internet* (Baltimore: Johns Hopkins University Press, 2010), 180–2; 189.

36   Charles Krauthammer, "Phony Theory, False Conflict," *Washington Post*, November 18, 2005.

37   Ray Suarez, *The Holy Vote: The Politics of Faith in America* (New York: HarperCollins, 2006), 55.

38   Michael Powell, "Judge Rules Against 'Intelligent Design,'" *Washington Post*, December 21, 2005.

3: 9/11

1   *The 9/11 Commission Report: Final Report of the National Commission on Terrorist Attacks Upon the United States* (New York: Norton, 2004), 7.

2   Ibid., 12–14.

3   Ibid., 41.

4   Ibid., 316.

5   Ibid., 311.

6   "President Bush's Remarks," *Washington Post*, September 12, 2001.

7   *The 9/11 Commission Report*, 50.

8   Ibid., 67.

9   Ibid., xvi.

10 Richard A. Clarke, *Against All Enemies: Inside America's War on Terror* (New York: Free Press, 2004), 242.

11 Condoleezza Rice, *No Higher Honor: A Memoir of My Years in Washington* (New York: Crown, 2011), xvi–xvii.

12 *The 9/11 Commission Report*, 259.

13 George Tenet, *At the Center of the Storm: My Years at the CIA* (New York: HarperCollins, 2007), 187; see also 145–49.

14 Rice, *No Higher Honor*, xvii, 65.

15 Bush, *Decision Points*, 154.

16 Edward Walsh, "Bush Encourages N.Y. Rescuers," *Washington Post*, September 15, 2001.

17 Laurie Goodstein, "After the Attacks: Finding Fault; Falwell's Finger-Pointing Inappropriate, Bush Says," *New York Times*, September 14, 2001.

18 Scott Simon, "Unrighteous Reverends," National Public Radio, September 22, 2001. www.npr.com

19 *The 9/11 Commission Report*, 337.

20 Bush, *Decision Points*, 207.

21 Gellman, *Angler*, 302–7; Comey, *A Higher Loyalty*, 84–99.

22 Cheney, *In My Time*, 352.

23 James Risen and Eric Lichtblau, "Bush Lets U.S. Spy on Callers Without Courts," *New York Times*, December 16, 2005.

24 Tom Ridge, *The Test of Our Times: America Under Siege . . . and How We Can Be Safe Again* (New York: Thomas Dunne, 2009), xi.

25 Ridge, *The Test of Our Times*, 52.

26 Carrie Johnson, Del Quentin Wilber, and Dan Eggen, "Government Asserts Ivins Acted Alone," *Washington Post*, August 7, 2008.

27 Ridge, *The Test of Our Times*, 99.

28 Bush, *Decision Points*, 444.

29 Katharine Q. Seelye, "A National Challenged: Captives; Detainees are Not P.O.W.'s, Cheney and Rumsfeld Declare," *New York Times*, January 28, 2002.

30 Rumsfeld, *Known and Unknown*, 569.

31 *The 9/11 Commission Report*, 145.

32 Dana Priest, "CIA Holds Terror Suspects in Secret Prisons," *Washington Post*, November 2, 2005.

33 Peter Finn, "Sept. 11 Suspects Will Be Tried by a Military Panel," *Washington Post*, April 5, 2011.

34   Bush, *Decision Points*, 169–71; Smith, *Bush*, 505.

35   Dana Priest and R. Jeffrey Smith, "Memo Offered Justification for Use of Torture,"
      Washington Post, June 8, 2004.

36   Cheney, *In My Time*, 358–59.

37   Tenet, *At the Center of the Storm*, 241–42.

38   Bob Woodward, "Detainee Tortured, Says U.S. Official," *Washington Post*, January
      14, 2009.

39   Linda Greenhouse, "Justices, 5–3, Broadly Reject Bush Plan to Try Detainees," *New
      York Times*, June 30, 2006; Jonathan Mahler, *The Challenge:* Hamdan v. Rumsfeld *and
      the Fight over Presidential Power* (New York: Farrar, Straus and Giroux, 2008), 283–4;
      298–301.

40   Michael Abramowitz, "Administration Strategy for Detention Now in Disarray,"
      Washington Post, June 13, 2008, and Robert Barnes, "Justices Say Detainees Can Seek
      Release," *Washington Post*, June 13, 2008.

41   Peter Finn and Anne E. Kornblut, "How the White House Lost on Guantanamo,"
      Washington Post, April 24, 2011.

42   William Glaberson, "Bin Laden Driver Sentenced to a Short Term," *New York Times*,
      August 7, 2008; John H. Cushman, Jr, "Appeals Court Overturns Terrorism Convic-
      tion of Bin Laden's Driver," *New York Times*, October 16, 2012.

43   William Glaberson, "Detainee Convicted on Terrorism Charges," *New York Times*,
      November 3, 2008; William Glaberson, "Judge Declares Five Detainees Held Illegally,"
      New York Times, November 20, 2008.

44   Cheney, *In My Time*, 420.

45   Gellman, *Angler*, 132–33.

46   Ibid., 138.

4: THE ENRON AND WORLDCOM SCANDALS

1   David Skeel, *Icarus in the Boardroom: The Fundamental Flaws in Corporate America and
      Where They Came From* (New York: Oxford University Press, 2005), 4–5.

2   Bethany McLean and Peter Elkind, *The Smartest Guys in the Room: The Amazing Rise
      and Scandalous Fall of Enron* (New York: Portfolio, 2003), xxiii, 114.

3   Roger Lowenstein, *Origins of the Crash: The Great Bubble and Its Undoing* (New York:
      Penguin, 2004), 129.

4   Peter Behr, "Hidden Numbers Crushed Enron; 'Partnerships' Shielded $600 Million
      Debt," *Washington Post*, January 12, 2002.

5   McLean and Elkind, *The Smartest Guys*, 366.

6   Ibid., 280.

7   Kurt Eichenwald, *Conspiracy of Fools: A True Story* (New York: Broadway, 2005),
      486–90.

8   Robert Barnes, "Ruling Threatens Enron Conviction," *Washington Post*, June 25,
      2010.

9   Rebecca Smith and John R. Emshwiller, *24 Days: How Two Wall Street Journal Reporters
      Uncovered the Lies That Destroyed Faith in Corporate America* (New York: HarperCollins,
      2003), 362.

10   Kurt Eichenwald, "Ex-Chief Financial Officer of Enron and Wife Plead Guilty," *New
      York Times*, January 15, 2004.

11   Alexei Barrionuevo, "Two Enron Chiefs Are Convicted in Fraud and Conspiracy Trial," *New York Times*, May 25, 2006; Alexei Barrionuevo, "Enron's Skilling is Sentenced to 24 Years," *New York Times*, October 24, 2006; Smith and Emshwiller, *24 Days*, 381.

12   Cynthia Cooper, *Extraordinary Circumstances: The Journey of a Corporate Whistleblower* (New York: John Wiley & Sons, 2008), viii.

13   Lynne W. Jeter, *Disconnected: Deceit and Betrayal at WorldCom* (New York: John Wiley & Sons, 2003), 29.

14   Ibid., 131.

15   Cooper, *Extraordinary Circumstances*, viii–ix.

16   Simon Romero and Alex Berenson, "WorldCom Says It Hid Expenses, Inflating Cash Flow $3.8 Billion," *New York Times*, June 26, 2002; Yuki Noguchi and Renae Merle, "WorldCom Says Its Books Are Off $3.8 Billion; U.S. Criminal Probe Reported," *Washington Post*, June 26, 2002.

17   Christopher Stern and Carrie Johnson, "WorldCom Files Record Bankruptcy Case," *Washington Post*, July 22, 2002; Jeter, *Disconnected*, 176.

18   Patrick McGeehan, "$100 Million Fine for Merrill Lynch," *New York Times*, May 22, 2002.

19   Gretchen Morgenson, "Bullish Analyst of Tech Stocks Quits Salomon," *New York Times*, August 16, 2002.

20   Alan Feuer, "Four Charged with Running Online Prostitution Ring," *New York Times*, March 7, 2008.

21   Jack Abramoff, *Capitol Punishment: The Hard Truth About Washington Corruption from America's Most Notorious Lobbyist* (Washington, DC: WND Books, 2011), 211.

22   Ibid., 153–54.

23   Peter H. Stone, *Heist: Superlobbyist Jack Abramoff, His Republican Allies, and the Buying of Washington* (New York: Farrar, Straus and Giroux, 2006), 23; Matthew Continetti, *The K Street Gang: The Rise and Fall of the Republican Machine* (New York: Doubleday, 2006), 153.

24   Susan Schmidt, "A Jackpot from Indian Gaming Tribes," *Washington Post*, February 22, 2004.

25   Susan Schmidt and James V. Grimaldi, "Abramoff Pleads Guilty to 3 Counts; Lobbyist to Testify About Lawmakers in Corruption Probe," *Washington Post*, January 4, 2006; Sheryl Gay Stolberg, "Tremors Across Washington as Lobbyist Turns Star Witness," *New York Times*, January 4, 2006.

26   Mike Lofgren, *The Party Is Over: How Republicans Went Crazy, Democrats Became Useless, and the Middle Class Got Shafted* (New York: Viking, 2012), 4.

27   Charles V. Bagli, "Due Diligence on the Donald," *New York Times*, January 25, 2004.

28   Paul Farhi, "A Caller Had a Lewd Tape on Donald Trump," *Washington Post*, October 8, 2016.

29   Jonathan O'Connell, David Fahrenthold, Jack Gillum, "As the 'King of Debt,' Trump Borrowed to Build His Empire. Then He Began Spending Hundreds of Millions in Cash," *Washington Post*, May 5, 2018.

30   Steve Eder, "Donald Trump Agrees to Pay $25 Million in Trump University Settlement," *New York Times*, November 18, 2016; Rosalind S. Helderman, "Trump Agrees to $25 Million Settlement in Trump University Fraud Cases," *Washington Post*, November 18, 2016.

31   Katie Zezima, "Boston Archdiocese to Sell Land to Raise $100 Million," *New York Times*, April 21, 2004.

5: THE IRAQ WAR

1   Tenet, *At the Center of the Storm*, 301.
2   David E. Sanger, "Bush Aides Say Tough Tone Put Foes on Notice," *New York Times*, January 31, 2002.
3   Clarke, *Against All Enemies*, 30, 32.
4   Tenet, *At the Center of the Storm*, xix.
5   Bush, *Decision Points*, 189.
6   Rumsfeld, *Known and Unknown*, 347.
7   Tenet, *At the Center of the Storm*, 305.
8   Rumsfeld, *Known and Unknown*, 427–28.
9   Bush, *Decision Points*, 229.
10 Tenet, *At the Center of the Storm*, 301.
11 "Text of Bush's Speech at West Point," *New York Times*, June 1, 2002.
12 Haass, *War of Necessity*, 5.
13 Robert Draper, *Dead Certain: The Presidency of George W. Bush* (New York: Free Press, 2007), 180, 184.
14 Smith, *Bush*, 309.
15 Elisabeth Bumiller and James Dao, "Cheney Says Peril of a Nuclear Iraq Justifies Attack," *New York Times*, August 27, 2002.
16 Haass, *War of Necessity*, 181.
17 Mann, *George W. Bush*, 77.
18 Rice, *No Higher Honor*, 180, 181.
19 Michael J. Mazarr, *Leap of Faith: Hubris, Negligence, and America's Greatest Foreign Policy Tragedy* (New York: PublicAffairs, 2019), 2–3; 5.
20 Bob Woodward, *Plan of Attack* (New York: Simon & Schuster, 2004), 3.
21 Rajiv Chandrasekaran, *Imperial Life in the Emerald City: Inside Iraq's Green Zone* (New York: Alfred A. Knopf, 2006), 115.
22 Michael R. Gordon and Judith Miller, "U.S. Says Hussein Intensifies Quest for A-Bomb Parts," *New York Times*, September 8, 2002.
23 "Top Bush Officials Push Case Against Saddam," CNN, September 8, 2002.
24 Tenet, *At the Center of the Storm*, 336, 341–43, 347–48.
25 Alison Mitchell and Carl Hulse, "Congress Authorizes Bush to Use Force Against Iraq, Creating a Broad Mandate," *New York Times*, October 11, 2002.
26 Woodward, *Plan of Attack*, 249.
27 Bush, *Decision Points*, 242; Cheney, *In My Time*, 395.
28 Woodward, *Plan of Attack*, 261–62.
29 Timothy L. O'Brien, "Blix Tells Security Council That Iraq's Cooperation is Limited," *New York Times*, January 27, 2003.
30 Colin Powell, *It Worked for Me: In Life and Leadership* (New York: HarperCollins, 2012), 223.
31 McClellan, *What Happened*, 144.
32 Keith B. Richburg, "'Old Europe' Reacts to Rumsfeld's Label," *Washington Post*, January 24, 2003; Craig S. Smith, "Threats and Responses: The Allies," *New York Times*, January 24, 2003.
33 Thomas E. Ricks, *Fiasco: The American Military Adventure in Iraq* (New York: Penguin, 2006), 117.

34   Smith, *Bush*, 660.

35   Rumsfeld, *Known and Unknown*, 724.

36   Chandrasekaran, *Imperial Life in the Emerald City*, 25.

37   Douglas Jehl, "U.S. Report Finds Iraq Was Minimal Weapons Threat in '03," *New York Times*, October 6, 2004; Mike Allen and Dana Priest, "Report Discounts Iraqi Arms Threat; U.S. Inspector Says Hussein Lacked Means," *Washington Post*, October 6, 2004.

38   Tenet, *At the Center of the Storm*, 332–33, 414; Charles Duelfer, *Hide and Seek: The Search for Truth in Iraq* (New York: PublicAffairs, 2009), 407.

39   Powell, *It Worked for Me*, 222.

40   Rice, *No Higher Honor*, 199.

41   Rove, *Courage and Consequence*, 339–40.

42   Bush, *Decision Points*, 262.

43   Rumsfeld, *Known and Unknown*, 449.

44   Bush, *Decision Points*, 262.

45   Rove, *Courage and Consequence*, 342.

46   Rice, *No Higher Honor*, 237.

47   Rumsfeld, *Known and Unknown*, 435.

48   Gellman, *Angler*, 218.

49   Cheney, *In My Time*, 369.

50   Tenet, *At the Center of the Storm*, 341.

51   Rice, *No Higher Honor*, 170.

52   Haass, *War of Necessity*, 278.

53   Powell, *It Worked for Me*, 210; Woodward, *Plan of Attack*, 150, 152.

54   Tom Shales, "Aboard the Abraham Lincoln, A White House Spectacular," *Washington Post*, May 2, 2003; Bush, *Decision Points*, 257.

55   Elisabeth Bumiller, "Amid Talk of War Spending, Bush Urges Fiscal Restraint," *New York Times*, September 17, 2002; "Iraq and the Economy," *Washington Post*, September 20, 2002.

56   John Nagl, "What America Learned in Iraq," *New York Times*, March 20, 2013.

57   Cheney, *In My Time*, 433.

58   Walter Pincus, "CIA Did Not Share Doubt on Iraq Data; Bush Used Report of Uranium Bid," *Washington Post*, June 12, 2003; Joseph C. Wilson, "What I Didn't Find in Africa," *New York Times*, July 6, 2003.

59   Robert Novak, "Mission to Niger," *Washington Post*, July 14, 2003.

60   "Novak: 'No Great Crime' with Leak," CNN, October 1, 2003; Gellman, *Angler*, 362,

61   Cheney, *In My Time*, 404, 410.

62   James Risen, "The Struggle for Iraq: Treatment of Prisoners," *New York Times*, April 29, 2004; Sewell Chan and Jackie Spinner, "Allegations of Abuse Lead to Shakeup at Iraqi Prison," *Washington Post*, April 30, 2004.

63   David Stout, "Bush Expresses 'Deep Disgust' Over Abuse of Iraqi Prisoners," *New York Times*, April 30, 2004; Rumsfeld, *Known and Unknown*, 551.

64   Draper, *Dead Certain*, 236.

65   Bush, *Decision Points*, 288.

66   Michelle Obama, *Becoming* (New York: Crown, 2018), 214.

67   Brian Knowlton, "Battle Ends Quietly as Kerry Concedes: Bush Wins 2nd Term by a Solid Margin," *New York Times*, November 4, 2004.

68   Bush, *Decision Points*, 203.

69 Rumsfeld, *Known and Unknown*, 660.

70 Graham, *By His Own Rules*, 3, 12.

71 "Transcript of President Bush's Address to Nation on U.S. Policy in Iraq," *New York Times*, January 11, 2007.

72 Thomas E. Ricks, *The Gamble: General David Petraeus and the American Military Adventure in Iraq, 2006–2008* (New York: Penguin, 2009), 303.

73 Bob Woodward, "Why Did Violence Plummet? It Wasn't Just the Surge," *Washington Post*, September 8, 2008.

74 Mickey Edwards, "Dick Cheney's Error," *Washington Post*, March 22, 2008.

75 Bush, *Decision Points*, 248.

76 Ernesto Londoño, "Iraq and Afghan Wars Will Cost Up to $6 Trillion, Study Says," *Washington Post*, March 29, 2013.

6: KATRINA

1 John McQuaid and Mark Schleifstein, *Path of Destruction: The Devastation of New Orleans and the Coming Age of Superstorms* (New York: Little, Brown, 2006), 75.

2 Ibid., 79–80.

3 Douglas Brinkley, *The Great Deluge: Hurricane Katrina, New Orleans, and the Mississippi Gulf Coast* (New York: William Morrow, 2006), 24.

4 McQuaid and Schleifstein, *Path of Destruction*, 185–186.

5 Brinkley, *The Great Deluge*, xiv.

6 Jed Horne, *Breach of Faith: Hurricane Katrina and the Near Death of a Great American City* (New York: Random House, 2006), 56.

7 Brinkley, *The Great Deluge*, 53–54.

8 Ivor Van Heerden and Mike Bryan, *The Storm: What Went Wrong and Why During Hurricane Katrina—The Inside Story From One Louisiana Scientist* (New York: Viking, 2006), 79, 82, 242.

9 McQuaid and Schleifstein, *Path of Destruction*, 252.

10 Bush, *Decision Points*, 310.

11 Ibid., 308.

12 Ridge, *The Test of Our Times*, 220.

13 McQuaid and Schleifstein, *Path of Destruction*, 332.

14 Brinkley, *The Great Deluge*, xiv.

15 Bush, *Decision Points*, 326.

16 Horne, *Breach of Faith*, 315–26.

17 McQuaid and Schleifstein, *Path of Destruction*, 335.

18 Ibid., 339.

7. A NATION OF MINORITIES

1 Blaine Harden, "America's Population Set to Top 300 Million," *Washington Post*, October 12, 2006.

2 Sabrina Tavernise, "Numbers of Children of Whites Falling Fast," *New York Times*, April 6, 2011.

3 Darryl Fears, "Hispanics in the U.S.," *Washington Post*, October 3, 2006.

4 Sam Roberts, "Minorities in U.S. Set to Become Majority by 2042," *New York Times*, August 14, 2008.

5   Carol Morello and Ted Mellnik, "Minority Babies Majority in U.S.," *Washington Post*, May 17, 2012; "The Browning of America," *Washington Post*, May 18, 2012.

6   Sinclair Lewis, *Babbitt* (New York: Bantam Dell, 1998), 159.

7   Krissah Williams, "Immigrants Sending $45 Billion Home," *Washington Post*, October 19, 2006.

8   Spencer S. Hsu, "Immigration Arrests Down 8% for Year," *Washington Post*, October 31, 2006; Brittany Renee Mayes, Aaron Williams, and Laris Karklis, "The History of U.S. Border Apprehensions," *Washington Post*, January 9, 2019.

9   S. R. Sidarth, "I am Macaca," *Washington Post*, November 12, 2006.

10   Nick Miroff and William Booth, "Border Arrests Fall Sharply, U.S. Says," *Washington Post*, December 4, 2011.

11   Shankar Vedantam, "U.S. Deportations Reach Record High," *Washington Post*, October 7, 2010.

12   Marc Lacey, "Hispanics Are Surging in Arizona," *New York Times*, March 10, 2010.

13   Carol Morello and Dan Balz, "Calif. Latino Population Burgeons," *Washington Post*, March 9, 2011.

14   Junot Díaz, *The Brief Wondrous Life of Oscar Wao* (New York: Riverhead Books, 2007), 1.

15   Junot Díaz, book signing, Politics & Prose Bookstore, Washington, D.C., September 10, 2008. Díaz signed my copy of *Oscar Wao* and we chatted briefly. He had been an intern at Rutgers University Press, which published my first book, *The Prohibition Hangover*.

16   Krissah Thompson and Felicia Sonmez, "To N.Y. Muslims, Islamic Center Near Ground Zero Would Be More Than a Mosque," *Washington Post*, August 19, 2010.

17   Alexander Burns, "Choice Words from Donald Trump, Presidential Candidate," *New York Times*, June 16, 2015.

8. GAY IN AMERICA

1   David Thorstad, "Can the LGBT+ Coalition Survive?" *The Gay & Lesbian Review Worldwide*, March–April 2019, 29–30.

2   Linda Greenhouse, "The Gay Rights Ruling," *New York Times*, May 21, 1996.

3   Carol Morello, "9 Million Americans Said to Be Gay or Bisexual," *Washington Post*, April 8, 2011.

4   Frank Newport, "In U.S., Estimate of LGBT Population Rises to 4.5%," Gallup, May 22, 2018.

5   Justin McCarthy, "Two in Three Americans Support Same-Sex Marriage," Gallup, May 23, 2018.

6   Joel Brinkley, "Supreme Court Strikes Down Texas Law Banning Sodomy," *New York Times*, June 26, 2003.

7   David Stout, "Bush Backs Ban in Constitution on Gay Marriage," *New York Times*, February 24, 2004.

8   Rove, *Courage and Consequence*, 374.

9   Ibid., 377.

10   Bush, *Decision Points*, 293.

11   Cheney, *In My Time*, 283.

12   Nathaniel Frank, *Awakening: How Gays and Lesbians Brought Marriage Equality to America* (Cambridge, Mass.: Belknap Press, 2017), 2.

13   Rove, *Courage and Consequence*, 374–75.

14   Harold Meyerson, "A Useful Nudge in California," *Washington Post*, May 21, 2008.

15   Karl Vick and Ashley Surdin, "Most of California's Black Voters Backed Gay Marriage Ban," *Washington Post*, November 7, 2008.

16   Frank, *Awakening*, 188–89.

17   Monica Davey, "Iowa Court Voids Gay Marriage Ban," *New York Times*, April 4, 2009.

18   Kate Zernike, "Amid Small Wins, Advocates Lose Marquee Battles," *New York Times*, December 3, 2009.

19   Craig Whitlock and Greg Jaffe, "Pentagon Now Backs Gays Serving Openly in Military," *Washington Post*, February 3, 2010.

20   Karen DeYoung, "Powell Reverses View on Gays in Military," *Washington Post*, February 4, 2010.

21   Ed O'Keefe and Jennifer Agiesta, "75% Back Letting Gays Serve Openly," *Washington Post*, February 12, 2010.

22   John Zogby, *The Way We'll Be: The Zogby Report on the Transformation of the American Dream* (New York: Random House, 2008), 97.

23   *Perry v. Schwarzenegger*, No. C 09-2292 VRW, United States District Court for the Northern District of California, August 4, 2010.

24   Ed O'Keefe and Craig Whitlock, "'Don't Ask' Opponents Get a Boost," *Washington Post*, December 1, 2010, and Sandhya Somashekhar, "Troops Express Views on Gay Ban," *Washington Post*, December 1, 2010.

25   "Remarks by the President and Vice President at Signing of the Don't Ask, Don't Tell Repeal Act of 2010" (official White House transcript), December 22, 2010.

26   Barney Frank, *Frank: A Life in Politics from the Great Society to Same-Sex Marriage* (New York: Farrar, Straus and Giroux, 2015), 332.

27   Peter Wallsten and Scott Wilson, "Historic Step by Obama on Gay Marriage," *Washington Post*, May 10, 2012.

28   Scott Clement and Sandhya Somashekhar, "Opposition to Gay Marriage Hits a Low," *Washington Post*, May 23, 2012.

29   Robert Barnes, "Victories for Gay Marriage," *Washington Post*, June 27, 2013.

30   Adam Liptak, "Supreme Court Ruling Makes Same-Sex Marriage a Right Nationwide," *New York Times*, June 26, 2015; Robert Barnes, "A Deeply Divided Supreme Court on Friday Delivered a Historic Victory," *Washington Post*, June 27, 2015.

31   David Nakamura, "Obama on Same-Sex Marriage Ruling," *Washington Post*, June 26, 2015.

32   Peter Hart-Brinson, *The Gay Marriage Generation: How the LGBTQ Movement Transformed American Culture* (New York: New York University Press, 2018), 216.

33   Richard Schneider Jr., "Pride Issue: Stonewall Special," *The Gay & Lesbian Review Worldwide*, May–June 2019, 5.

9: THE NATIONAL PASTIME

1   Michael S. Rosenwald, "AOL Tries to Navigate the Web It Helped You Find," *Washington Post*, December 9, 2009; Tim Arango, "How the AOL-Time Warner Merger Went So Wrong," *New York Times*, January 11, 2010.

2   Zogby, *The Way We'll Be*, x–xi.

3   Donna St. George, "Internet, Cellphones May Strengthen Family Unit, Study Finds," *Washington Post*, October 20, 2008.

4   Maggie Jackson, *Distracted: The Erosion of Attention and the Coming Dark Age* (Amherst, N.Y.: Prometheus Books, 2008), 13.

5   Steven Johnson, *Everything Bad is Good For You* (New York: Riverhead, 2005), 9, 14.

6   Chris Anderson, *The Long Tail: Why the Future of Business is Selling Less of More* (New York: Hyperion, 2006), 5, 183.

7   Walter Isaacson, *Steve Jobs* (New York: Simon & Schuster, 2011), 393.

8   Kevin Roose, "A Farewell for iTunes," *New York Times*, June 3, 2019.

9   Steve Lohr, "Smartphone Rises Fast from Gadget to Necessity," *New York Times*, June 10, 2009.

10   Nicole Perlroth, "The BlackBerry as Black Sheep," *New York Times*, October 16, 2012.

11   Michael Saylor, *The Mobile Wave: How Mobile Intelligence Will Change Everything* (New York: Vanguard Press, 2012), 2.

12   Isaacson, *Steve Jobs*, 569.

13   Philip Elmer-DeWitt, "Fortune Magazine Names Apple's Steve Jobs CEO of the Decade," *Fortune*, November 5, 2009.

14   Isaacson, *Steve Jobs*, xxi.

15   Richard L. Brandt, *One Click: Jeff Bezos and the Rise of Amazon.com* (New York: Penguin, 2011), 5.

16   Robert Spector, *Amazon.com: Get Big Fast* (New York: HarperCollins, 2000), 198.

17   Robert Frank, "Jeff Bezos is Now the Richest Man in Modern History," CNBC, July 16, 2018.

18   Gina Keating, *Netflixed: The Epic Battle for America's Eyeballs* (New York: Penguin, 2012), 4.

19   Michael V. Copeland, "Reed Hastings: Leader of the Pack," *Fortune*, November 18, 2010.

20   Keating, *Netflixed*, 248.

21   Dan Zak, "'Google:' After Searching High and Low, Group Picks 'Word of the Decade,'" *Washington Post*, January 9, 2010.

22   Ken Auletta, *Googled: The End of the World as We Know It* (New York: Penguin Press, 2009), 6–7, 122.

23   Ibid., 287.

24   Ibid., 257.

25   Ibid., 185, 297.

26   Ben Mezrich, *The Accidental Billionaires: The Founding of Facebook* (New York: Doubleday, 2009), 253–254.

27   David Kirkpatrick, *The Facebook Effect: The Inside of the Company That Is Connecting the World* (New York: Simon & Schuster, 2010), 10.

28   Mezrich, *The Accidental Billionaires*, 111.

29   Katherine Losse, *The Boy Kings: A Journey Into the Heart of the Social Network* (New York: Free Press, 2012), 107–108.

30   Kirkpatrick, *The Facebook Effect*, 244.

31   David Brooks, "When Trolls and Crybabies Rule the Earth," *New York Times*, May 30, 2019.

32   Hayley Tsukayama, "Facebook Nearly Flat After Glitches and Chaotic Trading," *Washington Post*, May 19, 2012.

33   Roger McNamee, "A Brief History of How Your Privacy Was Stolen," *New York Times*, June 3, 2019.

34   "CIA's 'Facebook' Program Dramatically Cuts Agency's Costs," *The Onion*, March 21, 2011, www.theonion.com

35   Kirkpatrick, *The Facebook Effect*, 205.

10: A SMALLER WORLD

1   Zogby, *The Way We'll Be*, 215.

2   Thomas L. Friedman, *Hot, Flat, and Crowded* (New York: Farrar, Straus and Giroux, 2008), 8.

3   Ibid., 5.

4   Thomas L. Friedman, "China Deserves Donald Trump," *New York Times*, May 21, 2019.

5   Fareed Zakaria, *The Post-American World Release 2.0* (New York: Norton, 2011), 104.

6   Dilbert, February 10, 2011.

7   Zakaria, *The Post-American World*, 43.

8   Daniel Yergin, *The Quest: Energy, Security, and the Remaking of the Modern World* (New York: Penguin, 2011), 160.

9   Steven Mufson, "This Time, It's Different," *Washington Post*, July 27, 2008.

10   Steven Mufson, "Calif. Field Goes from Rush to Reflection of Global Limits," *Washington Post*, July 29, 2008.

11   Ariana Eunjung Cha, "China's Cars, Accelerating a Global Demand for Fuel," *Washington Post*, July 28, 2008.

12   Yergin, *The Quest*, 184.

13   Michael E. Mann, *The Hockey Stick and the Climate Wars: Dispatches from the Front Lines* (New York: Columbia University Press, 2012), xiii–xv.

14   Andrew C. Revkin and Seth Mydans, "Climate Panel Reaches Consensus on the Need to Reduce Harmful Emissions," *New York Times*, May 4, 2007.

15   Eric Pooley, *The Climate War: True Believers, Power Brokers, and the Fight to Save the Earth* (New York: Hyperion, 2010), 11.

16   Robert Barnes, "Court Hears Global Warming Case," *Washington Post*, November 30, 2006.

17   Robert Barnes and Juliet Eilperin, "High Court Faults EPA Inaction on Emissions," *Washington Post*, April 3, 2007.

18   Friedman, *Hot, Flat, and Crowded*, 36.

19   Lenny Bernstein, "World's Fish on Move to Cooler Waters, Study Finds," *Washington Post*, May 16, 2013.

20   Yergin, *The Quest*, 8.

21   Steven Mufson, "Power-Sector Emissions of China to Top U.S.," *Washington Post*, August 27, 2008.

22   Juliet Eilperin, "Long Droughts, Rising Seas Predicted Despite Future CO2 Curbs," *Washington Post*, January 27, 2009.

23   John M. Broder, "Past Decade Warmest Ever, NASA Data Shows," *New York Times*, January 21, 2010.

24   Naomi Oreskes and Erik M. Conway, *Merchants of Doubt* (New York: Bloomsbury, 2011), 6.

25   Friedman, *Hot, Flat, and Crowded*, 124.

26   Andrew C. Revkin, "Climategate Fever Breaks," *New York Times*, July 7, 2010; Mann, *The Hockey Stick*, 209–10.

27   Oreskes and Conway, *Merchants of Doubt*, 215.

28   Mann, *The Hockey Stick*, 249–50.

29   Jad Mouawad, "Wind Power Grows 39% for the Year," *New York Times*, January 26, 2010.

30   Brad Plumer, "U.S. Oil Imports are Falling to Their Lowest Level Since 1987," *Washington Post*, January 9, 2013.

31   Juliet Eilperin, "Nation Set Record for Heat Last Year," *Washington Post*, January 9, 2013, and Sarah Lyall, "Heat, Flood or Icy Cold, Extreme Weather Rages Worldwide," *New York Times*, January 10, 2013.

11: THE NEW RETIREMENT

1   David Brown, "Life Expectancy Hits Record High in United States," *Washington Post*, June 12, 2008.

2   Susan Jacoby, *Never Say Die: The Myth and Marketing of the New Old Age* (New York: Pantheon, 2011), 287.

3   Roger Lowenstein, *While America Aged: How Pension Debts Ruined General Motors, Stopped the NYC Subways, Bankrupted San Diego, and Loom as the Next Financial Crisis* (New York: Penguin Press, 2008), 1.

4   George Magnus, *The Age of Aging: How Demographics are Changing the Global Economy and Our World* (Hoboken, N.J.: John Wiley & Sons, 2009), 52.

5   Mike Allen, "Confident Bush Vows to Move Aggressively; Second-Term Agenda Includes Social Security, Tax Code," *Washington Post*, November 5, 2004; Bush, *Decision Points*, 300.

6   Robert J. Shiller, "The Housing Boom is Already Gigantic. How Long Can It Last?" *New York Times*, December 7, 2018.

7   Financial Crisis Inquiry Commission, *Financial Crisis Inquiry*, 391.

8   Chris Farrell, *Unretirement: How Baby Boomers are Changing the Way We Think About Work, Community and the Good Life* (New York: Bloomsbury Press, 2014), 9.

9   Jacoby, *Never Say Die*, 211.

10   Samuel Harrington, MD, *At Peace: Choosing A Good Death After a Long Life* (New York: Grand Central Life & Style, 2018), 7.

11   Ibid., 139.

12   Ann Neumann, *The Good Death: An Exploration of Dying in America* (Boston: Beacon Press, 2016), 97–100.

13   Ibid., 210.

12: THE NEW URBANISM AND THE HOUSING BUBBLE

1   Tom Vanderbilt, *Traffic* (New York: Alfred A. Knopf, 2008), 15.

2   Eric M. Weiss, "Around D.C., a Cheaper House May Cost You," *Washington Post*, October 12, 2006.

3   Richard Florida, *The Rise of the Creative Class, Revisited* (New York: Basic Books, 2012), 8.

4   Ibid., viii.

5   Ibid., 11.

6   Bill Brubaker, "GWU Raises Tuition to Over $50,000 a Year," *Washington Post*, February 9, 2007.

7   Robert J. Shiller, "The Housing Boom is Already Gigantic. How Long Can It Last?" *New York Times*, December 7, 2018.

8   Robert J. Shiller, *The Subprime Solution: How Today's Global Financial Crisis Happened, and What to Do About It* (Princeton, N.J.: Princeton University Press, 2008), 4.

9   Tyler Cowen, *The Great Stagnation* (New York: Dutton, 2011), 69.

10   Ben S. Bernanke, *The Courage to Act: A Memoir of a Crisis and Its Aftermath* (New York: Norton, 2015), 176.

11   Financial Crisis Inquiry Commission, *Financial Crisis Inquiry*, 104; Alan S. Blinder, *After the Music Stopped: The Financial Crisis, the Response, and the Work Ahead* (New York: Penguin, 2013), 58.

12   Smith, *Who Stole the American Dream?*, 233.

13   Michael Lewis, *The Big Short* (New York: Norton, 2010), 23, 73; Andrew Ross Sorkin, *Too Big to Fail* (New York: Viking, 2009), 5.

14   Alec Klein and Zachary A. Goldfarb, "The Bubble, Part I: Boom," *Washington Post*, June 15, 2008, Zachary A. Goldfarb and Alec Klein, "The Bubble, Part II: Bust," *Washington Post*, June 16, 2008; Jill Drew, "The Crash: What Went Wrong," *Washington Post*, December 16, 2008.

15   Shiller, *The Subprime Solution*, 6.

16   Bush, *Decision Points*, 449.

17   "U.S. Stocks Gain on Speculation That Fed Will Cut Rates Again," *New York Times*, January 28, 2008.

18   Renae Merle, "Recession Weighs on Home Prices, Consumers," *Washington Post*, December 31, 2008.

19   "Home Prices Fell at Record Pace in October," *New York Times*, December 30, 2008.

20   David Streitfeld and Jack Healy, "Phoenix Leads the Way Down in Home Prices," *New York Times*, April 29, 2009.

21   Charles V. Bagli and Christine Haughney, "Fallout is Wide in Failed Deal for Stuyvesant Town," *New York Times*, January 25, 2010.

22   Robert J. Shiller, "The Housing Boom is Already Gigantic. How Long Can It Last?" *New York Times*, December 7, 2018.

23   Shiller, *The Subprime Solution*, 3.

13: THE GREAT RECESSION

1   Gretchen Morgenson, "Seeing a Fund as Too Big to Fail, New York Fed Assists Its Bailout," *New York Times*, September 24, 1998.

2   Blinder, *After the Music Stopped*, 57.

3   Ibid., 55.

4   Financial Crisis Inquiry Commission, *The Financial Crisis Inquiry Report* (New York: PublicAffairs, 2011), xvii.

5   Lewis, *The Big Short*, xviii, 107.

6   Wojtek Dabrowski, "Buffett: Bank Woes are 'Poetic Justice,'" Reuters, February 6, 2008.

7   Roger Lowenstein, *The End of Wall Street* (New York: Penguin, 2010), 127—28; Adam Tooze, *Crashed: How a Decade of Financial Crises Changed the World* (New York: Viking, 2018), 171.

8   Bernanke, *The Courage to Act*, 261.

9   Timothy F. Geithner, *Stress Test: Reflections on Financial Crises* (New York: Crown, 2014), 9.

10   Bush, *Decision Points*, 440.

11   Neil Irwin and Zachary A. Goldfarb, "U.S. Seizes Control of Mortgage Giants," *Washington Post*, September 8, 2008; Steven Pearlstein, "In Crisis, Paulson's Stunning Use of Federal Power," *Washington Post*, September 8, 2008; Henry M. Paulson Jr., *On the Brink* (New York: Business Plus, 2010), 3.

12   Lowenstein, *The End of Wall Street*, xxiv.

13   Sorkin, *Too Big to Fail*, 535.

14   Bernanke, *The Courage to Act*, 287.

15   Louise Story and Jo Becker, "Bank Chief Tells of U.S. Pressure to Buy Merrill Lynch," *New York Times*, June 12, 2009; Bethany McLean and Joe Nocera, *All the Devils Are Here: The Hidden History of the Financial Crisis* (New York: Penguin, 2010), 310.

16   Lewis, *The Big Short*, 262.

17   David Cho, "A Conversion in 'This Storm,'" *Washington Post*, November 18, 2008.

18   Bush, *Decision Points*, 458–59.

19   Lowenstein, *The End of Wall Street*, xxii.

20   Paulson, *On the Brink*, 261.

21   Tooze, *Crashed*, 15.

22   "Dow's 778-Point Tailspin is Bigger Loss Than First Trading Day After 2001 Attacks," *Washington Post*, September 30, 2008.

23   Neil Irwin and Amit R. Paley, "Greenspan Says He Was Wrong on Regulation," *Washington Post*, October 24, 2008.

24   Steven Mufson and Blaine Harden, "Around the World, the Signs of Slowdown Spiral Outward," *Washington Post*, October 25, 2008.

25   Nancy Trejos, "Retirement Savings Lose $2 Trillion in 15 Months," *Washington Post*, October 8, 2008.

26   V. Dion Haynes, "Downturn Pummels Consumer Confidence," *Washington Post*, October 29, 2008.

27   Paulson, Jr., *On the Brink*, 254.

28   Financial Crisis Inquiry Commission, *Financial Crisis Inquiry*, xv, 389.

29   Paulson, *On the Brink*, 436.

14: THE 2008 ELECTION

1   Dan Balz and Haynes Johnson, *The Battle for America 2008: The Story of an Extraordinary Election* (New York: Viking, 2009), 386.

2   Zogby, *The Way We'll Be*, 101–102.

3   David Maraniss, *Barack Obama: The Story* (New York: Simon & Schuster, 2012), xxii.

4   Balz and Johnson, *The Battle for America 2008*, 4.

5   Fredrick C. Harris, *The Price of the Ticket: Barack Obama and the Rise and Decline of Black Politics* (New York: Oxford University Press, 2012), 104.

6   Ibid., 99.

7   Jeff Zeleny, "Opponents Call Obama Remarks 'Out of Touch,'" *New York Times*, April 12, 2008.

8   Tim Alberta, *American Carnage* (New York: HarperCollins, 2019), 37.

9   Obama, *Becoming*, 407.

10   "Barack Obama's Speech on Race," *New York Times*, March 18, 2008.

11   Gwen Ifill, *The Breakthrough: Politics and Race in the Age of Obama* (New York: Doubleday, 2009), 206.

12   Helen Thomas and Craig Crawford, *Listen Up, Mr. President: Everything You Always Wanted Your President to Know and Do* (New York: Scribner, 2009), 144.

13   Balz and Johnson, *The Battle for America 2008*, 372.

14   David Plouffe, *The Audacity to Win: The Inside Story and Lessons of Barack Obama's Historic Victory* (New York: Viking, 2009), 3.

15   Balz and Johnson, *The Battle for America 2008*, xiii.

16   Alec MacGillis and Jon Cohen, "Democrats Add Suburbs to Their Growing Coalition," *Washington Post*, November 6, 2008.

17   "President-Elect Obama," *Washington Post*, November 5, 2008.

18   Neil Irwin and David Cho, "U.S. Offers Citigroup Sweeping Safety Net," *Washington Post*, November 24, 2008.

19   Renae Merle, "Stocks Tank as Recession Declared," *Washington Post*, December 2, 2008; Neil Irwin, "Economic Signs Point to Longer, Deeper Recession," *Washington Post*, December 2, 2008.

20   Steven Mufson, "Flight to U.S. Treasury Bonds is Bad News for the Economy," *Washington Post*, December 2, 2008.

21   Neil Irwin and Steven Mufson, "Economic Indicators Continue Nose Dive," *Washington Post*, December 6, 2008.

22   Neil Irwin, "Fed Cuts Key Rate to Record Low," *Washington Post*, December 17, 2008.

23   Louis Uchitelle, "Unemployment Hits 7.2%, a 15-Year High," *New York Times*, January 9, 2009.

24   Vikas Bajaj, "Markets Limp Into 2009 After a Bruising Year," *New York Times*, December 31, 2008, and Renae Merle, "Wall Street's Final '08 Toll: $6.9 Trillion Wiped out," *Washington Post*, January 1, 2009.

25   Lori Montgomery, "Obama Predicts Years of Deficits Over $1 Trillion," *Washington Post*, January 7, 2009.

26   David Leonhardt, "The Big Fix," *New York Times*, January 27, 2009.

27   Sean Wilentz, "George W. Bush: The Worst President in History?" *Rolling Stone*, May 4, 2006.

28   Smith, *Bush*, xv.

29   "Bush's Approval Rating," *Washington Post*, January 13, 2009.

30   Bush, *Decision Points*, 138.

31   Ibid., 181.

32   Ibid., 220.

33   Ibid., 306.

34   Cowen, *The Great Stagnation*, 58.

35   Smith, *Bush*, 176.

36   McClellan, *What Happened*, 210.

37   Bush, *Decision Points*, 452.

15: OBAMA

1   "Barack Obama's Inaugural Address," *New York Times*, January 20, 2009.

2   Jonathan Alter, *The Promise: President Obama, Year One* (New York: Simon & Schuster, 2010), viii.

3   Michael Grunwald, *The New New Deal: The Hidden Story of Change in the Obama Era* (London: Simon & Schuster, 2012), 20.

4   Ron Suskind, *Confidence Men: Wall Street, Washington, and the Education of a President* (New York: HarperCollins, 2011), 482.

5   David J. Garrow, *Rising Star: The Making of Barack Obama* (New York: HarperCollins, 2017), 1078.

6   Jonathan Alter, *The Center Holds: Obama and His Enemies* (New York: Simon & Schuster, 2013), xi.

7   Chuck Todd, *The Stranger: Barack Obama in the White House* (New York: Little, Brown, 2014), 10–11.

8   David Remnick, *The Bridge: The Life and Rise of Barack Obama* (New York: Knopf, 2010), 584.

9   Fredrick C. Harris, *The Price of the Ticket: Barack Obama and the Rise and Decline of Black Politics* (New York: Oxford University Press, 2012), 169, 173.

10   Ibid., 189.

11   Obama, *Becoming*, 396.

12   Richard Wolffe, *Revival: The Struggle for Survival Inside the Obama White House* (New York: Crown, 2010), 167.

13   Geithner, *Stress Test*, 4–5.

14   Binyamin Appelbaum and Neil Irwin, "Bank of America Gets New Round of U.S. Aid," *Washington Post*, January 16, 2009.

15   Annys Shin and Neil Irwin, "Layoffs Cut Deeper Into Economy," *Washington Post*, January 27, 2009.

16   Neil Irwin and Annys Shin, "598,000 Jobs Shed in Brutal January," *Washington Post*, February 7, 2009.

17   Edmund L. Andrews and Vikas Bajaj, "U.S. Plans $500,000 Cap on Executive Pay on Bailouts," *New York Times*, February 3, 2009.

18   Steven Pearlstein, "Big Lessons in Finance from a Little Bank You've Never Heard Of," *Washington Post*, February 11, 2009.

19   Shailagh Murray and Paul Kane, "Congress Passes Stimulus Package," *Washington Post*, February 14, 2009; Tooze, *Crashed*, 282.

20   Grunwald, *The New New Deal*, 13.

21   Ibid., 202.

22   Kenneth R. Feinberg, *Who Gets What: Fair Compensation after Tragedy and Financial Upheaval.* (New York: PublicAffairs, 2012), 92.

23   Neil Irwin and Annys Shin, "Fed Leaders Issue Bleak Forecast," *Washington Post*, February 19, 2009.

24   Lori Montgomery, "Deficit Projected to Swell Beyond Earlier Estimates," *Washington Post*, March 21, 2009.

25   David Leonhardt, "Job Losses Show Breadth of Recession," *New York Times*, March 3, 2009.

26   Edmund L. Andrews and Peter Baker, "A.I.G. Planning Huge Bonuses after $170 Billion Bailout," *New York Times*, March 14, 2009.

27   Annys Shin, "Stocks Soar, But Dismal Signs Remain," *Washington Post*, March 13, 2009.

28   Peter S. Goodman and Jack Healy, "663,000 Jobs Lost in March; Total Tops 5 Million," *New York Times*, April 3, 2009.

29   "A $1.33 Trillion Drop in Net Worth in First Quarter," *New York Times*, June 12, 2009.

30   Binyamin Appelbaum, "Stress Test Finds Strength in Banks," *Washington Post*, May 7, 2009.

31   Paul Ingrassia, *Crash Course: The American Automobile Industry's Road from Glory to Disaster* (New York: Random House, 2010), 4.

32   Ibid., 3.

33   Lowenstein, *While America Aged*, 10, 62.

34   Ingrassia, *Crash Course*, 158–59, 200.

35   Ibid., 176.

36   Lowenstein, *While America Aged*, 222.

37   Steven Mufson, David Cho and Cecilia Kang, "Aid in Hand, Clock Ticks for Detroit," *Washington Post*, December 20, 2008.

38   Peter Whoriskey and Kendra Marr, "In Auto Talks, No Cure-All for Health Care Costs," *Washington Post*, February 27, 2009.

39   Steven Mufson, "GM's New Road Map: Partial Nationalization," *Washington Post*, April 28, 2009.

40   Peter Whoriskey, "U.S. Gets Majority Stake in New GM," *Washington Post*, June 1, 2009.

41   Dana Hedgpeth and Jennifer Agiesta, "A Hard Downshift in Detroit," *Washington Post*, January 3, 2010.

42   Uwe E. Reinhardt, "The Fork in the Road for Health Care," *New York Times*, May 25, 2012.

43   Neumann, *The Good Death*, 169.

44   Bob Woodward, *Obama's Wars* (New York: Simon & Schuster, 2010), 3.

45   Scott Wilson, "Obama Calls for Fresh Start with Muslims," *Washington Post*, June 5, 2009.

46   Tenet, *At the Center of the Storm*, 257.

47   Woodward, *Obama's Wars*, 72.

48   Sheryl Gay Stolberg and Helene Cooper, "Obama Adds Troops, but Maps Exit Plan," *New York Times*, December 1, 2009.

49   Michael Hastings, "The Runaway General: The Profile That Brought Down McChrystal," *Rolling Stone*, June 22, 2010.

50   Peter Finn and Anne E. Kornblut, "How the White House Lost on Guantanamo," *Washington Post*, April 24, 2011.

51   Marc Lacey, "Killings in Drug War in Mexico Double in '08," *New York Times*, December 8, 2008.

52   Joel Achenbach, *A Hole at the Bottom of the Sea: The Race to Kill the BP Oil Gusher* (New York: Simon & Schuster, 2011), 1.

53   Joel Achenbach and David A. Fahrenthold, "Gulf Disaster is Biggest Accidental Spill in History, Analysis Says," *Washington Post*, August 3, 2010; Achenbach, *A Hole at the Bottom of the Sea*, 204.

54   Achenbach, *A Hole at the Bottom of the Sea*, 142.

55   Peter Whoriskey, "Weak Data Signal Grim Prospects for Workers," *Washington Post*, October 3, 2009.

56 Lori Montgomery and Neil Irwin, "Record-High Deficit May Dash Big Plans," *Washington Post*, October 17, 2009.

57 Neil Irwin, "Central Bank Chief Forecasts a Sluggish Recovery," *Washington Post*, December 8, 2009.

58 Remnick, *The Bridge*, 583.

59 Jackie Calmes, "U.S. Forecasts Smaller Loss from Bailout of Banks," *New York Times*, December 7, 2009.

60 Jackie Calmes, "Year-End Audit Finds TARP Program Effective," *New York Times*, December 9, 2009.

61 Neil Irwin, "In Crisis, Fed Made a Record Profit," *Washington Post*, January 12, 2010.

62 Tomoeh Murakami Tse, "Financial Firms Pay Out 17% More in Bonuses," *Washington Post*, February 24, 2010.

63 Binyamin Appelbaum, "Troubled Banking Industry Pulls Back," *Washington Post*, February 24, 2010.

64 Freeland, *Plutocrats*, 218.

65 Jackie Calmes, "TARP Bailout to Cost Less Than Once Anticipated," *New York Times*, October 1, 2010; Brady Dennis, "TARP at 2: Officials Assess Bailouts," *Washington Post*, October 1, 2010; Lori Montgomery, "U.S. to Pay $25 Billion for TARP, CBO Says," *Washington Post*, November 30, 2010.

66 Timothy F. Geithner, "5 Myths About TARP," *Washington Post*, October 10, 2010.

67 Geithner, *Stress Test*, 497.

68 Michael D. Shear and Peter Whoriskey, "Obama Takes Auto Bailout Victory Lap," *Washington Post*, July 31, 2010.

69 Vikas Bajaj, "Heart-Stopping Fall, Breathtaking Rally," *New York Times*, December 31, 2009.

70 Neil Irwin, Annie Gowen and Ben Pershing, "Job Losses a Blow to Still Fragile Economy," *Washington Post*, January 9, 2010.

71 "U.S. Home Price Index Rose Slightly in November," *New York Times*, January 26, 2010.

72 Suskind, *Confidence Men*, 460.

73 Joel Achenbach, "In Debate Over Nation's Growing Debt, a Surplus of Worry," *Washington Post*, December 8, 2009.

74 Frank, *Frank*, 318.

75 Feinberg, *Who Gets What*, 121.

76 Thomas L. Friedman, "Obama Should Seize the High Ground," *New York Times*, May 26, 2012.

16: THE TEA PARTY STRIKES BACK

1 Amy Gardner, "A Movement Without a Compass," *Washington Post*, October 24, 2010.

2 Lofgren, *The Party Is Over*, 66.

3 Geoffrey Kabaservice, *Rule and Ruin: The Downfall of Moderation and the Destruction of the Republican Party, from Eisenhower to the Tea Party* (New York: Oxford University Press, 2012), 388.

4 Theda Skocpol and Vanessa Williamson, *The Tea Party and the Remaking of Republican Conservatism* (New York: Oxford University Press, 2012), 8–9.

5 Adam Liptak, "Justices, 5–4, Reject Corporate Spending Limit," *New York Times*, January 21, 2010.

6   Skocpol and Williamson, *The Tea Party*, 79.

7   Alter, *The Center Holds*, 4.

8   Skocpol and Williamson, *The Tea Party*, 161.

9   Thomas E. Mann and Norman J. Ornstein, *It's Even Worse Than It Looks: How the American Constitutional System Collided with the New Politics of Extremism* (New York: Basic Books, 2012), 4.

10   Lofgren, *The Party Is Over*, 2.

11   Ibid., 3.

12   Obama, *Becoming*, 353.

13   Michael D. Shear, "With Document, Obama Seeks to End 'Birther' Issue, *New York Times*, April 27, 2011.

14   Neil Irwin, "Fed to Inject $600 Billion Into Economy," *Washington Post*, November 4, 2010.

15   Bernanke, *The Courage to Act*, 566.

16   Neil Irwin and Nia-Malika Henderson, "Recession is Officially Over, But Anxiety Lingers," *Washington Post*, September 21, 2010; Blinder, *After the Music Stopped*, 20.

17   Steven Mufson, "Debt Across U.S. Hits Post-WWII Levels," *Washington Post*, February 23, 2011.

18   Michael A. Fletcher, "Detailing How the Recession Imploded States' Finances," *Washington Post*, January 6, 2011.

19   Malcolm Harris, *Kids These Days: Human Capital and the Making of Millennials* (New York: Little, Brown, 2017), 167.

20   Freeland, *Plutocrats*, 3.

21   Smith, *Who Stole the American Dream?*, xiv–xv.

22   Cowen, *The Great Stagnation*, 51.

23   Jesse Eisinger, "Why Only One Top Banker Went to Jail for the Financial Crisis," *New York Times*, April 30, 2014.

24   Binyamin Appelbaum, "Family Net Worth Drops to Level of Early '90s, Fed Says," *New York Times*, June 11, 2012; Ylan Q. Mui, "Families See Their Wealth Sapped," *Washington Post*, June 12, 2012.

25   Neil Irwin and Dan Eggen, "Economy Made Few Gains in Bush Years," *Washington Post*, January 12, 2009; Neil Irwin, "Aughts Were a Lost Decade for U.S. Economy, Workers," *Washington Post*, January 2, 2010.

17: HISTORY IS NOT OVER

1   Jan-Werner Müller, *What is Populism?* (Philadelphia: University of Pennsylvania Press, 2016), 21.

2   Roger Lowenstein, "A Legacy of the Financial Crisis? The Makings of the Next One," *Washington Post*, September 7, 2018; Aaron Ross Sorkin, "From Trump to Trade, The Financial Still Resonates 10 Years Later," *New York Times*, September 10, 2018; Neil Irwin, "The Policymakers Saved the Financial System. And America Never Forgave Them," *New York Times*, September 12, 2018.

3   Jennifer Steinhauer, "Senate Races Expose Extent of Republicans' Gender Gap," *New York Times*, November 7, 2012; Dan Eggen and T. W. Farnam, "Spending a Lot, With Little Effect," *Washington Post*, November 8, 2012; Peter Wallsten, "Party Coalition at a Crossroads," *Washington Post*, November 8, 2012.

4   Charles Murray, *Coming Apart: The State of White America, 1960–2010* (New York: Crown Forum, 2012), 202, 243.

5   Yuval Levin, *The Fractured Republic: Renewing America's Social Contract in the Age of Individualism* (New York: Basic Books, 2016), 74, 89.

6   Joseph E. Stiglitz and Linda J. Bilmes, "The Book of Jobs," *Vanity Fair*, December 6, 2011.

7   Timothy P. Carney, *Alienated America: Why Some Places Thrive While Others Collapse* (New York: HarperCollins, 2019), 13, 51.

8   Thomas L. Friedman, *The World is Flat: A Brief History of the Twenty-first Century* (New York: Farrar, Straus and Giroux, 2005), 257.

9   Obama, *Becoming*, 397.

10   Charles J. Sykes, *How the Right Lost Its Mind* (New York: St. Martin's Press, 2017), xv.

11   Alberta, *American Carnage*, 612.

Index